The
Father's
Role

CROSS-CULTURAL PERSPECTIVES

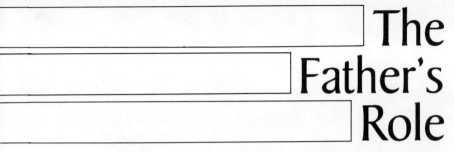

The Father's Role

CROSS-CULTURAL PERSPECTIVES

EDITED BY

Michael E. Lamb
UNIVERSITY OF UTAH

LEA LAWRENCE ERLBAUM ASSOCIATES, PUBLISHERS
1987   Hillsdale, New Jersey   London

Lawrence Erlbaum Associates, Inc., Publishers
365 Broadway
Hillsdale, New Jersey 07642

Library of Congress Cataloging-in-Publication Data

The Father's role.

Includes bibliographies and indexes.
1. Fathers—Cross-cultural studies.   2. Father and child—Cross-cultural studies.
I. Lamb, Michael E., 1953–   .
HQ756.F386   1987   306.8′742   86-29100
ISBN 0-89859-595-9
ISBN 0-8058-0016-6 (pbk.)

Printed in the United States of America
10 9 8 7 6 5 4 3 2 1

For Frank, Damon, and Darryn
Father and sons

Contents

Contributors

LAURA BENIGNI Istituto di Psicologica del Consiglio Nazionale di Ricerche, Rome, Italy.

BARRY HEWLETT Department of Sociology and Anthropology, Southern Oregon State College, Ashland, Oregon.

DAVID Y. F. HO Department of Psychology, University of Hong Kong, Hong Kong.

FRANCOISE HURSTEL Department of Psychology, University of Strasbourg, France.

CARL-PHILIP HWANG Institute of Psychology, University of Göteborg, Göteborg, Sweden.

NOBUTO IMAIZUMI Department of Psychology, Hiroshima University, Hiroshima, Japan.

SONIA JACKSON School of Social Work, University of Bristol, Bristol, United Kingdom.

ELLEN M. T. KOCHER Institut fur Entwicklungs-und Sozialpsychologie, Universität Dusseldorf, West Germany.

NINA KOREN School of Social Work, University of Haifa, Haifa, Israel.

MICHAEL E. LAMB Departments of Psychology, Psychiatry, and Pediatrics, University of Utah, Salt Lake City, Utah.

JUN NAKAZAWA School of Education, Chiba University, Chiba, Japan

REBECCA NEW Department of Child, Family, and Community Studies, Syracuse University, Syracuse, New York.

HORST NICKEL Institut fur Entwicklungs-und Sozialpsychologie, Universität Dusseldorf, West Germany.

AUGUSTINE B. NSAMENANG   Social Sciences Research Center, Yaounde, Cameroon.

KEVIN NUGENT   Child Development Unit, Children's Hospital Medical Center, Boston, Massachussetts.

GENEVIÉVE DELAISI DE PARSEVAL   Psychoanalyst, 118 Rue de Vaugirard, Paris, France.

GRAEME RUSSELL   School of Behavioural Science, Macquarie University, North Ryde, NSW, Australia.

ABRAHAM SAGI   School of Social Work, University of Haifa, Haifa, Israel.

DAVID SHWALB   Department of Psychology, University of Utah, Salt Lake City, Utah.

MAYAH WEINBERG   School of Social Work, University of Haifa, Haifa, Israel.

Preface

Little more than a decade ago, I wrote that fathers were "forgotten contributors to child development" so far as empirical research by psychologists was concerned. In the intervening years, happily, the situation has changed dramatically. The study of paternal influences has become quite popular, and we have made substantial strides in our understanding of them.

Most recently, psychologists have come to realize that fathers play multiple roles in the family, and that one needs to consider them all even when concerned narrowly about paternal effects on young children. This has promoted a laudable increase in multidisciplinary and multicultural approaches to the study of the family in general and fatherhood in particular. The many roles that fathers play within the family are socially defined and thus surely vary in subtle or substantial ways from society to society. Unfortunately, most researchers are familiar only with the research conducted in their own cultures. Even though most research continues to be conducted in the United States, we show in this volume that considerable research has been conducted in other countries, where interest in the father's roles is growing.

Because many of the studies conducted outside the United States are published in foreign journals and often in foreign languages, the volume represents the first opportunity for most American social scientists to become familiar with research conducted in several other cultures. These summaries are important in their own right, as portraits of fatherhood in 12 non-American cultures, as well as for the light they may cast on the association between culture and paternity more generally. Each author provides a brief introduction to the cultural context within which and by which the father's roles are defined; hence, the varying associations between context and fatherhood are emphasized. As a result, the chapters should be of interest to a broad array of social scientists and graduate students concerned with family roles and fatherhood in a selection of countries from each continent. I hope that the net effect is to increase our sensitivity to the importance of cultural assumptions and realities in shaping the realities and perceptions of social life. North America harbors some rather unique cultures: We may understand them better if we replace our ethnocentric assumptions of universality with an awareness of essential cultural relativity.

Michael E. Lamb

NORTH AMERICA

1 Introduction: The Emergent American Father[1]

Michael E. Lamb
University of Utah

In the last decade and a half, professional and public interest in the roles played by fathers in their children's development has increased enormously. Early in this era of paternal rediscovery, psychologists believed that fathers might have an important role to play in childrearing, even if their involvement (relative to that of mothers) was severely limited. Specifically, they questioned the implicit assumptions (a) of a direct correlation between extent of involvement and extent of influence and (b) that if mothers were more influential than fathers, they must be exclusively influential (e.g., Lamb, 1976, 1981c; Lynn, 1974). Interest in fathers was subsequently accentuated by popular and professional discovery of "the new fatherhood." The new father, immortalized for many by Dustin Hoffman's performance in *Kramer vs. Kramer,* was an active, involved, nurturant participant in all aspects of childcare and childrearing. Not surprisingly, belief in the existence and proliferation of such fathers led to further speculation about the importance of paternal influences on child development. As a result, rhetorical exchanges concerning the new father abounded; unfortunately, rhetoric continues to outpace serious analysis. My goal in this chapter is to redress that imbalance by providing a brief integrative overview of research and theorizing concerning the role (or multiple roles) that fathers play.

The thesis advanced here proposes that we are currently witnessing the fourth of a series of changes in popular conceptualizations of the father's roles and responsibilities. Today's fathers are expected to be more actively involved in

---

[1]This chapter was initially published in M. E. Lamb (Ed.), *The father's role: Applied Perspectives.* New York: Wiley, 1986. Copyright (1986) John Wiley & Sons; reprinted by permission.

childcare than in the past, and to a modest extent the average contemporary father is indeed more involved in childcare than his predecessor. It may be a mistake, however, to assume that this increased involvement is necessarily beneficial in all family circumstances (Lamb, Pleck, & Levine, 1985). Instead, one has to consider the individual circumstances in order to understand how children are affected by variations in paternal involvement.

In the recent debate about the changing role of fathers, much of the discussion has focused on the increasing role played by fathers in the direct care and rearing of their children. This refocus highlights a shift from a concern with fathers as persons primarily involved in the economic support of the family and perhaps in the discipline and control of older children (e.g., Benson, 1968; Bowlby, 1951) to a view that places increasing emphasis on the role that fathers play in the direct care of children of all ages. To fully appreciate this shift, and to explain better the ways in which contemporary fathers are influential, it is helpful to examine historical changes in the conceptualization of paternal roles and responsibilities. Consequently, the chapter begins with a brief historical review designed to place contemporary paternal roles into perspective. In the second section, I discuss evidence concerning the nature and extent of paternal involvement today, as well as data concerning the extent to which father involvement has changed over the last several years. I then discuss paternal effects on child development, summarizing the findings generated by research of three different genres conducted over the last four decades. Finally, I describe the factors that influence the degree and type of involvement that fathers have in their children's lives. Because the chapter surveys a broad range of topics and issues, the coverage is necessarily selective. To assist those readers moved to obtain further detail or documentation concerning the conclusions presented here, I include references to key empirical studies and major integrative reviews of the literature.

FATHERS IN AMERICAN HISTORY

To understand the contemporary concern with and confusion about fatherhood, it may be helpful to step back historically and examine the changes in the conceptualization of paternal roles that have taken place. The available data are obviously limited, but social historians argue that much can be learned by examining letters (admittedly, few wrote letters and even fewer thought to preserve them for posterity) and literature written or popular during particular eras. According to J. H. Pleck (1984a), one can actually discern four phases or periods over the last two centuries of American social history. In each of these, a different dominant motif came into focus, making other aspects of a complex, multifaceted role seem much less important by comparison.

The Moral Teacher

The earliest phase was one that extended from Puritan times, through the Colonial period, into early Republican times. During this lengthy period, the father's role was perceived as one that was dominated by responsibility for moral oversight and moral teaching. By popular consensus, fathers were primarily responsible for insuring that their children grew up with an appropriate sense of values, acquired primarily from the study of religious materials like the Bible. To the extent that a broader role was defined, fathers assumed responsibility for the education of children—not because education and literacy were valued in their own right, but because children had to be literate in order to read the Scriptures. Thus the father's responsibility for education was secondary; teaching literacy served as a means of advancing the father's role as moral guardian by insuring that children were academically equipped to adopt and maintain Christian ways. In their reviews, Demos (1982) and J. H. Pleck (1984a) point out that, during this era, "good fathers" were defined as men who provided models of good Christian living and versed their children well in the Scriptures.

The Breadwinner

Around the time of centralized industrialization, there occurred a shift in the dominant conceptualization of the father's role (J. H. Pleck, 1984a). Instead of emphasizing the father's role as moral teacher, his role came to be defined largely in terms of breadwinning, and this conceptualization of the father endured from the mid nineteenth century through the Great Depression (E. Pleck, 1976). An analysis of the then-popular literature and of letters written between fathers and children during that period confirms the dominant conceptualization of fatherhood in terms of breadwinning. Of course, this is not to say that other aspects of the father's role, such as the presumed responsibility for moral guardianship, had disappeared. Rather, breadwinning came into focus as the most important and defining characteristic of fatherhood and as the criterion by which "good fathers" could be appraised.

The Sex-role Model

Perhaps as a result of the Great Depression, the New Deal, and the disruption and dislocation brought about by the Second World War, the end of the war brought a new conceptualization of fatherhood. Although breadwinning and moral guardianship remained important, focus now shifted to concern about the father's function as a sex-role model, especially for his sons. Many books and articles in the professional literature focused on the need for strong sex-role models, and many professionals concluded that fathers were clearly not doing a good job in this regard (e.g., Levy, 1943; Strecker, 1946). Their inadequacies were also underscored in dramatic works, such as *Rebel Without a Cause,* and were ridiculed in comedies and cartoons like "All in the Family" and "Blondie" (Ehrenreich & English, 1979).

The New Nurturant Father

Around the mid 1970s, finally, a fourth stage was reached. For the first time, there was widespread identification of fathers as active, nurturant, caretaking parents. Active parenting was defined as the central component of fatherhood, and as the yardstick by which "good fathers" might be assessed. This redefinition of fatherhood occurred first in the popular media, where it was promulgated in works like *Kramer vs. Kramer* and *The World According to Garp.* Professional interest in the new fatherhood soon followed.

It is important to acknowledge the changing conceptualization of fathering because all four of the images or functions outlined above remain important today, although the extent to which they are deemed important varies across groups within our society. In a pluralistic society like ours, various conceptions of the father's role coexist, and it is important to bear in mind that while journalists and filmmakers here have been lauding active involvement and nurturant fatherhood for the last 10 years, there are many citizens whose conception of fathering is very different. In addition, one must recognize that fathers fill many roles, that the relative importance of each varies from one context to another, and that one must view active fathering—the key focus here—in the context of the various other things that fathers do for their children (for example, breadwinning, sex-role modeling, moral guidance, emotional support of mothers).

Modes of Paternal Influence Today

If one thinks about fatherhood simply in terms of the ways in which fathers are likely to influence their children, one can discern at least four ways in which fathers can have a substantial impact on their children and their children's development. Clearly, breadwinning remains a key component of the father's role in most segments of society today (Benson, 1968; Cazenave, 1979; J. H. Pleck, 1983) Even in the vast majority of families in which there are two wage-earners, the father is still seen as a primary breadwinner, if only because of continuing disparities between the salaries of male and female workers. Economic support of the family constitutes an indirect but important way in which fathers contribute to the rearing and emotional health of their children. A second important but indirect source of influence stems from the fathers' role as a source of emotional support to the other people—such as mothers—involved in the direct care of children (Parke, Power, & Gottman, 1979). When fathers function as sources of emotional support for mothers and others in the family, this tends to enhance the quality of mother-child relationships and thus facilitates positive adjustment by the children; by contrast, when fathers are unsupportive, children may suffer (Rutter, 1973, 1979). Fathers can also affect the quality of family dynamics by being involved in child-related housework, thus easing the mothers' workloads (J. H. Pleck, 1983, 1984b). (Paternal involvement in housework may also constitute a helpful model for children.) Fathers also influence their children by interacting with the children directly, and much of this chapter is concerned with paternal influences deriving from the caretaking, teaching, play, and one-on-one interaction with particular children (Lamb, 1981b). Most of the research on paternal influences is concerned with such direct influence patterns, even though there are multiple aspects of the father's role, and there are many ways other than direct interaction in which fathers can affect their children's development.

QUANTIFYING THE NEW FATHERHOOD

Much attention has recently been paid to the changing role of fathers, with particular focus on "the new father" who is, by definition, deeply involved in the day-to-day care and rearing of his children. Unfortunately, much of the evidence concerning the new fatherhood is journalistic in nature, and we do not know how representative the men featured in such accounts really are. Before pursuing our topic further, therefore, we need to ask: What does the average American father do and how has that changed over the last several years?

Components of Father Involvement

A large number of studies have been designed to determine both how much time fathers spend with their children and what sorts of activities occupy that time (Lamb, Pleck, Charnov, & Levine, 1985, 1987; J. H. Pleck, 1983). Many of these studies involve small and often unrepresentative samples—a perennial problem in developmental research. Fortunately, this area of research can boast of several studies involving nationally representative samples of individuals (both mothers and fathers) who were asked what fathers do and how much they do.

Given the availability of these data, it would seem easy to determine what contemporary fathers really do. Sadly, the task is not as easy as it sounds because the results of different surveys vary dramatically. One problem is that researchers have invoked very different implicit definitions of parental involvement in different surveys; because different activities comprise aspects of paternal involvement in different studies it becomes very difficult to compare results. To make sense of the data, therefore, it is first necessary to group studies in terms of similarities in the implicit definitions of paternal involvement employed (Lamb et al., 1987).

For purposes of analysis, one can distinguish three components of parental involvement. The first and most restrictive type of involvement involves time spent in actual one-on-one interaction with the child (whether feeding her, helping him with homework, or playing catch in the garden). These estimates, which Lamb et al. (1987) labelled estimates of *engagement* or *interaction,* do not include time spent engaged in child-related housework or time spent sitting in the living room while the child is playing in the family room next door. Lamb et al. (1987) included the latter in a second category comprising activities involving less intense degrees of interaction. The latter activities imply parental *accessibility* to the child, even if parent and child are not actually interacting with one another. Cooking in the kitchen while the child plays in the next room or even cooking in the kitchen while the child plays at the parent's feet would be examples of such types of involvement.

The final type of involvement is the hardest to define, but is perhaps the most important of all. This has to do with the extent to which the parent takes ultimate *responsibility* for the child's welfare and care, and can be illustrated by considering the difference between being responsible for childcare as opposed to being able and willing to "help out" when it is convenient. Responsibility involves knowing when the child needs to go to the pediatrician, making the appointment, and making sure that somebody takes the child to it. Responsibility involves making childcare and babysitting arrangements, ensuring that the child has clothes to wear, and making arrangements for the child's supervision when she is sick. Much of the time involved in being a responsible parent does not involve direct interaction with the child. Consequently, it is especially easy for survey researchers to lose sight of this type of involvement. It is hard to quantify the time involved, particularly because the anxiety, worry, and contingency-planning that comprise parental responsibility often occur when the parent is ostensibly doing something else.

When one distinguishes between the different components or types of parental involvement, one finds greater consistency from study to study than was apparent earlier, but a considerable degree of inconsistency remains. In part, this is because the distinction between the three types of involvement has been developed and applied retrospectively to the results of independent investigations conducted years earlier. As a result, there are still differences across studies in terms of specific definitions of engagement, accessibility, and responsibility. For example, in one of the major national surveys, "watching TV together" was grouped with activities of the interaction type, whereas in another study "watching TV together" was included as a component of accessibility.

To integrate and compare the findings of different studies, one must allow each researcher's idiosyncratic definition of involvement to stand, but employ *relative* rather than *absolute* measures of paternal involvement to compare results. Instead of comparing those figures in each study purporting to measure the amount of time that fathers spend "interacting with" their children, therefore, one must first compute figures (i.e., relative to the amount of time that mothers devote to this activity, how much of it do fathers do?) and then compare these proportional figures. The picture becomes much clearer when these relative figures are employed. Surprisingly similar results are obtained in different studies, despite major differences in the methods used to assess time use (diary vs. estimate), the size and regional representation of the samples employed, and the date when the studies were conducted.

The Extent of Paternal Involvement

Consider first those figures concerning the degree of involvement by fathers in two-parent families in which mothers are unemployed (Lamb et al., 1987; J. H. Pleck, 1983). In such families, the data suggest that fathers spend about 20 to 25% as much time as mothers do in direct interaction or engagement with their children. In the same types of families, fathers spend about a third as much time as mothers do just being accessible to their children. The largest discrepancy between paternal and maternal involvement is in the area of responsibility. Many studies show that fathers assume essentially no responsibility (as defined here) for their children's care or rearing.

In two-parent families with unemployed mothers, the levels of paternal engagement and accessibility are both substantially higher than in families with unemployed mothers (Lamb et al., 1987; J. H. Pleck, 1983). The figures for direct interaction and accessibility average 33% and 65%, respectively. As far as responsibility is concerned, however, there is no evidence that maternal employment status has any effect on levels of paternal involvement. Even when both mother and father are employed 30 or more hours per week, the amount of responsibility assumed by fathers appears negligible, just as it does when mothers are unemployed.

In light of the controversies that have arisen on this score, it is worth noting that fathers do not spend more time interacting with their children when mothers are employed. The proportions cited here go up not because fathers are doing more, but because mothers are doing less. Thus fathers are proportionately more involved when mothers are employed, even though their levels of involvement, in absolute terms, do not change to any meaningful extent. The unfortunate controversies in this area appear attributable to a confusion between proportional figures and absolute figures.

Child and Family Characteristics
Affecting Paternal Involvement

Researchers have also explored changes in paternal involvement related to the age of the child (J. H. Pleck, 1983). Interestingly, the changes that take place are the same for mothers and fathers. Parents spend much more time in childcare when there are younger rather than older children—a trend which, although understandable, contradicts the popular assumption that fathers become more involved as children get older. Fathers may know more about older children than about younger children, they may feel more comfortable and competent, and they may appear more interested, but they do not appear to spend more time with their older children. In part, this may be because older children no longer want to interact with parents as much; they prefer to interact with peers and/or siblings.

Popular presumptions are correct, however, so far as the effects of the child's gender are concerned (Lamb, 1981b). Fathers are indeed more interested in and more involved with their sons than with their daughters. They tend to spend more time with boys than with girls, regardless of the children's ages. Beyond these variations associated with age and gender, however, there are no consistent regional, ethnic, or religious variations in the amount of time that parents—mothers or fathers—spend with their children (J. H. Pleck, 1983).

Changes Over Time

Of course, the term "new fatherhood" implies that today's fathers differ from the fathers of the recent past. Unfortunately, few data are available concerning changes over time in levels of paternal involvement.

The best data available from a recent report by Juster (in press) who compared figures from a 1975 national survey with figures obtained in a follow-up survey undertaken six years later. In 1981, the average father spent much more time (26%) in the most intensive type of childcare (direct interaction) than in 1975. The percentage increase for mothers was substantially smaller (7%)—at least in part because the changes for mothers took place relative to higher baseline levels. In any event, the discrepancy between the levels of maternal and paternal involvement remained substantial: Mothers in 1981 still engaged in substantially more interaction with their children than fathers did, despite the larger increases in paternal involvement. In both 1975 and 1981, paternal involvement was about a third that of mothers, rising from 29% in 1976 to 34% in 1981.

Behavioral Styles of Mothers and Fathers

Thus far, we have considered only how much time parents spend with their children, ignoring the fact that there may be variations in terms of the content of their interactions. Both observational and survey data suggest that mothers and fathers engage in rather different types of interaction with their children (Lamb, 1981a, 1981b). Mothers' interactions with their children are dominated by caretaking whereas fathers are behaviorally defined as playmates. Mothers actually play with their children much more than fathers do but, as a proportion of the total amount of child-parent interaction, play is a much more prominent component of father-child interaction, whereas caretaking is much more salient with mothers.

Although mothers are associated with caretaking and fathers with play, we cannot assume that fathers are less capable of childcare. A number of researchers have attempted to investigate the relative competencies of mothers and fathers with respect to caretaking and parenting functions, and the results of these studies are fairly clear (Lamb, 1981a). First, they show that, in the newborn period, there are no differences in competence between mothers and fathers—both parents can do equally well (and/or equally poorly). Contrary to the notion of a maternal instinct, parenting skills are usually acquired "on the job" by both mothers and fathers. Mothers are "on the job" more than fathers are, however. Not surprisingly, therefore, mothers become more sensitive to their children, more in tune with them, and more aware of each individual child's characteristics and needs. By virtue of their lack of experience, fathers become correspondingly less sensitive and come to feel less confidence in their parenting abilities. Fathers thus continue to defer to and cede responsibility to mothers, whereas mothers increasingly assume responsibility, not only because they see it as their role, but also because their partners do not seem to be especially competent care-providers. As a result, the differences between mothers and fathers become more marked over time, but they are not irreversible. When fathers are thrust into the primary caretaking role by unemployment or by the loss of a partner, or when they choose to redefine their parental roles and their parent-child relationships, they are perfectly capable of acquiring the necessary skills (Hipgrave, 1982; Levine, 1976; Russell, 1982, 1983). In reality, of course, most fathers never get as involved in childcare as their partners, and so the differences between mothers and fathers tend to increase.

Summary

There have been increases over time in average degrees of paternal involvement, so the notion of a "new emergent nurturant father" is not entirely mythical. Mothers continue to spend more time and take responsibility for most of the day-to-day care of their children, however. The discrepancy between mothers and fathers is especially great in the area of what we have called responsibility, and in this regard there are few data available concerning secular changes in paternal behavior. In other areas, the changes, although significant, are still quite modest. In addition, the characteristics of mothers' and fathers' interactions with their children have for the most part remained remarkably consistent over time. Mothers are identified with caretaking, fathers with play.

PATERNAL INFLUENCES ON CHILD DEVELOPMENT

The focus of this chapter now switches from concern about fathers' actions to fathers' influences on their children's development. Over the decades of research on this topic, three bodies of literature have emerged; all are important in understanding paternal influences on child development. These three approaches—highlighting correlational strategies, the effects of father absence, and the impact of highly involved fathers, respectively—will be described and their results summarized separately in this section. The summaries presented here are by no means exhaustive. Indeed, in the first two subsections I limit my discussion to illustrative research involving fathers and sons. More detailed and comprehensive reviews are provided elsewhere (Adams, Milner, & Schrepf, 1984; Lamb, 1981c; Lamb, Pleck, & Levine, 1985); my goal here is to illustrate key features of the empirical research that have prompted major changes in our conceptualization of paternal influence patterns.

The Correlational Approach

Let us first consider those studies concerned with the search for correlations between paternal and filial characteristics. In such studies, researchers might try to measure either the warmth, closeness, or hostility of father-child relationships (for reviews see Biller, 1971; Lamb, 1976, 1981c) or else the masculinity or authoritarianism of fathers, and then correlate measures of those paternal or relational constructs with measures of some theoretically related characteristics in the children. This strategy was adopted in many of the earliest studies of paternal influences, the vast majority of which were focused on sex-role development—especially in sons. This is understandable, since many of these studies were done during the 1940s, 1950s, and early 1960s when the father's role as a sex-role model was considered most important. The design of these early studies was quite simple: The researchers assessed masculinity in fathers and in sons, and then determined how strongly the two sets of scores were correlated. To the researchers' great surprise, there was no consistent correlation between fathers' masculinity and sons' masculinity, a finding which puzzled many researchers because it seemed to violate a guiding assumption about the crucial function served by fathers. If fathers did not make their boys into men, then what role did they really serve?

It took a while for psychologists to realize that the guiding assumption may have been inappropriate. Researchers failed to ask: Why should boys *want to be like* their fathers? Presumably, they should only want to resemble fathers whom they liked and respected, and with whom relationships were warm or positive. In fact, the quality of father-son relationships was found to be an important mediating variable: When the relationships between masculine fathers and their sons were good, boys were indeed more masculine. Subsequent research suggested that the quality of the relationship was actually the crucial variable so far as the development of filial masculinity was concerned (Mussen & Rutherford, 1963; Payne & Mussen, 1956; Sears, Maccoby, & Levin, 1957). By contrast, the masculinity of the father was rather unimportant. In other words, boys seemed to conform to the sex-role standards of their culture when their relationships with their fathers were warm, regardless of how "masculine" the fathers were. Because of this, we might expect that the effects of close father-son relationships have changed over the last 15 years, during which cultural preferences for and expectations of male behavior have changed also. Today, for example, we might expect that warm fathers who have close relationships with their children would have more androgynous sons (since androgyny seems to be the contemporary goal) just as similarly close relationships to warm fathers formerly potentiated the development of masculine sons when that was the cultural ideal (Baruch & Barnett, 1979, 1983; Radin, 1978; Radin & Sagi, 1982).

As far as paternal influences on sex-role development are concerned, then, the key finding is that characteristics of the father (such as his masculinity) were much less important formatively than his warmth and the closeness and nature of his relationship with his son. This is an interesting and important finding because warmth and closeness have traditionally been seen as feminine characteristics. Thus "feminine" characteristics of the father—his warmth and nurturance— seems to be associated with better adjustment in sons, at least to the extent that adjustment is defined in terms of sex role.[2]

Similar findings have been obtained in studies concerned with paternal influences on achievement (Radin, 1981). Initially, the assumption was that fathers would influence achievement motivation positively because they were the family members who exemplified achievement in "the real world," and because their sons would surely want to emulate their fathers in this regard. Once more, it soon became clear that the father's warmth, closeness, and involvement were most important; fathers with these characteristics tended to have competent and achievement-oriented sons (Radin, 1978, 1981, 1982). The same characteristics are important where mothers' influence on children's achievement is concerned, again implying that fathers influence children not by virtue of "male" characteristics (like masculinity) but by virtue of nurturant personal and social characteristics.

A similar conclusion is suggested by research on psychosocial adjustment: Paternal warmth or closeness is advantageous, whereas paternal masculinity is irrelevant (Biller, 1971; Lamb, 1981b). Thus, across these three areas of development, better adjustment on the part of children seems to occur when the relationships between fathers and children are close and warm. In general, the same is true for mothers, so that children who have close relationships with both parents benefit from having two supportive, nurturant relationships and are psychologically better off as a result. As far as influence on children is concerned, there seems to be very little about the gender of the parent that is distinctly important. The characteristics of the father as a parent rather than the characteristics of the father as a man appear to influence child development.

---

[2]This is a questionable assumption, particularly given the ways in which sex roles are usually operationalized in the research literature. Readers are referred to J. H. Pleck (1981) and Lamb et al. (1985) for further discussion of these issues, which are not critical to the argument being developed here.

Father-Absence Research

While this whole body of research that I have termed "correlational" was burgeoning the 1950s, another body of literature was developing. This involved a series of investigations in which researchers tried to understand the father's role by studying families without fathers. The assumption was that by comparing the behavior and personalities of children raised with and without fathers, one could—essentially by a process of subtraction—estimate what sort of influence fathers typically had. The chief father-absence and correlational studies were conducted in roughly the same era; not surprisingly, therefore, the dependent variables studied were very similar and the nature of the results were in many ways similar. In the case of father-absence studies, the results also appeared consistent with popular assumptions. Unfortunately, the literature on father absence is voluminous and controversial; readers are referred elsewhere for more detailed discussions (Adams et al., 1984; Biller, 1974; Herzog & Sudia, 1973, Lamb, 1981). In the present context, suffice it to say that boys growing up without fathers seemed to have "problems" in the areas of sex-role and gender-identity development, school performance, psychosocial adjustment, and perhaps in the control of aggression.

Two related issues arising from the father-absence research must be addressed. First, even if one agrees that there are differences between children raised in families with fathers present and those raised in families with fathers absent, one must ask *why* those differences exist, and how we should interpret them. Second, it is important to remember that although there may be group differences between, say 100 boys growing up without fathers and 100 boys growing up with fathers, these findings do not mean that every individual child growing up without a father has problems in some if not all of the areas mentioned above, or that all boys whose fathers live at home develop normatively. One cannot make inferences about individuals from data concerning groups, simply because there is great within-group heterogeneity. This forces us to ask why such heterogeneity exists. Why do some boys appear to suffer deleterious consequences as a result of father absence while others do not? More broadly, the question is: What is it about the father-absence context that makes for group differences between children in father-absent and father-present contexts, and what accounts for the impressive within-group variance?

Researchers and theorists first sought to explain the effects of father absence in terms of the absence of a male sex-role model: In the absence of a masculine parental model, it was assumed that boys could not acquire strong masculine identities or sex roles, and would not have a model of achievement with which to identify (Biller, 1974). The problem with this interpretation is that many boys without fathers seem to develop quite normally, so far as sex-role development and achievement is concerned. Clearly, an explanation that emphasizes the absence in the home of a male sex-role model cannot be complete or inclusive. It has thus become increasingly clear that some other factors may be at least as important as (if not much more important than) the availability of sex-role models in mediating the effects of father absence on child development.

First, there is the absence of a co-parent—someone to help out with child-care, to be there when one parent needs a break, to supplement the parents' resources in relation to the demands of the child (Maccoby, 1977). Second, there is the economic stress that goes along with single parenthood, especially single motherhood. The median and mean incomes for single women who are heads of households are significantly lower than the average income for any other group, and the disparity is even larger when one considers per capita income, rather than income per household (Glick & Norton, 1979). Third, the tremendous economic stress oppressing single mothers is accompanied by social and emotional stress occasioned by a degree of social isolation and the largely disapproving attitudes that society continues to hold with respect to single or divorced mothers and children (Hetherington, Cox, & Cox, 1982). Lastly, there is the pre-divorce (and post-divorce) marital conflict—an important issue because, of all the findings in the area of socialization, the best validated is the fact that children suffer when there is marital hostility or conflict (Rutter, 1973, 1979; Lamb, 1981b). Since most single-parent families are produced by divorce and since divorce is often preceded by periods of overt and covert spousal hostility, pre-divorce conflict may play a major role in explaining the problems of children who do not live with their fathers. By contrast, these children—if they have good relationships with both parents before and after the divorce—tend to be better adjusted than children who do not have such relationships with both parents (Hess & Camara, 1979).

In sum, the evidence suggests that father absence may be harmful not necessarily because a sex-role model is absent, but because many aspects of the father's role—economic, social, emotional—go unfilled or inappropriately filled. It is essential to recognize the father's multiple roles as breadwinner, parent, and emotional support for partner in order to understand how fathers influence children's development.

Studies of Increased Paternal Involvement

Finally, we must consider a more recent series of studies concerned with the effects on children of increased father involvement, as exemplified by fathers who either share in or take primary responsibility for childcare (Lamb, Pleck, & Levine, 1985; Russell, 1983, 1986; Radin & Russell, 1983). This question has been addressed in three or four studies, which provide some remarkably consistent results with respect to preschool-aged children whose fathers are responsible for at least 40–45% of the within-family childcare. Children with highly involved fathers are characterized by increased cognitive competence, increased empathy, less sex-stereotyped beliefs, and a more internal locus of control (Pruett, 1983; Radin, 1982; Radin & Sagi, 1982; Sagi, 1982). Again, the question that has to be asked is: *Why* do these sorts of differences occur?

Three factors are probably important in this regard (Lamb, et al., 1985). First, because the parents assume less sex-stereotyped roles, it is not surprising that their children have less sex-stereotyped attitudes themselves about male and female roles. Second, particularly in the area of cognitive competence, these children may benefit from having two highly involved parents rather than just one; this assures them the diversity of stimulation that comes from interacting with different people who have different behavioral styles. A third important issue has to do with the family context in which these children are raised. In every study reported thus far, high paternal involvement made it possible for both parents to do what was subjectively important to them. It allowed fathers to satisfy a desire to become close to their children and it allowed mothers to have adequately close relationships with their children while also being involved in the pursuit of career goals that were important to them. In other words, increased paternal involvement in the families studied may have made both parents feel much more fulfilled. As a result, it is likely that the relationships were much warmer and much richer than might otherwise have been the case. My speculation, therefore, is that the positive outcomes obtained by children with highly involved fathers are largely attributable to the fact that the fathers' involvement created a family context in which parents felt good about their marriages and the arrangements they had been able to work out.

In all of these studies, fathers were involved because both their partners and themselves wanted this to be the case. The results might be very different when fathers were forced to become involved, perhaps because they were laid off while their partners could get and hold jobs. In such circumstances, wives might resent the fact that their husbands were ineffective breadwinners who could not hold jobs and support their families, while the men resented the fact that they were home doing "women's work" with the children when they really wanted to be outside the home earning a living and supporting their families (see Russell, 1983). This constellation of factors might well have adverse effects on children, just as the same degree of involvement has positive effects when the circumstances are more benign. The key point is that the extent of a father's involvement may be much less significant (so far as understanding the effects on children is concerned) than are the reasons for his involvement, his evaluation of that involvement, and his partner's evaluation of his involvement.

In sum, the effects may in many cases have more to do with the context of father involvement than with father involvement per se. What matters is not so much who is at home, but how that person feels about being at home, for his/her feelings will color the way he/she behaves with the children. Her/his behavior is also influenced by the other partner's feelings about the arrangement: both parents' emotional states affect the family dynamics.

Summary

The three genres of research on paternal influences together paint a remarkably consistent picture. First, fathers and mothers seem to influence their children in similar rather than dissimilar ways. The important dimensions of parental influence are those that have to do with parental characteristics rather than gender-related characteristics. Secondly, the nature of the effect may vary substantially depending upon individual and cultural values. A classic example of this can be found in the literature on sex-role development. As a result of cultural changes, the assumed sex-role goals for boys and girls have changed and this has produced changes in the effect of father involvement on children. In the 1950s, sex-appropriate masculinity or femininity were the desired goals; today androgyny or sex-role flexibility are desired. And whereas father involvement in the 1950s seemed to be associated with greater masculinity in boys, it is associated today with less sex-stereotyped sex-role standards in both sons and daughters. Third, influence patterns vary substantially depending upon social factors which define the meaning of father involvement for children in particular families embedded in particular social milieus. Finally, the amount of time that fathers and children spend together is probably much less important than what they do with that time and how fathers, mothers, children, and other important people in their lives perceive and evaluate the father-child relationships. All of this means that high paternal involvement may have positive effects in some circumstances and negative effects in other circumstances. The same is true of low paternal involvement. However, we must not lose sight of recent historical changes in average levels of paternal involvement (Juster, in press). If these trends continue, there will be increasing numbers of families in which greater father involvement would be beneficial.

THE DETERMINANTS OF FATHER INVOLVEMENT

Motivation

Four factors are crucial to understanding variations in the degree of paternal involvement (Lamb et al., 1987). First, there is motivation—the extent to which the father wants to be involved. Survey data suggest that 40% of fathers would like to have more time to spend with their children than they currently have available (Quinn & Staines, 1979). This implies that a substantial number of men are motivated to be more involved. On the other hand, the same data suggest that more than half of the fathers in the country do not want to spend more time with their children then they currently do. Clearly, there is no unanimity about the desirability of increased paternal involvement—an important point when one considers the need to evaluate parental motivations when attempting to understand parental influences (see previous section).

Recent changes in levels of paternal motivation have taken place, however, and can be attributed primarily to the women's movement and the questions it raised about traditional male and female roles. In addition, media hype about the "new father" has also affected motivation levels. The most impressive official program yet undertaken was initiated by the Swedish government in the early 1970s in an attempt to encourage men to become more involved in childcare (Lamb & Levine, 1983). Figures 1.1 and 1.2 depict images from the brochures and posters published by the Swedish government. Note that Figure 1.1 depicts a very large muscular man holding a tiny baby. This figure implicitly addresses one of the key attitudinal barriers to male involvement: the notion that it is effeminate for men to be involved in childcare. The illustration in Figure 1.2 likewise conveys the message that "real men" can be actively involved in child-care. The message is important because many men continue to feel that active parenting and masculinity are incompatible. Continuing fears of this sort help explain why some motivational shifts have been so slow and particularly why the number of fathers who take a major role in childcare has not increased very much (nationally or internationally) despite tremendous changes in female employment patterns.

FIGURE 1.1.

FIGURE 1.2.

Skills and Self-Confidence

Motivation alone cannot ensure increased involvement: Skills and self confidence are also necessary. Ostensibly motivated men often complain that a lack of skills (exemplified by ignorance or clumsiness) prevents increased involvement. These complaints can constitute excuses, but they can also reflect a very real fear on the part of many men.

When men are motivated, and the absence of skills poses a major barrier, formal skill development programs may be critically important. However, the best way to start getting men involved with their children may be to encourage them to do things that they enjoy doing together. The goal should be to develop a sense of self-confidence so that fathers come to enjoy being with their children, and come to feel increasingly self-confident. Once fathers realize that their children really are fun, absolutely adore them, and do not generate an endless succession of embarrassing crises, they will be willing to expand the range of activities and contexts in which fathers and children successfully function together. The key thing is to develop confidence—the skills themselves are easier to acquire later. Many fathers do not realize that most primiparous mothers are just as incompetent and just as terrified as they are. The difference is that women are expected to know how to parent, and cannot withdraw from the challenges involved. They have to pretend that they know what they are doing, and thus must learn the necessary skills as soon as they can.

In addition to self-confidence, sensitivity is also crucial (Lamb, 1980). Sensitivity involves being able to read the child's signals, know what he or she wants, know how to respond appropriately, know what expectations are realistic, etc. Both sensitivity and self-confidence are abstract characteristics, both of which are probably much more important than specific skills. Specific skills may provide useful vehicles by means of which sensitivity and self-confidence develop, however.

Support

The third factor influencing paternal involvement is support—especially support within the family from mothers. The same surveys that show a majority of men wanting to be more involved show that somewhere between 60% and 80% of women do *not* want their husbands to be more involved than they currently are (J. H. Pleck, 1982; Quinn & Staines, 1979). This suggests that, although many mothers would like their husbands to do more, a substantial majority are quite satisfied with the status quo.

There may be many reasons for these attitudes. Some mothers may feel that their husbands are incompetent and that their involvement may create more work than it saves. More importantly, increased paternal involvement may threaten to upset some fundamental power dynamics within the family (Polatnick, 1973–1974). The role of mother and manager of the household are the two roles in which women's authority has not been questioned; together, they constitute the one area in which women have had real power and control. Increased paternal involvement may threaten this power and preeminence. The trade-off is of dubious value because, although increasing numbers of women have entered the work force in the last two decades, they are usually restricted to low-paying, low-prestige, low-advancement occupations. In essence, women are thus being asked to give up power in the one area where power and authority are unquestioned in exchange for the possibility of power in another area. For many women, it is preferable to maintain authority in the childcare arena, even if that means physical and mental exhaustion.

Changes in women's attitudes toward paternal involvement have changed very little over the last 15 years or so (J. H. Pleck, 1982; Polatnick, 1973–1974). Their resilience is likely to endure until fundamental changes within the society-at-large change the basic distribution of power. Even among those women who say they would welcome increased paternal involvement, there may be more ambivalence than survey results indicate.

The heterogeneity of maternal attitudes regarding paternal involvement raises very important issues about father involvement and its likely effects on young children. As mentioned earlier, the effects on family dynamics may be most critical. Thus, when deciding whether or not father involvement should be encouraged in particular families, one must take into account the preferences and attitudes of *both* parents. To do so involves articulating individual assumptions and values and then negotiating in an attempt to achieve some satisfactory consensus.

Because women's attitudes and assumptions appear to be changing faster than men's, conflict between partners may become increasingly common as these societal changes continue. In this regard, it may be significant that in the two longitudinal studies of high father involvement, a remarkably high rate of family dissolution was evident when families were later relocated (Russell, 1983; Radin & Goldsmith, 1985). Thus, despite really good dynamics early on (at least in Radin and Goldsmith's subject families), there can often be substantial and fundamental problems around roles and responsibilities, particularly in this era of ambivalence and confusion. It is important to remember such negative aspects of paternal involvement even though, on the whole, father involvement is important and desirable for an increasing number of families.

Institutional Practices

The last of the factors influencing paternal involvement comprises institutional practices. The needs of families for economic support and the barriers imposed by the workplace rank among the most important reasons given by fathers to explain low levels of paternal involvement (e.g., Yankelovitch, 1974). Clearly this is an important issue for many men, and it will remain important as long as males take on and are expected to assume the primary breadwinning role. It is also true, however, that men do not trade off work time for family time in a one-to-one fashion. Survey data show that women translate each extra hour of non-work time into an extra 40 to 45 minutes of family work, whereas for men, each hour not spent in paid work translates into less than 20 minutes of family work (J. H. Pleck, 1983). Thus, while the pressures of work do have a significant effect on parental involvement, the effects on men and women are somewhat different. Being at work does reduce the amount of time that fathers can spend with their children, but even when they have time available, they spend only a small portion of it with their children.[3]

Paternity leave is the most frequently discussed means of enhancing paternal involvement. This near-exclusive focus is really misdirected, because paternity leave is unlikely to provide the answer to increased paternal involvement. One has to remember that less than one third of the working women in this country have any type of *paid* maternity leave, and if employers will not allow maternity leave, paternity leave must rank as an unrealistic goal. In addition, paternity leaves facilitate involvement only during a very narrow period of time at the beginning of the child's life, although their use does predict degree of subsequent involvement (Lamb, Hwang, Bookstein, Broberg, Hult, & Frodi, in prep.). Practices that allow men to be involved over the long-haul would be more helpful

---

[3]In addition to the constraints imposed by actual work time, it is also important to recall that the whole identification of fatherhood with breadwinning serves to limit male involvement in childcare.

than paternity leaves. Flexible time scheduling would certainly be of greatest value to many involved but employed fathers (and mothers), as J. H. Pleck (1986) suggests.

Summary

One can conceive of these four factors (motivation, skills and self-confidence, support, and institutional practices) as a hierarchy of factors influencing involvement. Favorable conditions must exist at each level if increased paternal involvement is to be possible and beneficial. Successful interventions will be those that can address people at each of these different levels, focusing on those areas in which the inhibiting factors are most prominent. Institutional barriers are much harder to change than any of the others. Nevertheless, institutions create much more flexibility than most people admit; while they pose major barriers, they might also allow many men to be more involved than they actually are.

SUMMARY

A number of issues pertaining to paternal involvement have been addressed—albeit briefly—in this chapter. As mentioned earlier, the currently high degrees of interest in paternal roles and functions on the part of scholars and researchers reflect the latest in a series of shifts in the ways in which American society conceptualizes and idealizes fatherhood. Consistent with the notion of a "new fatherhood," average levels of paternal involvement have increased in the last several years, although the increases have been modest. Mothers still spend much more time than fathers do interacting with or being accessible to their children, and this remains true even when both parents are employed. Furthermore, ultimate responsibility for childcare and childrearing remains the near-exclusive province of mothers, while fathers "help out when they can (or when it is convenient)." A number of factors—including motivation, skills and self-confidence, support, and institutional factors—appear to affect levels of paternal involvement, but many of these reflect manifestations of an underlying assumption: Men are first and foremost workers and breadwinners, whereas women are primarily nurturers.

Whatever the extent of their involvement, fathers do appear to influence their children's development, both directly by means of interaction and indirectly by virtue of their impact (positive and negative) on the family's social and emotional climate. Because attitudes concerning appropriate levels of paternal involvement vary widely, high and low levels of paternal involvement can be either beneficial or harmful to child development depending on the attitudes and values of the parents concerned. It is thus critically important to recognize inter- and intra-cultural diversity when exploring paternal influences on child development.

REFERENCES

Adams, P. L., Milner, J. R., & Schrepf, N. A. (1984). *Fatherless children.* New York: Wiley.

Baruch, G. K., & Barnett, R. C. (1979). *Fathers' participation in the care of their preschool children.* Unpublished manuscript, Wellesley College.

Baruch, G. K., & Barnett, R. C. (1983). *Correlates of fathers' participation in family work: A technical report.* Working Paper #106. Wellesley, MA: Wellesley College Center for Research on Women.

Benson, L. (1968). *Fatherhood: A sociological perspective.* New York: Random House.

Biller, H. B. (1971). *Father, child, and sex role.* Lexington, MA: Heath.

Biller, H. B. (1974). *Paternal deprivation: Family, school, sexuality and society.* Lexington, MA: Heath.

Bowlby, J. (1951). *Maternal care and mental health.* Geneva: WHO.

Cazenave, N. A. (1979). Middle-income black fathers: An analysis of the provider role. *Family Coordinator, 27,* 583–593.

Demos, J. (1982). The changing faces of fatherhood: A new exploration in American family history. In S. H. Cath, A. R. Gurwitt, & J. M. Ross (Eds.), *Father and child: Developmental and clinical perspectives.* Boston: Little Brown.

Ehrenreich, B., & English D. (1979). *For her own good.* New York: Anchor Books.

Glick, P. C., & Norton, A. J. (1979). Marrying, divorcing, and living together in the US today. *Population Bulletin, 32* (whole number 5).

Herzog, R., & Sudia, C. E. (1973). Children in fatherless families. In B. M. Caldwell & H. N. Ricciuti (Eds.), *Review of child development research* (Vol. 3). Chicago: University of Chicago Press.

Hess, R. D., & Camara, K. A. (1979). Post-divorce family relationships as mediating factors in the consequences of divorce for children. *Journal of Social Issues, 35,* 79–96.

Hetherington, E. M., Cox, M., & Cox, R. (1982). Effects of divorce on parents and children. In M. E. Lamb (Ed.), *Nontraditional families.* Hillsdale, NJ: Lawrence Erlbaum Associates.

Hipgrave, T. (1982). Childrearing by lone fathers. In R. Chester, P. Diggory, & M. Sutherland (Eds.), *Changing patterns of child bearing and child rearing.* London: Academic Press.

Juster, F. T. (in press). A note on recent changes in time use. In F. T. Juster & F. Stafford (Eds.), *Studies in the measurement of time allocation.* Ann Arbor, MI: Institute for Social Research.

Lamb, M. E. (Ed.) (1976). *The role of the father in child development.* New York: Wiley.

Lamb, M. E. (1980). What can "research experts" tell parents about effective socialization? In M. D. Fantini & R. Cardenas (Eds.), *Parenting in a multicultural society.* New York: Longman.

Lamb, M. E. (1981a). The development of father-infant relationships. In M. E. Lamb (Ed.), *The role of the father in child development.* (Rev. Ed.) New York: Wiley.

Lamb, M. E. (1981b). Fathers and child development: An integrative overview. In M. E. Lamb (Ed.), *The role of the father in child development.* (Rev. Ed.) New York: Wiley.

Lamb, M. E. (Ed.) (1981c). *The role of the father in child development* (Rev. Ed.). New York: Wiley.

Lamb, M. E. Hwang, C.-P., Bookstein, F. L., Broberg, A. Hult, G., & Frodi, M. (in preparation). *The determinants of paternal involvement.* Unpublished manuscript, University of Utah.

Lamb, M. E., & Levine, J. A. (1983). The Swedish parental insurance policy: An experiment in social engineering. In M. E. Lamb & A. Sagi (Eds.), *Fatherhood and family policy.* Hillsdale, NJ: Lawrence Erlbaum Associates.

Lamb, M. E., Pleck, J. H., & Charnov, E. L., & Levine, J. A. (1985). Paternal behavior in humans. *American Zoologist, 25,* 883–894.

Lamb, M. E., Pleck, J. H., Charnov, E. L., & Levine, J. A. (1987). A biosocial perspective on paternal behavior and involvement. In J. B. Lancaster, J. Altmann, A. Rossi, & L. R. Sherrod (Eds.), *Parenting across the life span: Biosocial perspectives.* Hawthorne, NY: Aldine de Gruyter.

Lamb, M. E., Pleck, J. H., & Levine, J. A. (1985). The role of the father in child development: The effects of increased paternal involvement. In B. S. Lahey & A. E. Kazdin (Eds.), *Advances in clinical child psychology* (Vol. 8). New York: Plenum.

Levine, J. A. (1976). *And who will raise the children? New options for fathers (and mothers).* Philadelphia: Lippincott.

Levy, D. M. (1943). *Maternal overprotection.* New York: Columbia University Press.

Lynn, D. (1974). *The father: His role in child development.* Monterey, CA: Brooks/Cole.

Maccoby, E. E. (1977). *Current changes in the family and their impact upon the socialization of children.* Paper presented to the American Sociological Association, Chicago.

Mussen, P. H., & Rutherford, E. (1963). Parent-child relations and parental personality in relation to young children's sex-role preferences. *Child Development, 34,* 589–607.

Parke, R. D., Power, T. G., & Gottman, J. (1979). Conceptualizing and quantifying influence patterns in the family triad. In M. E. Lamb, S. J. Suomi, & G. R. Stephenson (Eds.), *Social interaction analysis: Methodological issues.* Madison: University of Wisconsin Press.

Payne, D. E., & Mussen, P. H. (1956). Parent-child relations and father identification among adolescent boys. *Journal of Abnormal and Social Psychology, 52,* 358–362.

Pleck, E. (1976). Two worlds in one: Work and family. *Journal of Social History, 10,* 178–195.

Pleck, J. H. (1981). *The myth of masculinity.* Cambridge, MA: MIT Press.

Pleck, J. H. (1982). *Husbands' and wives' paid work, family work, and adjustment.* Wellesley, MA: Wellesley College Center for Research on Women (Working Papers).

Pleck, J. H. (1983). Husbands' paid work and family roles: Current research issues. In H. Lopata & J. H. Pleck (Eds.), *Research in the interweave of social roles* (Vol. 3), *Families and jobs.* Greenwich, CT: JAI Press.

Pleck, J. H. (1984a). Changing fatherhood. Unpublished manuscript, Wellesley College.

Pleck, J. H. (1984b). *Working wives and family well-being.* Beverly Hills, CA: Sage.

Pleck, J. H. (1986). Fatherhood and the workplace. In M. E. Lamb (Ed.), *The father's role: Applied perspectives.* New York: Wiley.

Polatnick, M. (1973–74). Why men don't rear children: A power analysis. *Berkeley Journal of Sociology, 18,* 44–86.

Pruett, K. D. (1983). *Two year followup of infants of primary nurturing fathers in intact families.* Paper presented to the Second World Congress on Infant Psychiatry, Cannes (France).

Quinn, R. P., & Staines, G. L. (1979). *The 1977 Quality of Employment Survey.* Ann Arbor, MI: Survey Research Center.

Radin, N. (1978). *Childrearing fathers in intact families with preschoolers.* Paper presented to the American Psychological Association, Toronto, September.

Radin, N. (1981). The role of the father in cognitive, academic, and intellectual development. In M. E. Lamb (Ed.), *The role of the father in child development* (Rev. Ed.). New York: Wiley.

Radin, N. (1982). Primary caregiving and role-sharing fathers. In M. E. Lamb (Ed.), *Nontraditional families: Parenting and child development.* Hillsdale, NJ: Lawrence Erlbaum Associates.

Radin, N., & Goldsmith, R. (1985). Caregiving fathers of preschoolers: Four years later. *Merrill-Palmer Quarterly, 31,* 375–383.

Radin, N., & Russell, G. (1983). Increased father participation and child development outcomes. In M. E. Lamb & A. Sagi (Eds.), *Fatherhood and family policy.* Hillsdale, NJ: Lawrence Erlbaum Associates.

Radin, N., & Sagi, A. (1982). Childrearing fathers in intact families in Israel and the U.S.A. *Merrill-Palmer Quarterly, 28,* 111–136.

Russell, G. (1982). Shared-caregiving families: An Australian study. In M. E. Lamb (Ed.), *Nontraditional families: Parenting and child development.* Hillsdale, NJ: Lawrence Erlbaum Associates.

Russell, G. (1983). *The changing role of fathers?* St. Lucia, Queensland: University of Queensland Press.

Russell, G. (1986). Primary caretaking and role sharing fathers. In M. E. Lamb (Ed.), *The father's role: Applied perspectives*. New York: Wiley.

Rutter, M. (1973). Why are London children so disturbed? *Proceedings of the Royal Society of Medicine, 66*, 1221–1225.

Rutter, M. (1979). Maternal deprivation, 1972–1978: New findings, new concepts, new approaches. *Child Development, 50*, 283–305.

Sagi, A. (1982). Antecedents and consequences of various degrees of paternal involvement in child rearing: The Israeli project. In M. E. Lamb (Ed.), *Nontraditional families: Parenting and child development*. Hillsdale, NJ: Lawrence Erlbaum Associates.

Sears, R. R., Maccoby, E. E., & Levin, H. (1957). *Patterns of child rearing*. Evanston, IL: Row Peterson.

Strecker, E. (1946). *Their mothers' sons*. Philadelphia: Lippincott.

Yankelovich, D. (1974). The meaning of work. In J. Rosow (Ed.), *The worker and the job*. Englewood Cliffs, NJ: Prentice-Hall.

II WESTERN EUROPE

2 Great Britain

Sonia Jackson
University of Bristol

THE BRITISH FAMILY CONTEXT

In considering the British family today, one is struck by several contradictions. The rhetoric of change is in the air but seems not to correspond with many measurable differences in the way people order their lives.

Economic, social, legal, and ideological factors appear to be pulling in one direction, political and administrative forces in the other. Major structural changes have occurred in British society over the past fifteen years, paralleled by a noticeable shift in the way that family organization and marital roles are discussed and reflected in the media. But the inertia of state institutions puts a powerful brake on the capacity of family structures to respond to changed conditions.

This can be clearly seen in relation to three trends in British society, which might be expected to have a dramatic impact on the family: the increase in the number of married women working outside their homes, the rise in the divorce rate, and the inexorable growth of unemployment, especially in the early 1980s. In addition, there is a new consciousness in women of the extent to which they may be disadvantaged by traditional patterns of economic and domestic life. The Sex Discrimination Act (1975) has made it illegal to disadvantage women in education and employment. This has had some effect in giving girls better access to scientific and technical qualifications. Among the professional and managerial classes, the education of girls is now more likely to approximate to that of their brothers; though this is still not true either of the upper or lower classes. However, because this is the class from which journalists, writers, broadcasters, lawyers, and managers are likely to be drawn, their influence may be out of proportion to their numbers.

29

The ideology of the family appears to be changing to the extent that there is a formal assumption of equality between husbands and wives. Edgell (1980) showed that this breaks down among professional couples when decision-making is analyzed by importance and frequency. Relatively unimportant decisions, which have to be taken repeatedly, tend to be made by wives. Major decisions that occur only occasionally (moving to a new home, for example) are made more often by husbands, though the wife may be consulted.

Cohabitation before marriage became increasingly common throughout the 1970s. Nearly 20% of those marrying for the first time in 1977 had previously lived together (Brown & Kiernan, 1981) compared with only 4% in 1970. If this trend continues, it will be less common for young men to move straight from a living situation (in which all their personal and domestic needs are catered for by their mothers) to receiving the same services from their wives. When young couples live together before marriage, there is usually some gesture at negotiating a division of domestic roles on an equitable basis, especially if both partners are working. After marriage, traditional expectations gradually reassert themselves, particularly when the birth of the first child takes the woman out of paid employment for several years.

Participation of married women in the workforce was very low (around 10%) throughout the first half of the century and did not alter significantly in peacetime until after the second World War (Davidoff, 1979). Since that time, the proportion of economically-active married women has increased steadily. By 1981, 57% of those under 60 were officially recorded as employed, although over half were employed part-time (less than 30 hours a week).

The most important determinant of whether a woman works outside the home is the age of the youngest child. The lack of child-care provision in Britain still makes it extremely difficult for a woman with a child under five to go out to work. Publicly-provided day care centers are now used almost exclusively for child protection purposes, and in most places it is not available to mothers with no male partners to support them (New & David, 1986). Because women command low wages and often cannot afford to pay economic rates for child care, there is little profit to be made from private child-care centers, which have been slow to develop. Home-based care, called childminding in Britain, is of variable quality and often hard to find (Jackson & Jackson, 1979).

Once the last child reaches the compulsory school age of 5, mothers have more freedom of choice. Even so, only 13% work full-time because it is expected that the domestic organization of the family will fit round the requirements of the school system with its short working day and long irregular holidays. A far larger number of mothers (44%) work part-time. Their hourly earnings are on average only two-thirds what men earn, and because of the shorter hours, their cash income is lower still.

As a result, the marked increase in the proportion of married women with children working outside the home has had little impact on the structure or expectations of the British family. Even those women who do combine paid work and motherhood are usually partially economically dependent. Moreover, the assumption that men are the chief breadwinners and women their economic dependents is backed by the laws on employment, social security, and taxation which define economic dependence as women's normal status (Land, 1986).

Thus women continue to think of themselves as "the maintenance staff for family members and the physical and emotional environment of the home." (New & David, 1985, p. 91). There are major social-class and occupational differences in the ways this role is interpreted by different women, but the role itself is generally accepted.

A second major change in British society has been the steep rise in the divorce rate, especially since the Divorce Law Reform Act of 1969, which came into operation two years later. In 1961 only 25,000 divorces were recorded in the U.K. By 1980 the figure had risen to 147,000 (Argyle & Henderson, 1985). If this trend continues, it can be predicted that one in three of all marriages currently being contracted will end in divorce (Haskey, 1982). The fact that divorce has now become a common experience has had the effect of destigmatizing it. Although the status of a formerly married person is still an uneasy one in contemporary British society (Hart 1976; Delphy, 1984), the greater possibility of escape from an unsatisfactory marriage has probably given women more power to negotiate their position within marriage.

When a marriage does break up, it is still more likely that the children will remain with the mother; nearly 90% of single-parent families are headed by females. The number of single fathers increased by 30% in the course of the 1970s, but the number of single mothers increased even more. Jackson (1982) pointed out that cross-sectional figures could be misleading, because being in a single-parent family is often a transitional state. Because men have a much higher and faster remarriage rate than women, far more families may have had the experience of being headed by a father alone than the figures would suggest.

Another social trend, which could have a stronger impact on family life, is the rise in unemployment. The dream of full employment was already slipping away in the early 1970s, but the really sharp increase occured between 1979 and 1983 when unemployment levels more than doubled to over 3 million. By that date, 15.6% of men and 8.7% of women in the workforce were officially registered as unemployed.

Unemployment is not evenly spread through the population but concentrated in the traditional urban centers of heavy industry: Scotland, Northern Ireland, North-east and North-west England, where whole communities may be jobless. Not only is the incidence of unemployment rising, but individuals are likely to be out of work for longer periods. Whereas, in 1979 only 29% of unemployed men had been out of work for a year or more, by July 1984 this figure had risen to 44% (Employment Gazette, 1979 and 1984). As yet there is little evidence of the impact unemployment is having on the family because most studies treat the unemployed as individuals and pay relatively little attention to their domestic and family arrangements (Allan, 1985). The financial effect is certainly very severe, with 80% of men who have been unemployed for more than 12 months living on or below the poverty line. Because of the inadequate rates paid for children, their families are likely to suffer the most deprivation and hardship (Clark, 1978).

In some areas of high unemployment there is still work for women, and role reversal might seem the obvious answer. However Bell and McKee (1984) argue that unemployment may well encourage a polarization of male and female activities rather than any convergence between them. The operation of state welfare programs, assuming a male income earner with a dependent female, provide wives of unemployed men with a strong disincentive to be in paid work. For this reason, wives with unemployed husbands are only half as likely to be employed as are married women in general (Allan, 1985). When both husband and wife are at home all day it seems that they may need to more clearly define their gender roles. Men's already-threatened self-esteem would be further undermined by undertaking 'female' tasks, while on the other hand, the woman may need to maintain her familiar routine and assert her superior expertise in domestic matters (Morris, 1983). From a number of studies of unemployed men, Allan concludes that "the ideology of the domestic division of labour is sufficiently embedded into everyday social life for it to be hardly threatened by the male's lack of employment" (1985, p. 166).

Although many researchers have come to similar conclusions, a closer examination of the evidence shows that most studies are concerned with men who have lost their jobs as a result of factory closures, not those who, as is increasingly common, have never had jobs at all. Secondly, they have paid very little attention to the man's relationship with his children or his contribution to child care as opposed to housework. There is a strong impression among teachers and child-care workers that men have become much more visible since the onset of mass unemployment. At Gateshead, near Newcastle, severely hit by the decline of heavy industry, the newly-built Metro station provides baby-changing facilities in male as well as female toilets. Yet this highly traditional community is the last place one would expect gender roles to crumble.

Do such indicators foreshadow a radical shift in family and household organization? Most commentators are skeptical. Detailed analysis of state welfare benefits (Land, 1986) shows a movement back to the position that the family maintenance is the responsibility of men. The role of the state, as Eleanor Rathbone, the great campaigner for family allowances, complained in 1924, is merely to ensure that the *man's* income is sufficient for him to indulge in "the praiseworthy leisure-time occupation of keeping a family" (Rathbone 1924/1986, p. 123).

It seems that despite the significant increases in cohabitation, wives' employment, divorce, and one-parent families, which all tend to undermine the traditional organization of family life, the underlying pattern remains strong.

Most men work to support their families, and most women work chiefly to improve the family's standard of living. The law, taxation, and welfare benefit systems, continue to enshrine the ideal of the male breadwinner and the dependent wife and mother while increasingly recognizing the possibility of other arrangements. New and David (1986) claim "men can push prams, women can be bank managers, but as the exceptions multiply, the rule itself is untouched"(p.43).

An alternative interpretation of the evidence might be that the conditions for change now exist but there has not yet been time for their effects to be felt. There are some signs that this is true of the father's role in the British family, which is the central issue addressed by this chapter.

The chapter begins by reviewing the state of fatherhood research in Britain and its development over the past 20 years. It is suggested that this in itself reveals a major change in perception of the father's role. A prominent theme in this research has been the male experience of transition to fatherhood, the subject of the next section. It is not disputed that fathers have become far more closely involved at the time of birth, especially that of a first child, but how far is this reflected in their later participation in child care?

What is the nature of fathers' interaction with their children? Does it differ from mother-child relationships, and if so in what ways? Do fathers, for example, transmit different attitudes to gender roles? What are the longer term effects of different degrees of father involvement?

A small number of British studies concern fathers in minority groups—those bringing up children alone, very young fathers, fathers in the army. These are of interest not only in themselves, but for the light they throw on the more general issue pervading British research—to what extent the role of fathers is or is not changing.

Finally this chapter discusses observer and researcher effect and how relevant they are in the interpretation of findings.

FATHERHOOD RESEARCH IN BRITAIN

Research on fatherhood in Britain started from a low base and the evidence is still limited compared with the vast body of data on mothers. However, a closer look at the latter reveals an almost exclusive interest in the implications of the mother's behavior for the child's development and rather little concern about the mother as an individual, or how the child (or more usually children) fit into the totality of her life. It was only when the primacy of the mother-child relationship began to be challenged, most notably by Rutter (1972), that the father came into focus. But much earlier, Gavron (1960) had pointed to the negative aspects of childcare and domesticity for women. It is this line of research, carried forward principally by Oakley (1974, 1979, 1980), which has done most to stimulate studies of the impact of parenthood on men, for whom previously it had been treated as a side issue.

It is significant that father-child relationships have from the beginning been seen as a two-way affair, with as much if not more interest in the father's feelings, attitudes, and experiences as in the child's. In contrast to the American research, there have been relatively few British observational studies of fathers and children. The major change in research design has been from interview studies where the mother was questioned about the father to studies involving direct interviewing of men.

Most reviews of fatherhood research (Beail, 1983; O'Brien, 1981), attempting to explain the dominance of the "mother-focused paradigm" (Rapoport, Rapoport, & Strelitz, 1977) in British research, cast the ethologist John Bowlby as the villain of the piece. It is sometimes overlooked that before Bowlby published his seminal work (1951) the strength of the emotional and psychological bond between mother and child was not, as now, a matter of common understanding. The emotional needs of children, if recognized at all, were considered entirely subservient to adult convenience, as accounts of the mass evacuation at the beginning of the Second World War illustrate (C. Jackson, 1985). Children were routinely separated from their mothers for reasons such as hospitalization, with complete disregard for the suffering on both sides (Robertson, 1953). An implicit understanding of attachment theory, articulated or not, is now part of the background against which maternal and paternal roles in Britain are negotiated (Backett, 1982; Boulton, 1983). Bowlby has long since modified his original position that fathers are of little direct importance to the child except in so far as they provide economic and emotional support to mothers.

By the late 1970s, interest in men's domestic and familial roles was developing fast, stimulated particularly by the work of Lamb (1976) and Levine (1976) in America and by the formation of the London-based Fatherhood Research Study Group. Although psychologists have been prominent in the Group, it has from the start been interdisciplinary, and includes practitioners as well as researchers. This can be seen in the influence of sociological and anthropological perspectives and methods in the writings of those associated with the Group, and in the concern which they show for social policy and practice implications.

The first wave of interest in fatherhood among British researchers culminated in two collections of papers, one psychological (Beail & McGuire, 1982) and the other multidisciplinary (McKee & O'Brien, 1982).

This was followed two years later (1984) by B. Jackson's posthumously published study of 100 first-time fathers which marked a shift of emphasis towards a closer examination of men's subjective experience of family life. It attempted to analyze the reasons for the mismatch between their aspirations and behavior.

This interest in masculinity and the male experience has been late to surface in Britain compared with the United States, but several British authors have pointed to its crucial importance in understanding the barriers to emotional closeness between fathers and children and to full participation by men in the parental role (Blendis, 1982; Lewis, 1986c).

The influence of cultural and situational factors on styles of fathering is a major concern of what might be called the second round of British fatherhood research, which gathered impetus in the early 1980s, but at the time of writing has not yet reached the stage of publication. The volume of work in progress, despite the hiatus in publication, justifies Beail's (1983) claim that fatherhood research is a major growth area in British psychology, and there is every indication that this will continue.

How far the surge in academic interest reflects a real change in social expectations in British society and in men's own perception of the fathering role is a matter of debate. In this chapter, I shall discuss findings in three main research categories which seem to throw some light on the matter, namely the transition to fatherhood, father's participation in child-rearing and father-child interaction.

BECOMING A FATHER

Having a baby is such a natural life event that researchers were slow to perceive its extremely problematic quality for many of the individuals concerned. Oakley (1979) demonstrated the profound psychological shock represented by motherhood for many women, but at least for them social expectations were clear, if often unwelcome. Men having babies in Britain today not only have to cope with their own confused feelings and uncertainty about what is appropriate behavior as they go through the new experience, but because the perceived role of fathers is changing so rapidly they also face uncertainty and contradictory messages from those around them.

B. Jackson (1984), in his semianthropological study in Bristol of 100 men having their first babies, charted the process from the time when the pregnancy was confirmed through the child's first year of life. In effect, although the experience is seen through the man's eyes, this was a study of how couples negotiate the transition to parenthood, since almost all the women insisted on being present during interviews (99/100) and the interchange between the man and woman often proved as revealing as anything said to the interviewer.

For example, it emerged that the decision to have a baby, far from being discussed and agreed upon by the couple, was almost always taken by the woman. The man concurred, though when this happened (whether before or after conception) is uncertain. Women had a clear idea of the appropriate moment, socially and biologically, to start a baby, and a sense, if they married late, of time running out. On the other hand, the men were more likely to see the time for fatherhood stretching infinitely before them. Jackson suggested that it is when "her finite line had crossed with his infinite one" that the decision to have a baby was taken or (more likely) emerged.

Very few of the men showed any awareness of the extent to which a baby would change their lives. Nearly a third entered pregnancy with an "innocent sense of minor disturbance" (p. 42). This was particularly evident when they were asked about their financial expectations. Most failed to appreciate the impact of the loss of the woman's earnings, and grossly underestimated the direct costs of babies and children.

In this sample only a very small proportion (9%) attended one parenthood class. All found the experience disappointing and usually did not return. There were practical reasons—the classes were generally held during working hours—and less tangible ones, such as the woman-dominated atmosphere. As one expectant father put it, "I'd be an alien" (p.52). Some of the women did not *want* the men inside this center of knowledge and preferred that the information be filtered through them, a finding echoed in other studies (Lewis, 1982). Russell's finding that over 20% of Australian fathers regularly attended preparation classes suggests that social expectations must have a powerful influence and that changes in timing, venue and style of presenting information would probably produce a much higher attendance rate among British fathers. There are signs, though as yet no published evidence, that this is occurring.

Both Jackson and Lewis (1982) discuss the appearance of "couvade-like" symptoms in the second trimester of pregnancy. These occurred in a minority of men in both studies in the form of marked weight gains or medical symptoms. The more bizarre forms of behavior tend to show up only in studies which combine interviews with direct observation. Jackson noted a heightened interest in pets displayed by one group of men, many of whom gave the dubious justification that the animal would be company for the baby. The most dramatic example was the prospective father whose mother had given the couple a cot for the coming baby. He had bought himself a dog and was continually kissing or nursing it and staring into its eyes; he spoke to it in baby talk and kept telling it, "You're such a baby" (p.55). It slept in the cot and he covered it with a blanket. Another extreme reaction observed in several men was a sudden fanatical interest in fitness or sports.

In the last part of the pregnancy many of the men seemed to feel an intense desire to get close to the baby, and a few felt excluded by the fact that it was enclosed in the woman's body. As one man expressed it:

> The time I like best is when she's fast asleep. She sleeps with her stomach to my back. . . . And sometimes I've woken up in the middle of the night and felt it kick me. That was good - just me and the baby in the dark. (p.58)

Almost all had tried to listen to the fetal heartbeat. Because they were rarely given the opportunity to do this by the medical staff they had to develop their own homespun methods. One man invented a very successful amplifying system using a set of five beer glasses.

In this study, most of the fathers took on a basic attitude towards the pregnancy at an early stage. Four typical reactions were identified, similar to those found in an earlier study by Richman and Goldthorp (1978). A small group of men could be classified as "refusers," swimming strongly against the cultural tide. They treated the pregnancy strictly as "women's business" having nothing to do with them, and saw themselves purely in the role of providers. A further group were classified as "observers," benevolent but detached, and also adopting a highly traditional view of men's and women's responsibilities in relation to babies. The third group, accounting for nearly half the sample, wanted to share the experience as fully as possible but more often than not were frustrated. Finally, there was a group, "identifiers," who would really have liked to have the baby themselves. Jackson found that these initial attitudes tended to persist and were reflected in the father's later participation in childcare and relationships both with the child and the mother.

This agrees with the finding by Scott-Heyes (1982) in a questionnaire study of 56 couples: Attitudes to pregnancy and childbirth were significantly related to a number of aspects of the marital relationship. Men with more positive attitudes to the pregnancy were reported to behave more affectionately towards their wives. This emerged particularly in their reaction to the woman's physical appearance and sexuality in late pregnancy.

At the initial interview in the Bristol study, 67% of the men said they intended to be present at the birth; when it came to the point, 81% actually attended. As in other countries, the 1970s saw an enormous increase in the proportion of British fathers present at the birth of their babies. The Newsons (1968) found only 13% of fathers attending the birth in 1958, even though the majority of births then took place at home. By 1970 when the Child Health and Education national longitudinal study began (Chamberlain, Chamberlain, Howlett, & Claireaux, 1975), almost all births took place in hospitals and fathers were firmly excluded from the delivery room, usually on the grounds that they might faint and get in the way of the medical staff. Kitzinger (1972) was one of the first writers on childbirth to suggest that the father's presence might be positively helpful, but at the time this usually meant a bitter fight with the hospital management. However, the battle was very swiftly won, and the presence of the father at birth is now so clearly expected in Britain that it is probably as hard for a man to stay out of the delivery room as it was for him to get in only a decade ago.

The extent to which this has now become conventional was underlined by the widely reported presence of the Prince of Wales at the birth of both his sons. At the time of the Prince's own birth, as several newspapers remarked, the Duke of Edinburgh was playing squash.

Some researchers (McKee, 1980; Woollett, White, & Lyon, 1982b; Jackson, 1984) see this "silent revolution" as indicating at least the potential for a major change in both men's and women's perceptions of the paternal role. Lewis (1982, 1986a) has strongly argued the opposite view: that attendance at birth has become a socially prescribed ritual act which bears no relation to the man's later behavior or involvement in childcare.

Jackson laid great emphasis on the intensity of the experience for the men, even those who were initially reluctant. He reported that "almost all the fathers who attended the birth reached an ecstatic peak of emotion: a personal Everest" (p.69). One said that he "felt like an astronaut who'd landed on the moon" (p.69). Even the more withdrawn ones became voluble, often rushing out after the birth and drawing total strangers into eager conversation. Of the fathers observed at 20 successive births, 18 were crying and the other 2 appeared numb. Given the absolute taboo against men's tears in British society, this is persuasive evidence. Questioned afterwards, most men said it was the first time they had cried since they were small children themselves.

However, the warmth and closeness which most men reported feeling towards mother and baby at this stage tended to be dissipated by the insensitive intrusion of medical staff and female relatives and by the demands of work. The opportunity for the father to remain close to the child and contribute substantially to his or her development is in many cases lost.

Lewis (1982, 1986a) also studied 100 fathers (first- and second-time) and many of his findings are similar, but his interpretation is radically different. As did Woollett et al. (1982) and B. Jackson (1984), Lewis reported that men feel that seeing a child born brings them closer to their wives and creates a bond between them and that child which may not exist with other children at whose births they were not present. However, Lewis suggests that it is also a public declaration of feelings for his wife and baby, "the culmination of a pregnancy career in which he has asserted his belief in the ideal of marital symmetry" (Lewis, 1982). He may even be laying a claim to the child in the event of marital breakdown in the future. Lewis sees the prescription of the father as the most suitable companion in childbirth not necessarily as a positive development but rather as a further extension of the power of the male-dominated medical profession over women. Given the choice, women might prefer a female companion. Not only does Lewis believe that the father's presence at birth will have no effect on his relationship with the child or commitment to the family, he suggests by analogy with anthropological evidence that such participation is no more than a cosmetic gloss over interpersonal and social conflicts (p.69).

In contrast to all other commentators, Lewis argues that more inclusion of fathers by official agencies may cause men to over-identify with the pregnancy, risking psychological maladjustment, and may erode the one area of family life in which women have personal and political power. This would seem a rather eccentric view, especially since Lewis himself (1982) comments on the striking ignorance of first-time fathers (54% had hardly touched a baby before their own) and on the fact that they felt confused and alienated by the information addressed to them. Like the fathers in Jackson's sample, they felt excluded by the official socializing agents—clinics, preparation classes, and procedures on the labor ward. It is hard to see how this can be desirable on any criterion.

FATHERS' INVOLVEMENT IN CHILDREARING

Division of responsibility within two-parent families has been a major focus for British research in the past 10 years. Young and Willmott (1973) while acknowledging that in the families they studied the primary responsibility for home and children rested firmly with the mother, suggested that the evolving family type in Britain was "symmetrical," with equal sharing of domestic and childcare roles. They believed that the shift to this pattern could be most clearly discerned within the professional class from which it might be expected to filter down the social scale, a point also made by B. Jackson (1984).

That some redistribution of family tasks has occurred seems not to be in doubt, but how evenly the change is spread throughout the population and the extent to which it represents a change in behavior as well as ideology remain open questions.

Lewis (1984) has pointed to the methodological problems whichever way these issues are tackled, either by asking men to compare their own parenting roles with those of their fathers, or by comparing data collected in studies on fathers in previous generations with that obtained in recent studies. This second option is rarely available because of the neglect of fathers in earlier research. However, the Newsons (1963) in their longitudinal study of 700 Nottingham children born in 1958 had the foresight to ask mothers fairly detailed questions about the involvement of their husbands. (It is perhaps no accident that a husband and wife team should have been ahead of their time in this way.) This enabled Lewis to make comparisons between their findings and his own study of 100 fathers in the same city 20 years later (Lewis, Newson, & Newson, 1982; Lewis, 1984).

At the time when their own children were a year old, more than half of these fathers had a clear perception of much greater involvement with their children than they had had with their own fathers. Over a third (35%) felt that their fathers had shown no interest in them at all, and only 14 remembered their fathers caring for them at any age.

In contrast, when they discussed their own involvement in childcare, 73% reported that they engaged in at least one activity with the child every day. Only one father admitted to performing no childcare task in the course of a week.

However, a comparison of the data from Lewis's study in 1980 and the Newsons' findings 20 years earlier suggest that changes in behavior may be rather less dramatic than they appear on the surface. Lewis (1984, 1986c) suggests that responses to questions about paternal involvement may be particularly sensitive to ideological shifts. For instance, at a time when it was considered demeaning for men to do "women's work" there may have been pressure on men to appear less involved than they were, whereas now the pressure, at least on middle class men, works the other way.

Lewis's comparison shows that the major change has occurred at the time of birth and in the immediate postpartum period when there is clear evidence of the father's much greater involvement (already discussed). Data on child care tasks when the child is a year old suggest fewer obvious differences between generations, with putting to bed the only activity to show a marked upward shift (see Table 2.1).

No similar comparisons have been attempted for older children as yet, but the Bristol-based longitudinal study started in 1970 (CHES) does provide some data on fathers' childcare activities in over 13,000 two-parent families when the target child was aged 5 (Osborn & Morris, 1982; Osborn, Butler, & Morris, 1984). Mothers were asked if in the previous week the father had (a) looked after the child for part of the day while the mother did other things, (b) put the child to bed, (c) took the child to school or nursery, and/or (d) read to the child. Although these measures are relatively crude and could not be said to represent a full range of child-related activities, they do tap forms of involvement other than physical caretaking, and by asking about the previous week are more likely to elicit accurate reports of behavior than mothers' general perceptions of *willingness* to help (cf. Backett, 1982). The results tend to support Lewis's view that the extent of fathers' involvement after the perinatal period has been exaggerated. No more than half the fathers helped with any one of the activities and only 4% helped in all four ways.

Socioeconomic differences proved rather less significant than would be expected. There were almost no differences among socioeconomic groups in the proportion of fathers who look after the child for part of the day. There was only a shallow gradient from most to least advantaged with respect to the number who put the child to bed and/or take the child to school, both of which might be related to working hours.

TABLE 2.1
Level of Fathers' Involvement with Their One-Year-Olds
in Caretaking Tasks: 1960 and 1980 Compared

Activity	Putting to Bed		Bathing		Nappy Changing	
	1960* %	1980 %	1960* %	1980 %	1960* %	1980 %
Involvement						
Little or none	29	26	54	62	37	40
Some involvement	29	24	21	9	38	37
A lot	30	48	16	24	16	28
"Yes"	11	—	9	—	9	—

*1960: Subsample of first- and second-time fathers with same socioeconomic status as 1980 sample, from Lewis (1984): Men's Involvement in Fatherhood: Historical and Gender Issues.

The fourth measure, reading to the child, showed much bigger differences. B. Jackson (1984), re-analyzing the data, found that these were related not only to Osborn and Morris's Social Index (1979), but even more closely to the father's educational background. Among fathers with no formal qualifications, 39% had read to the child during the previous week. For those with college degrees, the figure was 70%; if the father had a teaching qualification, it rose to 76%.

One explanation for these findings is that fathers have more freedom of choice whether to participate in "nonessential" activities, and they choose those which they regard as important or find congenial (as observation studies such as McGuire, 1982, have shown). Performance of more practical childcare tasks is determined by external factors, such as the number and ages of the children in the family or the need to give more help when the mother is working.

This interpretation is supported by the Newsons' finding (Lewis et al., 1982) that at age 7 father participation is higher in middle-class than working-class families and greater for boys than girls. Follow-up studies at 11 and 16 show an increasing differentiation with age between boys and girls, and a widening discrepancy between middle-class and working-class fathers, peaking at age 11 and reducing slightly during the following five years. Examination of the qualitative evidence shows that shared interests are a major factor in determining closeness between parent and child at later ages. These are more likely to develop with same-sex children and when there is money available for leisure activities.

THE EFFECTS OF FATHERS' WORK

The CHES study (Osborn et al., 1984) clearly illustrates the primacy of work over childcare tasks for men. Fathers fit childcare around their work commitments, mothers organize their work to accommodate childcare obligations.

This pattern is set from the beginning. B. Jackson (1984) asked how much time each man planned to take off work for the birth of the baby and then checked how much time they actually took. Only five men out of 100 stayed at home for more than two weeks. A quarter of the sample took two days or less, 31% took one week of their annual leave, and 21% took two. Even such a short break could be difficult to arrange, especially for manual workers (cf. Bell, McKee, & Priestley, 1983). And for self-employed fathers, continuing to work at a time of so many extra expenses was a matter of economic necessity.

Jackson argues that the failure of the working world—both at an institutional and a personal level—to recognize the significance of childbirth to men disrupts the developing bond between father and child, and perhaps contributes to the bouts of depression experienced by a third of the men in his sample. Most couples coped with the strains by retreating to traditional roles, the man seeking to maximize his earnings by working overtime or establishing his claim to promotion by long hours in the office. The consequence, as the CHES five-year follow-up showed (Osborn et al., 1984) is that 40% of fathers come home after the child is already asleep. Eleven percent are not there on weekends either so their opportunities to interact with the child are quite restricted.

However, the psychological primacy of work for the men seems to be as important as the practical obstacles it puts in the way of sharing domestic and childcare tasks. In Jackson's (1984) study, the fathers who spent the most time with the child in the first year were the 12 unemployed. In seven of these families the mother soon returned to part-time work to increase the household income. Superficially these men seemed well placed to reverse roles and become primary caregivers, but, although they become reasonably competent in looking after the child, none appeared to be conspicuously nurturing fathers. "The blockage was that they were with the child reluctantly and they held on as strongly as they could to their old sense of identity—an indentity defined by work" (p.108). There is a parallel here with the reluctant lone fathers ("passive acceptors") described by O'Brien (1984) in the study discussed below.

STUDIES OF FATHER-CHILD INTERACTION

The part played by fathers in sex-role development, or stereotyping, has attracted considerable attention as the feminist movement has alerted parents and childcare professionals to the fact that such socialization starts at a very early age. Indeed, leaving aside the very different role models still provided by mothers and fathers (as the evidence discussed in the previous section makes clear), there is much evidence from direct observational studies that male and female babies are treated differently *by fathers* from the moment of birth. These differences become increasingly larger and more significant as the child grows older.

OBSERVATIONS OF MOTHER/FATHER INTERACTION WITH NEWBORNS

Woollett et al. (1982) observed 29 births in an East London Hospital where 92% of the fathers were present at the birth. They note that there were large individual differences in fathers' behavior with newborns and that some may have felt inhibited by the hospital surroundings both in terms of their behavior and emotional expression. There was also clear evidence of observer effect when, for example, the father, mother, and child were left alone but their interaction continued to be recorded on videotape. The mothers were more actively engaged with the babies—smiling, stroking, exploring, and rocking them—when the observer was present than when absent. It is possible, though less likely, that this may also have influenced the different behavior of fathers to sons and daughters.

When the baby was a boy, fathers stayed longer in the delivery room (an extra 3½ minutes on average) and held their child considerably longer. They talked much longer to the newborns if they were boys: six times as many comments were recorded from fathers of boys as from fathers of girls.

White, Woollett, and Lyon (1982) looked at one aspect of fathers' involvement with their babies—how often, how long, and in what position they hold them. They argue that holding has been neglected as an index of involvement as opposed to physical caring functions. This is partly a methodological problem, in that it is far easier to ask factual and specific questions like "Did you bath your baby last week?" than about behavior like holding which is probably often unconscious and certainly not closely monitored by parents. However, holding may be a highly significant form of parent-child interaction, very important for increasing alertness (Bower, 1971).

White et al. (1982) found a holding rate by fathers immediately following delivery of 66%, higher than some American studies (e.g., Packer & Rosenblatt, 1979). They continued their study of behavior at birth with videotaped observations of the children up to 30 months. At 2 months most mothers, but only 18 (75%) fathers, held the babies for some time during the observation periods. By 4½ months 96% of the fathers held the babies during observations, girls slightly longer than boys, but the significant differences were in the hold position.

Already at birth there was a striking difference. The hold across position, with the baby held across the parent's body, either in the crook of the arm or on the knee, was used by every father for 87% of the holding time; "hold-inwards" position, with the fathers gazing into the baby's face, was used exclusively with boys. Boys were held inwards for 21% of the time. At 2 months, the differences were still greater: Girls were held across 66% of the observation time, boys only 31%. Boys were held inwards 46% of the time.

White et al. comment that the hold-inward position offers the best opportunity for rich interactive exchanges between father and child and allows each participant to respond sensitively to the other. The hold-inwards position maximizes the chance of the baby being alert and responsive to stimulation, which in turn might be an important determinant of parental attitudes to the baby.

The suggestion that the hold-inward position is more stimulating is supported by findings at 2 months and 3 months. Fathers talked considerably more to the babies when they were in the hold-inwards position than in the hold-across position, and at 5 months the babies were most active in the hold-inwards position. The hold-across position seems more associated with soothing, comforting and caretaking and may therefore contribute to or indicate greater emotional closeness between father and child. This is in line with evidence from other observational studies that fathers tend to be more active in stimulating the cognitive development of their sons but may be more emotionally attached to daughters.

The father's role in speech development has been seriously neglected in British research, which has focused almost exclusively on mother-child verbal interaction (cf. Tizard & Hughes, 1984). Early research assumed that fathers must have a negligible impact because of the very short periods during which they interact with infants at the language acquisition stage. However, studies of children whose mothers and fathers speak to them in different languages have shown this assumption to be false (Friedlander et al., 1972). A growing number of studies now compare mothers' and fathers' conversations with language-learning offspring, exploring the hypothesis that the child's experience of conversation with fathers vs. that of mothers is different but not less important. The evidence is conflicting, with some studies finding these differences between parents (Rondal, 1980) and others not. Lewis and Gregory (1986) suggest that some of these differences may be due to the activity in which the parents are engaged when observed.

They observed 6 father-child and 6 mother-child pairs; in each group there were 3 boys and 3 girls between the ages of 10 and 15 months, which span the period when the children might be expected to utter their first words. The mothers' and fathers' language to the children was observed in three different contacts: free play, structured play with toys, and looking at picture books. The observations were recorded on videotapes; the first three minutes of parental speech (after the child had settled down) were transcribed and analyzed. The amount, complexity, and functions of utterances were measured using a coding system developed by Gregory, Mogford, and Bishop (1979).

This study found some differences in parental style at 10 months (mothers said more during free play, fathers said more when playing with toys), but both the complexity and the functions of speech depended more on the context than on the sex of the parent. At 15 months, the major significant differences related to the play setting rather than the sex of the parent. For example, there were more directives during toy play and more comments during free play. Book play produced considerably more complex language, greater speech rate, a longer length of utterance, and more syllables per word. Therefore, studies which have found major differences attributable to the sex of the parent may have been confounded by the type of play considered, and studies which leave the choice of activity to the parent may have been examining situational rather than parental variables.

Lewis and Gregory have undoubtedly made an important point by suggesting caution in the interpretation of observational studies and by making an attempt to separate out sex and situational factors. However, this has to be set alongside the mass of evidence that fathers and mothers engage in different forms of play with their children, and that fathers, more than mothers, differentiate in their play between boys and girls. Thus, the differences that have been shown between mothers' and fathers' speech in naturally occurring language probably reflect differences in the language *experience* of children as coming from mothers and fathers; inferences drawn from these findings remain valid despite Lewis and Gregory's finding that the differences largely disappear once the play setting is taken into account.

McGuire (1982) has discussed the impact of the father on gender differentiation in early childhood. She suggests that studies focusing on the amount of time that a father spends with infants and young children may underestimate his influence. If, for example, his attitudes about appropriate behavior in boys and girls are more distinct, their potential influence may be more important than that of mothers in producing or accentuating differences between boys and girls. On the basis of social learning theory, one would predict that fathers would be particularly salient to sons as models of appropriate male behavior, though not perhaps until the age of 3 or 4. Bronfenbrenner (1961) found fathers more likely to treat children differently according to their sex, as did the 4-year and 7-year phases of the Nottingham longitudinal study (Newson & Newson, 1963, 1976).

McGuire (1982) studied 40 English fathers, 20 with 2-year-old boys and 20 with girls of the same age. Each family was observed twice and the mothers and fathers interviewed separately. The parents were given lists of toys and asked first to select those they would not consider suitable for their own child and then which they would think unsuitable if they had a child of the opposite sex. Fathers discriminated much more strongly on the basis of the child's sex than did the mothers. On the whole, both mothers and fathers agreed that aggressive toys, such as guns, were unsuitable for girls. Fathers disapproved of far more toys for boys than mothers did. For example, cooking, housework, or shopping items were picked as unsuitable more frequently by fathers than by mothers. Childcare toys were generally considered unsuitable for boys by both parents. One father, a teacher, said he could not imagine ever walking down the street accompanied by his son with a doll in a push-chair, even though the author observes he must often have pushed the same child in a push-chair himself.

The fathers who disapproved of the most toys for boys were the fathers of sons. Several mothers referred to their husbands' disapproval when explaining why they would not buy "girlish" toys for a boy—even though they might allow him to play with them, for example, in another child's house. These results are very similar to those obtained by Newson and Newson (1963) twenty years earlier.

When asked to describe their children to a stranger, more boys were described positively and more girls negatively ($p<0.05$). Even the positive statements about girls tended to emphasize their appearance (7 girls but no boys were described as pretty or beautiful), whereas size and strength were more valued for boys. These results agree with American studies (Rubin, Provenzano, & Luria, 1974).

Nineteen out of 39 men said they already had a special role in relation to their 2-year-old, but this was more likely if they had boys than girls (12 of the 19 fathers of sons; only 7 of the fathers of 20 daughters). Although they claimed to play equally with boys and girls, active play was mentioned far more often in relation to boys. Moreover, observations suggested that fathers much prefer playing with boys' toys and choosing those toys which they personally enjoy, whereas mothers do not discriminate.

The character of fathers' rough-and-tumble play was also observed to differ with the sex of the child. With girls this normally took the form of giving rides or "letting her jump on me," whereas with boys it was more often mock-fighting or specific sports.

McGuire notes that the sample was biased towards fairly well educated, middle-class parents whom one might expect to be more influenced by ideas about avoiding sex-role stereotyping and providing equal opportunities for girls and boys. However, already by the age of 2, very distinct patterns were emerging. The fathers studied, many of them still in their twenties, were apparently continuing the pattern of sex-role stereotyping with their children that was found by researchers a generation or more ago. They have well delineated ideas about which toys and activities are suitable for either sex child, and set firm guidelines about how girls should behave while letting boys get away with more mischief. Perhaps this helps to explain why girls are more often found to be over controlled but boys are more likely to exhibit conduct disorders. The results support the argument that the father-child relationship is of particular relevance when gender-specific differences in child behavior are being studied.

Lewis (1986b) provides further evidence from British studies that mothers and fathers contribute to sex-role development in distinctive ways. Discussing the reason why mothers and fathers interact differently with sons and daughters, he suggests that (a) they may have different goals; (b) fathers may have more stereotyped perceptions of children, as the data on parental behavior suggests (B. Jackson, 1984); or (c) men may be demonstrating their lack of experience with that individual child, as evidenced by the much shorter time they spend interacting with infants, and therefore have to fall back on male/female stereotypes.

Lewis suggests also that mothers and fathers may be influenced in different ways by the act of observation. He studied the language of mothers and fathers to 10-month-old children when they were being observed and when the observer was "called away to the telephone." The structure and function of the parents' language changed between the two conditions; for example, fathers used significantly more interrogatives with sons when being observed and with daughters when the observer left the room. Fathers may act differently when under pressure to demonstrate their parental skills to an observer, perhaps because they are less used to being with their children in public. Parental influence on sex-role socialization may nevertheless be important even if it only differentiates between boys and girls in *public* settings.

EFFECTS OF FATHER INVOLVEMENT

What effect does the degree of fathers' involvement and the division of childcare responsibility in the family have in the longer term?

The British evidence is sparse due to the fact that the design of the major longitudinal studies predated the current interest in the paternal role. Where questions were asked about the father they tended to be very general and to reflect the mother's view rather than attempting to elicit objective differences in behavior.

Lewis et al. (1982), in a longitudinal interview study, examined father participation at the ages of 7, 11, and 16 and related it to educational measures, career aspirations, and delinquency. They note that participation is a very relative term and that fathers are said to be "highly participant" when they do things that are simply taken for granted in the mothering role. Fathers remain "rather peripherally involved" with children; their perception of their status as subsidiary caregivers persists throughout childhood. They continue to see themselves and be seen by others as less skilled than their wives in understanding children's needs. At age 7, twice as many children were reported to be closer to their mothers than their fathers and, at 11, the gap was even wider. At 11 and 16, there were, however, class differences at the $p < 0.001$ level, with middle-class fathers more participant.

After controlling for class, sex, and family size, clear correlations were found between father participation at 11 and 16 and the child's educational and career aspectations. Participation scores at 7 and 11 also correlated significantly with later delinquency (defined as having acquired a criminal record by 18-20 years). It is suggested that the data need cautious interpretation. Maternal reports of father participation may well reflect the mother's satisfaction with the marital relationship rather than real differences in behavior; Backett (1982) argues this position convincingly. The enhanced cohesiveness of families with involved fathers might lead to a more coherent and constructive world view, tending towards high aspirations and low criminality.

However, in a follow-up study of 13,135 5-year-old children, Osborn and Morris (1982) assessed them on three measures of ability and related their scores to an index of the father's commitment to the paternal role based on the number of child-related activities in which he had been involved during the week preceding the survey interview. (Such activities included looking after the child for part of the day, putting to bed, taking to school, and reading to the child.) The effects of family size, maternal employment, and socioeconomic circumstances—all factors influencing father involvement—were separated out by analysis of variance. The results suggested that the cognitive development and vocabulary ability of the 5-year-olds were significantly increased by the father's involvement in child-centered activities, independent of other family and social influences.

FATHERS ALONE

Although role reversal of the kind studied by Russell (1982) in Australia is still extremely uncommon, increasingly fathers are considered competent to bring up children on their own. This is reflected both in the practice of the welfare services, which no longer think it necessary to take children into public care if, for example, the mother is hospitalized, and in the number of men seeking and being awarded custody of their children after divorce. Following George's (1972) study of motherless families, the topic attracted little interest until recently; most research on single-parent families continues to be strongly mother-focused.

O'Brien (1982, 1984) explored the phenomenon of lone fatherhood by comparing 59 separated or divorced men bringing up children on their own with a matched sample of married fathers. She proposes a three-way categorization of the path to lone fatherhood, somewhat similar to that suggested by Mendes (1976). O'Brien's three groups are "hostile seekers," whose child custody claims seemed to be activated as much by a desire for revenge on their (usually adulterous) wives as by a positive desire to care for the children; the "passive acceptors" whose wives simply left them with the children; and the "conciliatory negotiators," where custody and care arrangements were agreed between the couple at the time of separation (O'Brien, 1980).

A number of variables were significantly related to the respondents' feelings of competence in the lone-father role at the time of the interview. There were: high levels of childcare involvement before marital separation; becoming a lone father through the concilatory-negotiation route; having a small family and a satisfactory support system, being in regular contact with former wives, and, most strongly, expressing non-traditional beliefs about parental roles. Feelings of competence were *not* related to age, social class, length of marital separation, or sex or age of children. Thus Mendes's (1975) findings of a link between parental role anxiety and the rearing of opposite-sexed children was not upheld, but her proposition of a link between the route by which individuals become single parents and their later feelings about their competence was supported.

Marked differences were found among the three groups of lone fathers. Passive acceptors, even if they had often taken a major part in child-care before their wives' departure, reported the greatest unease with their situation; 80% expressed traditional beliefs about parental roles in the family and often relied quite heavily on older daughters. There is a similarity here with the unemployed fathers described by Jackson (1984). Clearly choice is a key element. One dimension extensively explored in this study is styles of discipline. It is interesting to note, in relation to the debate on fathering styles, that the anti-authoritarian ethos is strongly in the ascendant, with only 25% in each group approving of smacking their children.

Both samples showed identical social class patterns, with middle-class fathers in both groups less likely to believe in physical punishment (cf. Newson & Newson, 1976). There were, however, differences between fathers of girls and fathers of boys, and very distinct differences among the three categories of lone fathers. Hostile seekers, who had actively chosen single parenthood against the wishes of their wives, consistently appeared to be more severe than the other two groups in their orientation to discipline. Conciliatory negotiators, on the other hand, appeared to bring to parent-child relationships the same methods of handling conflict which they had displayed in their marital difficulties. Passive acceptors fell between these two groups.

A comparison of children's behavior in the lone-father and married-father families showed no significant differences, except a slight tendency for more lone than married fathers to describe their children as having difficulties in peer relationships.

YOUNG FATHERS

If perceptions of the father's role are changing as rapidly as some commentators suggest, one would expect age to be an important dimension, but no British study looks specifically at a subgroup of young fathers, and studies of teenage mothers have typically ignored their partners. However, Sims and Smith (1982) undertook the difficult task of tracing and interviewing 369 fathers of babies born to a national sample of adolescent girls. Two thirds of the fathers were themselves young (under 25) and one in five was under 20. The findings are open to the objection, recognized by the authors, that the men who could be traced and who agreed to be interviewed (59%), were by definition those who had accepted their situation. A comparison with census data (OPCS, 1980) shows that single men, men in unskilled jobs, and men born in the West Indies were underrepresented in the interviews. However, 87% were classified as working class, including 12% unemployed at the time of the interview, which contrasts with the middle-class bias of almost all other British fatherhood studies, and makes this by far the largest study of relatively disadvantaged fathers.

Despite the accidental nature of most of the pregnancies (only half of those not using contraception actively wanted a child), the men expressed a high degree of satisfaction with fatherhood and marriage and were closely involved in domestic and childcare tasks. Although these are not specified precisely enough for comparison with other studies, the rates reported were very high: 95% helped with housework and 96% fed the baby, at least occasionally.

This rather unexpected result, in view of the widespread perception of teenage pregnancy as a serious problem, illustrates the need to look at fathers in the context of their social situation and life experience. For these young men, family life, even on a very low income, may actually have represented a gain in freedom from living at home with their parents and, typically, four or more brothers and sisters. Having a baby, which for most middle-class couples involves a severe curtailment of social and recreational activity, gives these fathers access to public housing, a place of their own, and the choice of staying at home in the evening. Few seemed to regret their previous, more active social life, which in most cases consisted of drinking with friends in local pubs. The majority felt amply compensated by their current activities: pursuing hobbies at home, helping around the house, and being with the baby.

The interviews took place when the baby was under 7 months old, so it may be that problems would show themselves later when the child became more mobile and demanding, and the strain of living on a single low wage or possibly unemployment benefits might begin to tell. The very high level of satisfaction with marriage reported by these young working-class men is certainly not reflected in the statistics for marital breakdown. This suggests the need for repeated interview studies which combine qualitative and quantitative data and can draw a picture of men's experience over a longer time span than has yet been done.

FATHERS IN THE MILITARY

While research on the allocation of tasks within the family has produced mixed results, there seems no doubt that an ideological shift has occurred in the direction of more equal sharing of childcare and domestic tasks. But what about professions where the prevailing ethos pulls strongly in the other direction? Research in progress (Hockey, forthcoming) points to a conflict between the public personae of soldiers and their private expressive roles. A small study by Fanshawe (1985) in an English army town found that even in this highly traditional context the idea of shared parenting had gained a strong foothold. Only 1 woman out of the 50 said her husband did not help at all with childcare and another 8 that not much help was provided. Eighty-two percent perceived their husbands as helping to look after the children when they were at home, and 60% felt their husbands helped significantly with the housework. Analysis of tasks undertaken reveals a familiar picture, with 70% playing with their children, 56% bathing and putting them to bed, but only 16% ever taking full responsibility for the child in the home, freeing the mother to do other things. Overall, only 18 of the 50 (36%) fathers were considered by Fanshawe to provide really significant help with children.

Nevertheless, measures of maternal malaise (Rutter, Tizard & Whitmore, 1970) showed significantly different scores for women at times when the husbands were present and when they were away on overseas tours. The mean score for the whole sample at times when husbands were not away was 3.7 on a 24-point scale, similar to that obtained in a national sample of mothers of 5-year-olds (Osborn et al., 1984). During periods of separation, the mean score rose to 4.8 with over a quarter of the sample scoring 7 or more, a level considered to indicate severe stress. Twenty-one percent scored 9 or more when the father was absent, a figure which has been found to correspond with the appearance of serious psychiatric problems (Richman, 1976).

On the average, the husbands had been away for 5¾ of the previous 12 months with a mean period of absence of 9 weeks, but even the relatively short time which they spent at home seemed to provide important protection against depression and stress-related ill-health. Although on objective measures the practical help provided by these army fathers was quite small, it was rarely *perceived* as insignificant. It is possible that the expectations of army wives were different from those in the general population. Parker (1985) illustrates the persistence of extreme sex-role stereotypes in this enclosed society, especially in the officer class, which still adopts a paternalistic concern for soldiers' families and has a clear view of what is proper and fitting. In a community where the norm is a complete separation of marital roles, any contribution from the husband may be disproportionately appreciated. These data appear to support Backett's (1982) contention that fathers' participation in childrearing has a symbolic quality irrespective of the help actually given. Interestingly, she picks out bathing and playing with the child as tasks to which strategic importance is attached, and these were the activities in which husbands' participation was most frequently found by Fanshawe.

OBSERVER EFFECT AND RESEARCHER EFFECT

Several authors have pointed out the practical reasons for the relative scarcity of research on fathers as compared with mothers (B. Jackson, 1984). Both interview and observation studies are more easily conducted during the day, when men are normally at work and the majority of mothers, at least of young children, are likely to be free and available. Interviewing is skilled but poorly paid work; the people qualified and available to do it are also much more likely to be women. In both the CHES longitudinal study (Osborn et al., 1984) and the earlier National Child Development Study, the interviews were carried out by female community health visitors, so that the men's behavior and perceptions were filtered through not one but two women. This is true of almost all the earlier studies which involved questions about fathers.

More recent studies often involve the interviewing of men by women, and the special problems which this creates have been explored by McKee and O'Brien (1983). In their studies of new fathers and lone fathers, respectively, they encountered difficulty in persuading men to talk about pregnancy, childbirth, and family relationships. Interviews with men were significantly shorter than those with women. If a man's wife were present during the interview, she would often answer or interpret the interviewer's question for him.

The cultural component is clearly strong. Historical, geographical, and class dimensions can all be seen, for instance, in Cunningham-Burley's (1984) account of her interviews with Edinburgh grandfathers. They belonged to a generation in which gender boundaries were more clearly drawn and men's and women's worlds lay further apart. It is perhaps not surprising that in 16 cases out of 18 they contributed less to the interview than did the grandmother—even when the interviewer addressed herself directly to the man. Sometimes the man actually left the room during the interview. They seemed to have great difficulty in recalling their experience of becoming fathers or in describing their feelings about grandfatherhood, although they could be just as chatty as the women on neutral topics like homemade wine.

The need for men to demonstrate gender-appropriate behavior to the interviewer is not, however, confined to their interaction with women interviewers, and B. Jackson (1984) gives many examples of aggressive displays of masculinity, apparently designed to deflect embarrassing questions on "women's" subjects. He encountered the phenomenon of wives insisting on being present at interviews, or men reluctant to agree to be interviewed without their wives' support. Jackson also notes the fact that the woman often answered on the man's behalf, however clear it was made that fathers, not mothers, were the subject of the research.

In repeated interview studies where subject and interviewer became familiar with each other as individuals, some of these effects seem to diminish. In O'Brien's (1984) lone father study, the male-female research encounter sometimes appeared to mirror the conjugal relationship, leading to greater male self-disclosure and willingness to talk on topics normally discussed only with wives. Some men suggested that cross-gender talk about pregnancy and parenthood was easier, more appropriate, and less frightening. This appeared to be true in work settings as well as in social relationships. Fathers reported that women coworkers tended to be interested and sympathetic when the talk turned to such matters. Groups of men, however, were not merely indifferent but even punitive. They were likely to respond to any attempt to discuss babies and parenthood with jokes or teasing, and a rapid diversion to talk of men's traditional interests such as sports or politics.

However, B. Jackson's (1984) account of the same phenomenon suggests that, given sufficiently sensitive interviewing, men may be equally able to voice previously unexpressed feelings to another man. He wrote, "I often found that I was one of the few people, sometimes the only one, to whom the man had spoken his feelings."

Although McKee and O'Brien (1983) refer in passing to the fact that in order to deflect unwanted sexual advances they made "conscious decisions about make-up and clothes," the personal appearance and characteristics of the interviewer are not a factor which has been examined in the British research. It would seem likely, however, that the image represented by the interviewer might be as significant as the fact of being a man or woman. Is it easier for a male interviewer to give permission to another man to discuss taboo subjects if he himself presents a traditionally masculine image, or if he appears relatively androgynous? As yet, no studies have specifically examined this question.

A further unexplored question is that of researcher effect. In investigating such intimate and emotionally charged subjects as pregnancy, childbirth, childcare, and marital relationships, it seems improbable that the personal history and experiences of the researcher can be neutral elements. The choice of topics for research and the interpretation put on the results must be profoundly influenced by the researcher's personal experience, life history, and current situation. Within the confines of an academic paper it is not expected that writers will reveal anything about themselves, but when they do so in other contexts one's subsequent reading of their academic research work is informed (not discounted) by that knowledge. Few would have the courage to write as openly as Ann Oakley in her autobiography (1984), but, for example, the personal anecdotes in a popular book by Jackson (1980) do perhaps provide clues regarding the lens through which he viewed the 100 couples in his 1984 study. The distancing effect of the printed page causes us to forget that almost all parenthood researchers are themselves mothers and fathers, all are sons or daughters, and that the particular character of their relationships has implications for their direction of attention and interpretation of results.

CONCLUSION

British research on fatherhood, despite its dramatic growth over the past ten years, is still far from providing a complete picture of how men negotiate and perform their role in the family, or how this might be changing. In an attempt to escape the pathological focus of earlier work, there has been a tendency to aim for normality, excluding groups that might be perceived as in some way deviant, or simply less accessible. Thus the gaps noted by McKee and O'Brien (1982) largely remain. Fathers of older children, fathers in communal and cohabiting units, black fathers, and grandfathers scarcely appear in the literature, nor do the growing numbers of unemployed fathers.

Nevertheless, the trends reported in other English-speaking countries are clearly apparent in Britain. Fathers are expected to attend their children's birth, even if they are not formally married to the mother. They are considered competent to care for mother and child and any other children in the family during the postpartum period. The ideology of more equally shared parenting is dominant even if the reality may fall short of it.

The cultural prohibition against the expression of tender feelings and nurturant behavior by men appears to be weakening rapidly, although it seems that many men still attempt to impose on their sons a much sharper definition of sex-appropriate behavior than they adopt themselves. Fathers have been observed to reinforce gender stereotypes more strongly than mothers.

Possibly mothers are trying to influence their sons in what they see as a desirable direction. There is evidence that it is important for women's self-esteem and perception of the marital relationship to be able to see the man as willing to participate in childcare, irrespective of what he actually does. In this way they may be trying to accommodate to the highly participant image of fatherhood currently presented in the media, particularly in women's magazines.

The view that men can simply choose how involved they wish to be in domestic and childrearing tasks (and many feminist writers suggest that men generally choose to do less rather than more) now appears oversimplified. Many husbands have a delicate sense of the point at which "help" becomes trespassing, and women are unlikely to give up their command of the home territory any more willingly than men have allowed women full admission to the world of work.

However, particular factors in British society make it probable that men will increasingly share both the pleasures and the hard work of childrearing on a more equal footing. The continuing rise in male unemployment makes men available for childcare and puts more pressure on women, if they can find jobs, to go out to work. Thus, although planned role reversal remains unusual, unstable (as in Australia), and virtually confined to the professional classes, involuntary role reversal is becoming more common.

The proportion of women with young children in paid employment has continued to rise but there has been no parallel increase in the provision of day-care facilities, either public or commercial. Nurseries provided by local authorities are almost entirely reserved for children considered to be at risk of abuse or neglect. Although the quality and accessibility of home-based daycare (child-minding) has improved, several studies have shown that care by the father, when available, is strongly preferred (Bone, 1975; Jackson & Jackson, 1979; Osborn et al., 1984).

A third factor is the increased tendency for men to apply for and be awarded custody of children after divorce (O'Brien, 1984). At present, lone fathers are still a small minority, but the sight of men publicly caring for children and venturing into settings such as childcare facilities and health clinics (previously the preserve of women) is likely to become much more familiar. As a result, one might expect the social forces—which at present push men back into the traditional role—to operate less powerfully. We may then begin to see a significant shift towards the position envisaged by Schaffer (1977) when family roles will be allocated on the basis of temperament and personal inclination rather than gender.

ACKNOWLEDGMENT

Thanks to Charlie Lewis, Margaret O'Brien and Albert Osborn for helpful discussion and for supplying unpublished material.

REFERENCES

Allan, G. (1985). *Family life,* Oxford: Blackwell.

Argyle, M., & Henderson, M. (1985). *Anatomy of relationships,* London: Heinemann.

Backett, K. C. (1982). *Mothers and fathers: A study of the development and negotiation of parental behavior.* New York: Macmillan.

Beail, N. (1983). The psychology of fatherhood. *Bulletin of the British Psychological Society,* Vol. 36, 312–314.

Beail, N., & McGuire, J. (Eds.) (1982). *Fathers: Psychological perspectives.* London: Junction Books.

Bell, C., McKee, L., & Priestley, K., (1983). *Fathers, childbirth and work: A report of a study.* Manchester: Equal Opportunities Commission.

Bell, C. & McKee, L. (1984). *His unemployment, her problem: The domestic and marital consequences of male unemployment.* Paper presented to the Annual Conference of the British Sociological Association.

Blendis, W. (1982). *Men's experiences of their own fathers.* In N. Beail & J. McGuire (Eds.), *Fathers: Psychological perspective.* London: Junction Books.

Bone, M. (1975). *Day Care for Pre-School Children.* London: Office of Population Censuses and Surveys.

Boulton, M. G. (1983). *On being a mother, a study of women with pre-school children.* London: Tavistock.

Bower, T. G. R. (1971). The object in the world of the infant. *Scientific American,* October, 30-38.

Bowlby, J. (1951). *Maternal Care and Mental Health.* Geneva: WHO.

Bronfenbrenner, U. (1961). Some familial antecedents of responsibility and leadership in adolescents. In L. Petrullo & B. M. Bass (Eds.), *Leadership and interpersonal Behaviour,* New York: Holt, Rinehart & Winston.

Brown, A., & Kiernan, K. (1981). Cohabitation in Britain: Evidence from the General Household Survey, *Population Trends, 25:* 4–10.

Chamberlain, R., Chamberlain, G., Howlett, B. C., & Claireaux, A. (1975). *British Births: Vol I, The First Week of Life.* Heinemann: London.

Clark, M. (1978). The Unemployed on Supplementary Benefit. *Journal of Social Policy,* 7, 385–410.

Cunningham-Burley, S. (1984). 'We don't talk about it. . . .' Issues of gender and method in the portrayal of grandfatherhood. *Sociology, 18,*

Davidoff, L. (1979). The separation of home and work? Landladies and lodgers in nineteenth and twentieth-century England. In S. Burman (Ed.) *Fit work for women.* London: Croom Helm.

Delphy, C. (1984). *Close to home: A materialist analysis of women's oppression,* London: Hutchinson.

Edgell, S. (1980). *Middle-class couples,* London: Allen & Unwin.

Employment Gazette (1975, 1984). London: HMSO.

Fanshawe, P. G. (1985). *Mothers in an army town.* Unpublished dissertation. Bristol: University of Bristol.

Friedlander, B., Jacobs, B., Davis, B. & Wetstone, H. (1972). Time-sampling analysis of infants' natural language environments in the home. *Child Development* 43, 730–740.

Gavron, H. (1960). *The captive wife.* London: Routledge & Kegan Paul.

George, V. (1972). *Motherless families.* London: Routledge & Kegan Paul.

Gregory, S., Mogford, K., & Bishop, J. (1979). Mothers' speech to young hearing impaired children. *Journal of British Association of Teachers of the Deaf,* 3, 2.

Hart, N. (1976). *When marriage ends,* London: Tavistock.

Haskey, J. (1983). Children of divorcing couples, *Population Trends, 31,* 20–26.

Hockey, J. (1986). *Squaddies: Portrait of a subculture,* Exeter: Exeter University Press.

Jackson, B. (1980). *Living with children,* London: Sphere.

Jackson, B. (1982). Single-Parent Families. In R. N. Rapoport, M. P. Fogarty & R. Rapoport (Eds.), *Families in Britain,* London: Routledge & Kegan Paul.

Jackson, B. (1984). *Fatherhood.* London: George Allen & Unwin.

Jackson, B., & Jackson, S. (1979). *Childminder: a study in action research.* London: Routledge & Kegan Paul.

Jackson, C. (1985). *Who will take our children?* London: Methuen.

Kitzinger, S. (1972). *The experience of childbirth.* London: Gollancz.

Lamb, M. E. (Ed.). (1976). *The Role of the Father in Child Development.* New York: Wiley.

Land, H. (1986). Women and children last: The reform of social security. In M. Brenton & C. Ungerson (Eds.), *Yearbook of Social Policy 1985–86.* London: Routledge & Kegan Paul.

Levine, J. A. (1980). *Who Will Raise the Children: New Options for Fathers and Mothers.* Philadephia: Lippincott.

Lewis, C. (1982). A feeling you can't scratch?: The effect of pregnancy and birth on married men. In N. Beail & J. McGuire (Eds.), *Fathers: Psychological Perspectives.* London: Junction Books.

Lewis, C. (1984). *Men's involvement in fatherhood: Historical and gender issues.* Paper presented in the Symposium, "Gender Issues and the Life-Span," at the Developmental Section of the British Psychological Society, Lancaster.

Lewis, C. (1986a). *Becoming a father.* Milton Keynes: Open University Press.

Lewis, C. (1986b). Early Sex-role Socialization. In D. Hargreaves & A. Colley (Eds.) *The Psychology of Sex Roles.* New York: Harper & Row.

Lewis, C. (1986c). The role of the father in the human family. In W. Sluckin, and M. Herbert, (Eds.), *Parental Behaviour.* Oxford: Basil Blackwell.

Lewis, C., & Gregory, S. (1986). Parents talk to their infants: Interpreting observed differences between mothers and fathers. Unpublished manuscript, Reading University.

Lewis, C., Newson E. & Newson, J. (1982). Father participation through childhood and its relation to career aspirations and delinquency. In N. Beail & J. McGuire (Eds.), *Fathers: Psychological perspectives.* London: Junction Books.

McGuire, J. (1982). Gender-specific differences in early childhood: The impact of the father. In N. Beail & J. McGuire (Eds.), *Fathers, Psychological Aspects.* London: Junction Books.

McKee, L. (1980). Fathers and childbirth: Just hold my hand". *Health Visitor,* 53, 368–372.

McKee, L., & O'Brien, M. (Eds.). (1982). *The father figure.* London: Tavistock.

McKee, L., & O'Brien, M. (1983). Interviewing men: Taking gender seriously. In E. Gamanicow, *The public and the private.* London: Heinemann Educational Books.

Mendes, H. A. (1976). Single fathers. *The Family Co-ordinator.* 25, 439–444.

New, C., & David, M. (1986). *For the children's sake,* London: Penguin.

Newson, J., & Newson, E. (1976). *Seven years old in the home environment,* London: Allen & Unwin.

Oakley, A. (1974). *The sociology of housework.* Oxford: Martin Robertson.

Oakley, A. (1980). *Women confined: Towards a sociology of childbirth.* Oxford: Martin Robertson.

Oakley, A. (1984). *Taking it like a woman.* Oxford: Martin Robertson.

O'Brien, M. (1980). Lone fathers: Transition from married to separated state. *Journal of Comparative Family Studies,* X1, 115–127.

O'Brien, M. (1981). Some recent trends in fatherhood research. *Early Childhood. 2, 3.*

O'Brien, M. (1982). Becoming a lone father: Differential patterns and experiences. In L. McKee & M. O'Brien (Eds.), *The father figure.* London: Tavistock.

O'Brien, M. (1984). *Fathers without wives: A comparative psychological study of married and separated fathers and their families.* Unpublished PhD. thesis, London School of Economics.

Office of Population Census and Surveys (1980). Birth Statistics 1977. HMSO, London.

Osborn, A. F. & Morris, T. C. (1979). The Rationale for a Composite Index of Social Class and its Evaluation. *British Journal of Sociology, 30,* 39–60.

Osborn, A. F., Butler, N. R., & Morris, A. C. (1984). *The social life of Britain's five-year olds:* A Report of the Child Health & Education Study. London: Routledge & Kegan Paul.

Packer, M., & Rosenblatt, D. (1979). Issues in the study of social behaviour in the first week of life. In D. Schaffer & J. Dunn (Eds.), *The first year of life: psychological and medical implications of early experiences.* New York: Wiley.

Parker, T. (1985). *Soldier, soldier.* Heinmann.

Rapoport, R., Rapoport, R. N., & Strelitz, Z. (1977). *Fathers, mothers, and others.* London: Routledge & Kegan Paul.

Rathbone, E. (1924). *The disinherited family.* (Reprinted in 1986 with an introduction by S. Fleming). Bristol: Falling Wall Press.

Richman, N. (1976). Depression in mothers of pre-school children. *Journal of World Psychology & Psychiatry, 17,* 75–78.

Richman, J., & Goldthorp, W. O. (1978). Fatherhood, the social construction of pregnancy and births. In S. Kitzinger & J. David (Eds.), *The place of birth.* Oxford: Oxford University Press.

Robertson, J. (1953). Some responses of young children to loss of maternal care. *Nursing Times, 49,* 382–386.

Rondal, J. A. (1980). Fathers' and mothers' speech in early language development. *Journal of Child Language, 7,*353–369.

Rubin, J. Z., Provinzano, F. J., & Luria, Z. (1974). The eye of the beholder: parents' view on sex of newborns, *American Journal of Orthopsychiatry,* 44, 512–519.

Russell, G. (1982). Shared-caregiving families: An Australian study. In M. E. Lamb (Ed.), *Nontraditional families: Parenting and child development.* Hillsdale, N. J.: Lawrence Erlbaum Associates.

Russell, G. (1983). *The changing role of fathers.* St. Lucia: Queensland University Press.

Rutter, M., Tizard, J., & Whitmore, K. (Eds.) (1970). *Education, health and behaviour,* London: Longman.

Rutter, M. (1972). *Maternal deprivation: Reassessed.* London: Penguin.

Schaffer, R. (1977). *Mothering.* London: Fontana/Open Books.

Scott-Heyes, G. (1982). The experience of perinatal paternity and its relation to attitudes to pregnancy and childbirth. In N. Beail, & J. McGuire, (Eds.) *Fathers: Psychological Perspectives.* London: Junction Books.

Sims, M., & Smith, C. (1982). Young fathers: Attitudes to marriage and family life. In L. McKee & M. O'Brien (Eds.) *The Father Figure,* London: Tavistock.

Tizard, B., & Hughes, M. (1984). *Young children learning: Talking and thinking at home and at school,* London: Fontana.

White, D., Woollett, A., & Lyon, L. (1982). Fathers' involvement with their infants: The relevance of holding. In N. Beail & J. McGuire (Eds.), *Fathers: Psychological perspectives,* London: Junction Books.

Woollett, A., White, D., & Lyon, L. (1982). Observations of fathers at birth. In N. Beail & J. McGuire (Eds.) *Fathers: Psychological perspectives.* London: Junction Books.

Young, M., & Willmott, P. (1973). *The symmetrical family.* Harmondsworth: Penguin.

3

Paternity "A la Française"*

Geneviève Delaisi de Parseval
Psychoanalyst, Paris

Françoise Hurstel
Université Louis Pasteur

The past throws light on the present. This present, that of French paternity, is characterized by "a mutation" or "a new phase of debate . . . which we are currently experiencing," according to historian Duby (1976). In this present explodes a certain status of the father's authority and allpowerfulness, the status of paterfamilias. This present, finally, raises questions never asked before, such as the place of the parent in the new methods of procreation (artifical insemination with a donor, for example). The past, then, can be used as a reference to what has changed so that we can appreciate the true value of the present. The diachronic, historical perspective can therefore be the vital theme for research on paternity "à la française." This is the perspective we have chosen to adopt.

Our plan is as follows: We will describe some of the terms given to the fathers, our ancestors, who have marked out the history of France so as to be able to outline the characteristics of the 20th century French father and the current upheavals in fatherhood. How have the French moved away from the paterfamilias who had absolute authority over property and people, to the "new fathers" who are close to their children with parental authority held by mother? Why are the paternal functions as educator, genitor, and name-giver, held for centuries by a single man, now divided among several people? And what are the psychological effects of these social transformations? Are fathers doomed to disappear with the new forms of medically assisted procreation, the increasing

---

*Translated from French by Helen Dykins

power of women governing contraception, and the new laws on filiation rights? Or is it rather the contrary, that various forms of fatherhood, with their numerous and rich possibilities for relationships between father and child, are in the process of being created? These are the questions, at the heart of an inquiry into fatherhood "à la française," which we will consider.

Let us consider some definitions: What do we mean by paternity? What is a father?

Let us first clarify the distinction we make between *paternity* and *fatherhood*. In this article we will use the term paternity in the abstract meaning of notion or concept. For example, we analyze in the third part the new changes in the notion of scientific paternity. On the other hand, we will use the term fatherhood to deal with the psychological paternal function (e.g., "deficient," "excluded," or "new" fathers, as in the second part).

While they are presented as being evident notions, paternity and fatherhood are in fact extremely complex terms. We will distinguish between them and define the notions which mark out the field of paternity so as to be able to understand it and to situate our intentions (Hurstel, 1985b).

The characteristics of the paternal function lie in two distinct domains: the social domain, where the references and the particularities of the father in a given society are established, and the field of the psyche, where the rooting of the father in the subjectivity of each one of us is established. That there are intricate links between the two is certain, but these links are neither automatic nor mechanical. We shall therefore define paternity as a complex unity of both social and psychological functions. These functions can be fulfilled by one or more men, or sometimes (rarely) by women.

Within the social function, the terms *status* and *role* do not cover the same aspects of paternal function. Within the psychological function, we will differentiate among the possibilities for a subject to assume fatherhood, but distinguishing the multiple identities of real fathers who mark the personal and family history of each individual. These distinctions are useful since, according to the historical periods brought forward, that which dominates and that which changes within the paternal function do not stem from the same aspects of the function. Therefore we can only evoke the social function and, in particular, the status, we mean the place of authority and power which society, in a given moment in history, accords paternity. But of their role, by which we understand "totality of concrete behavior expected of fathers either by society or by his family" (Segalen, 1981), we know very little. French fathers of the past are still relatively unknown to us. No complete presentation of the history of fathers has been done to this day, contrary to the history of mothers attempted by historians Knibielher and Fouquet (1977). As to the psychological function, nothing can be said since casework and biographies from that period hardly existed at all. This is not, moreover, a matter of chance. It was Freud and psychoanalysis who caused studies to multiply, and the psychological question specific to fatherhood to develop. But there is more to it than that. For a long time, probably up to the end of the 17th century, the very notion of individual and psychological being remained for the most part a secondary reality in relation to the reality of the group. The individual did not consider himself as being isolated or having an existence or a self-awareness outside his group. The notion of individuality is, in itself, a reality that is historically dated (Mauss, 1950).

We are saying that the question of the father from his origins to the present day has not only varied in his social and psychological characteristics, but also on the very emphasis which a society puts on certain aspects of his function.

FRENCH FATHERS OF THE PAST: THE ALL-POWERFUL FATHER

We will distinguish between the deep roots, located in Roman Law, and the images of God within Middle Aged Christianity. It was during this latter period that a type of society was established which was to engender a form of family and marriage, which, with a few changes, has been maintained until the last few decades. The institution of marriage, which was settled at this period, was to designate who the father was, and to invest him with a social, political, military, and economic power, while at the same time joining all the paternal functions within one man.

Of course, important historical and mythical elements have influenced the images of the occidental father: the father in ancient Egypt, in ancient Greece, and in the Old Testament. These are fathers of whom we know little unless we accept the remarkable series of studies published by the German Tellenbach (1976). But we feel that the roots specific to French paternity are found principally in Roman Law and in the Christian Gospel.

Far-reaching Roots: Paterfamilias and Roman Law

The father of us all is Roman Law! Laws from the Ancient Regime to the French Civil Code, the laws which determine the legal status of the father, all have their roots in Roman Law. One can say that the different types of fathers which have succeeded one another in France—from the feudal father to the contemporary "new" fathers, via the bourgeois father of the 19th century—are all tinkered products of the paterfamilias of ancient Rome.

Who was the Roman paterfamilias? He drew his power and his authority, which were absolute, from the Law, to the extent of having the power of death—and therefore the power of life—over his children. Laws such as the power of the father in Rome were exercised beyond time and space, beyond the practices and customs. Whether he was present or absent, it was the father who held the authority and the power. Whether the son was 2 or 50 years old, the father ruled the son until his death. He had no need of brutality or gestures to be obeyed; he should even do without them—that being the epitomy of recognized authority. Thus, old Caton, the roman orator said, "a model of conservatism and severity, found it shameful that a father should raise a hand against his sons" (Thomas, 1984). For the Roman father was not tyrannical: he was all-powerful. He drew this all-powerfulness from a social and political power, that belonged to the "fathers" (*patres* in Latin). "Patres" was the name given to the senators, "patrici" to the patricians," paterpatriae" to the emperor, and "Jupiter" to the god who represented the sovereign function. Thus, fathers and magistrates were invested in the same way.

Numerous effects ensue from this political and legal definition: the Roman father was not the parent. The function of begetting did not give the right to the title of father. Adoption was therefore attached to the principle of Roman paternity. This was a widespread adoption: "By a transfer from one man to another, the son of one man becomes the son of another. While, in these man to man contracts, the boys are a mean of an alliance, paternity turns out to be a pure product of the law" (Thomas, 1984). Paterfamilias is both a political and an economic power; it is he that transmits the name and the inheritance. During his life he possesses patrimonies, and is the guardian of his sons and those who live in his house. Master of his children's lives, the father brings the son into the world with a special rite: *amphidromies* (the father takes the newborn child and, in front of the whole household, he walks round the house three times, holding the child in his arms). And so we have his function and his legal, economic, political, and social status. His daily role consists in being his son's educator (not his daughter's: he will only pay attention to her when the time comes to marry her off!). He teaches his son gymnastics, equitation, grammar, and law. If he cannot do this himself, he chooses a tutor, either an uncle or an old friend. But above all, he transmits a system of values to his son, and trains him to become a citizen of the city: in this society where the family is so much more than a unit of reproduction, where it is "the archetype of the social order, the father is the compulsory means of getting to the city" (Thomas, 1984). And the son? The absolute power of the father corresponds to the absolute submission of the son. When there are rebellions against the father, they are quite radical: there are cases of parricide. But rebellions among the aristocracy are rarely due to personal conflicts of an affective nature, or due to the "generation gap"; they are almost always political acts. One famous example is that of Caesar and Brutus. But all this does not mean that there are no sentiments in the father-son relationship; they are sublimated by the ideals of the times and dominated by civic relations.

Thus the roman paterfamilias, who is the ancestor of the French father, was above all, a master with a political, social, and legal power. Because of this, the function of genitor was laid aside and adoption formed the foundation of paternity. From this standpoint sons were privileged, since they were their father's successors; daughters only had value as instruments in alliances. It is this founding paternity of social relations and of the city, which is used in expressions such as "fathers of the Church" or "founding fathers" which were to find themselves transformed during the feudal period.

The Feudal Father

During the feudal period, the paterfamilias, stemming from the Roman Law, combined with characteristics of the Christian image of God and with forms which were specific to that society, to constitute a father whom we will call "feudal father."

Through the Gospel, Christianity offers an image of an all-powerful father, who adopts those who believe in him and is adopted by those who believe in him. The specifically Christian meaning of God's fatherhood is that of the pact of filial adoption which was God's historic initiative. And so we find once more the notions of adoption and power which were already present in Roman Law, but here with the notion of power dominates, characterized by the Christ figure (Kyrios in Greek, a term which means "Lord"). That designation of majesty marked the feudal period, and not the idea of "brother Jesus," which is a relatively recent notion. The tympanums of *Autun* Cathedral (one of the most beautiful cathedrals in romanesque *Bourgogne*), with their severe Christ figures, full of majesty, bear witness to this image of Jesus as an "all-powerful Lord".

How do the characteristics of the paterfamilias and the specific forms of the feudal society fit together?

It was between the second half of the 10th century and the first half of the 11th century that society became organized into a hierarchical order which was to last for a long time. Duby (1976) tells that it functioned according to a tripartite model: the people of the Church, those who pray; the lay noblement and knights, those who fight; and the vast mass of workers (traders, artisans, and peasants). It was a hierarchical system characterized by the relationships among people: the peasants were dependent on the nobles, the nobles themselves were dependent on each other. The most powerful men (economically, militarily, and socially speaking) were themselves submitted and dependent on the supreme suzerain on earth, the King of France. The King enjoyed immense prestige because he was the "greatest of all suzerains," he was nobody's vassal unless he was God's. In this society, God was experienced and imagined as the "almighty Father, the Creator." Inversely, each earthly father, from the peasant to the lord, would be experienced, by analogy, as "Lord." The family was the basic unit of society and, according to the feudal society's image, it was both a hierarchy and a community. This was an extended family: it included several generations and had multiple functions. Termed a "Mesnie," or household family, it was a socio-economic unit (the father was also the "head of the firm"), and a unit of military command, reproduction, men, good, and culture. The father was the master over his sons even when they are old: violent conflicts would break out between the "elder" or "Senior," and the "Youths" (even when the latter were in their fifties!)

What establishes permanently the father's position of strength is the institution of marriage, which knits together the functions of the father in a single man.

Historians and anthropologists, in particular Goody (1983) for the 5th and 6th centuries, and Duby (1981) for the 11th and 12th centuries, have brought to light the slow hand of the Catholic Church's power concerning matrimonial practices, the long struggle to make cohabitation illegitimate, then to make it disappear, and finally change children born in non-conformist unions into "bastards."

Two conceptions of marriage were violently opposed in Latin Christianity at about 1100. At this time a conflict reached its height, a conflict which was to end in the institution of practices which have remained more or less stable to the present day. About 900 years ago, therefore, the forms of marriage were established which "are being broken up now"; this disintegration: "is our whole concept of world, our whole way of looking at life, of seeing the relationship of work and familiarity which are breaking apart" (Duby, 1981).

Indeed, marriage was to perpetuate forms of the family and society: for "the rites of marriage were instituted to assure the allocation of women between men, to discipline male competition around them and to officialize and socialize procreation. By designating who the fathers are, they are adding a single obvious filiation to that of the mother" (Duby, 1981). They were also to give the children born of the marriage the status of heirs, ancestors, a name, and some rights. Thus, marriage founded the relationship of kinship: it is the keystone of the structure of society, and the father is the central pillar. Thanks to this institution, different aspects of the paternal function join in the person of the father.

With the "feudal father" of the Middle Ages, paternity and the institution of marriage were linked together around the 11th century. This linkage was to provide French paternity with the definition and power which we recognize up until 1970 (in legal documents): the father became the name-giver, thus assuring his descent, the genitor (in theory), and the educator. Father in the image of God and the prince, he had authority over property and people.

We can see from this, how deep the mutation is that we are experiencing today, since it is that order which is collapsing especially in the figure of the all-powerful father, which had found its typically French expression as far back as the 11th century.

This change was progressive: history works over a long period, and transformations within paternity are clearly discernable well before its present form. We will ask, along with Tellenbach (1976) a question which he put to the occidental father and which we put to the French father: "When did the decline of the image of the "paterfamilias" begin? When did his status begin to falter?"

Close Roots; Monarchical Parricide

On the quiet, slow transformations of the France of Ancient Regime, then in the upsets of the French Revolution, and finally in the visible return of paternal authority in the 19th century, points of rupture concerning paternal power were to be marked out.

Can we not say that the first parricide on a social scale was the execution of King Louis XVI? And that "domestic royalty" was to be rejected at the same time as the monarchy? In "Mémoires de deux jeunes mariées," Balzac (1841) wrote: "When it decapitated Louis XVI, the Republic effectively decapitated all the fathers of families . . ." And further on, he underlines that it was not only this fact that played a part, but also that the whole society and the vision men had of themselves had completely changed: "There are no more families today, there are only individuals." This view is testified by the work of the encyclopedists and Rousseau (1755). The latter had already said in his *Discourse on the Origin of Inequality:* "Instead of saying that civil society is derived from paternal power, we should have said the contrary, that this power draws its main force from the former." This assertion was the inverse of that of the traditionalist lawyer Merlin, who in the *Universal and Reasoned Book of Jurisprudence* (1787), in the article on "Punishment" (paternal), wrote: "Paternal power is not a law which stems from men; nature put it inside us." Two conceptions of man, family, and fatherhood are in confrontation here. And the first one was to prevail over the second one.

The first conception, that of Rousseau's, prevailed over the second one, that of the defenders of absolute paternal power. The power of the father was no longer referred to as a natural law and, therefore, as untouchable. Instead it was recognized in the context of its relationships with the society which produced it. Thus, the change within society and the dispute over the King's power will lead to the dispute over the father's power.

Two examples allow us to evaluate the contradictory ideas which, on the eve of the Revolution, characterized the appraisal of paternal power.

1. In the article "Child" from the *Encyclopédie* of 1755, a dispute appears concerning the father's power. Here is an enlightening excerpt: "The father is the Master of the Child only as long as his word is necessary to him; beyond this term they become equals, and then the Son is totally independent of his father and only owes him respect and obedience." This is not so far from the first article of the Declaration of Human and Civil Rights proclaimed in August 1789: "Men are born and remain free and equal in the eyes of the Law."

2. We must not forget that, in parallel to this enlightened current from which the Revolutionaries were to draw their inspiration (the 18th century was the century of "leading lights"), Merlin (1787) still held that the law of the father was a natural fact.

The revolution was to bring a spectacular but transitory mutation to the father's law. The revolutionaries appeared, according to the historian Schnapper (1980), like "prophets"; indeed, their laws went beyond everything that has been wished for and dreamed of. For 10 years, the status which was put forward to the father was strangely to foreshadow that which is offered today, 200 years later, as we shall show in the following examples.

Let us judge for ourselves!

March 1790: The abolition of "lettres de cachet." Fathers could no longer imprison their children.

April 1790: institution of the "family court," to give advice concerning difficult children. What has happened to the "power" of the father, the unique head of the family?

August 1793: *the abolition of paternal power.*

But the Revolution went too far and too fast; the mentality was not ready for this great change. The right of paternal punishment was re-established in 1801, and with the Civil Code of 1804 the father rediscovers (under the name of "paternal authority") his status of power over his children, his wife, and her property. Thus, an initial point of rupture in the father's social and political all-powerfulness can be found, in the 18th century, in the ideas prevalent at this time and in the French Revolution. This is testified by the revolutionary laws which give to the father and mother a relatively equal status and abolish paternal power. Does not this time, which lasted for ten years, in a way foreshadow the legal status of the father today?

The "Padre Padrone" of the Nineteenth Century

A second line of rupture was to make the figure of the all-powerful father fall from his pedestal: this was the rise of industrialization in the 19th century.

The "padre padrone" is the father-head of the firm, the bourgeois-owner. It is also the title of a recent Italian movie by the Taviani brothers. In this story the father, the head of a small agricultural concern in Sardinia, dictates everything. He forces his son to work with him. But this father-owner learns in the last sequences of the movie that he can no longer compete with the prices and that his son is leaving him to study to become a teacher. This movie symbolizes the power of the father in the 19th century. Although it is absolute within the family, it is no longer a social, political, and religious power since it is not upheld by the State anymore. On the contrary, we witness here the State's supervision of families and, in particular, the father: "Since 1804, paternal power as seen by the Law has been progressively altered by the multiplication of legal and administrative inspection, which the exercise of paternal power gave rise to." (Labrusse, 1982). This was an alteration which was literally to undermine paternal authority. The list of these inspections is impressive. We have picked out nine of these supervisions between 1880 and 1912. The most important are the following. In 1889, the law of *paternal degeneration* is introduced, in which the State takes charge of the child when the father is incapable of bringing it up. In 1912, juvenile courts are given the authority for social investigation, to supervise families and parents suspected of being "bad" for the child and for the society.

Two phenomena accompany this inspection. The first is a distinction between the "good" and the "bad" father. Until now, all fathers were, according to the law and in theory, "good fathers." But now, some will be suspected, watched, and excluded. Following which criteria? Social and personal criteria: bad fathers are those who do not observe or transmit the social norms. They are "ignorant, fallible and wicked." In her book on mother love, Badinter (1980) gives an ironical description of these "bad fathers": "Contrary to the bad mother, who does not belong to any social background in particular, the bad father is usually a poor or penniless man, a worker or a minor artisan placed, already at the end of the 19th century, in flats which were too small, or a drunkard who drinks in the pub and only goes home to sleep and work off his frustrations with excessive violence on his wife and children . . . This is the father of the future, delinquent vagabond." Here we recognize a portrait of the poor worker such as described in Tristan's *Diary* (1843–1844). We are far from the father as "God's lieutenant" (17th century), the substitute of the King within his family! Inversely, the "good father" would be the man from the wealthier classes, the head of a firm, the business man, or the "padre padrone."

The second new phenomenon: In between the "good father" and the "bad father" a new species of father is going to appear, the *specialists* (Hurstel, 1984). Whether these were magistrates (representatives of the law, charged with safeguarding children's rights), physicians, schoolmasters, or social workers they took over from the declining parent. And, today, what about the pediatricians, psychiatrists, psychologists and gynecologists? This is a phenomenon which has become more widespread! And while some bourgeois fathers still have, in certain cases, the economic and family power, the social image of the father is definitively marred by the suspicion that weighs on father in general. Indeed, another aspect of industrialization was to deal a severe blow to the "padre padrone" himself: this was the distance usually erected between the home and the place of work. "Politics and business absorb the head of the family, the father, who has been handling figures all day, can hardly be preoccupied with the development of his son's moral conscience in the evening," wrote Chambon, author of a work on mothers in 1909 (quoted in Badinter, 1980). The status and the actual educative role which were part of the father's functions, were thus taken from him. It was the mothers (at least in bourgeois households) who had the monopoly on family education. School, which was obligatory, would then take over. A new notion appeared in the vocabulary of child specialists: that of "absent fathers" which would, in the 20th century, engender the notion of "deficient fathers."

The 19th century would, little by little, bring some changes in the role of father. While the Civil Code still recognized his power, it was subversively undermined by the rise of industrialization which considerably modified society and family. In the reduced urban families composed of father, mother, and children (nuclear families), it was the mother who held the actual authority over the children; it was the mother who had the educative function. In the 19th century society, parents are watched over by different institutions: the child is obliged to go to school, and the childhood "specialists" appear. For the first time in the history of paternity, comes the idea that there may be "good" and "bad" fathers. The idea of a "paternal deficiency" will become typical in the discussions on paternity during the first half of the 20th century. But are fathers truly "deficient?"

FRENCH FATHERS IN THE 20TH CENTURY: FROM "DEFICIENT" FATHERS TO "NEW" FATHERS

Up to now, we have put the emphasis on the evolution of the father's social function and authority status. As there is a lack of in-depth studies by historians, we cannot picture the possible psychological problems which may have existed in the father-child relationship. Neither do we know the nature of the father's everyday role in these periods. What is certain in the 20th century, however, in this age of psychological discovery and also of the "humble father", is that the role and psychological function of the father is now somewhat better known to us. Nevertheless, it was only in the last part of the 20th century—since the 1970's—that numerous works and research studies on fatherhood psychology began to appear.

In this part of the chapter, we will look first at the area covered by the notion of "paternal deficiency," followed by the notion of "new" fathers.

The "Deficient" Fathers (1950–1972)

We can truly speak of the "mutation" of the paternal status between 1900 and 1972. The assessment of this first part of the 20th century up to 1972 is impressive; let us remember the elements. As far as the legal status is concerned, the fall of the father would be marked from decade to decade by new laws which would whittle away his prerogative by favoring children's rights and later, women's rights. Here are three important dates. The legislation of 1935 abolished the right of "paternal punishment" (the father's right to imprison his children). The 1970 law accorded parental authority to the mother as well as to the father, so that the father was devoid of any particular authority. Finally, the law of 1972 recognized natural filiation and set it in equal terms with legitimate filiation: in this case, the mother's right prevails over that of the father's.

As far as economic status and role are concerned, the exodus from country to town in the 1950s was to make the salaried class widespread, deprive the father of his status as head of the firm (agricultural or artisanal), and take him away from home. The father became the "absent father." In the vocabulary of child specialists, he is practically excluded from his children's education. The mothers were recognized by these specialists as the only valid educators.

All this culminates in the generalized idea of "paternal deficiency" of which all fathers are now suspect, the figure of a "deficient father" becomes apparent.

Let us not forget, finally, that such deficiency lies within a demographic reality. We should remember that France has suffered three wars in less than a century (from 1870 to 1945), a dramatic loss of men and loss of potential fathers. As for those who escaped the slaughter, is it really surprising that they were considered deficient?

What does this paternal deficiency represent in the years from 1955 to 1972? To what does it correspond in French society? How is it marked out in family life?

We will present a few types of fathers termed deficient. We shall then go on to examine the notion of deficiency using a survey as a basis for our discussion.

The Excluded Father in French Pediatrics
from the Beginning of the Century Until the 1960s

Delaisi de Parseval and Lallemand (1980) have undertaken a study on the images of the father as seen by French baby-care manuals from the beginning of the century up to the post-war period.

The images are as follows. First, the *Great Absentee*. The first diktat of the manuals rests upon the presence of the mother and the absence of the father. The second assumption is that the mother and children are at home, and the father is at work. The implicit ideology of this discourse about conception, birth, and motherhood highlights pregnancy, delivery, breast-feeding, and mother-child relationships in the first years as essential moments—but all basically feminine. The man, the father, remains a trivial element throughout the whole of this process.

But if the absence of the father is important, then his presence (that is, as it is referred to by the authors), is no less important. The father is described as a "big baby" during the first months of his offspring's infancy: "The image of this husband-father-big-baby-who-must-be-fed is, with no doubt, one of the components of the complementary fantasies of the nursing mother, of the "mama" of the latin world."

Another privileged image is the *father "Saint-Joseph."* He is presented as being the calming influence in the home, looking after everything while his wife is pregnant. This is an apparently contradictory image, but it is just as derisive as the others; it joins the image of the "embarrassed father."

From the beginning of the pregnancy, physicians only accord him a minimum, if not inexistent role. One of them wrote on the subject of the male parent's fantasies during this period: "He is unable to act, to decide, to do. He, who wants to guide, and to get things moving, has no role. In *theatrical terms, he is an extra.*"

This abstract father, quite ill at ease in his role, is the eternal intruder into the mother-baby couple and appears to be a character that no one has authorized to "father." Neither society (to begin with, the baby-care books) nor his wife (for the most part) really recognize his right, competency, know-how, tenderness, or patience; these we are led to believe are the prerogative of the mothers.

This study, which is based on the works of childhood specialists, enables us to state that if we can really call fathers deficient it is essentially because they are relegated to this place by these very specialists, who normalize the activities surrounding the child. Yet while fathers are termed deficient, they are in fact excluded by educational theoreticians. But in everyday life, things do not necessarily happen according to this stereotyped scenario, as we shall now see.

Is the Absent Father a "Deficient" Father?

We have undertaken a survey (Hurstel, 1978, 1982) of 10 families who experienced the great rural-urban exodus which took place in France during the mid-fifties. This exodus towards the town, and the change of profession which resulted from this, were the cause of the transformation of the father's economic status: from being the head of a company ("padre padrone") he became an employee or worker. These phenomena caused his role to change: fathers were taken away from home during the day, and came back tired in the evening, leaving the care of and the responsibility for the children in the hands of the mother. They became absent fathers.

These men, aged between 40 and 45 when the survey was undertaken in 1978, are among those who, in the 1960s, exchanged their status of farmer or artisan for the status of worker. With their wives, they left their villages to come and live in the industrial town of Montbeliard in East France and became employed in the production unit belonging to Peugeot cars. The study of their biographies, collected through semi-directive interviews, enables us to clarify the psychological and social effects of this change in status.

The results of the survey permit us to state the following:

1. These men have destabilized social positions. The change in status entails a depreciation of the father's image as seen by the people in his immediate environment, especially in the eyes of his wife, who compares her husband with her own father. This depreciation of the father's social image is felt more or less strongly from one family to another, depending on the number and seriousness of the conflicts between husband and wife.

2. Not only does the immediate and indirect environment accuse the father, recently become a worker, of being deficient, but the man himself thinks he is "insufficient" and a "bad father." This judgment is always made through a comparison with the fathers and grandfathers—of preceding generations all of them farmers. In all the interviews, the men made the following bitter remark: "How can you possibly be a father here, when you haven't even got a corner to put up a workbench in your apartment to show your son what you can do?" These comments do not signify that the fathers are bad fathers in the eyes of their

children, but that they experience things as if they were. The problem here concerns paternal identity.

When we have just stated accounts for the psychological effects on the adult family members, of the change in the fathers's social status, a status which is less actualized than before. We perceive a "decline in the social image," in the words of psychoanalyst Lacan (1938).

But going beyond this depreciated social image of fatherhood, can we say that fathers are deficient in the eyes of their children in everyday life?

Our results show that if they are truly deficient, it is not through the direct relationship of status transformation and psychological effects.

3. Let us examine the father's role, as demonstrated in this survey, that is, what fathers do, want, and are for their children. The change in the status gives rise to a break between private and working life. The mother has the upper hand concerning the private life, and the father, who is absent from the home so that he can earn a living for the family, may also be absent from his children's education. This absence becomes a psychological absence if the mother, now responsible for the home, considers the father's opinion and moral authority as being without value—if she actually excludes him. Thus we see that it is not the real absence of the father which is the essential determining factor for terming the father deficient, but the meaning this absence assumes for each member of the family.

In fact, the fathers studied here do have a role in the daily life of their children. With their sons, the fathers are educators. With their daughters, they stay within the bounds of an affectionate relationship. Indeed, the education of the daughters within this originally rural population depends on the competence of the mother. In one of interviews, one man gave the following statement: "The mother is all for her son, the father for his daughter. The mother teaches her daughter, the father his son—to make a man out of him." What does a father teach his son? These men, cut off from the techniques and know-how of the rural environment, can no longer transmit their knowledge to their sons. In the evening after the day's work and during the weekend, the men take up activities based on rural and artisanal practices: some repair their cars, others do odd jobs about the apartment, other work in allotments rented on the outskirts of the town.

They all have a manual activity which they transmit to their sons. But it must be stated that they do not oversee their children's school activities, this being a domain reserved for the mother. They do not take part in caring for the babies either, this also being a domain reserved for the mothers.

4. The father tries to achieve his conception of the ideal image of his role. It is through this that he revalues himself.

5. The notion of deficiency is also the result of a theoretical confusion. It is a superficial analysis of paternal realities, which confuses the historical and sociological analysis with the psychological analysis.

From a historical perspective, there is indeed a loss of the father's all-power-fulness. One of the sociological effects of this—on a level of fatherhood prac-tices—can be seen in the social decline of the father's image in France. We have already shown that this decline began at the end of the 18th century, and we could say that its climax is at its top in the first part of the 20th century. Every man who becomes father *de facto* takes on a depreciated social function; thus, if we want to speak of a father's deficiency, an additional and truly psychological factor must be present in the evaluation: the necessary taking into account of the weight of the family history, as well as the story of the individuals who assume parental functions.

Thus the life of men-fathers in the first part of the 20th century was a paradox: They assumed a function which was depreciated to the extreme, socially speak-ing. This paradox came to a head between 1968 and 1970. Indeed, in May 1968 there was a cultural revolution which was a sort of second "French Revolution". It was no longer the father king who was killed, but the "paterfamilias" insofar as he still existed in people's memories. May 1968 is the pregnant pause which gives emphasis to paternal deficiency. After the absent father and the excluded father, the father becomes the "dead father." But paternity was not dead any-way: This paradox found an outlet when fathers began to claim recognition of their own paternity. Indeed, from 1979 onwards, *mass media* announced the birth of a "new" father.

The "New" Fathers (1972–1985)

Who are these "new" fathers who emerged in France in 1972 (Delaisi de Par-seval, 1981)? If we look at the images presented to us, we see that this sup-posedly new character is in fact a young father (belonging to the 20–35 age group) who changes his baby's nappies, gives the child a bottle, takes him or her for walks, and even goes as far as looking after him or her while the mother goes out to work. We should not forget the "must" of the contemporary obstetric imagination: the inevitable image of the father at the scene of the birth, a character whose experience is supposedly fantastic and indispensable (see the success of the movement created by Leboyer).

What Do They Do? Father's New Role

Surveys enable us to clarify what fathers do with their children, what they do in the way of household activities, and what fatherhood signifies in their eyes.

1. Working life is of paramount importance for the majority of men inter-viewed: "Their plans concern their work." They wish to become fathers, but "this will come naturally" (Ferrand, 1982) in their eyes. This differs from women, who have family *and* professional plans. Many men say that they have tried to find a job which is compatible with taking care of their children.

2. The father's tasks with his children remain traditional in an urban environment: overseeing their schoolwork, games, walks, sport, and doing odd jobs (Ferrand, 1982). This is what men call "doing the same things as the mother."

There is, therefore, a limited characteristic in the masculine participation in parental tasks. Moreover, this participation implies a contact with the children. The only families where there is a real division of household tasks and care have been seen within artistic and student populations (Hurstel, 1985a). The division of tasks in the majority of cases is performed in the following manner: skilled parental tasks (awakenings, games, teaching, etc.) are done by the father; while the unskilled parental tasks (food, washing, upkeep, etc.) are left to the mother (Segalen, 1982).

3. For all men, fatherhood is an additional status. This is what a 38 year old technician had to say: "Having a child gives you a certain weight; when I announced that I had a son, the others looked on me differently. All of a sudden I was taken seriously" (Ferrand, 1982). This status gives a man a certain standing in the eyes of his contemporaries. These results converge with those of Levine (1982) for the U.S.A. and Christensen (1982) for Denmark.

While fatherhood does not give a social status of power, it nevertheless confers an actualized personal status. This status can be appreciated if we consider the growing number of specialists who are studying the question. Since 1975, work on different aspects of paternity has been continually increasing, particularly in the fields of psychology, psychoanalysis, psychiatry, and education. These studies enable us to present the situation of the father in the 1980s.

Who Are They? The Father's Identity

The major research studies undertaken in France on this question converge on a set of points.

1. Becoming a father corresponds to a complex psychological process. The authors note down in detail the decisive moments. First of all, the announcement of fatherhood which sparks off the process of fantasy and symptomization (couvade-syndrome). The birth will then direct the fantasies according to the child's sex. Giving birth is often experienced by men as something which is impossible to look at. Finally, the first relational demonstrations between father and child represent the third important moment in the psychological process of "paternalité" (Delaisi de Parseval, 1981).

2. We have noticed that, even if the father does the same thing as the mother, the relational demonstrations are different and never double the mother-child relationship. Indeed, beyond the differences pertaining to two human beings (each one having a particular relational style) we can see a difference in the psychological position in relation to the child. Men who father are in the position of separator in relation to the mother-child couple. The very first relations be-

tween father and child comfort the man in this still traditional paternal function (Hurstel, 1985a).

3. A study undertaken in the field of pediatrics (Bydlowki & Levy-Leblond, 1982) underlined the psychological characteristics of men who have the opportunity of caring for their hospitalized babies. An identification with the mother who carries the baby, gives birth to it, and cares for it is emphasized in their case. This identification is present in all men, but is reinforced and allowed by the present actualization in the *mass media* of the new father. Another study (Cukier, 1982), which observed fathers at the time of the premature birth of one of their children, confirms the importance of the father's possibility of playing a role early on in his relationship with the baby, although institutions and tradition often impose a necessarily secondary and different paternal role. The author reports the case of a father whose second child was born prematurely. He took care of the baby in a special way because the new-born was hospitalized far from the mother in a neonatal clinic. The father said: "The first time, the mother was the most interesting, at this time, it was the child. I saw him straight away, when he was very ill and I became attached to him earlier and more than with the first one. I also felt useful as I brought the milk to him." The author informs us that this father underwent a severe depression several months after the birth—in short the equivalent of the maternal postpartum depression.

This and other studies confirm the importance that the father can have for the baby—if he is given the opportunity to approach the child.

Thus, we should try to understand this "new father" phenomenon as an element which renews the question of paternity. But we must go beyond the everyday life and experience of fathers in order to grasp the nature and extent of the mutations which have affected the paternal function since the early 1970s. Since then, the definition of fatherhood and the very concept of filiation have been undergoing some important changes, and this is what we will now go on to show. But first, a definition: Filiation is defined as the adjudication of paternity, a social process of assignment of paternity.

CURRENT CHANGES IN PATERNITY: TOWARD NEW DEFINITIONS (1972–1986)

Three phenomena explain the new concepts of paternity which have raised in France during the last decade: modifications in marriage forms and new family types; changes concerning the filiation rights; and rapid progress in biomedical science.

These new concepts are characterized in three ways:

1. Fatherhood split between several individuals, sometimes not seen as cumulative, sometimes considered as additional.

2. Intentional fatherhood (psychologically or morally speaking)—or in other words—fatherhood through preconceptional adoption.
3. Delayed or delayable fatherhood, of which we will give four examples: (AID fatherhood, AIH fatherhood, fatherhood after cancer, *postmortem* fatherhood).

The present time is perhaps at such a moving point that we start to doubt notions that have been until now beyond any doubt, such as the notion of father (or the notion of mother). Whereas the father of *Ancien Regime,* during the 11th and 12th centuries, was characterized by a total linking up of function, fatherhood today is split according to the separation of its defining functions. In the case of artificial insemination with donor (AID), for example, we shall see that the genitor is separated from the educator, who is also the name-giver. In the case of divorce and multiparentage, the name-giver, who is here the genitor, is no longer the child's educator (or sole educator).

Three Contemporary Phenomena, Causes of Changes

Three contemporary phenomena with their specific interference in the French context can account for this radical change, which has been translated into new forms of paternity for about a decade.

The first one is linked with the institution of marriage.

Marriage, the supporting institution for paternity, is decreasing significantly. Marriage rate (number of marriages per 1000 inhabitants) was, in the beginning of the 19th century, on average 7.5%. By 1979, this rate had decreased to 6.4%; by 1983, it had further decreased to 5.5%. The totals were: in 1972, 416,000 marriages; in 1983, 300,000 marriages (Sullerot, 1984).

Between 1975 and 1981, the number of unmarried people increased significantly. And the number of divorces increased tremendously. With the slowdown of marriage, the institution that specifies who is the father, we are faced with the problem of filiation laws. Filiation rights were considerably modified in France with the law passed on January 3, 1972, which made blood relationship an essential element when establishing an individual's filiation, and induced or "permitted" a real revolution in the field of paternity. With the extraordinary progress of biomedical sciences, we have witnessed a spectacular watershed compared with the Civil Code of 1804, to such an extent that it was possible to write that "fatherhood had definitely left the domain of belief, and had entered the domain of certainty" (Deniniolle, 1983). Obviously, this movement did not abruptly come to pass: Since 1955, French jurisprudence has allowed serological analyses, which can prove non-paternity or be an element leading to a repudiation of paternity. This was formalized by the law of 1972 which legislated the equality of filiation and truth of relationships from a double standpoint, both biological and affective. From this point onwards, the vision of fatherhood moves away from the secret of conception and invalidates the options given in the Code of 1804, which were all based on the impossibility of proving fatherhood with certainty. According to a jest made by a lawyer, the old saying *"Pater est quem nuptiae demonstrant"* could be parodied in the following terms: *"Pater est quem sanguis demonstrat."* From now on paternity must be proven; it can therefore, as an inevitable consequence, escape the true genitor even when he is the husband of the mother, if the latter should wish it so!

Indeed, another quite innovative characteristic of this law is that the married mother can dispose of paternity herself, as she can declare the child under her maiden name. We can see that the power of the mother is impressive: "In the words of Article 374, the mother alone has parental authority (which is incorrectly termed under the circumstances), even if natural fatherhood is legally established" (Deniniolle, 1983). This is a measure which deserves to be underlined: it totally deprives the father of his authority over the child.

Fatherhood can now be proved with a success rate of 99.8%, thanks to progress in biology. One can say that it is from now on a scientific paternity. Obviously, it is the whole concept of filiation which has changed. We see that paternity is no longer the prerogative of the father. As well as the mother's power, the child's right is also a notion which has become increasingly important. This can mean, for example, that a child can choose between his mother's two successive husbands, providing that he was born less than 300 days after the dissolution of the marriage and is legitimized by the mother's second husband. In the case of paternal conflict, the child's interest is from now on the important factor. In anticipation of a possible evolution of this case, lawyers think that if society allows the insemination of single women, or the postmortem insemination of widows, then a new law is likely to be needed, of a sort never known before: the woman's absolute right over her child, mixed with a paternity which will remain secret forever, as if it were definitely effaced. As to the name, it will no longer be so much the name of the father, as we have seen; we are entering the era of the "maternal grandfather's name" (the name of the mother's father) since the mother has the right to declare the newborn child officially under her maiden name.

As for the father, it is sure in any case that the combination of these three phenomena we have just put forward (new family types, new rights, and the rapid progress of biomedical sciences) have dealt a cruel blow to his status, and even to his stature. Perhaps the death of the father is no longer a myth, from the moment one can freeze "paternity" in an anonymous test tube and conserve it, sell it, and so forth. Has the age of the father-object really come? Would paternity, as defined until now, be basically changed by the biology of reproduction? The manipulation of time concerning human life constitutes quite obviously a revolution in the paternal imagination. To define this particular phenomenon, we have proposed the notions of additional fatherhood, preconceptional adoptive fatherhood and delayed fatherhood.

First Characteristic in the Concept of Paternity:
Split, Additional, Dependent on Several Individuals

Several forms of fatherhood have recently appeared in western societies. One of the foremost techniques is AID, which enables a sterile man to be a child's father without being his genitor. Added to this is a unique element: the fact that this genitor is unknown to the couple, and he gives his sperm to a sperm bank which freezes it and conserves it with the aim of inseminating an unknown woman.

AID fatherhood thus has cast doubts about the traditional vision of fatherhood since it creates an original form of paternal filiation. We have studied in detail the question of fatherhood in AID, the fatherhood of the man whom we called the "AID father" or "father-who-came-in-from-the-cold" (Delaisi de Parseval & Janaud, 1981). We will come back to the particular case of fatherhood through AID, very organized in France, which plays a pilot role and constitutes for the specialists in this field a model unique in the world. Here are some figures to give an idea of the situation: there are 20 "sperm banks" in France, called CECOS, spread over all the territory. (CECOS stands for: Center for Study and Storage of Sperm.) More than 15,000 children have been born in this way since 1972. More than 1,000 families have at least two children born through AID, and there are families with three, four, and five AID children. In 10 years (1973–1983), 5,000 sperm donors (who are voluntary and unpaid) have turned up (David, 1985).

Another technique lends a different characteristic to the idea of fatherhood: as well as being split (*pater* differing from *genitor*, AID father differing from sperm donor), it is becoming dependent on one or several women. This is due to the technique of in vitro fertilization (IVF) and also to the usage of "surrogate mothers," with or without artificial insemination.

"Straight" IVF, which consists in fertilizing an ovum from the mother with the sperm from the father in a test tube, does not fundamentally change fatherhood. Only the parameter of medicalization—which is, certainly, not neutral—comes into play. But when IVF is used due to sterility of the husband, the wife's ovum is fertilized with the sperm of another man, a donor. This case is close to that of AID, as far as fatherhood is concerned: there is the same split between the father and the genitor, the latter being considered simply as a donor of gametes. There are hundreds of cases of this type in France, and it is increasing rapidly.

The IVF technique also enables a man to become a father through the intervention of two women, one of them being unknown to the couple and giving her ovum, the other, the wife of the husband, carrying the child and giving birth to it. This is a recent practice in California and Australia, and it started in France. To give a further illustration, this can also be done with the participation of three women, including the wife of the father: the woman-donor provides the ovum which will be fertilized in a test tube, the surrogate mother who will carry the embryo and then give it to the initial couple, and, finally, the wife who becomes the social mother. Other variations are also foreseeable (see Singer & Wells, 1984). But what is essential to analyze is the fact that the notion and biological roles pertaining to fatherhood are, from now on, closely related to the biological truth which can be manipulated according to the wishes of the physician and the couple.

A final word about the practice of surrogate mothers, which is likely to become widespread, and its consequences concerning fatherhood. Men, in the role of potential fathers, are scarcely present, or even totally absent. However, as there are two women in question, there are also two men in the shadow of the gestation: the husband of the inseminated surrogate mother, who will not be the father of the child to be born (although he may already be the father of other children with his wife); and, on the other hand, the future social mother's husband, the candidate for surrogate fatherhood. He is both the future social father and the biological father. In this case, he plays the role of sperm donor for the insemination of the surrogate mother, but he "makes" the father-mother couple with an unknown woman, since the child to be born will be the product of his gametes along with those of the surrogate mother! There are a few cases of this kind now in France.

Psychological consequences of split paternity are complex. They require a study of parenthood on completely new bases. This brings to a notion of *additional* parenthood. It looks like a kind of moral fostering by the genitor. So far, there are just a few studies about actual experiences of these fathers. We have personally studied with numerous AID fathers as well as with AID sperm donors. We have also been doing clinical work with AID parents (fathers and mothers) (Delaisi de Parseval, 1981, 1985). Our work addresses the questions about AID fatherhood which come out of the study by Snowden and Mitchell (1981) interviewing 66 English couples who were parents of one or more AID children.

Second Characteristic: Adoptive, Intentional, Preconceptional Adoptive Paternity

But let us get back to the philosophy of paternity which emerges from the application of these new techniques: it is not exactly a question of progress in science or biology, but more a question of revolution. New types of fatherhood are being formed before our eyes. First, the "absolutely well known" and "completely certain" notions which were unconcerned in the concept of paternity before 1970 are being confronted. Moreover, the question of knowledge changes into that of a deliberate wish. A lawyer comments on this change in direction as follows: "You feel as if you were under the rule of biology, because it has succeeded in piercing nature's mysteries, but really we are under the rule of the most absolute, that of desire. . . . This means filiation through desire, of which our law, as with most others, practices in the shape of adoption, will meet an unexpected field and an important application" (Robert, 1984).

The notion of adoption therefore comes back with some force, but with a content that is appreciably different from adoption historically. Indeed, it is more a question of preconceptional adoption. The main theme running through all these situations stemming from the different techniques is in fact constituted by the wish of the people asking to have a child. This is why, for a number of specialists in filiation law, full adoption and filiation through desire, seem to be well adapted to the new needs. In this way, there is no legal gap: In France, the 1976 law on adoption can break the tie of a child's filiation to his blood family from the moment of his plenary adoption by another individual, even if this person is the spouse of one of the parents (e.g., in the case of divorced parents) (Gobert, 1985).

Two philosophies come to light here. The first stems from a medical conception: It is a question—in the case of AID fatherhood—of repairing the psychologically impossible fatherhood of a man who wants to be a father, through the fatherhood of another man who is expressed in an anonymous way. The other is a social option: It reflects the idea that, from the time that procreation is separated from sexuality (since the arrival of modern contraception), everyone is free to use this experience as he so wishes. This is how, thanks to AID, a single woman may, in fact, use a man as a "stallion" only, without any notion of fatherhood. A widow can also use the intentionality of fatherhood of her late husband (if his sperm has been frozen) in the case of *post mortem* fatherhood.

The fatherhood of the sperm donor is more precarious than that of the AID father, because the former is not even named in the AID. The AID system is based on paternity since it has to repair the impossible fatherhood of one man by the possible fatherhood of another; the paradox is that the very word paternity is never used. It would be more fair to refer to the sperm donor as the "donor-father", and the husband as the "AID-father." Because the donor-father is living an original experience of fatherhood—absolutely unique in our history— We conducted a survey of 50 men who had given sperm for AID some years before (Delaisi de Parseval, 1981, 1985). What emerges from this work is that it is impossible for a man to see himself only in the image of a sperm donor, rejecting completely the paternal dimension. This is the reason we suggest the notion of "additional fatherhood" in order to qualify this particular type of sharing of the parental experience. Besides, in France, the great majority of these men are married and fathers themselves. This is not by chance: It is specifically this status of fathers which is in great demand by the managers of sperm banks—as if it were a caution that the sperm these men give is not only a gift of genes, but a gift of paternity.

The distinction made between father and genitor and between social mother and biological mother have been a part of our cultural heritage for a long time. This difference has always been effective in traditional adoption. But what is new is the possible dissociation between sexuality and procreation. Also the fact that the traditional roles concerning the child (wanting it, carrying it, educating it, etc.) can now be played by different people who do not necessarily have affective or social ties with the child. For example: an unknown person can give the sperm, or the ovum; a second person, can carry it; another couple (or, possibly, one man or woman alone), can educate it. These modifications call for all sorts of revision concerning the notions of fatherhood and motherhood, which now need a more subtle distinction to define them than the previous one based on biological or physiological attributes (Delaisi de Parseval & Janaud, 1983).

All these characteristics give the notion of "reconceptualized" paternity. As Fletcher (1974) wrote, "Paternal (and kin) relationships need to be reconceptualized. They cannot any more be based on blood or wombs or even genes. Parenthood will have to be understood non-biologically or, to be more specific, morally."

From the moment that paternity is no longer defined by law or by explicit social rules of filiation, the responsibility is thrown back into the domain of psychology. This is why we have put forward the hypothesis that only *a new adoption tie* can take into account the new modes of procreation.

We propose the notion of preconceptional adoption as much for AID fatherhood as for the forms of delayed fatherhood which we will now touch upon.

What are the workings of the mind achieved by the man who becomes a father through AID? Unique father within our history, he is like the traditional adoptive father, who is the social father only. There are, however important differences: He has adopted the project of having a child through AID, has lived through the experience of insemination of his spouse, has been an "expectant father" during pregnancy, has been present at delivery, and has known the particular psychological feeling of "engrossment" in the first hours and days following the birth of his child (Greenberg & Morris, 1974).

Reverse question: How should we deal with the genetic contribution of the sperm donor, whom we deliberately call the "co-genitor" or additional father or even father-in-law, in the etymological sense of the word? We put forward the hypothesis that if the AID father has really mourned his fertility, he can authentically adopt the genes given (or lent) by the donor, the additional father of his future child. It is in this sense that the term preconceptional adoption can take on all its dimension. The history and the projects for this particular fatherhood covers a very rich and original area for human parenthood research.

Third Characteristic: Delayed Fatherhood

Let us come now to the notion of delayed fatherhood. Another technique—indeed, different than simple freezing—is applied to human gametes. Sperm can be stored for a number of years (this will be also the case of embryos) and, in this way, it becomes possible to master the moment of fatherhood. The time may come soon when it will not be the moment of conception which will determine the child's age, but the moment of de-freezing the gametes. And this is revolutionary data.

We will distinguish between delayed fatherhood in AID and delayed fatherhood in AIH (artificial homologus insemination).

Delayed Fatherhood in AID

The sperm donor is one of the men who lives this particular experience of fatherhood. His participation in the AID fatherhood is, by definition, delayed, since he never knows when his sperm is going to be used. It may perhaps occur on the day after his visit or after years of storage. Certain donors are aware of the fact that an insemination performed with their sperm may take place after their death. We personally know of the case of a donor involved in an accidental death some months after donating his sperm, a donation with has enabled five conceptions with five different women, all made after his death. Although it is an exceptional case, it forms a natural part of the AID system, which uses frozen semen for periods of 10 years and possibly more (Delaisi de Parseval, 1981).

As for the man who becomes father by his spouse's insemination with donor sperm, he experiences also a delayed fatherhood. Aware of his sterility, he knows that he must postpone his desire of fatherhood. And, particularly, the "repairing" by AID weakens him, to the extent that he loses time control. Indeed, he will be a father if his spouse is registered on a AID waiting list, if she is receptive to insemination, and so forth it is a delayed fatherhood in a double way: in the fantasy and in the technique.

Delayed Fatherhood in AIH

Other men meet up with a more traditional form of delayed fatherhood, but still within the system of insemination. There are cases of AIH, however, performed with stored semen. Three cases of AIH-fatherhood appear to some extent in France nowadays:

Fatherhood of the sterilized man.   A typical French case is that of delayed fatherhood following male sterilization. The protocol used by the CECOS involves asking the candidates for vasectomy to store sperm for themselves before the operation, so as to avoid reanastomosis (the reverse operation) or to prevent them having to turn to AID, if ever in the future they would wish another child. If we keep in mind the very high separation and divorce rate, it is then not surprising that a divorced man may wish to have other children some years later, with another partner. We have specifically studied these cases of fatherhood: We have considered in detail the cases of sterilized men who have had a child conceived with their sperm which had been frozen for several years and then de-frozen before the insemination of their partners (Delaisi de Parseval & Jouannet, 1985). Once more, this is a form of fatherhood which, owing to biomedical techniques, can be considered as a new form of paternity.

Fatherhood after cancer.   There is still another form of delayed fatherhood. It exists not only in France, but perhaps longer here than anywhere else, due to the vast CECOS network. We are dealing here with delayed fatherhood after cancer. Autopreservation of semen is proposed men suffering from Hodgkin disease or carcinoma of the testis, before the sterilizing treatment. This conservation is usually well accepted by these men—often very young—who can thus picture a time in the future when they are cured (Hodgkin disease does in fact have an excellent prognostic). In one of the two CECOS of Paris, 173 cases of auto-preservation before sterilizing treatment in cases of cancer were carried out between 1973 and 1978. These figures have risen rapidly since then. Some children have already been born (Czyglick et al., 1982).

Fatherhood after death.   At the present moment, the last cases of delayed fatherhood which has recently had many repercussions in France is the question of fatherhood through the *postmortem* insemination of a widow with the sperm of her late husband. In these cases, the latter clearly expressed the desire to have a child when he was alive, otherwise there would be no reason to speak of delayed fatherhood. It was precisely because of the desire and the intentionality of the *living* father that the legal event was played in France. The Court of Créteil (in the outskirts of Paris) gave a judgment in favor of *postmortem* insemination on August 1, 1984, which was the first judgment of this type in the world. It is likely to set a precedent even at an international level, as these cases are few.

Beyond the precise case put forward here (but many other cases are waiting to be heard in different CECOS), it is interesting to note that the judgment was based on notions which mark modern paternity: the expressed desire or, in other words, the paternity of intention. The Court, "basing its decision on the testimonies recorded during the proceedings, believes that the formal wish of Corinne's husband to make his wife the mother of a joint child is unequivocally established, whether the conception of the child should come to pass during his lifetime or after his death" (Robert, 1984). The judgment therefore ordered that the stock of sperm from Corinne's husband which was conserved by the CECOS should be returned to her, now a widow—in other words, returned to the woman for whom it was meant by the desire of her husband, be he dead or alive. (Corinne's husband had suffered from carcinoma of the testis and, according to the protocol in current use, he had undergone auto-preservation of his sperm before having treatment.)

Among the numerous legal commentaries on this judgment, we can read the following one: "It would be no more disconcerting for a human being to be born the child of a dead father—which enables him to know where he comes from and to which family he belongs—than to be the child of an unknown father, which cuts him off from a part of himself" (Labrusse, 1985). These cases of postmortem fatherhood, although they are exceptional, present a significant change in the mentalities.

These forms of medicalized fatherhood strip the different levels of paternal construction.

CONCLUSION

Characteristics and Changes of French Paternity

A social and all-powerful father.   As with all human societies, but systematically in France, an examination of the laws of filiation shows that using the blood community as a basis for kinship is misleading (Meulders, 1973). The French system of filiation (contrary to our neighbors in northern Europe, for example) is dominated by the supremacy of law over nature (in its biological sense). Paternity boils down first and foremost to its social and political function. It is society which recognizes and designates who is the man-father, and it is society which invests him with his function and power, whether it be in line with Roman Law, or by means of the institution of marriage. The parent's desire and the biology had not the importance they have nowadays. Medical advances enables us to separate the biological father from the social father.

Two consequences resulted from this social investiture: the notion of adoption and the notion of paterfamilias. While adoption was written down in Roman Law as being a general rule for filiation, in France it was to become linked to the institution of marriage. Adoption is never defined in biological terms: it is always defined by law. For a long time it was reserved for particular cases, but it has become more general today. We can, for instance, say that artificial insemination with a donor is a form of special adoption. In the same way, the notion of "*possession d'Etat*" (that is, the actual and daily presence of a man) is another form of adoption which is becoming more and more important in French jurisdiction.

If the notion of paterfamilias (a term which comes from Roman Law) is accountable for the absolute power of the father over his children, it is not an exaggeration to say that, until the beginning of the 20th century, French fathers remained sorts of paterfamilias.

For this paternal power was to be characterized by modes which were specific to each era. It would be "tinkered with" in many ways, in the sense that Levi-Strauss (1962) uses this term: namely, modified according to the social systems and mental categories. Some examples of tinkering follow: At the time of conversion of Christianity and during the entire feudal period, the Paterfamilias was the earthly lord (the knight) but also the divine Lord (God and Jesus). There was, therefore, some tinkering with the term in the Middle Ages between its Roman and its Christian meaning. He was also the head of artisanal or rural industry, and also the possessor of patrimonies. It is in this way that the term finds the meaning of "father-owner" in the 19th century—but, this time, in the context of industrialization and small firms. In 1968 in France, the man to be knocked down was still the paterfamilias, and yet the father had already lost his statute of power. This term, then, came to represent all forms of family, social, and economic ascendancy.

Functions which can be called "totalitarian".   Up until the last few years, the father was characterized by a remarkable unity of functions brought together in a single man. Like the giant Atlas, the father in France has shouldered the weight of all aspects of the paternal function. He must be—at one and the same time—the parent, educator (for the sons), nourisher (in the sense of providing material goods), name-giver, guarantor of the rules of kinship, and, above all, the husband of the mother! In other societies, these roles are often shared between several persons.

A clear point where the present breaks away from the past can be drawn here. Another disjunction has taken place with the forms of medicalized procreation, separating the biological father from the social father.

From these two characteristics, the social and all-powerful father designated by the law, and a totalitarian definition of paternal functions, a third characteristic element of paternity "a la française" will ensue.

The paternal, affective, and carnal experience is repressed.   This experience had not been socially recognized. While fatherhood is first and foremost a social function, the affection and care of the children is officially reverted to the mother. During a long time, motherhood (with exceptions such as queens, whose maternity had a political weight), belonged to private life, and even to the most intimate part of private life, as Knibielher and Fouquet (1977) emphasize in *History of Motherhood*. The history of fatherhood is, on the contrary, particularly mixed up with the social and political history of France. This probably did not prevent men from loving their children and having affectionate relationships with them, but it is certain that, until 30 years ago, they hardly ever took care of young children.

We should underline one paradox. If the father was originally the legal father, why do we have such difficulty today in separating genitor and social father? A law, which could enable a separation of the father's functions, has not yet been made. Is not another fantasy brought to light here? If the father is not longer the "total" father, assuming all the paternal functions, does he not then become father of "nothing"? This is a hypothesis which has some foundations for, since 1968, the period of the great "paternal crisis," some people still go on writing: "Father is dead" (Florenne, 1983).

We have defined some names given to fathers and their history, milestones of a specifically French genealogy. From the paterfamilias, the prototype (or ancestor) of French fathers, to the "new" fathers, numerous and unusual forms of fatherhood have emerged.

Does this mean that fatherhood is dissolving in a test tube and that the paternal function no longer has any grounds for existence? Have we clearly entered the age of the matriarchy? We are far from believing this.

Should we emphasize the revolutionary side of these techniques or, rather, the forms of fatherhood which they have made possible? The single example of surrogate mothers—and the new types of father which are connected to this practice—brings out the fact, if we look at it closely, that we have drawn on one of the finite—*not* infinite—possibilities of human parenthood.

At the end of the 20th century, behind the coldness of clinical cases, a wealth of human cases paradoxically emerges, which have nothing to do with any scene from science fiction. Thus, human fatherhood is enriched by the contributions of biomedical techniques.

ACKNOWLEDGMENT

This paper was supported by LADISIS (research laboratory, n°668, of the National Center for Scientific Research). LADISIS (Dimensions sociales et incidences subjectives du langage) is located at the University of Strasbourg I.

REFERENCES

Badinter, E. (1980). *L'amour en plus. Histoire de l'amour maternel 17ème-20ème siecles*. Paris: Flammarion.

de Balzac, H. (1841). *Mémoire de deux jeunes mariées*, Paris: Gallimard.

Bydlowski, M., & Levy-Leblond, E. (1982). La paternité à l'épreuve de la première année [Fatherhood in the first year], Proceedings on the international symposium "Les pères aujourd'hui" [Contemporary fathers]. Paris, INED (National Institute for Demographic Studies).

Christensen, E. (1982). Jeunes pères aujourd'hui [Young fathers today]. Proceedings of the international symposium "Les pères aujourd'hui" [Contemporary fathers]. Paris: INED.

Cukier, F. (1982). Attitude des pères lors d'une naissance prématurée. [Fathers attitude in case of premature birth]. Proceedings on the international symposium *Les pères aujourd'hui* [Contemporary fathers]. Paris: INED.

Czyglick, F., Auger, J., Albert, M., David, G. (1982). L'autoconservation du sperme avant thérapeutique stérilisante [Semen preservation before therapeutic sterilizing], *La Nouvelle Presse Médicale*, 11, 37.

David, G. (1985). Don et utilisation du sperme [Gift and sperm use]. Proceedings of the international symposium "Génetique, procréation et droit" [Genetics, procreation and law]. Arles: Actes-Sud.

Delaisi de Parseval, G., (1981). *La part du père* [The share of the father]. Paris: Seuil.

Delaisi de Parseval, G. (1985). Le don du sperme [Sperm gift]. Les conceptions induites [Induced conceptions]. In Audebert, Bourgeois, Emperaire, Meunier, (Eds.). *Fondazione per gli studi sulla reprodizione umana:* Palermo.

Delaisi de Parseval, G., & Janaud, A. (1981). Le père qui venait du froid, ou le père-IAD [The AID-father]. *L'Information Psychiatrique,* 57, 10.

Delaisi de Parseval, G., & Janaud, A. (1983). *L'enfant à tout prix* [The child at all costs]. Paris: Seuil.

Delaisi de Parseval, G., & Jouannet, P. (1985). Semen storage, delayed fatherhood and vasectomy. *Psychosomatic obstetrics and gynecology.* Leiden: University of Leiden.

Delaisi de Parseval, G., and Lallemand, S. (1980). *L'art d'accomoder les bébés. Cent ans de recettes francaises de puériculture* [One century of french recipes of childcaring]. Paris: Seuil.

Deniniolle, S. (1983). Qu'est-ce qu'un père? [What is a father?], In *La Liberté de l'Esprit.* Paris: Balland, 4.

Duby, G. (1976). *Le temps des cathédrales.* Paris: Gallimard.

Duby, G. (1981). *Le chevalier, la femme et le prêtre.* Paris: Hachette.

Encyclopedie (1755). Article *Enfant,* Tome 5 (18th century Encyclopedia, Entry "Child").

Ferrand, M. (1982). *Paternité et vie professionnelle* [Fatherhood and professional life]. Paper presented at the Xth World Conference of Sociology, Mexico City.

Fletcher, J. (1974). *The ethics of genetic control.* New York: Doubleday.

Florenne, Y. (1983). La mort du père [Father's death]. *Le Monde,* 27.

Gobert, M. (1985). Les incidences juridiques de progrès des sciences biologiques et médicales sur le droit des personnes [The legal effects of biological sciences progress on individual law]. In *Génétique, Procréation et Droit* [Genetics, procreation and law]. Arles: Actes-Sud.

Goody, J. (1983). *L'évolution de la famille et du marriage en Europe,* Paris: Colin.

Greenberg, N., & Morris, M. (1974). The engrossment, *American Journal of Orthopsychiatry, 44,* 520-531.

Hurstel, F. (1978). Fonction paternelle et déracinement culturel: qu'est-ce qui fonde la paternité? [Paternal function and cultural eradication]. *Bulletin de Psychologie.* 30, 355.

Hurstel, F. (1982). Identité du père et classe ouvrière à Montbéliard aujourd'hui [Father identity and working class in Monteliard]. *La Pensée,* 228.

Hurstel, F. (1984). Une espèce en voie de disparition [A disappearing type], *Autrement,* special issue: *Pères et fils* (Fathers and sons), 61.

Hurstel, F. (1985a). Les changements dans la relation père-nourrisson en France: qui sont les pères qui paternent? [Changes in the father-infant relationship: who fathers?]. Proceedings of the Second World Conference of Child Psychiatry in Cannes, France.

Hurstel, F. (1985b). La fonction paternelle aujourd'hui: problèmes théoriques et questions d'actualité [Paternal function: Theoretical problems and current questions] *La fonction parentale.* Paris: ANPASE.

Knibielher, Y., & Fouquet, C. (1977). *Histoire des mères* [History of mothers]. Paris: Montalba.

Labrusse, C. (1982). La notion de paternité en droit [Notion of paternity in law]. Proceedings of the international symposium "Les pères aujourd'hui" [Contemporary fathers]. Paris: INED.

Labrusse, C. (1985). Don et utilisation de sperme et d'ovocytes. Le point de vue d'un juriste [Gift and use of sperm and ovum. The view of a jurist]. *Genetique, precréation et droit* [Genetics, procreation and law]. Paris: Actes-Sud.

Lacan, J. (1938). *Les complexes familiaux* [Family complex]. Paris: Navarin.

Levine, J. (1982). La nourvelle paternité aux Etats-Unis [New fatherhood in the U.S.A.]. Proceedings of the international symposium "Les pères aujourd'hui" [Contemporary fathers]. Paris: INED.

Levi-Strauss, C. (1962). *Les structures élémentaires de la parenté.* Paris: Presses Universitaires de France.

Mauss, M. (1950). *Sociologie et anthropologie* [Sociology and anthropology] Paris: Presse Universitaires de France.

Merlin (1787). *Puissance paternelle* [Paternal Power] Répertoire universel et raisonné de jurisprudence. Tome 14. Paris.

Meulders, M. (1973). Fondements nouveaux du concept de filiation [New foundations of the concept of filiation]. *Annales de Droit,* 4.

Robert, J. (1984). La révolution biologique et génétique face aux exigences du droit [Biological and genetic revolution opposite to the demand of law]. *Revue du Droit et de la Science Politique en France et à l'Etranger.*

Rousseau, J. (1983). *Discours sur l'origine et les fondements de l'inégalité parmi les hommes.* Paris: Editions Sociale.

Schnapper, B. (1980). La correction paternelle et le mouvement des idées au 19ème siècle (1789– 1935) [Paternal thrashing and state of ideas in the 19th century]. *Revue Historique,* 263, 2.

Segalen, M. (1981). *Sociologie de la famille* [Sociology of the family]. Paris: Colin.

Segalen, M. (1982). La nouvelle femme [The new woman]. *Etudes,* 11.

Singer, P., & Wells, D. (1984). *The reproduction revolution: New ways of making babies.* Oxford: Oxford University Press.

Snowden, R., & Mitchell, G. (1981). *Artificial family. A consideration of artifical insemination by donor.* London: George Allen and Unwin.

Sullerot, E. (1984). *Pour le meilleur et sans le pire* [With the best, without the worst.] Paris: Fayard.

Tellenbach, H. (Ed.) (1976). *L'image du père dans le mythe et dans l'histoire* [The image of the father in myth and in history]. Paris: Presses Universitaries de France.

Thomas, Y. (1984). Caton et ses fils [Caton and his sons]. *Autrement,* 61.

Tristan, F. (1980). *Le tour de France—Journal* (Ship's log 1843–1844). Paris: Maspero.

4 West Germany and the German-Speaking Countries

Horst Nickel
Ellen M. T. Köcher
University of Düsseldorf

PUBLIC OPINIONS, POLITICS AND STATISTICAL DATA

Change of Women's and Men's Roles in Public Discussion

The traditional role-pattern (wife's role: housewife and mother; husband's task: working for the family's economic safety/provision) has been critically discussed the last two decades. Influenced especially by women's liberation movements, women began to reject more and more a one-sided commitment to the role of housewife and mother and to seek self-fulfilment by participating in professional and public life on the basis of equal rights. Later on, after women's roles had been eagerly argued about, men's situation became a new focus of interest.

On the one hand, traditional male roles were increasingly criticized, especially by public media. On the other hand, first approaches of nontraditional-role opinions and behaviors of some men were enthusiastically welcomed and generalized. For example, in the 1980s, catchwords like "the new fathers" and "the first love: the father and his child," drew the reader's attention to popular parents' magazines.

We have to differentiate the diverse factors influencing individual men's role understanding and behaviors. The most striking of them is age. In young people, for example, we can observe a broad approximation between the sexes in the way they dress. Young men's public demonstration of traditional maternal tasks seems to be rather common. On the street, fathers pushing prams (baby carriages) or carrying infants in baby slings and baby carriers no longer attract special attention as they did only a few years ago. Similarly, fathers looking after their children and playing with them on playgrounds or taking them to the grocer's when shopping have become a matter of course.

Except for some regional differences, these observations are true for all German-speaking countries. But there are some distinct differences in the field of social policy, especially between the three Western-oriented countries (the Federal Republic of Germany, Austria, and Switzerland) and the German Democratic Republic. These differences and a question—whether the preceding observations are only superficial changes, or do they mark systematic trends as to the father's role—will be treated in the next chapter. In order to give answers, first let us present some numbers, facts, and laws.

Sociological Data and Politics

Introductory Remarks

The problem we meet is that past national or international reports contain mainly information as to the situation of women and mothers. But this is the only kind of statistical material allowing us to draw some conclusions regarding fathers.

Statistics on the subject "father" do not reflect the broad public interest in this topic. There are only some exceptions (e.g., single fathers, paid leave). A further difficulty is to compare the figures from the four different countries, in which different samples were assessed in different years, by different methods, and with different aims.

Therefore, the following information is structured separately for each of the German-speaking countries. We shall present numbers and describe the situation and conditions of female professional work and opinions on role-distribution, for these aspects enable us to draw preliminary conclusions on the father's role.

The Situation in the Federal Republic of Germany

In the Federal Republic of Germany (FRG), 17.2 million men and 10.5 million women are employed—that is half of the nation's women who are aged 15–65. About one third of the women have children aged 0–18 years and work part-time. (They hold 90% of the part-time jobs.) Their situation in professional life (as compared with that of men) is characterized by low salaries, repetitive and underrated work, and shorter education (Grieswelle, 1985). According to a recent survey of 9800 adults from 10 European countries (Commission of the European Community, 1984), there have not been any progressive trends in the FRG over the last decade: In 1975, 56% of the women wished to take part in professional life and, in 1983, only 52% of them felt that way.

However, nowadays West German men seem to accept women's professional ambitions and achievement, according to the latest broad inquiry conducted by Metz-Göckel and Müller in 1985 (Lebert, 1985). Four-fifths of the men agreed to the statement that the best condition of partnership is both partners' contentment in professional life. When asked what sort of partners' role distribution they thought to be most favorable (Commission of the European Community, 1984), 26% of the West German sample preferred equality, 30% voted for the conventional housewife-and-mother role for women, 34% thought women should care for the household to a greater extent than men, and 10% didn't give any clear statement. Interestingly, the question was put already prejudiced as two of the three answering-alternatives referred to traditional roles, and men's preference of the role as househusband and father had been totally excluded.

In another inquiry (Grieswelle, 1985), popular opinions seemed more progressive in that 72% of the women and 69% of the men demanded to abandon traditional sex-role patterns in favor of a fair distribution of tasks. They voted for men's contributions in the household. But the facts were very discrepant: 72% of the women reported that they worked in the household in the evening and only 16% of the men did so. Similarly, the Ministry of Youth, Family, and Health states that there are only slight improvements in the partnership of men and women: 39% of the men helped in the household and 51% in childcare. It seems that, to most men, the role of the father is more acceptable (or appealing) than that of househusband (Der Bundesminister für Jugend, Familie, und Gesundheit, 1980).

In the latest inquiry (Lebert, 1985), 92% of the men did not feel stressed by household activities—for they hardly participated in these tasks! Even when their partners were not housewives, 87% of them never ironed, 76% never laundered, only 1.6% prepared the meals, and so forth. As to childcare, traditional roles were favored: 44% preferred the husband working outside the house and the wife staying at home, 1% preferred the reverse, and 14% voted for an egalitarian concept (husband and wife each working half-time). Even more conservative opinions were held concerning young parenthood. Three out of four men wanted women to stay at home when their children are very young. They would not agree to extrafamilial childcare.

Under the laws in effect before 1986, expectant mothers need not work (and were paid their usual wages 6 weeks pre- to 8 weeks postnatally. They could stay at home for and with their baby till his 6th month of life and were paid maximally 17 Deutsche Mark (about $8) per day, and they could not be called in until the 8th month. The months of maternity leave were acknowledged for the annuity insurance. Ninety-five percent of the women exploited these "motherhood-holidays" and about half thereafter gave up their professional work at least temporarily, mostly when their children were very young. (Numbers of working mothers in relation to child(ren)'s age: 500,000 mothers with child(ren) under 3 years; 1,597,000 with child(ren) under 6 years; and 2,900,000 with children under 15 years.) Correspondingly, mothers in an inquiry (Grieswelle, 1985) wished to receive so-called "education money" (for raising their child instead of working outside the home) till the 3rd year of life, more opportunities to work part-time, and extrafamilial childcare. The number of crèches has doubled from 438 (in 1965) to 871 (in 1977), but it is still rather small. Besides, the problem of childcare still exists for mothers of older children: In most schools (by the way, also in Austria and Switzerland) lessons are finished at noon and pupils then return home, where an adult (usually the mother) has prepared lunch and is waiting for them.

The dependency of mothers' but not fathers' professional work on child(ren)'s age and the necessity of extrafamilial childcare let us suppose that fathers' contributions in family tasks are not yet very many. Interestingly, mothers did not even mention fathers' involvement as a means of alleviating their burden of education (Grieswelle, 1985).

Nevertheless, the father's function, especially for infants and toddlers, has been taken up by the political parties to an increasing extent. With a view to social and political change, the conservative Christian parties recently have begun to discuss a bill, which in the meantime has been resolved by the Parliament. This bill enables fathers to assume primary care functions without suffering complete financial loss. After the birth of a child, either the mother or the father has the opportunity of taking state-funded maternity or paternity leave (first of 10 and later of 12 months). This leave is combined with a so-called job guarantee ensuring that they will be able to return to their previous professional position.

Beyond directly subsidizing those who apply for parent leave, governmental measures of this kind could have a broader sociological effect by signaling the path of social development as far as the changing role of the father is concerned. It is conceivable that even fathers who do not make use of this right nevertheless become more aware of their indispensable responsibilities in childcare and prepare themselves for their forthcoming parental task before the event. In this context it should be mentioned that, in the last years, many fathers have taken part in prenatal courses together with mothers (Bartoszyk & Nickel, 1986a, 1986b). The same applies to fathers who take the initiative in organizing parent-run crèches. Along this line we should note that the number of fathers who raise their children alone has more than doubled from 69,000 (in 1972) to 145,000 (in 1982), accounting for 16% of one-parent-families in the FRG (Fthenakis, 1985). In these cases, the traditional pattern is turned upside down by extremely engaged fathers.

In order to understand these discrepancies regarding men's and fathers' roles, it is important to look at some variables modifying the ideals as well as the reality. It is not possible to speak of "the new father" (to use the mass-media expression) without mentioning certain factors, that affect the new role-patterns. Age, education, and religious commitment seem to be such influences, e.g., in Catholic regions traditional role patterns are more important than in Protestant regions. Women had more positive attitudes towards their own lifelong professional work the younger and better educated they were (Frauenforschung, 1985).

Eckert (1985) reports that better schooling of men correlates with openness to their wives' professional wishes and with individualized strategies of problem solving.

So from a sociological point of view—as in other similar processes of societal change—the upper social classes prove to be the trendsetters. This is true both for the importance attached to the family and professional life as well as for the active participation of fathers in childcare. A representative study in North Rhine–Westfalia (western FRG) showed that lower-middle-class and upper-lower-class fathers (and mothers) were primarily interested in professional success, while upper-middle-class fathers (especially university men) tended to value the family equal to or even higher than professional success (Döpkemeyer, 1981; Schmidt-Denter, 1984, cf. 2.4).

Similarly, social differences became apparent when analyzing the extent to which the legal possibilities for supporting the father's function are exploited. Both fathers and mothers are entitled to special paid leave under the terms of the statutory sickness-insurance schemes if their child is ill. In 1981, more than half (62.7%) of the voluntarily insured parents who made use of this opportunity (the majority of whom belong to the middle classes) were fathers. The corresponding figure for the predominantly lower-class fathers under the obligatory sickness-insurance scheme was 12%. But their number had doubled since 1976 (Fthenakis, 1985).

There are other signs that opinions concerning the father's role are changing in the lower classes due to the extensive discussion of this topic in the public media. This is shown most distinctly in the rapid increase of the number of fathers attending the child's birth. This trend holds for all social classes. An inquiry conducted by us in Düsseldorf, for instance, revealed that only 10% of the fathers were not present at the birth of their first child (Bartoszyk & Nickel, 1986b, p. 356). It is not yet clear whether this phenomenon really represents an accepted change of roles or whether it merely reflects a superficial conformity to changing public opinion in terms of social desirability.

The Situation in Austria, Switzerland, and the German Democratic Republic

In Austria, in 1984, 1.3 million women were working; they made up 44% of all working inhabitants. (Statistisches Handbuch für die Republik Österreich, 1985). In 1977, one quarter of the employed women had children younger than 15 years. As to the number of children, 46% of the working married women had one child and 38% of them had four and more children (Szinovacz, 1979).

Since 1957, expectant mothers have been paid motherhood-leave 8 weeks prenatally and 8–12 weeks postnatally. They can stay at home with their baby for one year (which is excepted in the annuity insurance) and they are guaranteed a job on their return (Dorrer & Rowhani, 1978).

From microcensus data assessed from 1969 to 1977, Szinovacz (1979) concluded that there was a trend for fathers' increasing involvement, especially in childcare (it didn't matter whether their wives were working or not). There was a slight trend toward increasing involvement in household chores (but this depended on their wives' work). According to Szinovacz many factors besides the wives' occupation influenced familial role distributions: People were most likely to chose egalitarian functions for men and women when they were upper social class, living in urban areas, and lacked relatives who would help in household tasks and childcare. These trends parallel those data observed by Schmidt-Denter (1984) in North Rhine–Westfalia (FRG).

But in spite of the growing engagement of fathers in familial domains, reports of the Ministry of Social Administration and Szinovacz (1979) conclude that women—now as before—carry the main load and responsibility for the household and for childcare. At least this fact has been recognized as essential for the family income by law. This also applies to the FRG. The recent legislation and jurisdication also consider the man's share of household duties and child-care responsibilities.

In Switzerland in 1980, 1,117,000 women and 1,980,000 men were professionally working (Statistisches Jahrbuch der Schweiz, 1984). In a study in western Switzerland[1] (n = 1033 households), 47% of the married women without children were employed as were 39% of the married women with one child and 31% of the married women with two or more children were working. The proportion of working women among the married is about the same as in the FRG and smaller than in Austria, this might be related to the higher economic prosperity of Switzerland and FRG in comparison with Austria.

Pregnant mothers are allowed to take leave without being called in at least 8 weeks each pre- and postnatally. They are paid differently depending on the facultative insurance (in Switzerland, people can choose the level of their sick insurance.) Their postpartum leave varies a little depending on the area of Switzerland where the mother is living. Currently, the longest postpartum leave is 4 months, but that is still an exception. Even this seems to be rather short when compared with the conditions in the other three countries. As one point there was a referendum on a parenthood leave (for mothers or fathers) lasting the first 9 months of the baby's life, but this was rejected by the majority.

Similarly, it was reported that household and family work are generally undervalued and that men—independent of social class and wives' work—hardly participate in household tasks. At least half of the men never do household tasks. For example, 79% of the men never launder, and 52% never cook. These figures resemble those assessed in the latest West German inquiry (Lebert, 1985). A little

---

[1]This study was conducted by the "Mouvement populaire des familles" and was cited by the Eidgenössische Kommission für Frauenfragen (1982). It is the basis of the following sociological data.

discrepant with the results for the FRG (Schmidt-Denter, 1984) is the finding that men's engagement decreases in the upper classes of income. This may be due to different sociological classification systems or to Swiss-German differences.

Besides these questions focusing on household roles, families with different age-groups of children were asked questions concerning the father's role: 30% of the fathers of very young children (0–6 years old) put them to bed regularly (some of them together with the mother); 4% of fathers helped their children aged 7–11 with homework. In nearly half of the families, both parents discussed sexuality with their adolescent children (in the other half, it was the mother alone); some of the young adults confided in both parents and some only in their mother. Obviously, Swiss men in their role as house keepers and fathers are not very active. Their father-role seems to become more important to them as their children grow older—but, even then, fathers are only addressed (by the children) together with their wives and hardly ever preferred.

All in all, Switzerland seems to be a rather conservative country as to the role distribution of men and women. However, even there single progressive approaches are made, examples of which are the institution of a commission of women's problems and the above-mentioned legal initiative (i.e., possibility of paternity leave).

In the German Democratic Republic (GDR), 78% of all married women are employed and, the proportion of *mothers* who are employed is even greater. Most of them have full-time jobs (8¾ hours per day and 43¾ hours per week). Mothers of two and more children have 40-hour workweeks and, in the case of shift-work, they get additional holidays. Besides, all women and single fathers are entitled to stay at home one additional day per month in order to care for their household.

Correspondingly, state-run day nurseries for infants and toddlers had been introduced already in the fifties and sixties. Since 1976, expectant mothers have holidays 6 weeks pre- and 20 weeks postnatally, which are paid by the social-insurance fund. Further, they can take leave until the baby's first birthday. This is a paid leave only when a second child or further children are born. The so-called "baby-year" (= year spent raising one's baby and not working on one's profession) for mothers is exploited by 90%. If a lack of crèches exists, mothers are even allowed to stay at home for the first 3 years (unpaid).

In spite of these relatively generous measures related to motherhood, women have to carry the main burden of the housework and of childcare (Eckert, 1985), for the orientation is one-sidedly to both sexes' full-time work and not to their family work. On the contrary, the task of child raising has been delegated from the parents to institutions. But, ultimately, household tasks and childcare have remained in women's domain of responsibility: All of the state-run measures directed at supporting motherhood seem to be intended to further population-politics, but not parenthood in the sense of equality for men and women in the domains of profession and family. The man's role in the family is hardly ever discussed. It is only of interest when the mother is absent (e.g., household-days for single fathers). So the father's role in the GDR seems rather comparable to Western countries. Normally, the father does not have the major responsibility for his child(ren)'s education.

Summary

In all of the four German-speaking countries the subject of women's role has been discussed earlier and more intensely than that of men's role. Probably the extent of discussion corresponds to the extent of change in both sexes' role definitions and behaviors. Women seem to have enlarged their life-sphere by entering the professional domain—but often to the debit of a doubled load of duties in work outside and inside the house (household and child-raising). Man's family role generally is not considered to be an enrichment in his life.

In the GDR, the question of men's engagement in the familial setting is hardly ever discussed because the educational role has been delegated *from* the parents to professional educators. However laws are ultimately directed to motherhood (and not to fatherhood or parenthood) in a very conservative way. The father's role in, GDR currently seems to lack any new concept.

By contrast, men's participation in family duties in the three Western German-speaking countries is a subject of current discussion. Interestingly, fathers' engagement is accepted more as a necessity caused by women's double load than as an opportunity for enriching men's lives. Perhaps this is the reason why very different attitudes toward men's and father's roles have been documented in the reports from these countries, and why a lack of fathers' activities in the family and (especially) in the household has been lamented. When comparing the two fields, men seem to prefer the role of the father (i.e., the educational tasks) to that of househusband (i.e., the household tasks). Nevertheless, there are some fundamental approaches toward "the new father"; for example, by legal initiatives concerning paternity leave.

Whether and how the current gaps within the conceptual frames and between ideals and reality can be bridged will be answerable only through a long developmental process. A large variety of interdependent sociological, political, and individual factors must be investigated.

THE FATHER'S ROLE AS SUBJECT OF EMPIRICAL RESEARCH

Previous Acknowledgment of the Father's Importance

As in other Western European countries and in America, scientific discussion in the German-speaking countries attributed to the father no more than indirect significance for child development, especially in the first years of life, until the mid 1970s. In agreement with the dominant theory of attachment, mothers were seen as the primary caregivers for the child; they had the responsibility of furthering the child's capability of emotional attachment in addition to their functions of nursing and care (Ainsworth 1964, 1969, 1972, 1979a, 1979b; Bowlby 1952, 1969, 1976). Fathers were prevented from fulfilling these tasks not only by their professional obligations but (according to the psychoanalytic and ethological concepts upon which the attachment theory was founded) they also lacked basic requirements. The father's contribution to the care and education of small children consisted primarily of earning a living for the mother and child and, within limits, offering the mother emotional support.

In developmental and pedagogical psychology, the importance of the father for the young child has only very rarely been investigated and in these rare cases almost exclusively with a view to analyzing the significance of his absence in so-called fatherless families (Lehr, 1978; Meyer-Krahmer, 1980). The role of the father as a direct or indirect figure of identification was only acknowledged for children of school age and for adolescents. It was discussed particularly in the context of detachment (cf. Nickel, 1979).

Yet, two decades ago, Hetzer (1967) pointed out that it is the father (rather than the mother) who tends to urge the child to progress from one step of life to the other. Following the trend of the times, she mainly analyzed the significance of fathers in fatherless families. In this context, she pointed to the dangers involved when fatherless children have to replace the mother's partner and experience adult problems too early in life.

A basic change in scientific approaches did not take place in the German-speaking countries until the end of the seventies, triggered off by the reception of American studies (cf. Lehr, 1978; Meyer-Krahmer, 1980). Those reports were followed by popular scientific journals and mass publications that were all too quick in deducing practical tips for parents—which were by no means always supported by the data available. This applies especially to the participation of fathers at preparatory courses and their presence at births as well as to the reintroduction of births at home and to the contact between parents and neonates in hospitals.

As a result, not only psychologists and educators but also pediatricians and gynaecologists were called upon to take a stand, and the subject of "fathers" was increasingly discussed in medical journals. In recent years, the subject has been taken up in a whole variety of additional scientific disciplines, particularly child psychiatry, family sociology, and family law (cf. Remschmidt, 1983). For example, the "Role of the Father in the Development of the Child" was one of the main subjects of the 1985 conference of the German Society of Child and Juvenile Psychiatry. In family sociology, the changing role of the father has been under discussion for some years in the context of the changing functions of family members (Mitterauer & Sieder, 1980).

Empirical research was long in coming and, for this reason, there are only few results concerning this subject in the German-speaking countries. This was revealed through an inquiry conducted by the authors (see the following section). But the reception of international research has led to diverse overviews and summaries in recent years which concentrate—as did the first empirical studies—on the importance of the father in early childhood. Beyond this, the father's role is discussed in the contexts of divorce cases and judgments concerning the care and custody of children (Fthenakis, Niesel, & Kunze 1982; Fthenakis, 1983), and in special situations such as illegitimate children, single fathers, stepfathers, and fathers not having the care and custody of their children (Fthenakis, 1984, 1985; Peters, 1985).

The position of the GDR is quite different. In line with the political decision in favor of comprehensive crèche education from a very early age, scientific discussion and empirical research have mainly focused on this aspect of child development (Schmidt-Kolmer, 1977) with the emphasis on the comparison of different forms of institutionalized care vs. family education. No distinctions are made between mothers and fathers, as educators, again in line with the prevailing political opinion. In the last years there are plans for a research project in which a differentiation is to be made between the mother's, father's, and professional educator's roles in the promotion of children's creativity.[2]

A Survey of Current Research in German-Speaking Countries

The parent-child relationship in the first year of life, with special regard to the father's role, has been a central topic of research in the Institute of Developmental and Social Psychology at Düsseldorf University since 1982. Investigations have been conducted under the guidance of the first author and financially supported by the Ministry of Science in North Rhine–Westfalia (cf. Bartoszyk & Nickel, 1986a,b; Nickel, Bartoszyk, & Wenzel, 1982, 1985a, 1985b; Wenzel, Bartoszyk, & Nickel, 1985).

Centering around the father's preparation for his role in infant care, this project is closely related to a representative inquiry conducted by the Institute concerning the social environments of children aged zero to 6 years, in which special regard was also paid to the father's role (Döpkemeyer, 1981; Schmidt-Denter, 1984; Zamponi, 1983).

Within this frame, we conducted an inquiry addressed to all research institutes in the FRG, GDR, Austria, and Switzerland whose orientations or functions suggested that they might be carrying out research on the importance of the father in child development. These included university psychological institutes and institutes of child psychiatry, pediatrics, and social medicine as well as all other state-run or private research institutions working in this field. The aim of this inquiry was to provide a comprehensive documentation of all research activities

---

[2]Letter from the Psychological Section of Karl Marx University, Leipzig, GDR, Nov. 1984).

concerning the role of the father in the German-speaking countries (cf. Köcher & Nickel, 1985; Nickel & Köcher, 1986).

Approaches were made to a total of 193 institutes, and replies were received from 36 of them—a return rate of about 18%. Of these, 20 respondents replied they worked on the subject, and 16 said that they did not. The non-responses of 157 institutes were interpreted as negative reports, too, for the inquiry was formulated in a way that answers were expected in cases of positive feedback only.

Not all of the 20 affirmative replies reported the results of studies that had been carried out; 9 of them only outlined the plans of studies or of studies just being carried out. All the positive answers came from the Federal Republic of Germany. They can be roughly grouped according to two main dimensions.

Studies centering around or directly addressing the father-child relationship: Only three of the reported studies directly investigate father-child interaction. So, counting the Düsseldorf project, we are aware of only four studies concerning this subject in the whole German-speaking area of inquiry. These studies focus on the following topics:

(a) the father's role in the first 5 years of the child's life (Gauda, 1983);
(b) relationships between parents and their 3-month-old infants (Zimmermann, 1985);
(c) relationships between the father and his child in the first year of life, especially aspects of comfort, care, and play (Wutz, 1985); and
(d) father-child interaction in the first year of life and the importance of infant-caretaking courses (Nickel et al., 1985a).

None of the presented works are explicitly concerned with the father-mother-child triad; only one investigates the transition from triad to tetrad by means of case studies (Kreppner, Paulsen, & Schütze, 1982).

Studies dealing with fathers' role only in an indirect manner: Seventeen answers fall into this group. They can be classified as follows:

(a) perinatal partner relations and interactions, fathers' attitudes (n = 4; Grossmann & Volkmer, 1984; Jäger, Lindemann, & Beckmann, 1984);[3]
(b) fathers as sources of stress vs. sources of support for the mother-child relation (n = 1; Engfer & Gavranidou, 1984);

---

[3]Authors are mentioned in parentheses only if they have already published their research. Therefore, the number of authors mentioned is smaller than the number of studies (n) because some of the studies are in progress or only being planned.

(c) fathers' engagement in terms of the time they spend in childcare (n = 2; Jennewein & Matzanke, 1983);

(d) the importance of the father for specific aspects of child development, e.g., language, learning, creativity, psychopathological phenomena (n = 3);

(e) family research and family epidemiology (n = 4; Fisch & Lüscher, 1981; Olbrich & Brüderl, 1986);

(f) clinical questions, e.g., the influence of educator behavior on psychosomatic illness, partnership problems of parents of schizophrenic children (n = 3; Behringer et al., 1982).

Altogether we can conclude from the results of this inquiry that the number of studies focused on the father-child interaction in the German-speaking countries is still very small.

Furthermore, it can be stated that relevant research refers exclusively to the father's importance for children below school age (that is 6 years of age). On the one hand, this is probably due to the fact that special efforts were required to fill the research gap uncovered by the awakened awareness of the significance of the father's role by the international scientific community in the 1970s. On the other hand, this trend is also explained by the increased interest in early childhood by German-speaking developmental psychologists during that decade (Nickel, 1980).

It could also be of significance that the educational importance of parents in child development decreases as the child grows, while the importance of extra-familial persons increases. As a result, the parents' functions for children of school age are often analyzed within the context of a whole number of educational interactions and influences without differentiating the sex of the educator, as in the GDR. Finally, there are difficulties in methods and research-economy when trying to find an appropriate approach to the parents of pupils or adolescents. In view of this situation, the following analysis is restricted to a preliminary assessment of the role of the father for children below school age. It is structured around three focal points: the father's role during pregnancy and birth and during the child's first year of life, and his role with preschool children. Due to the scanty data base we can do no more than point the way for further research.

The Father's Role in the Contexts of Pregnancy and Birth

More and more fathers attend pregnancy courses for birth-preparation and infant care together with their wives. The majority of today's fathers are present in the delivery room. However, the figures for the frequency of the father's presence at birth vary widely from region to region and generally range between 50% and 80%.

In the Düsseldorf study (Bartoszyk & Nickel, 1986b, p. 356), 91% of the fathers participated in the birth of their child; 78% of them were present during the whole time and 13% part of the time (i.e., either at the beginning or at the end of the birth). Nearly all of the mothers (97%) experienced the fathers presence as supportive and all of the fathers described the birth itself and the experience of birth positively. However, both mothers and fathers criticized some of the conditions in the delivery room and made proposals for improvement, particularly with a view toward promoting father-child contact. There were strong recommendations for a room in which the young family could be alone for a while and for fathers to have the opportunity and receive encouragement to bathe and diaper the newborn baby (Bartoszyk & Nickel, 1986b).

Some hospitals have already tried to meet these wishes by reorganizing the labor room to make it homier and by allowing the father to maintain physical contact with the mother. In addition, parents are prepared for the perinatal situation at special informational meetings (cf. Olbertz, 1983).

According to Gauda's studies (1983), nearly all pregnant women wished the expectant fathers to be present at birth, and 56% of the fathers themselves wanted to participate. Grossmann and Volkmer (1984) established in a retrospective study (n = 100) that the father's wish to be present at birth has a greater impact on his approach and behavior towards the child than whether he actually attended birth or not. Only this wish (not actual attendance) covaried with other parameters of paternal involvement such as frequent participation in infant care courses, interest in the birth process and infant development, and the actual assumption of baby-care duties.

The perinatal emotional state of the fathers, measured at various times shortly before and after birth, was more stable than that of the mothers (Olbrich & Brüderl, 1986). The prenatal and postnatal anxieties, exhaustion, introvertedness, and depressive moods often observed in mothers were hardly ever seen in fathers. Similarly, the emotional state of the fathers appeared to depend less on the state of the partnership than for mothers. At the same time, the mothers seemed to cope with stress more adequately than fathers, who showed more passive and evasive strategies than their wives. However, there was one subgroup of fathers who showed signs of extreme emotional stress, namely, those whose children had not been planned. Grossmann, Thane, and Grossmann (1981) also emphasize the importance of this factor for the mother's behavior.

Before birth, fathers generally expect the changes brought by their new role to be less profound than mothers (Gauda, 1983). Answering a questionnaire in the infant's fourth week of life, both mothers and fathers separately stated that they had experienced the first period of adaptation to the child as a stressful one with distinct transitional difficulties. Fathers and mothers attributed their insecurity about physical contact with the child to the following reasons, here ranked in order of perceived importance (Bartoszyk & Nickel, 1986b):

(a) lack of practical experience with infants;
(b) the individuality of the child;
(c) lack of knowledge about childcare and child development; and
(d) contradictory information in handbooks, magazines, etc.

Father-Child Interaction in the First Year of Life

In the mass media and parents' journals, "the new father-infant relationship" and "the expectant father and birth" are topics that receive a great deal of coverage. The "new father" is described as cooperative in household management, sharing daily in childcare duties, and actively participating in building up an affectionate and tender relationship with the infant. However, empirical results show that changes in this direction are only beginning.

By means of pre- and postnatal diaries referring to daily tasks, Jennewein and Matzanke (1983) found that fathers changed their daily routines before and after delivery. But the women's daily routines had changed more drastically in the direction of the traditional housewife role-pattern. After studying 20 families with their first children, Gauda (1983) was unable to give a clear answer to the question whether there is such a thing as the "new father." On the one hand, many of the fathers wanted to participate in daily childcare and some of them were willing to get up in the night when the baby cried. But, in the author's opinion, demands on the mothers were less since nearly all of them had given up their professional activities. All in all, Gauda found that fathers are mainly play partners for very small children.

In an exploratory study conducted as part of the "Bielefeld Longitudinal Study" (initiated by Grossmann), Wutz (1985) analyzed whether there are different areas of father-child relations and whether these change during the first year of life. She held informal interviews with 49 mothers when their children were 2, 6, and 10 months old and made notes on familial interactions. Interview and observation data were grouped into three function categories: care, comfort, play. The results showed that fathers were involved in all of these functions; in each of them more than a third of the fathers participated to a very great extent (as defined by scales of involvement). While the fathers' comfort and care activities remained constant over the 3 age groups, an increasing involvement in play activities can be inferred from the results. The same applies for the fathers' emotional understanding of their children, which seemed to grow in the first year of life in the play and comfort areas but not as far as care was concerned. Involvement and understanding were not related to child attachment at the age of 18 months but very much related to the quality of play at the age of 2 years.

The percentage and duration of eye contact were examined in two studies as indicators of quality of the father-child relationship (Gauda, 1983; Zimmermann, 1985). Gauda found that the eye-contact of both parents with the child was very similar, but that father-child dyads had shorter yet more frequent eye-contact sequences than mother-child dyads.

Zimmermann also observed higher frequencies in father-infant eye contacts (in comparison with mothers and infants) in a home play situation with 3-month-old babies. She also identified qualitative differences in the methods used to influence the child's behavior. While fathers tended to react to their children and practiced less control, mothers tended to be more directive and stimulating to a moderate degree. This suggests that fathers employ an educational style comparable to that proven in earlier studies on extrafamilial educators to be promotive for the child (Nickel, 1985; Nickel, Schenk, & Ungelenk, 1980).

The effects of expectant fathers' participation in preparatory courses on father-child interaction in the first year of life were studied in the Düsseldorf Longitudinal Study by Nickel et al. (1985a, 1985b). The sample could not be randomly assigned because of the principle of voluntary participation in infant care courses: It was not possible to assign people against their wish to a preparation group or to hinder voluntary participation. First, contacts with parents were made by asking doctors, midwives, and heads of birth-preparation courses to distribute questionnaires. Participants were 69 married parents and their firstborn children (27 boys and 42 girls). Most of the adults were aged 23–30 years and were of German nationality; each father's profession was outside the fields of medicine, psychology, childcare, education, and the social sciences. Before delivery, 71% of the mothers had been working full-time jobs and 32% of them wanted to continue professional life after their legal pregnancy pause. Most parents were middle-class and lower-middle-class (cf. Kleining & Moore, 1968), which is comparable to other empirical studies on parent-child interaction.

A group of prepared fathers (those having attended infant care courses with their wives prenatally) was compared with a group of unprepared fathers (those who had not attended preparation classes). According to questionnaires answered by both parents, prepared fathers scored significantly higher with regard to changing diapers, helping the baby go to sleep, and pushing the pram or carrying the baby in a baby sling. The study also analyzed the quantitative and qualitative features of father-child interaction under laboratory conditions in the children's 3rd and 9th months of life. Compared with the unprepared fathers, prepared fathers kept closer physical contact with their 3-month-old babies and were rated warmer in face-to-face interaction with them. In the 9th month of life, this seemed to have a positive effect on infant behavior: Prepared fathers' children were rated higher in responsivity and the quality of vocalization (fewer negative, more happy vocalizations) than the children of unprepared fathers. The behavior of the 2 groups of fathers still tended to differ as described above; however, the differences were no longer statistically significant. To a certain extent, the scores of the unprepared fathers were now closer to those of the prepared fathers. We can cautiously infer from these findings that participation in preparatory courses is of particular importance in the first months of interaction with the infant. While non-prepared fathers experience their initial learning "on the job," the prepared fathers show from birth favorable behavior patterns toward the infant which have a positive long-term impact on child development. It is not yet clear which role the father's initial motivations (as well as other factors) play.

Another result of the Düsseldorf Study is worth mentioning: Only 2 out of 26 children distinctly chose their father over their mother in an experimental decision-and-attachment situation. (The infant was placed near a strange person while the father and mother stayed in different directions but equidistant from the child.) This demonstrates that in a stress situation mothers still play the main role for most infants.

In a feeding situation with newborn babies, Parke, Grossmann, and Tinsley (1981) found that American mothers and German fathers scored higher in rocking and visual attention than their partners. These behavioral differences may express different parental role-patterns in the two countries.

Fathers of Toddlers and Preschool Children

In recent years, the father's role with toddlers and preschool children has been increasingly discussed in popular science journals but not as much as his role at birth and in the first year of life. This could be due to the fact that fathers' functions for infants have changed more drastically than for older children with whom fathers have traditionally been more involved, if only part of the time and for certain activities.

In this connection a new practical concept in West Germany must be mentioned. This is represented by the so-called "parent-child-playgroups," which explicitly offer mothers and fathers the possibility of playing systematically with their infants and pre-kindergarten children. These groups usually meet weekly for about 2 hours, some of them under pedagogical guidance.

This concept, which seems promising from a developmental and pedagogical point of view, has hardly been researched at all. Exceptions are the studies of Ruppelt (1982), Tobola (1983), and Knödel (1983) concerning one special form of parent-child-playgroup, the "Prager Parent-Child Program" for parents and babies in the first year of life.

To fill the research gaps, we initiated a research project concerning parent-child playgroups within ecological contexts (Köcher & Nickel, 1984, 1985). As to the father's role we have made the following preliminary observation: Either fathers are totally absent in these groups or they represent a small minority. In groups of about 10 adult participants, maximally two fathers were present. So "parent-child play-groups" seem to be more of a program than a fact. Most of them should rather be called *"mother*-child playgroups." The absence of fathers in these groups may be due to two reasons: The first one is that fathers' professional obligations and the times of playgroups' meetings often clash. This fact points to the classical role-sharing of men and women which still dominates especially when the children are very young. The second reason seems to be a psychological one: It was revealed in a pure "father-child playgroup" which excluded mothers, not accepting them even on a visiting basis. The head of this group explained this attitude by observing that young men had great difficulties in showing paternal feelings even among themselves and found it difficult to sing and play freely with their children without embarassment. So we can suppose that the common lack of fathers in parent-child playgroups is connected with their difficulties in practicing a new role pattern in the openness of a group setting.

Only three recent studies concerning the fathers of toddlers and older preschool children were named in our inquiry (Gauda, 1983; Fisch & Lüscher 1980/81; Schmidt-Denter, 1984). Perhaps this points to the fact that the father's role in this age group does not change as radically as it does in the early weeks and months of the new baby's life.

Through a longitudinal study, Gauda studied the father-child interaction during the first five years of life. The sample consisted of 20 well educated, middle-class adults (sociologically above the population average). Mothers ranged in age from 18 to 32, and fathers from 18 to 40. Their children's birth weight varied from 2500g to 4000g, with Apgar scores of at least 8 (first minute, no complications in pregnancy and birth).

Interviews were held with the parents each year until the children were aged 5; they were asked about the course of the preceding year.

The question asked in the third year of life was: "What does the father do with the child?" An attempt to classify playful activities showed that in 9 of 14 cases (the other 5 could not be evaluated) fathers preferred typical "paternal" games, such as soccer, gymnastics, romps, and building blocks. In contrast to the games the children played with their mothers, these were characterized as "physical" and "wild" (cf. Clarke-Stewart, 1978; Lamb, 1977b).

In the fourth year of life, father-child contacts decreased. Only 10 of 19 children had an opportunity to see their father daily for any significant period of time. Another question asked was: "How often does the father play with his child?" It was answered in 9 cases by "almost daily," the other 10 played with their child once or twice a week or "occasionally." Only 8 of 17 fathers enjoyed playing with their children, 9 would have preferred other activities. In 13 of 17 families, joint activities were undertaken with the child but in 10 families these were restricted to the weekends.

When the children were 5 years old, there was no question specifically referring to father-child contacts; these were inferred from observational data. In 9 cases the whole family came to the interview, in 7 cases the mother (and once the grandmother) came alone with the child, but the child was never accompanied by the father on his own. When both parents were present the child was asked with whom he wanted to go to the playroom. All of the children chose the mother. Fathers almost always observed the play scene from behind a window and only participated in play in cases when the mother was otherwise engaged (e.g., calming or breast-feeding a younger brother or sister). Even then the mother dominated in most cases (Gauda, 1983).

This increasing withdrawal of fathers from parent-child interaction and their decreasing importance for child development was not confirmed by Fisch and Lüscher (1980, 1981). They found that fathers played a substantial role in family life and in rearing their 4- and 5-year-old children. They reported clear indications that partners were beginning to approach the parent-child relationship on a joint basis. These more favorable results may be explained by different assessment methods. Gauda based parts of her study on observations while Lüscher and Fisch referred mainly to interview data. It is conceivable that conformism to prevailing social desirabilities may have played a role in influencing the fathers' answers in the interview situation, especially for those wishing to present themselves as the "new fathers." This interpretation is supported by the fact that the mothers interviewed by Fisch and Lüscher rated the fathers' involvement in household tasks and child-rearing lower than the fathers themselves.

Fathers' Involvement in the Ecological Context

The most comprehensive research work in the German-speaking countries dealing with ecological conditions and the father's participation in the care and rearing of children aged 0–6 was conducted by the Institute of Developmental and Social Psychology at Düsseldorf University (Schmidt-Denter, 1984, cf. Research in the German-Speaking Countries). This representative inquiry involved 1033 families in North Rhine–Westfalia (the FRG state with the greatest population density.

Parents answered questions concerning the type and scope of their activities in different functional areas: care, protection, attachment, control, play, stimulation/learning (Döpkemeyer, 1981; Schmidt-Denter, 1984; Zamponi, 1983). Compared with other child reference persons, especially the mothers, the fathers showed the greatest inter-individual functional variability. The following determinants of the type and scope of their paternal involvement were identified:

(a) social class (more involvement by those in the higher classes);
(b) regional origin (more involvement by city-dwellers than by country-dwellers);
(c) age (more involvement by younger fathers as well as higher scores on control and stimulation/learning measures); and

(d) number of children (higher scores on attachment and stimulation/learning measures by fathers with fewer children).

Three groups of fathers were identified by cluster analysis:

Group 1: Active fathers. They developed the closest relationship to their children, participated regularly in childcare, and were particularly active in play and stimulation/learning functions.

Group 2: Less active fathers. They scored similarly to Group 1 in attachment and "control" and to Group 3 in protection. They had scores between these two groups in other functions (i.e., care, play, stimulation/learning).

Group 3: Inactive fathers. They reached very low scores in 5 of the 6 functions. Some variability was evident in scores for the control function.

It is interesting to note that the mothers' behavior varied according to the activity group in which the spouse was categorized. For example, mothers married to active fathers stimulated their children to a greater extent than mothers married to less active and inactive fathers. In general, mothers and fathers married to one another showed clear accordance in certain functional areas which promote the creation of certain familial care and educational climates (e.g., in play and stimulation/learning). On the other hand, there were also distinct but complementary differences, especially with regard to childcare. The more the fathers were involved here, the less the mothers were forced to participate and could turn their attention to other tasks.

Schmidt-Denter (1984) draws the following conclusions from his results. Due to the fact that fathers are (still) the main breadwinners in the family, they can only relieve the mothers comparatively little in household and education. Nevertheless, they appear to have great flexibility in deciding on their paternal involvement—as reflected in the above mentioned variability. Something approaching a "new" quality in the father's behavior was demonstrated in one subgroup, especially with regard to closer emotional father-child relationship. The fathers most resembling the new type idealized in public media were, in the majority, younger men, members of upper social class, and residents of cities. These data correspond with the sociological findings mentioned above (cf. Eckert, 1985).

SUMMARY AND CONCLUSIONS

Current Discussion

Summing up the current public discussion and empirical research on the importance of the father for child development, one can observe progress as well as discrepancies.

Without question, it can be stated that this problem has increasingly come into the focus of public discussion in recent years. Empirical research has also begun to treat this problem, albeit with a delay. The studies are exploratory, initiated by individual researchers independent of each other and drawing on international—predominantly American—investigations. The role of the father is by no means the major focus of all these studies; in some, it is only touched upon marginally.

There are several research efforts being conducted in the German-speaking countries that are as yet at their beginnings and uncoordinated (cf. Fthenakis, 1985). However, there is also lack of coordination in those countries in which the father's role has been taken up by empirical research for some time. Lamb, Pleck, Charnov, and Levine (in press) emphasize that a considerable amount of descriptive information has been collected as to the father-child relationship but that systematic research and analysis is urgently needed, especially dealing with aspects of provisioning, protection, and procreation from a biosocial perspective.

Cautiously summing up the West German findings—recall that positive feedback arrived from FRG only and not from Austria, Switzerland, and GDR—we can observe a change of attitudes regarding the role patterns of men and women, especially with regard to women's professional activities and the sharing of household duties and childcare responsibilities. Fthenakis (1985) points out that men are developing new conceptions of their roles and tasks as fathers, and the presented findings (e.g., Schmidt-Denter, 1984) support this assumption especially for some subgroups of fathers. However, investigations specifically directed toward this problem have, at best, only been able to confirm this trend in "not only but also" terms. The assurance and definiteness with which the mass media, especially those with parents as their target group, report about this role change cannot be justified.

It is interesting to note our findings that, in scientific research as well as in public discussion, the change in the father's role is being considered primarily with reference to the first years of the child's life. Until recently, fathers were almost exclusively seen as having an important role for older children, particularly their sons.

Connected with this change, the meaning of the emotional father-child relationship has been emphasized more and more. Formerly, fathers' behaviors were primarily viewed under cognitive aspects and with regard to their modeling functions. Now, however, variables such as sensitivity and empathy are considered as relevant research material.

This new research trend may be due to several different reasons: First, we can observe an international focusing of developmental psychology on babyhood and on the first years of life. Second, the strong achievement ideology of the sixties and seventies, with its priority of cognitive development, has widely decreased. Third, the availability of pupils and their parents (at least in Germany) has become difficult by several administrative demands. And, last but not least, parents' meaning for their children is, in fact, greatest during infancy and early childhood.

West German Results and International Findings

When comparing the findings from the FRG with the results gained by international research (especially American), there are many surprisingly clear correspondences in fundamental aspects. However, there are signs of regionally determined discrepancies and shifts of emphasis in the design of the various studies, the types of results gained, and the interpretation of these results.

There are obvious parallels between West German and American studies as to the importance of the father's responsibility and involvement, his understanding and sensitivity in interaction with small children (cf. Lamb, Pleck, & Levine, 1985; Sagi, 1982), and the quality of play (Pedersen et al. 1979; Yogman, 1981). It has been shown to hold true for West German fathers that they develop a greater sensitivity and come to feel themselves equally confident and efficient as their partners in this domain by taking on responsibility for the child and gaining experience in direct father-child contact situations. This was clearly confirmed in the Düsseldorf Study comparing fathers who had participated in preparation courses during pregnancy with a non-prepared control group. The more engaged fathers had the more responsive children (Nickel et al., 1985a, 1985b). This finding corresponds to the conclusion drawn by Sagi.

German studies have also been able to confirm American findings (cf. Lamb, 1976a, 1977b) that fathers play with their children more than mothers do and develop different activities from the mother. Additionally, Schmidt-Denter (1984) identified a subgroup of fathers which has become involved in other functions in addition to play. With the exception of some subgroups of families, the conclusion drawn by Barry and Paxson (1971) from the comparison of 80 cultures that, in 90% of all cases, the mothers have the main role in infant care is generally true for all the German-speaking countries.

On the other hand, there were differences between German and American fathers with respect to care. In an intercultural study (Parke et al., 1981), American fathers and German mothers (and vice versa) resembled each other in some behaviors more than did the fathers from the two countries or the mothers. But in order to decide whether these are substantial differences we need further investigation. As to attachment, there were discrepancies as well as agreements between the American sample and various German samples (cf. Escher-Gräub & Grossmann, 1983).

Conclusions

To date, father research in the German-speaking countries has not yet been explicitly based on the concept of triadic interaction, long proposed by Lamb (1977a,b) and Clarke-Stewart (1978). At best, the findings reveal the similarities and differences between the father's and mother's behavior with the child or the retrospective effects of the father's behavior on mothers. This, together with the urgently needed coordination of the various approaches being applied, remains a

distinct desideratum for future empirical research in the German-speaking countries. From a methodological point of view, sophisticated procedures have to be
applied in order to analyze the sociological and sociopsychological variables that
influence fathers' role attitudes and self-concepts. Some studies (e.g., Eckert,
1985; Schmidt-Denter, 1984) established that the simple dichotomy of traditional
vs. non-traditional families and the exclusive use of socioeconomic criteria often
prominent in international studies do not reflect complex realities. They confirmed the demand of Lamb, Pleck, Charnov, and Levine (in press; cf. also
Lamb, Pleck, & Levine, 1985) that adequate consideration of ecology within the
frame of a comprehensive biosocial perspective be required as an essential condition of fathers' behavior and experience. Furthermore, regard must be paid to
epochal psychological trends of regional significance; these are heavily influenced by the mass media and attract various population subgroups.

REFERENCES

Ainsworth, M. D. S. (1964). Patterns of attachment behavior shown by the infant in interaction
    with his mother. *Merrill-Palmer Quarterly, 10,* 51–58.
Ainsworth, M. D. S. (1969). Object relations, dependency and attachment: a theoretical review of
    the infant-mother-relationship. *Child Development, 40,* 969–1025.
Ainsworth, M. D. S. (1972). Attachment and dependency: A comparison. In J. L. Gewirtz *Attach-
    ment and dependency.* Washington, D.C.: Winston.
Ainsworth, M. D. S. (1979a). Attachment as related to mother-infant interaction. In: J. S. Rosen-
    blatt, R. A. Hinde, C. Beer, & M. Busnel, (Eds.) *Advances in the Study of Behavior* (Vol. 9).
    New York: Academic Press.
Ainsworth, M. D. S. (1979b). Infant-mother attachment. *American Psychologist, 34,* 932–937.
Barry, H., & Paxson, L. M. (1971). Infancy and early childhood: Cross-cultural codes. *Ethnology,
    10,* 467–508.
Bartoszyk, J., & Nickel, H. (1986a). Die Teilnahme an Säuglingspflegekursen und das Be-
    treuungsverhalten von Vätern in den ersten Lebenswochen des Kindes [Fathers' Participation in
    infant-caretaking courses and their caretaking-behaviors in the children's first weeks of life].
    Praxis der Kinderpsychologie und Kinderpsychiatrie 1, 35, 245–260.
Bartoszyk, J., & Nickel, H. (1986b). Geburtsvorbereitung, Geburtserlebnis und Eltern-Kind-Kon-
    takt während des Klinikaufenthaltes: Eine empirische Untersuchung unter besonderer Berück-
    sichtigung der Rolle des Vaters [Birth: Preparation, experience and parent-child contact during
    clinical postpartum stay. Empirical study especially regarding the father's role]. *Geburtshilfe und
    Frauenheilkunde, 46,* 452–462.
Bowlby, J. (1952). *Maternal care and mental health.* Geneva: WHO.
Bowlby, J. (1969). *Attachment and loss,* Vol. 1. *Attachment.* New York: Basic Books.
Bowlby, J. (1976). *Trennung* [Separation]. München: Kindler.
Clarke-Stewart, K. A. (1978). And daddy makes three: The father's impact on mother and young
    child. *Child Development, 49,* 466–478.
Commission on the European Community—see "K"
Der Bundesminister für Jugend, Familie und Gesundheit (Ed.) (1980). *Leben in der Bundesrepublik
    Deutschland—Frauen '80* [Life in the Federal Republic of Germany—Women '80]. Bonn.
Döpkemeyer, M. (1981). *Merkmale familiärer Betreuung von Kindern im ersten Lebensjahr*
    [Features of familial child care in the first year of life.] Diplomarbeit am Institut für Ent-
    wicklungs- und Sozialpsychologie, Universität Düsseldorf (unpublished).
Dorrer, R., & Rowhani, J. (1978). *UNO-Dekade der Frau 1976–1985—Katalog von öster-*

reichischen Maßnahmen [UNO Decade for women 1976–1985—Catalogue of Austrian measures] Wien: Bundesministerium für soziale Verwaltung.

Eckert, R. (1985). Familien- und Erwerbsarbeit und ihre Zuordnung auf die Geschlechter [Work in family and profession and its attribution to both sexes] In K. Weigelt, (Ed.), *Familie und Familienpolitik - Zur Situation in der Bunderepublik.* Forschungsbericht 44 der Konrad-Adenauer-Stiftung, Melle: Knoth.

Eidgenössische Kommission für Frauenfragen (1982). *Die Stellung der Frau in der Schweiz, Teil II: Biographien und Rollennorm* [Women's situation in Switzerland, part II: biographies and role-patterns].

Engfer, A., & Gavranidou, M. (1984). *Sources of stress and support - their impact on the mother-child relationship* Paper presented at Inaugural European Conference on Developmental Psychology, Groningen.

Escher-Gräub, D., & Grossmann, K. E. (1983). *Bindungsun sicherheit im zweiten Lebensjahr - die Regensburger Querschnittstudie* [Insecurity of attachment in the second year of life - the Regensburg cross-sectional study.] Forschungs, bericht (unpublished) Universität Regensburg.

Fisch, R., & Lüscher, K. (1980). *Feldbericht zu den Untersuchungen über die Lebensverhältnisse junger Familien in Konstanz und Mannheim* [Report on the Studies about young families' life-settings in Konstanz and Mannheim]. Universität Konstanz und Zentrum für Umfragen, Methoden und Analysen, Mannheim.

Fisch, R., & Lüscher, K. (1981). *Feldbericht II zu den Untersuchungen über die Lebensverhältnisse junger Familien in Konstanz und Mannheim* [Second report on studies about young families' life-settings in Konstanz and Mannheim.] Universität Konstanz.

Frauenforschung [Research on women] (journal) Heft 1, pp. 118–131.

Fthenakis, W. (1983). Gemeinsame elterliche Sorge nach der Scheidung. [Cooperative parental care after divorce]. In H. Remschmidt (Ed.), *Kinderpsychiatrie und Familienrecht.* Stuttgart: Thieme.

Fthenakis, W. E. (1984). Die Vaterrolle in der neueren Familienforschung [The father's role in recent family research]. *Psychologie in Erziehung und Unterricht, 31,* 1–21.

Fthenakis, W. E. (1985). *Väter.* Bd. 1: *Zur Psychologie der Vater-Kind-Beziehung.* Bd. 2: *Zur Vater-Kind-Beziehung in verschiedenen Familienstrukturen.* [Fathers - first vol.: Psychology of the father-child relationship, second vol.: The father-child relationship in different family structures]. München - Wien - Baltimore: Urban & Schwarzenberg.

Fthenakis, W. E., Niesel, R., & Kunze, H. R. (1982). *Ehescheidung. Konsequenzen für Eltern und Kinder* (Divorce. Consequences for parents and children). München - Wien - Baltimore: Urban & Schwarzenberg.

Gauda, G. (1983). Die Rolle und der Einfluß des Vaters in den ersten fünf Lebensjahren. [The father's role and influence in the first five years of life] In K. E. Grossmann, & P. Lütkenhaus (Eds.): *Bericht über die 6. Tagung Entwicklungspsychologie,* Regensburg: Universität Regensburg.

Grieswelle, D. (1985). Probleme heutiger Familien und Familienpolitik. [Problems of today's families and family politics] In K. Weigelt (Ed.): *Familie und Familienpolitik - Zur Situation in der Bundesrepublik.* Forschungsbericht 44 der Konrad-Adenauer-Stiftung, Melle: Knoth.

Grossmann, K., Thane, K., & Grossmann, K. E. (1981). Maternal tactual contact of the newborn after various postpartum conditions of mother-infant contact. *Developmental Psychology, 17,* 158–169.

Grossmann, K. E., & Volkmer, H.-J. (1984). Fathers' presence during birth of their infants and paternal involvement. *International Journal of Behavioral Development, 7,* 157–165.

Hetzer, H. (1967). *Kind und Jugendlicher in der Entwicklung* [The developing child and adolescent]. 10. Aufl. Hannover: Schroedel.

Jäger, M., Lindemann, A., & Beckmann, D. (1984).Paarbeziehung und Geburtsverlauf. [The couple's relationship and course of birth]. In J. W. Scheer (Ed.), *Ärztliche Maßnahmen aus psychologischer Sicht: Beiträge zur medizinischen Psychologie.* Berlin: Springer.

Jennewein, K., & Matzanke, C. (1983). *Einflüsse des Kindes auf die Eltern* [The child's impact on his parents. Students' research guided by L. Brüderl]. Studentische Semesterarbeit unter Anleitung von L. Brüderl. Universität Giessen (unpublished).

Kleining, G., & Moore, H. (1968). Soziale Selbsteinstufung (SSE). [Sociological self-rating]. *Kölner Zeitschrift für Soziologie und Sozialpsychologie, 20,* 502–552.

Knödel, P. (1983). *Erziehungseinstellungen, Einstellungs veränderungen und Mutter-Kind-Interaktionen* [Educational attitudes, their changes and the mother-child interaction]. Diplomarbeit, Universität Münster (unpublished).

Köcher, E. M. T., & Nickel, H. (1984). Qualitative und quantitative Erhebung entwicklungs- und erziehungspsychólogisch relevanter Merkmale von Eltern-Kind-Spielgruppen. [Parent-child playgroups: qualitative and quantitative assessment of features relevant from a developmental and educational psychological point of view]. *DGfE-Informationsdienst, Kommission: Pädagogik der frühen Kindheit, 5,* 10.

Köcher, E. M. T., & Nickel, H. (1985). Die Berücksichtigung des Vaters in der gegenwärtigen Forschungspraxis: Ergebnisse einer Umfrage im deutschsprachigen Raum. [The father's role as subject of research — results of an inquiry in the German speaking countries]. *Psychologie in Erziehung und Unterricht, 32,* 288–292.

Kommission der Europäischen Gemeinschaften (Hrsg.) (1984). *Frauen und Männer in Europa 1983* [Women and men in Europe 1983]. Brüssel.

Kreppner, K., Paulsen, S., & Schütze, Y. (1982). Infant and family development: From triads to tetrads. *Human Development, 25,* 373–391.

Lamb, M. E. (1976a). Interactions between eight-month-old children and their father in child development. In M. E. Lamb (Ed.): *The role of the father in child development.* New York: Wiley.

Lamb, M. E. (1976b). Twelve-month-olds and their parents: Interaction in a laboratory playroom. *Developmental Psychology, 12,* 237–244.

Lamb, M. E. (1977a). The development of mother-infant and father-infant interaction in the second year of life. *Developmental Psychology, 13,* 639–649.

Lamb, M. E. (1977b). Father-infant and mother-infant-interaction in the first year of life. *Child Development, 48,* 167–181.

Lamb, M. E., Pleck, J. H., Charnov, E. L., & Levine, J. A. (1987) A biosocial perspective on paternal behavior and involvement. In J. B. Lancaster, J. Altman, A. Rossi, & L. Sherrod (Eds.), Parenting across the lifespan: Biosocial perspectives. Chicago: Aldine.

Lamb, M.E., Pleck, J. H., & Levine, J. A. (1985). The role of the father in child development: The effects of increased paternal involvement. In B. B. Lahey & A. E. Kazdin (Eds.), *Advances in clinical child psychology* (vol. 8). New York: Plenum Press.

Lebert, U. (1985). Der Mann (The Man). *Brigitte, 21,* 98–110.

Lehr, U. (1978). Die Bedeutung von Mutter und Vater für die Persönlichkeitsentwicklung des Kleinkindes [The mother's and father's importance for the child's personality development]. In R. Dollase (Ed.), *Handbuch der Früh- und Vorschulpädagogik,* Düsseldorf: Schwann.

Meyer-Krahmer, K. (1980). Die Rolle des Vaters in der Entwicklung des Kindes [The father's role in child-development]. *Psychologie in Erziehung und Unterricht, 27,* 87–102.

Mitterauer, M., & Sieder, R. (1980). *Vom Patriarchat zur Partnerschaft* [From patriarchy to partnership]. München: Beck.

Nickel, H. (1979). *Entwicklungspsychologie des Kindes- und Jugendalters* [Developmental psychology of childhood and adolescence]. Band I und Band II. 3. Aufl., Bern - Toronto: Huber.

Nickel, H. (1980). Child psychology: A review of thirty years of research in the Federal Republic of Germany. *The German Journal of Psychology, 4,* 313–334.

Nickel, H. (1985). Vorschulisches Erzieherverhalten im Spiegel empirischer Untersuchungen [Preschool educational behaviors in empirical studies]. In H. Nickel (Ed.), *Sozialisation im Vorschulalter.* Weinheim/Bergstraße: edition psychologie.

Nickel, H., Bartoszyk, J., & Wenzel, H. (1982). *Parent-infant-interaction and preparation for parenthood*. Twentieth International Congress of Applied Psychology, International Association of Applied Psychology, Abstracts, Edinburgh, p. 220.

Nickel, H., Bartoszyk, J., & Wenzel, H. (1985a). *Eltern-Kind-Beziehung im ersten Lebensjahr: Der Einfluß von Vorbereitungskursen auf das Verhalten des Vaters und seine Bedeutung für die Entwicklung des Kindes* [The parent-child relationship in the first year of life: the influence of preparation courses on fathers' behaviors and its importance for child development]. Forschungsbericht Universität Düsseldorf.

Nickel, H., Bartoszyk, J., & Wenzel, H. (1985b). Fathers as caregivers for infants: The importance of participating in preparation-courses. *Cahiers de psychologie cognitive, 5,* 493.

Nickel, H., & Köcher, E. M. T. (1986). Väter von Säuglingen und Kleinkindern - zum Rollenwandel in der Bundesrepublik Deutschland [Fathers of infants and toddlers - role change in the Federal Republic of Germany]. *Psychologie in Erziehung und Unterricht, 33,* 171–184.

Nickel, H., Schenk, M., & Ungelenk, B. (1980). *Erzieher- und Elternverhalten im Vorschulbereich* [Behaviors of professional educators and parents with preschool-children]. München - Basel: Reinhardt.

Olbertz, F. (1983). *Informationsabende für werdende Eltern in der Klinik* [information meetings for expectant parents in hospitals]. 7. Tagung internationale Studiengemeinschaft für Pränatale Psychologie (ISPP). Düsseldorf.

Olbrich, E., & Brüderl, L. (1986) Frühes Erwachsenenalter: Partnerwahl, Partnerschaft und Übergang zur Elternschaft [Early adulthood: Partner's choice, partnership and transition to parenthood]. *Zeitschrift für Entwicklungs psychologie und Pädagogische Psychologie 18,* 189–213.

Parke, R. D., Grossmann, K., & Tinsley, B. R. (1981). Father-mother-infant-interaction in the newborn period: A German-American comparison. In T. M. Field, A. M. Sostek, P. Vietze, & P. H. Leidermann (Eds.), *Culture and early interactions*. Hillsdale, NJ: Lawrence Erlbaum Associates, New York: Hillsdale.

Pedersen, F. A., Yarrow, L. J., Anderson, B. J., & Cain, R. L. (1979). Conceptualization of father influences in the infancy period. In M. Lewis, & L. A. Rosenblum (Eds.), *The child and its family, genesis and behavior*. (Vol. 2). New York: Plenum Press.

Peters, M. (1985). *Die Situation Alleinerziehender und ihrer Kinder aus ökopsychologischer Perspektive* [The situation of single parents and their children form an ecopsychological perspective]. Diplomarbeit am Institut für Entwicklungs- und Sozialpsychologie der Universität Düsseldorf (unpublished).

Remschmidt, H. (Ed.) (1983). *Kinderpsychiatrie und Familienrecht* [Child psychiatry and family law]. Stuttgart: Thieme.

Ruppelt, H. (1982). Eltern-Kind-Gruppen in der Sicht der Teilnehmer [Parent-child groups from the participants' view]. *Der Sozialarbeiter, 5,* 117–123.

Sagi, A. (1982). Antecedents and consequences of various degrees of paternal involvement in child rearing: The Israeli project. In M. E. Lamb (Ed.), *Nontraditional families: Parenting and child development*. Hillsdale, NJ: Lawrence Erlbaum Associates.

Schmidt-Denter, U. (1984). *Die soziale Umwelt des Kindes* [The child's social environment]. Berlin-Heidelberg-New York-Tokyo: Springer Verlag.

Schmidt-Kolmer, E. (1977). *Zum Einfluß von Familie und Krippe auf die Entwicklung von Kindern in der frühen Kindheit* [The impact of family and creche on children's development in early childhood]. Berlin (Ost): VEB-Verlag Volk und Gesundheit.

Statistisches Handbuch für die Republik Österreich (1985). Wien: Österreichisches Statistisches Zentralamt.

Szinovacz, M. E. (1979). *Lebensverhältnisse der weiblichen Bevölkerung in Österreich. Teilnahme am Erwerbsleben und familiäre Situtation* [Living conditions of Austrian women. Participation in professional life and familial situation]. Wien: Bundesministerium für soziale Verwaltung.

Tobola, A. (1983). *Eine Analyse von Interaktionen zwischen Mutter und Kind im ersten Lebensjahr*

[An analysis of mother-child interactions in the first year of life]. Diplomarbeit, Universität Münster (unpublished).

Wenzel, H., Bartoszyk, J., & Nickel, H. (1985). Väter als Bezugspersonen von Säuglingen - Zur Bedeutung der Teilnahme an Vorbereitungskursen (Fathers as reference persons of infants - the meaning of participating in preparation courses). In D. Albert (Ed.), *Bericht über den 34. Kongreß der Deutschen Gesellschaft für Psychologie in Wien 1984*, Band I Grundlagenforschung. Göttingen - Toronto - Zürich: Hogrefe, 398–399.

Wutz, C. (1985). *Die Vater-Kind-Beziehung im ersten Lebensjahr:* Trost, Spiel, Pflege [Father-child relationship in the first year of life: comfort, play, care]. Diplom-Arbeit, Universität Regensburg (unpublished).

Yogman, M. W. (1981). Games fathers and mothers play with their infants. *Infant Mental Health Journal, 2,* 241–248.

Zamponi, M. (1983). *Kennzeichen väterlicher Betreuung von Kindern im ersten bis sechsten Lebensjahr* [Features of paternal child-care form the first to the sixth year of life]. Diplomarbeit am Institut für Entwicklungs- und Sozialpsychologie, Universität Düsseldorf (unpublished).

Zimmermann, C. (1985). *Die Eltern-Kind-Beziehung mit drei Monate alten Säuglingen* [The parent-child relationship with three-months-old infants]. Frankfurt: Peter Lang.

5 The Changing Role of Swedish Fathers

Carl Philip Hwang
University of Göteborg

THE CHANGING ROLE OF SWEDISH FATHERS

What does the father's role in Sweden today look like? This question has been the topic of lively debate in Sweden during the past few years. Popular books have been written (e.g., Kjellman & Wizelius, 1983; Johansson, 1982; Uddenberg, 1982), investigations have been made, and the Minister of Equality (between the sexes) has formed a special task force to study this question. (Does any other country have a minister of equality?) The mission of this so-called "men's group" is to suggest measures that might hasten the development of equality between men and women. In 1985, the group published its first major report, entitled "Mannen i förändring" ("Men's changing role").

In a similar vein, the importance of the relationship between father and child has been emphasized for its role in the well-being of the child, of the father, and of the family as a whole. Advertising campaigns and pamphlets have been used to convince fathers that it is good for them to learn to take care of their child right from the start, and to share the responsibility for the child with the mother. There is also accurate statistical documentation as to how many fathers exercise their legal rights to take parental leave to stay home and take care of their sick child, or to shorten their working day from 8 hours to 6.

In other words, one might think that it is easy to answer the question as to what the father's role in Sweden today looks like. Unfortunately, this is not the case. On the one hand, many people make statements in which they openly approve of the legislation and official policy statements. They do this before they have had time to examine more carefully whether social reality has changed. On the other hand, there are those who are overcritical of the failures of the system

FIGURE 5.1.   The father of Alfons Åberg. Alfons Åberg is the main figure in popular books of the Swedish author and illustrator, Gunilla Bergström. Alfons lives with his father; no mention is made of his mother.

and draw the conclusion that the father's role in Sweden is the same as it is in other countries.

In the present chapter we will attempt to answer the question: What does the father's role in Sweden look like today? In the first part, we describe the historical development within the realm of the family during the 19th and 20th centuries. It is during this period that the modern fatherrole in Sweden developed. In the next section, we discuss whether or not Swedish parents enjoy equality with one another. How do the mother and father divide the work of home and children, and what do they think about their division of labor?

In the third section, we describe the Swedish system of parental insurance with particular attention to the question of who uses the system and its effects on fathers, mothers, and children. We also present briefly a few possible future changes in the system of parental insurance. In the last section, we describe the situation of divorced fathers in Sweden.

THE SWEDISH FATHER—PAST AND PRESENT

In Sweden, as in other countries, the transition from an economy based on domestic production to one based on wage earning had a particularly great impact on the mother's and father's roles within the family. The father's role as a trainer of the young was important in the agrarian society, where he passed on knowledge of farming, taught his children handicrafts, and taught them how to read and pray (Frykman & Löfgren, 1979). By the middle of the 19th century, the family no longer functioned as a unit of production, that is, both the need to work together and the direct dependency on one another had diminished. A new type of family grew up—the middle-class and working-class families in the city—both of which had the father as the primary provider. Thus, the father left the family to work in the labor market (i.e., he left home), whereas the mother remained with the children and the household work. The family became increasingly a unit of consumption where the woman had the role of housewife and the man the role of provider (Kyle, 1985).

The poet and social philosopher, Erik Gustav Geijer (1773–1847), was perhaps the one person who has most clearly described how the father's role in raising children changed at the beginning of the 19th century in Sweden. Geijer's basic position was that the family was the foundation of society, and model citizens come from model homes (Kyle, 1985). In 1825, when Geijer was a member of a committee on raising children, he wrote:

> The child's first teachers are naturally his parents, and here I emphasize no less paternal instruction than maternal, although the latter comes earlier, and both ought to work together . . . The child understands the value of knowledge . . . if the father himself teaches him the rudiments, even if this is only to read a book. No one is above this task, who is fortunate enough to be a father. (pp 128, in Kyle, 1985)

In other words, Geijer described not only an active role for the father but also a division of labor between the sexes: The mother took care of the small children and the father was responsible for reason and rationality.

Fifteen years later, in 1840, when Geijer reconsidered the subject of parental roles, changes had come about. The father was no longer a teacher and mentor of his children; the priest, the teacher, and, of course, the mother had assumed these roles (Kyle, 1985). The father was instead obliged to assume social duties, not only for himself but for the whole family.

Geijer's attitude towards the mother was, however, ambivalent. On the one hand, her role as the caretaker was emphasized; on the other hand, she was forced to relinquish certain social rights. The improvement of the mother's position in the home went hand in hand with a deterioration of the position of women in society.

Geijer's ambivalent attitude towards women as both mothers and women, and his emphasis on motherhood as a social role, became the dominant factor during the whole of the 19th century and a good part of the 20th century.

Sweden was industrialized relatively late—not until the second half of the 19th century. In connection with industrialization, men came to be "absent fathers." The ethologists Frykman and Löfgren (1979) describe the middle-class father's role in Sweden at the end of the 19th and beginning of the 20th century in the following way:

> The father is respected and honored at a distance, while the mother represented light, warmth and love. Love of the father largely built on respect and distance, but the view of the father was also divided and ambiguous. In many descriptions of childhood during this period, the father was portrayed as a person to be respected, admired, and feared. Behind this double image of the father lay the duplicity of the male role in a middle-class environment. In contrast to the mother, the housewife, he moves freely between his home and the outside world. Every morning he disappears into the world of production and of his career, pressed by feelings of duty and diligence as a provider. There was an element of mystery and of the unknown in this double life. Children had only vague ideas about their father's "other life." If he worked at home, he shut himself into his office where no one was permitted without good reason (pp. 97–98).

What was the father's role like in Swedish working-class homes at the end of the 19th and beginning of the 20th century? In comparison to the middle-class homes, there were similarities but also differences. The father was still a distant person who came home from work tired, or else hurried out to meet his friends. The home was, however, not a place where the family was brought together as it was for the middle-class family, but rather a base of operation from which members of the family were sent out to help support the family as a whole. Fathers were in many cases forced to lead a busy life, roaming about looking for work (Frykman & Löfgren, 1979).

The year 1921 is often called the year of the breakthrough of democracy in Sweden. In that year, a new family law was passed in Sweden, along with other reforms. Prior to 1921, according to the old law, the father was the sole guardian of his children. He had the final word when it came to their upbringing and education. In the same way, the husband had the right to make all decisions which concerned the household. He acted as guardian of his wife, having the right to control her work, her sexuality, and her economic assets (Kyle, 1985).

The new family law implied not only that women received full civil rights (including the right to vote) but also that custody of the children was shared between the parents and that marriage was a state which concerned only the man and woman. The man's sole rights of control over his children, his wife, and his household thus came to an end. From then on, parents shared the responsibility for raising children, and men and women each had control over their own lives. Although this law did not cause equality to suddenly exist in the Swedish family, it is clear that the law contributed to a gradual change in the role of men and fathers.

Much has happened in Sweden since 1921 that has affected the area of family life. The threat of a population decrease created a political climate in which family policy oriented towards increasing fertility (Myrdal & Myrdal, 1934). Patterns of life together for men and women changed dramatically, primarily as a result of women's liberation and the official equality between the sexes. The Social Democratic Party which came into power in the 1930s had a particularly important role in developing family policy in Sweden.

Swedish society continued to change. In 1930, the number of people employed in industry was equal to the number employed in agriculture. By the end of the seventies, only 3% of the work force was employed in agriculture. In 1930, 30% of the population lived in densely populated areas; by 1976, this figure had risen to 83% (SOU, 1978).

The number of employed women also increased. However, most women usually quit working in factories when they got married and had children. In the 1930s and 1940s, the ideal was still that a "real man" should support his family. A woman's place was in the home (SOU 1978).

After World War II, the demand for labor rose sharply in Sweden. At the same time, there were significant changes in demographic patterns. More women were getting married, and people of both sexes married at an earlier age. There was no longer any large group of unmarried women available for the labor market. Married women were thus needed in the paid work force (Qvist, 1973).

However, married women could not join the work force on the same terms as men or unmarried women. They had the major responsibility for the home and children. Part-time work was one way for women to maintain contact with professional life. During this time, the ideology of "women's dual role" replaced the ideal of the man as supporter of the family and the wife as housewife. Swedish women thus were given both a professional role and a family role (SOU 1978:28; see also Liljeström, 1980).

During the 1960s, a new perspective began to emerge in Swedish labor and family policy. In 1964, a program for future policy called "The Equality of Women" was presented. The Social Democratic prime minister, the late Tage Erlander, wrote the following in its preface:

"Equality between the sexes implies . . . that men get an increased opportunity to be close to their children, and to exert an influence over the upbringing of new generations. Women's rights thus imply men's rights." (Mannen i förändring, 1985).

In the 1960s, however, issues of equality between the sexes were still focused mostly on strengthening the position of women in working life, and on reforms in the area of family policy. It was not until the beginning of the 1970s that interest was directed at the man and the father. Evidence for this change includes a book published on the subject (Paulsen, Andersson, & Sessler, 1975), a government inquiry (SOU 1976:71), and a special committee that was appointed in 1972 in order to make recommendations for measures to increase equality between men and women.

Children were no longer the responsibility of women alone. Parenthood began, little by little, to replace motherhood (e.g., Dahlström, 1971). Parental insurance (see below) replaced motherhood insurance. A greater number of men began to take an active role in caring for their children. At least on paper, it is not only the women who today have a "dual role" in Sweden. Both men and women are expected to take responsibility both for the home and for a job. We will discuss the realization of these possibilities in the next sections of this chapter.

DOES SEXUAL EQUALITY EXIST BETWEEN SWEDISH PARENTS?

In 1968, the Swedish government presented a report to the United Nations' Economic and Social Council describing a policy towards sex roles, more radical than any proposed by any government previously or since. Even as the modern women's movement was just beginning in Europe and America, Sweden had decided to aim for complete equality between men and women in the labor market, politics, and the family. It was in the latter sphere that the Swedish model was particularly radical. Women were supposed to be economically independent from their male partners and just as responsible for the economic support of children. Men were to be equally responsible for housework and childcare. Role-sharing in the family was regarded as a prerequisite for women's full participation in the economy, politics, and trade unions, as well as a way to enhance men's opportunities for self-fulfillment as fathers and persons with interests outside the marketplace.

In sum, a new perspective on the family was presented, in which men and women shared many aspects of life—including an equal responsibility as parents. Has this vision been realized? Can we truthfully speak of this sort of equality in Swedish homes? Before we attempt to answer this question, it is necessary to give some background information concerning patterns of family life in Sweden today.

CONTEMPORARY SWEDISH FAMILIES

Family patterns have changed dramatically in Sweden during the past few decades. Marriage patterns and decreasing fertility have resulted in new kinds of families being formed (Liljeström, 1978). A larger proportion of the adult population is part of a family-with-children subgroup, so more people have a parental role to play. The period of time they play this role, however, is probably shorter than it was for past generations of Swedes, due to such factors as the smaller number of children and the increased number of single-parent families (SOU, 1975). Additionally, there is a tendency for men and women to become parents at a later age than before—due (in part) to their extended schooling (Official Statistics of Sweden, 1982).

If we look at this picture of family structure from the point of view of the child, we find that most children in Sweden live in families with two cohabiting parents. However, in 1980, 15% lived in single-parent families, usually with the mother. Only 12% of the children living with a single parent lived with their fathers (SOU, 1983).

Swedish families rarely include more than two generations: parents and children. In 1977, only 0.5% of the children living with both their parents lived in households with three generations (Official Statistics of Sweden, 1982; For a description of the informal social networks of Swedish mothers and fathers, see Gunnarsson, 1982.)

If we turn to the effects of the parents' occupations on the family situation, the most obvious effect is that the parents' job regulates both the amount of time they can spend with their children and their need for childcare outside of the family.

The proportion of fathers in Sweden who are employed outside the home is significantly higher than the proportion of mothers. In 1977, fathers of young children were as actively employed as men in the age group 25–54 (Official Statistics of Sweden, 1982). Ninety-two percent of the men in families with preschool children were gainfully employed, while this figure was 98% for men with school-age children (Winander, 1982).

The proportion of mothers in the paid work force has risen dramatically in the last two decades. In 1964, less than one third of all employed women had children; by 1980, this figure had risen to almost one half. The increase has been particularly rapid among mothers of preschool children, where the proportion of those who work outside the home more than doubled during the 60s and 70s (Petterson, 1981). In 1981, about 80% of the women with preschool children were gainfully employed (Official Statistics of Sweden, 1982).

The number of working hours has been reduced successively in Sweden so that today, compared with people in other countries, Swedes are involved in paid work relatively few hours per day. The group with the longest average workday is married men with children. In 1977, 34% of the men with children under 7 had a average working day of over 10 hours. This figure was not related to whether the wife was employed full-time or part-time; the father's paid working time was equally long in both cases (Official Statistics of Sweden, 1982; Winander, 1982).

In sum, we can see that most Swedish women work outside the home. While in the past there was one wage earner per family, the most common pattern in today's two-parent family is that both parents are gainfully employed: the father full-time and the mother part-time (see Näsman, Nordström, & Hammarström, 1983, for a review). This is a pattern which we recognize in many other Western societies. The question is: Who does the work that was previously done by housewives, that is, taking care of the children and the housework? Is it true that Swedish parents enjoy more equality in this respect than those in other countries, or is this a myth?

Division of Housework and Childcare

It seems that responsibility for the care of the home and the children still largely rests with the mother, even if she works outside the home. In Sweden, as in other countries, we can rightfully speak of a double work load for women. Women are the ones who take responsibility for and perform most household work (i.e., cooking, washing dishes, laundry, cleaning, and shopping). For example, two thirds of the women who work full-time prepare most or all of the meals for the family. Washing dishes and grocery shopping are the two chores that Swedish men take part in relatively often; in one out of every three families, the parents share these jobs on equal terms (Official Statistics of Sweden, 1982).

Regardless of whether women work full-time or part-time, the differences between the sexes remain. In 1972, the number of hours per week (Monday–Friday) spent doing household work in families with preschool children, was estimated to be 17 hours for the mothers and 3½ hours for the fathers. Women with part-time jobs worked an average of 4–5 hours per weekday on household chores, while those who were not gainfully employed worked 5–6 hours. When women worked part-time, or not at all, the men's work time in the home decreased from 3½ hours to between 10 and 25 minutes per day (SOU, 1979:89). It is interesting to note that these figures have not changed substantially in the last 10 years. In a recent study, it was found that men devoted an average of 7–8 hours per week to household chores or childcare (Trost, 1983a), while women spent an average of 35 hours per week on these tasks (SOU, 1979).

It is quite remarkable that the division of labor is less equal among couples with children than among childless ones (see Fig. 5.2.). The difference is surprisingly large. Once again, the differences remain regardless of whether the woman works full-time or part-time. When children are born and the household work becomes more of a burden, it seems as though Swedish parents fall into the traditional sex roles; this is true today in a similar way as in the past. The extra work that children give rise to is laid almost entirely on the mother's shoulders. They have the major responsibility for laundry, putting the children to bed, taking care of clothing, contacts with day-care centers, schools, and so forth (Official Statistics of Sweden, 1982; Sandqvist, 1985).

The difference is particularly obvious among men over 45, and among those who are poorly educated. Probable explanations for the inactivity of these older

Sharing of household chores in Swedish families

All couples

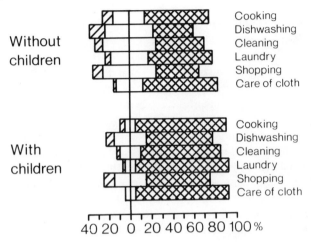

Without children

Cooking
Dishwashing
Cleaning
Laundry
Shopping
Care of cloth

With children

Cooking
Dishwashing
Cleaning
Laundry
Shopping
Care of cloth

40 20 0 20 40 60 80 100 %

Couples where the women works full-time

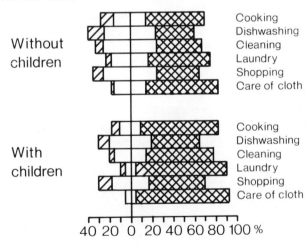

Without children

Cooking
Dishwashing
Cleaning
Laundry
Shopping
Care of cloth

With children

Cooking
Dishwashing
Cleaning
Laundry
Shopping
Care of cloth

40 20 0 20 40 60 80 100 %

Man does most
Share equally
Women does most

FIGURE 5.2. Sharing of household chores in Swedish families.

men are that more of them are married to housewives and that fewer of them have young children and homes that require a lot of work. The difference is less significant for families where the man is well educated and between 25 and 35, and where the children are under 3 (Trost, 1983a).

When we compare both parents' commitment to the care of the children we find that mothers have the major responsibility for the actual care and upbringing. A small portion of parents share the responsibility equally. The major portion of fathers take some responsibility for the children, even if it is quite limited. This is particularly true when the children are a bit older. One third of the fathers claim to have close emotional ties with their children. This is true primarily for those fathers who have shared responsibility on equal terms with the mothers, but it is also true for those who are less involved but still show an active interest in their children (SOU, 1976).

In Sweden, the amount of contact between parents and children differs from one social class to another. Working-class fathers have been traditionally described as being family-oriented. Many studies have shown, for example, that working-class fathers spend more time with their families than other fathers who worked full-time but earned higher incomes (Holter, Henriksen, Gjertsen, & Hjort, 1975). Working-class fathers' greater orientation towards the family is usually interpreted as a reaction to a tedious job, and less often as a genuinely greater interest in the children (Gardell, 1976).

One recent study has documented a strong orientation towards the family in fathers of other social strata. For example, upper-middle-class fathers in Sweden were found to be more actively involved in infant care (Nettlebladt, Uddenberg, & Engelsson, 1981).

Work Role—Parental Role

When the limited involvement of fathers has been discussed in Sweden, it has been assumed that they would spend more time doing household chores and caring for the children, if only their work permitted it. In other words, people think that the father's work schedule largely determines how much time he can devote to housework and children. The shorter his working hours, the more time he has for the family.

Notably enough, this line of reasoning does not seem to hold. Instead, it seems that the Swedish men with relatively short working hours also spend fewer hours in the home than those who work full-time (Trost, 1982a). Studies from other countries confirm that the relationship between working hours and involvement in the home and family is not at all as clear as one might imagine (Pleck, 1983).

In the same way, it is assumed that, if the woman is gainfully employed, the man compensates for her absence by devoting more time to his family. A number of investigations of Swedish parents suggests that there is a correlation between women's employment and men's involvement in the home and family. Haas (1982), for example, showed that responsibility for childcare was more equally divided between the parents in families where the mother worked outside the home.

In other words there is a definite tendency for men to take a greater part in housework when the woman is employed outside the home. In a comparison between 1974 and 1977, Petterson (1981) showed that household chores became redistributed: Men increased their share of the chores if the woman was employed full-time or part-time. The proportion of Swedish families where the man was employed full-time and the woman part-time, and where the woman claimed to do all or almost all the housework, decreased from 50% to 37%.

Attitudes Towards Present-Day Roles

Despite the fact that women in Sweden take care of the lion's share of both housework and childcare, often in addition to work outside the home, almost all of them are satisfied with the division of labor in the home. Less than one tenth of Swedish women declare a definite dissatisfaction with the distribution of household chores. Somewhat more women, but still only a small minority, report that they are dissatisfied with their spouse's limited involvement in childcare (Official Statistics of Sweden, 1982).

It also seems to be the case that Swedish women expect to shoulder the major responsibility for home and family in the future (SOU, 1979:89). In a study of working-class women, it was found that mothers did not believe that men could take the same sort of responsibility for childcare that they could. Those who believed in the man's good intention in this respect still doubted that the labor market would allow him to be a parent on the same terms as a woman (Liljeström & Dahlström, 1981).

As far as men are concerned, very few felt that men's and women's roles in the home and at work will change enough so that men's roles become more similar to women's and vice versa. The less the man is involved at home, the more traditional is his view on equality between the sexes (Trost, 1983a). Most men feel that they devote enough time to household chores and childcare, but that men in general ought to become more involved in these activities (Jalmert, 1983). A probable explanation for this finding is that men in Sweden have learned that equality between the sexes is a good thing. In other words, their view of what men in general ought to do seems to be lip service, which has little relation to what they actually do. In reality, they are not prepared to change their own behavior to any great extent (Hwang, 1985b).

At the same time, some studies suggest that Swedish men are not as satisfied with their roles as fathers as one might expect. For example, Winander (1982) found that, when asked, men reported that they felt they spent too little time working in the home, taking care of the old and the sick family members, and being with their children. In another study, Swedish men described the barriers they encountered when they tried to reevaluate their roles as fathers. These barriers included: a one-sided view of themselves as providers for the family; their emotional inability to work with children; their wives' monopoly with regard to the children, and perfectionism and interference in housework; their own leisure-time activities; work in another area, overtime; work which is physically or psychologically taxing hard manual work; long working hours; and attitudes at work (SOU, 1976).

At the beginning of this section, we posed the question as to whether Swedish parents enjoy equality between the sexes. Equality in the home is many-sided. In some cases, it means an equally large contribution towards all the household chores, or sharing the total burden by specializing in different areas; it can mean taking equal responsibility at home, or equal opportunities for leisure and relaxation (Sandqvist, 1984).

The answer to the question regarding equality between Swedish parents depends on what perspective we have. If we concentrate on differences between mothers and fathers, we find a traditional pattern: mothers take care of home and family, while fathers work outside the home. If one takes the traditional standards of 30 to 40 years ago as a basis (i.e., when mothers mostly worked at home and fathers were only providers), one finds considerable equality today. Both the mother and the father provide for the family economically; both the father and the mother take care of the children. It is clear, however, that there still is a considerable difference between the roles of Swedish parents. The pattern is a traditional one, even if the differences between parents in Sweden are probably smaller than in many other Western societies. Swedish fathers and mothers are not equal, but it can no longer be said that the daily life of parents in Sweden is strictly compartmentalized (Sandqvist, 1984).

FATHERS ON PARENTAL LEAVE

When men become fathers in Sweden today, the "old" male role and the new one come face-to-face. If we say that the former role implied that men should support the family financially, the latter role demands that he also takes responsibility for, and an active interest in, the everyday life of the family (i.e., participate in work around the house). This latter demand becomes particularly relevant when children are born, since a family without children generally involves much less household work (Jalmert, 1984).

In 1974, a new law for parental insurance came into effect in Sweden. This law represents a new policy in family affairs, which strives for more equality between the parents. Fathers are now able to share the parental leave with their employed wives, and they now have the same right to stay home from work when the children are sick. Even before this reform, a tradition had developed in Sweden whereby fathers were allowed to be present at the birth of their children.

It is difficult to say exactly in what year this possibility was opened up but (in modern times) Sweden is probably one of the first countries where fathers were allowed to be present during the delivery of their children. (For a study of how Swedish fathers behave with their infants shortly after delivery, see Rödholm, 1981; Rödholm & Larsson, 1979.) This tradition, coupled with the parental insurance reform, represent a very positive attitude towards fathers' participation in childcare (see Lamb & Levine, 1983, for a review).

In the section that follows, the current form of the parental insurance scheme is described. First, each part of the scheme is described together with figures as to how it is used. We then discuss Swedish fathers' views of parental insurance.

The Parental Insurance Scheme

When a child is born, fathers in Sweden have the possibility of receiving parental compensation for their short-term care of children up to a maximum of 10 days. During these 10 days, the father can stay home from work with the mother to help out with the new baby or to take care of older children. The compensation during this period is equivalent to 90% of the father's regular salary. This part of parental insurance is reportedly used by about 85% of new fathers (Riksförsäkringsverket, 1981). An interesting question is why the remaining 15% do not take advantage of this possibility, especially as these days are "earmarked" (whether or not fathers take leave does not affect the amount of other types of leave available), and provide almost full economic compensation.

During the first 180 days of the child's life, parental compensation in connection with the child's birth is paid to one or both parents. As before, compensation represents 90% of the parent's salary up to a stipulated maximum SEK 403 (US $58) and not less than SEK 48 (US $7) per day. In comparison, it can be noted that the median income for men and women in Sweden in 1986 is SEK 222 (US $32) per day (information obtained from Riksförsäkringsverket). The parents decide themselves who should stay home and take care of the child and who should receive the compensation. This part of the parental insurance can be divided as whole or half days, and must be taken within the first 9 months of the child's life.

Each parent is then entitled to another 180 days of leave that can be taken immediately, transferred to the other parent, or taken at any time in the first 7 years of the child's life. Remuneration is paid at 90% of full salary for the first 90 days and the remainder of the 180 days at SEK 48 per day. This special leave can be used to reduce the employee's working day from 8 to 6 hours per day for some portion of the child's life. In addition, all parents in Sweden who have children under 8 years of age are entitled to decrease their working hours from 40 to 30 hours per week (without receiving economic compensation).

Despite nationwide advertising campaigns picturing wrestlers, soccer players, and other decidedly "masculine" men holding, feeding, and strolling with babies and exhorting other men to share the joys of parenthood, only about 10% of the fathers take advantage of the first 180 days of parental leave. The proportion of days during which leave is taken is also very small: about 2%. Thus, 98% of the leave days are used by the mothers (SOU 1982). Generally, mothers nurse their babies during the greater part of these 6 months, so it is quite possible that the father does not wish to compete with her during this time.

As regards the next 90 days, almost 28% of the men take leave during some part of this time. However, their leave represents only approximately 9% of the total number of leave days. The remaining 90 days (i.e., those for which the parent receives only SEK 48 per day) are almost never used by fathers and, in many cases, not by mothers either. Many families do not feel they can afford to use the last three months of parental leave since the compensation represents only a small part of what they would earn at their regular jobs (SOU, 1982).

If we consider the child's first year of life as a whole, we find that four out of five fathers do not take leave for a single day. Of the total number of days of leave used, 4% are used by men and 96% by women.

Another part of parental insurance gives parents the right to stay home and receive 90% of their salary to take care of a child who is sick or who has a contagious illness. The parents have the right to this compensation for a maximum of 60 days per child per year until the child is 12 years old. During 1980, 34.5% of the fathers took advantage of this part of the parental insurance. This is obviously the part of the parental insurance where the Swedish parents have most equality. Interestingly, 51% of the families who had the right to parental compensation for short-term care of children used this right during 1980 (SOU 1982:36).

We are forced to conclude that Swedish men use their right to be with their children to an extremely limited extent. In other words, we can say that a large proportion of men in Sweden give up the chance to be with their children. The question is why men do not use parental insurance more. There is no definite answer to this question, but certain clues can be found in the results of some recent Swedish investigations.

Fathers' Engagement in and Experience of Parental Leave

In a questionnaire survey, men were asked about their attitudes towards parental leave (SOU 1982:36). Six percent of those surveyed had been on leave. As could be expected, these men were considerably more positive toward parental leave than those who had not been home on leave themselves. In this study, the age of the man was clearly related to his attitude towards parental leave. Not unexpectedly, the younger men were more positive about leave than the older ones. The age of the child also seems to be related to the man's attitude. Among the men who had teenage children, only about one fifth were clearly positive about parental leave; among those with children under 3 years of age, parental leave was more highly appreciated. A final factor of importance seemed to be the man's profession and place of employment. The men who were most negative to parental leave were self-employed or worked in male-dominated places of employment. The ones most positively oriented worked in places of employment dominated by women (see also Hwang, Eldén, & Fransson, 1984).

Similar results were obtained in another study of 918 men and women (SOU 1982). About 45 of the families (10%) had split the parental leave at least partly. As in the earlier study, it was found that parental leave was shared by the parents least of all in families where the father was employed in private business or was self-employed. The mother's employment situation had no effect on whether or not the father stayed home.

In an effort to discover the reasons why parents are reluctant to share parental leave, we recently made a study of 50 men on parental leave (Hwang et al., 1984). The fathers were interviewed concerning their views on the leave of absence, and what problems arose, for example, when they returned to work. The average length of leave was 4.7 months. About two thirds of the men were satisfied with the leave. Most fathers were surprised, however, that is was so time-consuming and such hard work to be done on a full-time basis.

The problems these fathers mentioned often had to do with adjustments to the child's rhythm and the difficulties in planning one's day. One father commented on this problem by saying: "At work, at least I knew when the coffee break was!" A common complaint was that the fathers felt lonely and isolated during their parental leave.They had no contact with other fathers on similar leave and it did not seem natural to them to associate with mothers on leave. Many missed their social contacts at work. For example, one father said: "It wasn't exactly a bed of roses, I felt very isolated."

For most of the men, however, the leave of absence was a positive experience. They felt they had had a chance to follow their child's development. Several fathers felt that it was fruitful on a personal level and that it put the importance of their work in perspective. In addition, several fathers, during their leave, felt that they had come to a better understanding of the situation of the average housewife.

What did the women think of sharing the leave? Interestingly enough, almost all the women were satisfied with having the men stay home too. Each felt that her husband was able to participate in caring for the child in a different way then he could have otherwise. One woman recounted her experiences as follows: "I remember so well when my husband said 'of course we'll divide the first year.' It was so nice to know that we would continue to share the responsibility just as we had done with the housework during the two years we had lived together."

When the reasons for men's reluctance to take advantage of parental leave are discussed in Sweden, mention is often made of man's professional role, the family's economic situation, and the demands of the man's job (SOU 1975; Trost, 1983b). When fathers are asked why it is the woman who is going to stay home during the child's first year, they usually answer: "I would be glad to stay home, if only I could for my job"; "My boss would never go along with it." It is difficult to say how much truth there is in this argument.

Several investigations have shown that employers in Sweden are, in many cases, suspicious of—or directly negative towards—a male employee taking parental leave (Hwang et al., 1984). Many employers presumably consider a man to be untrustworthy if he stays home to look after his child in the same way a woman does. This can result in the man missing a promotion, or in some other way getting left behind in competition with his colleagues. Employers know what rights are given the employees by law, but often they feel that the man is not being loyal towards his work if he takes leave. A manager at a middle-sized Swedish company said, for example: "Of course, I can't *prevent* an employee staying home and taking care of his children, but . . . anyway, I think it's unfair to the co-workers to take leave" (Hwang, 1985b).

Although many employers, particularly within the private sector, are negative towards men staying home to take care of their children, the picture is not altogether clear. References to negative reactions on the part of the employer are sometimes pretexts for other reasons. In reality, many Swedish fathers do not want to stay home. Evidence for this was obtained when we asked the fathers who had been on parental leave what the reactions were when they went back to work. About half of the bosses either had not indicated any negative reaction, or had even been openly positive. Three out of four fathers had not noticed any particular reaction on the part of coworkers or else had received positive reactions (Hwang et al., 1984).

Effects of Parental Leave

So far we have discussed what opportunities Swedish fathers have to take care of their children, how often they do this, and various reasons for and against sharing the parental leave of absence. The next question is what the effects are of men staying home and taking care of their children. One way of answering this question is to compare families where the father goes to work and the mother is at home taking care of the child, with families where the father is on leave and takes the major responsibility for the child while the mother works. We have completed two studies of this sort.

In the first study, our subjects were 52 middle-class couples, all recruited while expecting their first child. Half of the fathers initially planned to take at least a month of paid paternity leave, although several changed their minds for various reasons. In the end, only 17 actually took leave. For those 17, the average amount of time away from work was about 3 months. The leave generally began at the time when the child was weaned, that is, when the child was about 5 months old. Although the sample was small and the results must thus be interpreted cautiously, our findings were surprising. One of our major goals was to see what effects major responsibility for childcare had on parental behavior toward the child. Observations before, during, and after the time when the fathers were home with the child produced surprisingly similar results. We found, in general, no differences between fathers who stayed home and fathers who worked. In other words, in relation to the children, it did not matter if the father stayed home or not. On the other hand, we found major differences between the fathers and mothers—regardless of who had been home and who had worked (Frodi, Lamb, Hwang & Frodi, 1982).

Observations of behavior when the child was 8 and 16 months old produced especially clear differences. Regardless of whether the mothers worked or not, the mothers were consistently more affectionate towards the children than their partners were: They talked to them, smiled, and laughed more often; they performed more activities to care for the child; and they held the child more than the fathers did (Lamb, Frodi, Hwang, Frodi, & Steinberg, 1982; Lamb, Frodi, Frodi, & Hwang, 1982; Hwang, 1981).

Our second goal in this study was to examine the effects of increased paternal participation on infant preferences for mothers and fathers. Which of the parents did the child smile, laugh, and talk with most often, and who did the child go to when she or he wanted to sit on someone's lap, be carried or comforted? As before, the results showed that there was no difference between fathers who stayed at home and fathers who worked. The children, on the other hand, showed clearcut preferences for their mothers regardless of the extent to which their fathers had been involved in their care (Lamb, Frodi, Hwang, & Frodi, 1983).

When the Swedish children were one year old, we observed them with their parents in a standardized laboratory procedure designed to assess the quality of infant-parent attachment (Ainsworth, Blehar, Waters, & Wall, 1978). We found that the children showed a close and secure attachment to the father as often as to the mother, and that there was no difference between "home fathers" and employed fathers (Lamb, Hwang, Frodi, & Frodi, 1982).

We obtained similar results when we studied a new group of fathers on parental leave. We found, once again, that when the mother was present, there was no major differences between what "home fathers" and working fathers did with the children. Interestingly enough, the results changed when the fathers were alone with the children. When the mothers were not present, the fathers on parental leave were more anxious to take care of the children (change diapers, etc.) as compared with the working fathers. The working fathers, on the other hand, spent more time cuddling and playing with the children than the home fathers did (Hwang, 1985). These results are not amenable to simple explanation. One possibility is that home fathers, like mothers, are used to assuming responsibility for childcare even if the partner is not present. In a sense, these fathers are more likely to share caregiving responsibilities on an equal basis with the mother. Working fathers, on the other hand, tend to "help out" while their partners are the ones meeting the major proportion of caregiving needs.

In conclusion, Swedish fathers' opportunities to be at home and take care of their children do not seem to have particularly great importance in regard to how they act towards their children. However, results of a recent study of 145 other Swedish families show that the amount of paternal leave significantly predicts subsequent parental involvement (Lamb, Hwang, Brookstein, Broberg, Hult, & Frodi in preparation).

In recent years, there has been considerable discussion in Sweden about possible negative effects on the child when the father takes parental leaves. Based on Mahler's theories (Mahler, Pine, & Bergman, 1975), it has been said that fathers taking leave can be dangerous for younger children. A father who is home with his child, a so-called "Velour Daddy," might disturb the "symbiosis" between mother and child too early; because the man acts as both mother and father towards the child, he would interfere with the child's sex identification. The findings presented above suggest that the risk for problems in the child's sexual identification are not very great. If fathers take on the major responsibility for the child early in her or his life, problems in the child's development do not seem to follow (Hwang, 1985a). However, it should be noted that no investigation has yet been made where the hypothesis regarding possible effects on the child's sexual identity has been tested.

Before we can give a final answer to why changes in parental roles did not produce changes in the characteristic maternal and paternal styles, we must come to terms with several problems. First, most children are cared for by the mother initially; fathers in Sweden normally do not have charge of the children from birth. Second, most mothers have been at home for a longer time than the fathers (in our study of 52 parents, the father who had been on the longest parental leave had taken care of his child for 5 months). In other words, parents do not switch roles or even share the responsibility for the child equally. Third, almost all contemporary parents had been brought up traditionally by their parents. It is likely that, in terms of sex roles, these years of upbringing are more important than 3 months of being home taking responsibility for a child.

It will take time before we know definitely what the implications are of Swedish fathers' being home and taking care of their children. It is quite possible that we cannot get a definitive answer to this question until the children who have been raised by so-called nontraditional parents have grown up and become mothers and fathers themselves. (See Nettlebladt, 1981, for studies concerning the importance of a man's relationship with his own father when he becomes a father himself.)

Parental Insurance in the Future

Parental insurance in Sweden has been changed and expanded over the years since it was introduced in 1974. At present, different ways of achieving a more equal division of parental leave (between the parents) are under discussion. One version of a reform that would directly affect fathers has been suggested by a task force on the male role, which was appointed by the Swedish government (Mannen i förändring, 1985).

As we mentioned before, parental insurance includes 9 months with almost full compensation for loss of income, and three months with compensation of SEK 48 ($7) per day. The reform proposed by the task force would allow parents who share parental leave to be home more days with compensation as compared with those who do not share it. According to the task force, families who share parental leave so that each parent takes at least 3 months' leave, ought to be entitled to compensation for loss of income (90% of one's salary), even during the last 3 months of leave. The motivation for such a measure is that it stimulates men to take parental leave in a concrete and determined way. It allows an improvement in compensation for those families who share the leave, and it would not imply any decrease of benefits in any respect for those families who, for one reason or another, do not wish to share the leave. This reform is, however, still only a proposal from a task force. The political developments in Sweden during the next few years are probably crucial for whether or not this reform is passed.

DIVORCED FATHERS

So far, we have described the role of fathers who live in so-called "complete" families (i.e., with both wife and children). In concluding this chapter, we will mention some things about the situation of divorced fathers in Sweden.

In Sweden in 1981, one out of every four children between 0 and 17 years of age lived with only one parent. The vast majority of these children lived with their mothers; less than 12% lived with their fathers (SOU 1983:51). As in most other countries, Swedish fathers are, thus, in an inferior position in any discussion of child custody (Trost & Hultåker, 1985). When the custody of a child is disputed, most courts assume that the mother is the parent who can best take care of the child.

There are many divorced Swedish fathers who seldom, if ever, see their children. It may be the case that, prior to divorce, the father already had a weak position in the family. After divorce, contact between fathers and children is often totally or partially broken (Ekselius, 1982). Twenty-eight percent of the children living with only one parent never see the other parent, and the latter parent is primarily the father (SOU 1983). Interestingly, when the father has custody, the child tends to have more contact with the "other parent" (i.e., the mother): 9 out of 10 children living with their father had contact with their mothers. A reasonable explanation for this is that women, who have had greater contact with their children prior to divorce, are more attached to them, and are thus more anxious to be with them.

Contact between the father and the child, when the mother has custody, is affected by factors such as the age of the father, his current marital status, and the length of the marriage (SOU 1980). For example, fathers who live alone tend to have more frequent contact with the child than those who have remarried and/or are living with another woman. When the parents were married more than 15 years prior to the divorce, the father and child have more frequent contact than if the marriage was shorter. (See Magnusson, 1985, for a review of how person-environment factors influence development). There is a clear relationship between the mother's situation and the amount of contact between father and child: Contact is less if the mother remarries than if she lives alone.

Finally, two other factors—the number of years since divorce, and the distance to be traveled—also affect contact between father and child. The proportion of children in Sweden who have extensive contact with their father decreases dramatically with the number of years after divorce. At the same time, the proportion who have no contact whatsoever increased. As regards the distance to be traveled, contact decreases quite naturally as the distance to be travelled by fathers or children increases (SOU 1980).

Since 1971, parents in Sweden have had the opportunity to share custody of the children after divorce. This means that both parents have a joint legal responsibility for care of the child, even after the marriage is dissolved. Shared custody can be set up in two ways, either as *shared care*, where the child lives about the same amount of time with each parent, and *sole care*, where the child lives mainly with one parent, but has a certain amount of contact with the other parent.

Up until 1982, shared custody was an option only for married parents who divorced. In other words, unmarried parents who split up did not receive shared custody. Today it is generally applied to parents who get divorced (irrespective of whether the parents are married or not), A prerequisite for receiving shared custody in a divorce case, however, is that the parents both agree to it. Otherwise, one of the parents (generally the mother) is given custody, while the other parent has visiting rights.

Quite naturally, a high rate of contact is usual when the parents have shared custody. However, it does not follow automatically that a particular type of custody affects the type of contact between parent and child. It is probably the type of custody, together with various other characteristics of the parents who choose the form of custody, which determine the quantity and quality of contact between the child and the parent he or she does not live with (SOU 1983:51).

Several investigations have recently been made in Sweden which study the effects of shared custody (Trost & Hultåker, 1985; Öberg & Öberg, 1985; see also Lenneér-Axelson, 1985, for an overview). Öberg and Öberg concentrated their study on the type of shared custody in which children live about an equal amount of time with each parent (shared care). They found that shared care is a good thing, primarily for fathers and children. The so-called "man's group" (Mannen i förändring, 1985) states that shared care does not necessarily imply that the child lives exactly equal amounts of time with each parent. What is important is that neither parent is deprived of everyday contact with his child. To be a Sunday father—and to drift gradually further and further away from one's former family—is not a good alternative, they feel.

SUMMARY AND CONCLUSION

What is the father's role in Sweden today? This question was posed at the beginning of this chapter. If we look at the possibilities Swedish fathers have to enjoy daily contact with their children, it is clear that, in an international perspective, their situation is unique. As far as I know, there is no other Western country which affords fathers such excellent opportunities for close contact with their children as Sweden. Fathers can, like mothers, take parental leave during the child's first 12 months of life, the first 9 of which are compensated for almost fully. He can stay home and take care of a sick child, and has the right to reduce his working time up to 2 hours per day until the child is 8 years old. Even divorced fathers have a relatively advantageous position, with the option for obligatory shared custody.

In terms of family policy, then, fathers have a very strong position in Sweden. If one is not satisfied with viewing the opportunities, and looks beyond them to see how Swedish fathers actually take advantage of them, the results are, however, discouraging. The differences between mothers and fathers are still great. While the average father in Sweden spends 7–8 hours per week doing housework and caring for children, mothers spend five times as many hours doing these jobs. The differences remain regardless of whether the woman works full-time or part-time.

FIGURE 5.3. Alfons Åberg's father reading a good-night story to Alfons.

If one wishes to have a balanced picture of Swedish fathers, one ought not be too overwhelmed by their inability to take advantage of the opportunities that exist. There are certain indications that fathers in Sweden have begun to see that they are important for their children, and that their children are important for them. This is particularly true for young, well educated fathers with small children, but it seems as if even other categories of fathers are in the process of reevaluating their roles as fathers. Many Swedish fathers feel pressure from their spouses, friends, colleagues, and others to take more active interest in their children and, in this way, to share parental responsibility.

It is no longer very easy for fathers to avoid their share of responsibility. The knowledge that love develops through simple, everyday actions—such as feeding, comforting, bathing, and playing with the child—is gradually seeping into most fathers' consciousness. Even if all of them are not like Alfons Åberg's dad (see picture), there are still indications that a new role for fatherhood is gradually developing in Sweden.

ACKNOWLEDGMENT

This paper was supported financially by the Swedish Council for Research in the Humanities and Social Sciences. I am grateful to this organization for their support.

REFERENCES

Ainsworth, M. D. S., Blehar, M. C., Waters, E., & Wall, S. (1978). *Patterns of attachment*. Hillsdale, NJ: Lawrence Erlbaum Associates.

Dahlström, E. (1971). *The changing roles of men and women*. New York: Beacon Press.

Ekselius, E., (1982). *Ensam far, ensam mor* [Single father, single mother]. Stockholm: Bonniers.

Frodi, A. M., Lamb, M. E., Hwang, C. P., & Frodi, M. (1982). Father-mother-infant interaction in traditional and non-traditional Swedish families: A longitudinal study. *Alternative Lifestyles, 1*, 3–22.

Frykman, J., & Löfgren, O. (1979). *Den kultiverade människan* [The cultured man]. Malmö: Liber Förlag.

Gardell, B. (1976). *Arbetsinnehåll och livskvalitet* [Work content and life quality]. LO: Prisma.

Gunnarsson, L. (1982). *Fäders och mödrars informella sociala nätverk: Resultat från en intervjuundersökning.* [Fathers and mothers informal social network: Results from an interview study]. Institutionen för Praktisk Pedagogik, Göteborg universitet, rapport No. 117.

Haas, L. (1982). Parental Sharing of Childcare Tasks in Sweden. *Journal of Family Issues*, Vol. 3, 389–412.

Holter, H., Henriksen, H. V., Gjertsen, A., & Hjort, H. (1975). *Familjen i klassesamfunnet* [Family in the class society]. Oslo: PAX Förlag A/S.

Hwang, C. P. (1981). *Parent-infant interaction during the first eight months of life*. Unpublished Doctoral dissertation, Universität Göteborg.

Hwang, C. P. (1985a). *Småbarnspappor* [Fathers with small children]. In C. P. Hwang (Ed.), *Faderskap*. Stockholm: Natur och Kultur.

Hwang, C. P. (1985b). *Varför är pappor så lite engagerade i hem och barn?* [Why are fathers involved to such a small extent in home and children?]. In C. P. Hwang (Ed.), *Faderskap*. Stockholm: Natur och Kultur.

Hwang, C. P. (in press). The behavior of Swedish primary and secondary caretaking fathers in relation to mothers presence. *Developmental Psychology*.

Hwang, C. P., Eldén, G., & Fransson, C. (1984). *Arbetsgivares och arbetskamraters attityder till pappaledighet* [Attitudes of employers and colleagues to parental leave]. Psykologiska institutionen, Göteborgs universitet, rapport no. 1.

Jalmert, L. (1983). *Om svenska män: fostran, ideal och vardagsliv* [The Swedish man: upbringing, ideals and everyday life]. Stockholm: Arbetsmarknadsdepartementet (DA 2).

Jalmert, L. (1984). *Den svenske mannen* [The Swedish man]. Stockholm: Tidens Förlag.

Johansson, P.-G. (1982). *Pappa-Pappa barn* [Father-father-child]. Stockholm: Rabén & Sjögren.

Kjellman, K., & Wizelius, T. (1983). *Pappa kom hem* [Come home daddy]. Stockholm: Wahlström & Widstrand.

Kyle, G. (1985). *Från patriark till pappa* [From patriarch to daddy[. In P. Hwang (Ed.), *Faderskap*. Stockholm: Natur och Kultur.

Lamb, M. E., Frodi, A. M., Frodi, M., & Hwang, C. P. (1982). Characteristics of maternal and paternal behavior in traditional and non-traditional Swedish families. *International Journal of Behavioral Development, 5,* 131–141.

Lamb, M. E., Frodi, M., Hwang, C. P., & Frodi, A. M. (1983). Effects of paternal involvement on infant preferences for mothers and fathers. *Child Development, 54,* 450–459.

Lamb, M. E., Frodi, A. M., Hwang, C. P., Frodi, M., & Steinberg, J. (1982). Mother- and father-infant interaction involving playing and holding in traditional and non-traditional Swedish families. *Developmental Psychology, 18,* 215–22.

Lamb, M. E., Hwang, C. P., Bookstein, F. L., Bröberg, A., Hult, G., & Frodi, M. (in preparation). Determinants of paternal involvement. Unpublished manuscript, University of Utah.

Lamb, M. E., Hwang, C. P., Frodi, A. M. & Frodi, M. (1982). Security of mother- and father-infant attachment and stranger sociability in traditional and non-traditional Swedish families. *Infant Behavior and Development, 5,* 355–367.

Lamb, M. E., & Levine, J. (1983). The Swedish paternal insurance policy: An experiment in social engineering. In M. E. Lamb & A. Sagi (Eds.). *Fatherhood and family policy*, Hillsdale, NJ: Lawrence Erlbaum Associates.

Lenneér-Axelson, B. (1985). *Skilsmässopappor och styvpappor* [Divorced fathers and stepfathers]. In P. Hwang (Ed.), *Faderskap*. Stockholm: Natur och Kultur.

Liljeström, R. (1978). *Yrke och Barn* [Professional life and children]. Stockholm: Natur och Kultur.

Liljeström, R. (1980). *Våra barn, andras ungar* [Our children, others' kids]. Stockholm: Liber Förlag.

Liljeström, R., & Dahlström E. (1981). *Arbetarkvinnor i hem-, arbets-och samhällsliv* [Working-class women at home, at work and socially]. Stockholm: Tiden.

Magnusson, D. (1985). Implications of an interaction paradigm for research on human development. *International Journal of Behavioral Development, 8,* 115–137.

Mahler, M., Pine, F., & Bergman, A. (1975). *The psychological birth of the human infant*. New York: Basic Books.

Mannen i förändring. (1985). *Idéprogram från arbetsgruppen om mansrollen* [The changing role of man]. Stockholm, Tidens Förlag.

Myrdal, A., & Myrdal, G. (1934). Kris i befolkningsfrågan. Stockholm.

Nettlebladt, P., Uddenberg, N., & Engelsson, I. (1981). Sex-role patterns. paternal rearing attitudes and child development in different social classes, *Acta Psychiatrica Scandinavica, 64,* 12–24.

Nettlebladt, P. (1981). *The man and his family*. Unpublished thesis, University of Lund. Sweden.

Näsman, E., Nordström, K., & Hammarström, R. (1983). *Föräldrars arbete och Barns villkor - en kunskapsöversikt.* Parents work, children's demands - a review. Forskningsrapport 41. Stockholm: Liber Tryck.

Öberg, G., & Öberg, B. (1985). *Den delade familjen* [The split family]. Forskningsrapport från Pedagogiska institutionen. Stockholm universitet. Nr. 26.

Official Statistics of Sweden (1982). *Women and children—interviews with women about family and work.* Stockholm: National Central Bureau of Statistics.

Paulsen, M., Andersson, S., & Sessler, G. (1975). *Rätten att vara människa* [The right to be a human being] Stockholm: Raben & Sjögren.

Petterson, M. (1981). *Deltidsarbete i Sverige* [Part-time work in Sweden]. Rapport 23, Arbetslivscentrum, Stockholm.

Pleck, J. H. (1983). Husbands' paid work and family roles: current research issues. In H. Lopata & J. H. Pleck (Eds.) *Research in the interweave of social roles (Vol. 3). Families and jobs.* Greenwich, CT: JAI Press.

Qvist, G., (1973). *Statistik och politik. Landsorganisationen och kvinnorna på arbetsmarknaden* [Statistics and politics. Trade unions and women on the labor market. Stockholm: *Tvärsnitt.*

Rödholm, M. (1981). Effects of father-infant postpartum contact on their interaction 3 months after birth. *Early Human Development, 5,* 79–85.

Rödholm, M., & Larsson, K. (1979). Father-infant interaction at the first contact after delivery. *Early Human Development, 3,* 21–27.

Rydin, I. (1981). *Fakta om barn i Sverige* [Facts about children in Sweden]. Rädda Barnen, Akademilitteratur.

Sandqvist, K. (1984). *Jämställda pappor - finns dom.* [Do fathers enjoy equality?]. Paper presented at the Conference for Changes in Family Structure in Sweden.

SOU (1975). *Förkortad arbetstid för småbarnsföräldrar* [Swedish Official Report: Shortened working hours for parents with small children]. No. 62.

SOU (1976). *Roller i omvandling* [Swedish Official Report: Changing Roles]. No. 71.

SOU (1978). *Jämställdhet i arbetslivet* [Swedish Official Report: Sexual equality at work]. No. 38.

SOU (1979). *Kvinnors arbete.* Swedish Official Report: [Women's work]. No. 89.

SOU (1980). *Ensamförälder 1980* [Swedish Official Report. One-parent families 1980]. No. 18.

SOU (1982). *Enklare föräldraförsäkring* [Swedish Official Report: Easier parental insurance]. No. 36.

SOU (1983). *Ensamföräldrarna och deras barn* [Swedish Official Report: One-parent families and their children]. No. 51.

Trost, J. (1983a). *Män och hushållsarbete* [Men and housework]. Rapport från familjeforskningsgruppen, Uppsala universitet. Nr. 3.

Trost, J. (1983b). *Mäns åsikter om ledighet från arbetet* [Men's views on leave of absence]. Rapport från familje-forsknings-gruppen, Uppsala universitet. Nr 3.

Trost, J., & Hultåker, Ö. (1985). Legal changes and the role of fathers: Swedish experiences. *Journal of Marriage and Family, 9.*

Uddenberg, N. (1982). *Den urholkade fadern* [The hollow father]. Stockholm: Wahlström & Widstrand.

Winander, B. (1982). *Jobs in the 80's.* Jobbet i livssammanhanget. stencil [Work in the life contents]. stencil. SIFO, Skrift-serie.

6

Italian Fathers and Infants: Cultural Constraints on Paternal Behavior

Rebecca S. New
Syracuse University

Laura Benigni
Institute of Psychology
Italian National Council of Research

The following discussion of fathers and infants is based on two studies of infant care and development conducted simultaneously in a small industrial town in Central Italy. Together, the two studies produced qualitative and quantitative data on the father's transition to parenthood during pregnancy and childbirth, patterns of father-infant interaction, and attitudes regarding the paternal role in infant care and development during the first year of life (Benigni, Giorgetti, & Sasso, in press; New, 1984). In addition to providing descriptive data on paternal behavior in this Italian sample, goals specific to this chapter are to examine the status of Italian men as fathers and to gain insight into why some fathers, yet not others, choose an active paternal role. This investigation of the paternal role in infancy acknowledges the need for an ecological perspective on human development (Valsiner & Benigni, in press), which in turn mandates the study of paternal behavior within the context in which it occurs. Before presenting findings from the two studies, the chapter will therefore begin with a depiction of the Italian family from a sociohistorical point of view, followed by a review of contemporary research on Italian fathers. The second half of the chapter will proceed with an ethnographic description of family life in this Central Italian town, thereby completing a frame for viewing the findings from these two studies on paternal behavior during infancy.

SOCIOHISTORICAL PERSPECTIVES ON THE ITALIAN FAMILY

Italy as we know it today has been described as at least two countries—the North and the South—(Sirey & Valerio, 1982). Contemporary sociologists (Ardigò & Donati, 1976; Bagnasco, 1977) have defined a "third" Italy, referring to those regions of North-Central Italy that have a homogeneous socioeconomic structure (levels of production, wages, labor market) and cultural traits which, while still traditional, are in the process of modernization (Donati & Cipolla, 1978). It is therefore increasingly difficult to make general statements about the country without acknowledging the enormous dissimilarities in history, language, economic, and sociocultural characteristics (Moss, 1981). Yet several characteristics have been sufficiently documented across Italy to enable a brief historical glimpse of Italian family life, particularly as it influences the nature and extent of the father's contributions to infant care and development. These are: the significance attributed to the family as a social unit (Peristiany, 1977); the ubiquitous strength of kinship ties independent of family structure (Klapisch-Zuber, 1985); and the heritage of "too much mother and not enough father" (Rolle, 1980, p. 113).

For brevity's sake, the following discussion will integrate the largest body of literature—that on the traditional Southern Italian agricultural family—with information on families in the industrial North as well as that recently defined area of Italy (which includes Tuscany, Marche, Umbria, and bordering regions). Patterns or events which are typical of only one of the three geographic regions of Italy will be acknowledged. This historical overview will conclude with a contemporary perspective on the Italian family.

The Centrality of the Family as a Social Unit

The bulk of the literature on the status and conditions of family life in Italy results from fairly recent investigations, with a disproportionate interest in the South (Silverman, 1975). Yet historians have long recognized the power of the Italian family. Certainly, there are ecological reasons why the medieval peasant family rather than the individual formed the fundamental unit of labor, as was the case throughout most of Europe (Herlihy & Klapisch-Zuber, 1978). Yet the continued subjugation of the individual Italian's needs to those of the family goes beyond the economic concerns of traditional as well as contemporary sharecroppers (Kertzer, 1984). The salience of the family has been attributed to sociopolitical factors particular to Italy—specifically, the lack of faith in government institutions (Berkowitz, 1984) amidst the need for dignity and solidarity in the face of continued and varied foreign domination (Sirey & Valerio, 1982). Such a national distinction has been translated into the popular belief that neither the law, the state, nor the Italian society can function if they "interfere with the family's supreme interest" (Barzini, 1964, p. 190). It was the cornerstone of the controversial theory (DeMasi, 1976) of "amoral familism" in which such dedication to the nuclear family was seen as the primary cause of the incapacity of cooperation and the resulting poverty throughout the South (Banfield, 1958).

One of the ways in which this familistic orientation has traditionally been enacted is through the preservation of *la via vecchia* ("the old way of life"). This maintenance of traditional life patterns is especially apparent in rural Italian communities. Within most small towns in Italy, this notion of stability through the family continues to be accepted, evident in such seemingly innocent practices as the use of nicknames. Although nicknames conceivably highlight unique characteristics of individuals, a recent investigation confirmed that nicknames among contemporary Italian families are passed on from one generation to the next for the primary purpose of affirming the family unit (Mabilia, 1980).

Throughout most of this century, Italian civil law continued to assign important powers and functions to the head of the family, and the family as a whole assumed a series of unavoidable social obligations (Acquaviva & Santuccio, 1976). Only within the past decade have these laws changed to acknowledge egalitarian principles and individual rights (Ronfani, 1983). In spite of dramatic modernization processes throughout the country, including the progressive decrease in family size (Livi Bacci, 1977) and the rise in the social status of women, the contemporary family continues to play a central role throughout Italy. As a nation, Italy persists in being described as a "country of families" (Sirey & Valerio, 1982, p. 179).

Family Structure and Extended Family Networks

The Italian family is well-recognized for its ability to adapt to the changing conditions of Italian socioeconomic and political life. Yet the nature and structure of the traditional Italian family remained essentially undocumented other than through novels and biographies (Barbagli, 1984). Historians focused on sociocultural events and studies of great leaders until the beginning of the twentieth century (Moss, 1981). Even then, writings by economic and political historians on the nature of the Italian family have been flawed. For example, the claim that the nuclear family had emerged by the fifteenth century (Goldthwaite, 1968) has been criticized on the basis of the small sample of wealthy families examined, to the exclusion of the "common masses" (Klapisch-Zuber, 1985, p. 3).

During the last two centuries, as interest in the family as a domain of scholarship grew on the part of historians and social anthropologists, a large body of literature accumulated on the patrilineal extended family as a predominant Italian ideal (Paci, 1982). The idealized sharecropper family of central Italy, for example, was ruled by a male head of the senior generation, with two or more conjugal families. A woman would move in with the family of her husband, and was in charge (under supervision of the mother-in-law) of most aspects of running the household. The fluctuation of census reports for such arrangements has been blamed on the desire for independent households by some daughters-in-law as well as the biological constraints of the average short life expectancy for males (Douglass, 1980). Regardless, at the turn of the century these complex households were much more likely to be found in Italian households of *all* occupational categories than elsewhere in Western Europe (Kertzer, 1984).

In the South, this configuration of the family is perceived and described as "an indivisible whole" (Siebert, 1984), and has traditionally precluded any sort of romantic or private relationship between the members of a married couple. Major events within the nuclear family (engagement, marriage, birth of children) are seen as not so much concerned with the couple itself as with the evolution of the relative roles and social behavior of man, woman, and child with respect to their extended families (Littlewood, 1978; Schreiber, 1977).

The bonds that have been described historically as uniting families and kin beyond the physical boundaries of the home are now seen as complex, often only indirectly perceptible, and highly personal as opposed to institutional (Klapisch-Zuber, 1985). Such familial relationships have been extensively documented and described in Italian proverbs and, in fact, represent the most detailed and voluminous category. In support of ethnographic depictions of inevitable conflicts (Berkowitz, 1984), most of these proverbs refer—in positive or negative terms—to the ideal of close and harmonious social ties between the *casa* of close relatives versus those referring, in more ambiguous terms, to social relations beyond the lineal group (Gabaccia, 1984).

For the past 50 years, there has been a clear and steady trend away from the extended family (Mabilia, 1980), paralleling changes—particularly increased industrialization—in the occupational structure of villages throughout Italy (Saunders, 1979). Currently, the debate continues over whether or not the historically low statistical incidence of the extended family household, as well as its current decline, affirms the nuclear family as the basic social unit of Italian society, particularly in the South (Douglass, 1980).

Yet current research suggests that these ties with kinsmen outside the nuclear family, which traditionally remained so strong and so geographically localized that extended family members were considered "far away" if they resided on the other side of town (Kertzer, 1984), continue to be reflected in family life throughout much of Italy. Contact with extended family kin remains a viable option in the North (Saraceno, 1981); a regular family practice in Central Italy which occurs significantly more often than in other Western countries (Paci, 1982); and a hidden feature of life in small Southern Italian towns, leaving little time or reason for couples to develop a relationship among themselves and their children (Siebert, 1984). Thus, interpretations of Italian family life should also continue to be declared inadequate, as was the case with studies of Renaissance families (Klapisch-Zuber, 1985), if the immediate household is the only unit of observation and such kin ties are not taken into account.

Italian Men and Women at Home:
"You Can't Put Two Feet in One Shoe"

Anthropologists and sociologists investigating Mediterranean cultures have concentrated on the dichotomy of men's and women's lives, and publications abound which attempt to support or refute conceptualizations of male dominance and female subservience. The resolution of each claim appears entirely dependent upon the context of the investigation. There is widespread recognition of the official Italian ideology which proclaims "the ultimate authority of the male" as breadwinner, decision maker, and spokesman to the outside world, deserving of deference and respect from not only his children but his wife as well (Berkowitz, 1984, p. 86). Until recently, this ideology has been interpreted legally and economically as a result of the powerful patrilineal bias in Italian legislative thought (Maraspini, 1968). The psychological distance between husband and wife may have been further encouraged by the traditional practice of typically large age gaps between Italian spouses, such that historically the husband and wife have been as far apart in age as a mother and her children (Klapisch-Zuber, 1985).

In spite of this unequal relationship between males and females, it has been argued that Italian women need not necessarily be considered inferior. Instead, the sharp distinction between women's and men's roles may account for what some have described as the relative superiority of women over men within their "assigned sphere of activity"; or, put another way, "what a woman loses on the swings she gains on the roundabouts" (Maraspini, 1968, p. 189). Among ethnographers of the South, such domestic power has matriarchal tones, given that the woman's function is virtually indistinguishable from the family's well-being (Cornelisen, 1976); hence the well-worn expression "The mother *is* the family" (Giovannini, 1981, p. 415). Yet the matriarchal concept has been cited as superficial—given the surrogate quality of the woman's life, her limited resources outside the home, and the fact that what power she had—until recently—was derived from masculine authority (Berkowitz, 1984; Maraspini, 1968).

Conceptions of the Italian father have been challenged as well. The theory of male supremacy has been interpreted as a cultural illusion (Cornelisen, 1976), even though the notion of the paternal authority figure has some historical support. In studies of Tuscans and their families during the thirteenth and fourteenth centuries (Herlihy & Klapisch-Zuber, 1978), upper-class fathers demonstrated their authority regarding the care of infants (particularly sons), assuming major responsibility in deciding whether or not to put them out to a wet nurse, as well as supervising their diet following weaning. As the perception of infant vulnerability changed (from one with a precarious hold on life to one who had some assurance of survival, given adequate attention to physical health), so too did the role of the father. By the fifteenth century (if not before), the primary goal of a good father was to function as a manager of his household's prosperity. The care of infants and children was left to the mother, and the father demonstrated his authority without overt involvement in childcare routines or decisions.

By the eighteenth century, the paternal figure had become victim to frequent attacks by philosophers of the Enlightenment. Responding to the passing of absolutism in Europe, with the goal of arriving at a free and equal society, the family—and the father—came under increasingly close scrutiny (Campanini, 1985). In more recent discussions of the father's position in the family, particularly in the poverty-stricken South, the wife's domestic authority has provided sharp contrast to the inadequacy of the husband's economic endeavors. Intrafamilial behavior in these families has been characterized by rivalry between the husband and the children for the attention of the mother (Parsons, 1970); she has often contributed to this conflict by pitting the children against the father (Rolle, 1980). Yet the myth of the dominant male continues even in Southern Italy. The maintenance of this ideal has been attributed to peasants' resentment of women's social prowess as well as their need to disguise the discrepancy between the father's actual role and the ideal model (Gabaccia, 1984; Rogers, 1975). Outside the South, prestige and importance continue to be attributed to the male's actual contributions to the family. The father's role as chief breadwinner and his status as final authority remain virtually unchallenged.

Ethnographers prone to compromise suggest that Italian families have simply encompassed, simultaneously, both matriarchal and patriarchal principles: The father remains head of the family and guides it in its economic endeavors, while the mother runs the household (Gabaccia, 1984). This complex set of attitudes, which is thought to be derived from religious ideologies as well as cultural role expectations and the dynamics of family structures (Parsons, 1970), fosters strength and power in members of each sex while simultaneously imposing severe restrictions on them (especially in the case of women).

The current state of the Italian family is considered to be in a period of major transition, reflecting changes in the Italian social system in general. Rapid modernization in the past decades has wreaked havoc on the family as well as educational and religious institutions (Fraser, 1981). There has been a noted increase in attempts to set up nuclear family households (or at least to avoid the extended-family phase of the domestic cycle)(Saunders, 1979). Correspondingly, as a result of the women's liberation movement of the 1970s and the social and political push for change stemming from recent laws relevant to family life (abortion, divorce, paternity leave, and family rights), there has been a change in the status of women (Acquaviva & Santuccio, 1976; Ronfani, 1983; Saraceno, 1984; Sirey & Valerio, 1982). Contemporary debate has focused on the future of the family itself, and many assume that the paternal authority figure "is disappearing" (Saraceno, 1976, p. 113). Given the association of somewhat similar social changes in the United States and other Western nations with increased paternal involvement, these transformations within the Italian family might reasonably be expected to increase the odds of paternal involvement in childcare.

This potential has not been realized. In fact, economic pressures in Italy (such as housing shortages and unemployment) are beginning to reverse the trend to more "liberated" (nuclear) households; many women have been forced back to (or continue in) traditional family roles, in part as a result of the weak demand for female labor (Fraser, 1981). These circumstances, in combination with the increasingly specialized tasks facing the contemporary Italian housewife, have resulted in the "professionalization" of the Italian woman's domestic role, one which is enacted in a manner described as rigid and inflexible (Acquaviva & Santuccio, 1976; Balbo & May, 1975-76). This shifting, among highly educated urban families, from a somewhat egalitarian relationship to a lowered status for fathers has been described as representative of a "new matriarchy" (Donati, 1985). Concomitantly, Balbo and others describe the situation of the contemporary woman as *doppia presenza* (double presence) in that she is now expected to manage major responsibilities both in the home and at the workplace (Balbo, 1978). Regardless of whether or not this conception of the mother's role is new or true, few ethnographers disagree with the observation that contemporary Italian women exercise more power and influence in the household than the notion of partriarchy implies (Berkowitz, 1984). Both the mother-centered feature of traditional Italian family life and the increasing professionalization of contemporary woman's domestic role are associated with minimal involvement on the part of the Italian father within the context of childcare.

To summarize, sociohistorical studies on the Italian family concur with respect to the following:

1. Throughout Italy the family has traditionally dominated the individual's interest as well as loyalties.

2. The conception of *la famiglia* goes beyond those nuclear family members sharing a dwelling. In fact, the very term *casa* ("home") refers *not* to the nuclear family but to the intergenerational bilateral group of close kin which, for the young married couple, includes both sets of parents as well as all brothers and sisters, single and married.

3. Italians throughout Italy have clung tenaciously to traditional conceptions of appropriate gender roles, even in cases where the real is far removed from the ideal. The image of the family as father-dominated and mother-centered associates masculine power with the procurement of prestige and income outside the domestic realm, while feminine authority remains confined to interfamilial concerns, including the care of children.

Current literature suggests that these characteristics continue to be applicable to a majority of Italian families. Collectively, these features appear to be mutually supportive, contributing to the successful preservation of *la via vecchia*—the traditional way of life—in many parts of contemporary Italy. The continued availability of the extended family network (in spite of household structure) facilitates the transmission of commonly held values, thereby providing support for family unity. Such intergenerational bonding, however, surely competes with the development of a communicative relationship between husband and wife according to the romantic model (Shorter, 1980). These extended family charac- teristics have been associated in other cultures with the maintenance of tradi- tional values—including gender role specialization—and appear to mitigate against anything other than minimal paternal involvement in childcare (West & Konner, 1976; Whiting & Whiting, 1975). Such findings do not, therefore, bode well for increased participation by Italian fathers in the care of infants and children.

A review of contemporary Italian research including examinations of the pater- nal role follows.

RESEARCH ON ITALIAN FATHERS

Studies focused specifically on the Italian father-child relationship remain excep- tionally rare, and published reports are few. While it is unfortunate that Italian fathers have thus far not been viewed as warranting psychological investigation, there is a small body of research (with reference, albeit brief, to Italian men as fathers) which illuminates some of those very dimensions addressed in this chapter. A majority of these studies has been primarily concerned with contem- porary models of the Italian family, including the marital relationship and the changing role of women in the family setting. Some of these studies were discussed in the previous section; those which specifically address the corre- sponding changes—or lack of them—in the role of the father will be summa- rized below.

Discussions on parenting in Southern Italian families continue to focus on the centrality of the maternal figure and the authoritarian nature of the father (Mar- aspini, 1968). This stability in the division of labor between men and women parallels the continued reference to the greater extended family as "the family" rather than those members of the nuclear family. In a recent field study (Siebert, 1984) examining childcare practices and the relationship between husbands and wives in a small town in Calabria (Southern Italy), the appearance of the nuclear family did not reflect the functioning family model. The network of family ties left little privacy available to the couple. When questioned about their roles as fathers, the men in the Calabria study were unable to describe their specific duties apart from reference to their authority and the abstract notion of helping the mother (while refusing to do housework). The investigators also noted the expressed fear of some to touch their infant(s), a response which was surely reinforced by the social stigma of appearing effeminate, as well as the distaste in "dirtying one's hands."

A similar study (Littlewood, 1978), conducted in a small agricultural town in the region of Puglia, noted that (except for their period of engagement) couples described daily routines which in icated virtually separate lives—a pattern which became more rigid following the birth of their first child. Even in old age, intimate relationships between husband and wife proved difficult, since each spouse described separate roles with respect to their extended families. For example, the social role of *la nonna* ("the grandmother") was exalted, while the role of *il nonno* ("the grandfather") noticeably declined.

Studies conducted in Northern and Central Italy have focused on the potential redistribution of power among adult members as a result of recent transformations in the family. This potential is apparently far from being realized; instead, the move toward an egalitarian relationship between husband and wife has actually resulted in an increase in both the authority and the domestic responsibilities of the mother. This interpretation is supported by several recent investigations on the work loads and daily routines of Northern Italian women. In one study involving 500 families (Saraceno, 1980), the bulk of the household responsibilities—including involvement with children—continued to be assumed by the women, regardless of social class status or maternal employment. While there was a limited tendency for middle-class working women to divide the family work load with the husband, and fathers occasionally assumed the role of playmate, none of the men in a sample of 500 did laundry, mended clothes, or cared for a child who was ill.

The extent to which Italian women have been socialized for, and have accepted, their strictly functional role in the family (Saraceno, 1975) was evident in another study conducted in the same city (Avanzini & Lanzetti, 1980). Among this Milan sample, in which there were numerous family models (including those of a more symmetrical nature), fathers reported spending significantly less time with their children than did the mothers. They also reported a reluctance to send their children to kindergarten or nursery school. The mothers did not acknowledge the discrepancy between their supposed change in status and their increased household responsibilities, and responded to interviews with more traditional responses than did the men regarding both the value of women's work as well as stereotypic sex roles.

Psychosocial aspects of parenting were the focus of a third group of investigators, in which 300 middle-class Trieste couples were interviewed before and after the birth of their first child (Nordio, Piazza, & Stefanini, 1983). The insignificant role of the father was evident in their self-descriptions. They described their activities in expressive rather than instrumental terms, with feeding and cleaning interactions seldom reported. Many of these couples reported less willingness to ask grandparents for assistance. There was also the same hesitation reported in the previous study to send children to nursery school.

Hence, in Northern Italy the scaling down of the authoritarian dimensions of the paternal figure and the reduced dependency on the extended family network (especially in terms of childcare assistance) seem to have resulted in increased demands related to the contemporary woman's domestic role rather than provoking increased participation on the part of fathers. Assistance in the areas of domestic responsibilities appears to come in the form of a "culture of services" (Bianchi, 1982), in which mothers turn to social services such as daycare centers, community health programs, and public playgrounds.

The most extensive findings of minimal paternal involvement in childcare have resulted from an nationwide investigation (representing five different parts of Italy) of parenting responsibilities in 2000 families with young children (CENSIS, 1984). Throughout the sample, the organization of family life remained the mother's responsibility, even if she were employed in a position of high salary and prestige. The father, in contrast, played a marginal role in the care of his children. The major difference in childcare practices between families included in this study was in the tendency on the part of professional couples to have their children cared for outside the home—sometimes, but not always, by familiar resources (relatives, neighbors, or baby-sitters). Working-class families, by contrast, tended to care for infants within the home—a practice that surely reflects the limited access to childcare services in the South (Benigni et al, in press).

In sum, in spite of dramatic differences across Italy in terms of family structure, socioeconomic status, and characteristics of daily living, it appears that the role of the Italian father in childcare remains minimal at best, his contribution as breadwinner deemed necessary and sufficient. Yet we know little more than we did when we started regarding other dimensions of the role the Italian father might play in infant and child development. None of the studies previously mentioned included attention to the patterns of social interaction that characterize the father-infant relationship, the settings in which these interactions typically take place, nor fathers' attitudes regarding their paternal role.

The remainder of this chapter—by nature of its selected focus (fathers' attitudes as well as actual involvement in infant care and social interactions), the research setting (Central Italy), and the research orientation (comparative/developmental)—breaks new ground in the examination of Italian men as fathers. The two studies on which the following discussion is based were characterized by a multi-method approach to data collection, including ethnographic observations, fact-oriented interviews, structured parent-child interactions, and naturalistic observations of infant care patterns and social interactions within sample infants' homes. Findings culled from these sources will be integrated to provide descriptive data on the attitudes, behaviors, and ecological circumstances of 30 fathers of infants during the first year of life.

FATHERS AND INFANTS IN A SMALL TOWN IN CENTRAL ITALY

The Field Site

Both studies to be discussed took place in the same small town of 16,000 inhabitants, approximately 50 km north of Rome, in the region of Lazio. Formerly the site of an Etruscan capital city, the town was rebuilt as a medieval fortress in the ninth century; much of its history is evident in the remaining medieval architecture. The town is situated on a plateau, somewhat isolated from the surrounding countryside where wheat and tobacco as well as vineyards and olive groves are cultivated. Although the area is (and has been) predominantly agricultural, most town residents are now wage earners involved in the production of artistic and industrial pottery. The rapid growth during the 1970s of ceramic factories on the outskirts of town has been a major source of employment to Southern Italian immigrants, and has brought a sense of economic well-being to residents. Census figures from 1981 revealed low unemployment rates, with the female participation in the labor force on par with the rest of Italy, where males outnumber females three to one (Balbo & May, 1975–76; ISTAT, 1983).

Types of housing reflect major social divisions in the community. Working-class families, predominantly Southern Italian *immigranti,* live in either the centuries-old historic center (*Centro Storico*), isolated farms or the new public housing apartments. Middle-class families, most of whom have been town residents for generations, live in condominiums, villas, or the rapidly growing suburbs. Intergenerational cohabitation is rare; the most common household configuration includes four people, with the average household size 3.1 members (ISTAT, 1981). In spite of the changing patterns of town life in the direction of an urban-industrial model, many links with tradition remain.

Family Life in a Small Town

As is characteristic of most small Italian towns, the family as a social unit is nurtured and protected by community norms and daily routines. Adult status for both men and women is typically withheld until they become parents. Such status—or the lack of it—is inferred, in this community, by the continued use of the term *sposi* ("newlyweds") for couples without children, regardless of how long they have been married. The message to young couples is clear in such commonly heard expressions as "A family without children is like a garden without flowers."

The community does more than encourage the formation of family units; it also supports what might be called "family time." The pivotal point of the day is *pranzo* (the midday meal), when all business shut down and workers as well as schoolchildren return home. After this meal, everyone is busy. Men take a nap, play pool, or return to a second place of employment. Children join peer groups, while women return to their domestic tasks. In mid-afternoon, shops slowly reopen while a good proportion of the community—especially adolescents—turns out for the daily stroll up and down the bridge leading west out of town.

In the late afternoon, children again disperse to join friends in the park or to play in the cobblestone streets, while women shop for the evening meal and return to their homes. Men who had participated in the afternoon stroll either return to their homes or, more likely, join each other for a card game and/or conversation at one of the several recreation centers or coffee bars. By sundown, the entire family is together again, and after a light evening meal they typically spend the rest of the evening watching television or visiting with friends and relatives. Children are present during most of the evening, frequently staying up until the entire family goes to bed. Men also use this time as an opportunity for a final *cafe*.

Throughout these daily routines, extended family members are present. Grandmothers supervise children in the park or accompany them on the daily walk; grandfathers take toddlers to the coffee bars to purchase *gelato* ("ice cream"). Aunts, sisters-in-law, and adult female cousins work together in someone's kitchen in the preparation of holiday pastries or the canning of seasonal produce. Entire families, including multiple grandparents, aunts, uncles, and cousins, frequently join together to share an evening meal. For a majority of town residents, the availability of extended family relationships provides a culturally homogeneous network of economic and social support, in spite of the fact that cohabitation rarely occurs other than in the case of a widowed parent or unmarried sibling.

Numerous encounters between adults and children occur during the day, as children of all ages are integrated into the adult social world. While daily routines (particularly mealtimes) serve to bring entire families together, with little or no distinction made between activities which are suitable for children versus those exclusive to adults, adult behavior conforms to previously described gender roles. Even when sharing the same physical setting, men and women are seldom seen in joint participation of normal daily activities. The town square or *piazza* is a center of predominantly male social activity; and several bars, the theaters, and most of the recreation centers are off-limits to women. Men, on the other hand, are seldom seen in the markets, and only the elderly among community males frequent the park benches.

In short, this setting is not only typical of other small towns in Central Italy but reflects those previously described characteristics of the greater Italian culture in terms of its orientation to the family, the continued presence of large extended family networks, and its interpretation of appropriate spheres of male and female activity. As such, it functions as a natural laboratory in which to study Italian paternal behavior.

In spite of the strict sex segregation of the daily routines of adults, ethnographic observations suggested that the Italian men in this community, young and old alike, are considerably more interested in infants and young children than would be predicted on the basis of previous research, and certainly more than males in other Western societies. For example, bank administrators and grocery store clerks not only talked and played with infants accompanying their mothers but appeared, to the foreign eye (New, 1984), to actively seek out such opportunities. School-age boys who might be expected to resist such activities were often seen playing with toddlers who had joined them outside. These observations suggest that there was sufficient masculine interest in young children—coupled with multiple opportunities for men to be with their families—to promote paternal involvement in some fashion. Hence we approached the examination of the father's role in infant care and development with less than clear expectations.

Research Methods

The nature of the two studies to be discussed differed somewhat in terms of sample characteristics (first- vs. second-born) and methodology (structured vs. naturalistic observations). They both, however, shared an interest in fathers and infants, and included attitudinal, behavioral, and contextual data. Detailed descriptions of the two studies are available elsewhere (Benigni et al., in press; New, 1984). For purposes of this chapter, results will be combined when appropriate to present a general picture of the paternal role during infancy.

Description of the Sample

The combined sample included 10 first- and 20 later-born infants of working- and middle-class families. Most of these families were native to the area. Also included in the sample were a number of Southern Italian families, many of whom had lived in the area for more than a decade but, because of the Southern birthplace of their extended families, were still categorized by the community as *immigranti.*

A number of the sample fathers worked in the ceramic industry; other occupations ranged from physician to factory owner to truck driver. Most of the mothers in each sample were employed either before or following marriage, yet only three continued to work after childbirth.

Those families with more than one child still reflected a contemporary trend toward smaller nuclear families. Two children were considered ideal by most parents, and many agreed with one father's remark that "*Uno non basta; due sono troppi*" ("One is not enough; two are too many"). Other than the four sample families which shared their homes with widowed grandparents, the nuclear family household was the norm. As was the case throughout the community, a major characteristic of most sample families was the geographic accessibility of extended family members, including parents, brothers and sisters, in-laws, as well as other relatives. With rare exception, these extended family members lived in the vicinity of sample homes—some within walking distance. Most parents reported weekly if not daily contacts with one or more *parenti* ("kin").

Although the sample size in each study is small, these families are representative of the population in general, sharing employment situations and living conditions with the majority of the town's inhabitants.

Findings will be presented in three parts, begining with observations of fathers' naturally occurring involvement in childcare from birth through the first year of life as well as styles of interaction (assessed in semistructured settings). The second portion of the discussion will focus on psychological dimensions of the father's involvement in infant care and development, including parents' attitudes regarding their respective roles in infancy; and the third will address the issue of individual differences within the sample.

Transition to Fatherhood: Pregnancy and Childbirth

Information regarding the first-time father's role during pregnancy and childbirth was collected via joint and separate interviews with the husband and wife during the third trimester of pregnancy, interviews with a member of the hospital staff following childbirth, and spot observations of parent-infant interaction in the hospital setting. Paternal involvement in subsequent pregnancies was reported by the mothers.

The cultural prescription for parenthood was apparent in the early timing of first birth following marriage (generally less than two years) for couples in both studies. The husband was typically the first to know of the wife's pregnant state, and the good news was quickly passed on to extended family members. Yet the actual pregnancy did not seem to be the subject of great changes or reflection on the part of either the expectant women or their husbands.

When asked about their expectations regarding the impact of the pregnancy (and subsequent childbirth) on their marriage, first-time fathers predicted either no change or a positive one—a closer husband-wife relationship. Most women predicted no change at all, although one mentioned that she expected the mother-child bond to exceed that between husband and wife.

Few women followed any systematic course of prenatal care, with visits to the gynecologist neither frequent nor regular. If the woman was accompanied on such visits, it was by her mother or another female relative rather than her husband. Mothers-to-be were as likely to turn to female relatives for advice during pregnancy as they were to the local gynecologist. Women reported little or no help from their husbands with their domestic responsibilities during even the latter months of pregnancy. The physical demands and psychological dimensions of pregnancy seem to be regarded as the sole concern and responsibility of the mother-to-be.

Only one first-time father was present at the birth of his child. The rest of the fathers were denied access to the delivery room—a situation that was acceptable to most of the women and a majority of the men. Even though rooming-in was in effect at the local hospital (there was no option, given the lack of a nursery), fathers' visits were limited to two 1-hour periods per day, and most saw their newborn infants for the first time during the prescribed "fathers' hour" from 6–7 p.m.

Early interactions between the new father-infant dyads were virtually nonexistent. In those cases where the father approached the child, it was typically at the mother's suggestion or insistence, and interaction sequences were brief. His more likely mode of behavior was to concentrate on his wife.

Fathers were not the only ones who visited the newborns and their mothers during the hospital stay (which typically lasted from 4 to 7 days). With a single exception, members of one or both extended families welcomed the newborns. Grandparents represented a major proportion of the visitors, many of whom were more likely than the father to engage in animated interactions with the infant.

When asked about the type and source of assistance given to the mother upon her return from the hospital, one woman reported aid from her husband with household tasks while the maternal grandmother helped with childcare, and another said that her husband helped with older siblings. In all other cases, female extended family members (mothers, mothers-in-law, sisters, sisters-in-law) were predicted and/or reported to provide assistance with domestic tasks and care of any older siblings. In general, there were no exceptions of paternal assistance in childcare following childbirth.

Patterns of Infant Care and Social Interaction

The following discussion of paternal behavior during infancy is based on two sets of data: a series of naturalistic observations on the second- or later-born infants (New, 1984, in preparation); and semistructured observations on firstborns (Benigni et al., in press). Because the foci and analyses of the two studies varied, their results will be discussed separately.

Naturalistic observations at 3-month intervals in the homes of the second- or later-born infants produced observational data on 90% of the fathers at 4 months; 90% at 7 months; and 75% at 10 months. This high rate of fathers present in the home reflects the degree to which work schedules allowed for family time. These observations revealed a number of physical and social characteristics of the infant care environment, summarized as follows:

1. Infants spent little or no time alone with their mothers, sharing the caretaking environment with a variety of familial and non-familial individuals, including fathers, siblings, neighbors, and extended family members. The amount of social contact, as measured by the number of people recorded during each observation period, was consistently high and frequently involved as many as five or six people in addition to the mother-infant dyad.

2. The number of people observed in the infant care environments resulted in a high level of social activity on the part of the infant. The infant was also the object of a great deal of attention throughout much of the observation. In spite of this attention, there were relatively few instances of playful interaction, with

physical caretaking a more likely focus of this infant-directed activity. Play rarely co-occurred with caretaking tasks and was unlikely to involve objects.

3. Infants had limited opportunities for locomotor exploration throughout the first year of life. Instead, they spent a large portion of their time being held or in some form of restraint apparatus. During the first 6 months, the carriage or infant seat was the most common placement of sample infants. As motor skills increased, several infants had more frequent access to walkers, although not necessarily for purposes of locomotor activity; furniture arrangements were somewhat crowded, and few accommodations were made to encourage exploration of the physical environment. By the end of the first year, when many infants were walking, they still spent, on the average, over half of each observation period in a walker, playpen, or on someone's lap.

4. Mothers assumed virtually all responsibility for the physical care of the infant; socialization was shared by a wide array of other individuals present in the infant care setting (New, 1984).

Given this brief description of the infant care environment, we will now turn to the issue of how, and to what extent, fathers were involved with their infants in this setting.

Paternal Style of Interaction with Infants

Although most of the fathers were off work during the period of observation, they typically only remained in the same room with the infant for brief intervals of time, during which dyadic father-infant interactions were infrequent. Given that a majority of the naturalistic observations took place in the kitchen, it may be that fathers were uncomfortable remaining in a room so clearly associated with female activities. Most fathers, however, appeared to have other things to do; they napped, watched television, or went out for a cup of coffee during those periods of time that they were not at work. When asked if the fathers left the room (or home) because of the observer's presence, most mothers reported that such behavior was typical; fathers rarely remained in the home following meal times. Yet most fathers were relatively infant-focused (directing some sort of behavior to the infant) for much of the time that they were in the same room. This ratio of infant-directed behavior as a proportion of time present in the infant care environment was only exceeded by the mother, who monitored or interacted with the infant for most of the time that she was in the same room (New, in preparation).

Distal rather than proximal behaviors characterized fathers' interactions with their infants; looking and talking represented the bulk of fathers' infant-directed activities. Fathers were more likely to call or whistle from across the room than they were to pick up and play with their infants. When fathers *did* touch their infants, albeit in a tentative and awkward way, they generally did so briefly, only to return to a distant location away from the infant's position. If a father held his infant, it was often while waiting for the mother to prepare the baby's bottle or meal. Such holding was rarely accompanied by conversation or playful interaction.

With a few exceptions, fathers were minimally involved in the physical care of their infants. They had nothing to do with feeding, unless it was to serve as a distraction (whistling, waving a toy) while the mother rapidly spoon-fed the unwary infant. On the rare occasion that a father was observed attempting to groom or dress an infant, his act was generally ridiculed or criticized, and his efforts were either undone or unacknowledged.

Aside from the major difference between the father's behavior and that of the mother in terms of physical caretaking, the father's role was not so clearly articulated when compared to other figures in the caretaking environment. In fact, the distribution of fathers' behaviors at 10 months was identical to that of visiting women; looking and talking were their most common modes of infant interaction, followed by physical contact and holding. Differences were limited to variations in the form of physical contact and in the frequency of holding. Fathers' patterns of physical interactions typically included tickling and poking; they also occasionally assumed a pedagogical role by holding the hands of infants learning to walk. Fathers were the least likely of all adults, including visitors, to hold their infants.

Playful interactions between fathers and infants were infrequent, yet when they occurred they were often similar in form to those of other (non-maternal) women present in the infant care setting. Such interactions were characterized by vigorous physical handling, with infants being tossed, bounced, and playfully spanked. During early infancy, however, fathers were not as likely to participate in such forms of play as were other adults—especially females (aunts, cousins, grandmothers, and next-door neighbors). Mothers were not necessarily averse to this type of interaction; they were just more likely to be involved in other types of infant interactions, specifically those related to physical care.

The overall impression of these observations is that the father served as one among many social partners for the infant, with distal behaviors his predominant mode of activity. The fact that looking represented the major proportion of all the father's infant-directed behavior suggests that the father's interest in the infant was coupled with a hesitancy to demonstrate any more overt behavior. For many fathers, this hesitancy was reinforced by, if not the result of, criticisms of his infant-directed activity. One father, for example, was slapped when he attempted to reach into his infant daughter's mouth to feel for a new tooth. Even when infants turned to their fathers and attempted to initiate social exchanges, they often received little more than a smile and a poke in return. Most fathers behaved as if the most appropriate thing for them to do within the infant care environment was to assist the mother if she needed it prior to or during feeding, but otherwise to stay out of the way.

Videotaped observations of firstborn infants and their parents confirmed the described inhibition on the part of fathers to interact with their infants, including the developing tendency to keep a distance between themselves and their young infants. These observations varied from the naturalistic ones in that they were purposefully scheduled for a time when both parents would be present and the infant would be awake and *already dressed and fed*. The setting, in fact, closely approximated that of "company."

At the time of the first videotaped observations (average infant age: 20 days), fathers in this "neutral" setting touched, tickled, and patted the infant on the average as often as the mothers. The father's style of physical contact was distinguished by the increased likelihood of touching the infant's mouth, while the mother was more likely to touch the feet. Mothers talked more to the infants, yet fathers were equally likely to engage in the highly stylized form of baby talk common to the community. Fathers and mothers were also similar in their frequency of visual contact with the infant, although mothers were more often observed engaged in eye-to-eye contact.

At 2 months, patterns of paternal interaction became more clearly differentiated from those of mothers in several key ways. Mothers increased their frequency of physical contact, exceeding the fathers' use of proximal modes of behavior in all categories. Both mothers and fathers increased their visual monitoring of the infant, with fathers achieving eye-to-eye contact almost three times as often as did the mothers. Fathers also increased their frequency of verbal stimulation to approximately the same rate as the mothers. While mothers used their natural voices more often than fathers to elicit the infant's attention, fathers relied on baby talk for most of their verbal interactions, exceeding the mothers by almost 200% in their use of this exaggerated style of infant communication.

By 6 months, fathers' patterns of distal rather than proximal modes of interaction were clearly established. Their physical contact remained significantly less than that by the mother, with one exception; fathers were the primary source of such behaviors as tickling. Distal interaction on the part of the father was now primarily through looking; he talked only a third as often as did the mother, and his use of baby talk dropped to a lower frequency than the mother's. Most mothers' frequencies of eye-to-eye contact also increased, while the fathers' decreased.

This quality of minimal paternal interaction was further apparent in home observations 6 months later of fathers with their year-old firstborn infants in structured and free-play sessions. Summary characteristics of fathers' interactions in the free-play setting included only the occasional display of a toy without comment or manipulation. When *asked* to play (in the structured setting), more fathers talked about and displayed the toys. An almost equal number, however, made either no or feeble attempts to attract the child's attention, again often merely holding up the toy without comment (Benigni et al., 1986).

Combined results of these two observational studies suggest that these sample fathers were, for the most part, minimally involved in actual infant care and were infrequent interaction partners with infants. Yet most fathers' initial interest in and curiosity about their infants was apparent to observers in both studies. This early paternal interest was manifest in several ways (each more similar to than different from the mother's behavior): fathers watched, talked to, and physically interacted with their infants. However, rather than developing, over time, a strategy of interaction strengthened by experience and familarity, most fathers appeared to move in the direction of an increasingly passive role characterized by, at best, distal behaviors; and, at worst, noninvolvement.

One interpretation of this decreased involvement over the first year of life is simply that the novelty of the new infant had worn off. It is also possible that these fathers were simply more uncomfortable than were the mothers in the presence of the observer and, therefore, inhibited the natural course of their interactions with their infants. Other data, however, suggest that neither of these explanations is sufficient.

Parental Attitudes Regarding the Paternal Role in Infancy

In an effort to gain an understanding of how cultural values and beliefs mediated the paternal role, mothers and fathers (interviewed separately) were asked a number of questions regarding their perceptions of parental responsibilities during infancy.

The stereotype of a father "unable to cope with the fragile infant and un-knowledgeable in the ways of babies" (Lewis & Weinraub, 1976, p. 165) was far from obsolete in this sample. In fact, it was a self-proclaimed reality. Most fathers saw their role in infancy and early childhood as a passive one, with few responsibilities. Particularly in the case of the very young infant, fathers actually expressed fear that they would inadvertently harm the child: "Until six months, I won't *touch* the baby."

At one extreme, several parents (both fathers and mothers) said that fathers should not be involved at all in infant care other than to "give a hand" to the mother. While many noted that the fathers did "*poco o niente*" ("little or nothing"), most said that it was appropriate for fathers to be involved in infant care in some fashion. The involvement was limited, however, by the father's sense of his own competency. With rare exception, fathers decribed themselves as incapable of doing much more than holding the infants. Repeatedly, fathers claimed that the best they could do was to help the mother if she needed it, and that under normal circumstances it was better for all concerned if he stayed out of her way. Mothers reiterated fathers' beliefs about their caretaking competencies, declaring that the father could do little that would be of any help.

When pressed, during the interview, to consider whether or not a father *could* perform some of the caretaking responsibilities traditionally assigned to the mother if, for example, she was suddenly called away from home, less than half of the parents felt that it would be possible. Most men immediately responded to the effect that "I don't know how to do anything," and came up with a workable solution that would relieve them of the necessity of coping with responsibilities which they felt were beyond their capabilities: "I would call my sister" or "my mother" or "my mother-in-law". Mothers agreed that one or more such women would need to come to the rescue.

The mystique surrounding the tasks and responsibilities of infant care was further elaborated when parents were asked to describe characteristics of good and bad parenting. While the general attitude was that "bad mothers don't exist!" the composite picture of a good Italian mother included one who cares for the child, feeds it well, keeps it clean, and always watches to see that it is safe. Fathers, on the other hand, clearly varied in their ability to live up to relatively minimal standards. The paternal characteristic most frequently mentioned by fathers was that they be good providers. They also believed that a good father should serve as a role model and assume responsibility for his children's education. The one specific behavior mentioned by men was that a good father should play with his children. What most mothers wanted was a father who was "interested and involved," yet the level of involvement mothers specified generally only included playing.

The significance attributed to the respective roles of parents varied tremendously. When asked to compare the "unique" contributions of mothers and fathers to infant care and development, few felt that there was anything special that an infant could gain from the father; the only thing mentioned—by three parents—was paternal affection. Mothers, on the other hand, were considered solely capable of performing numerous and essential childcare tasks, including washing, changing, feeding, and "understanding the cries of the child." The differing perceptions of maternal and paternal contributions were highlighted by one mother, who claimed that only a mother "can hide the eventual recognition" that the father pays no attention to the child.

The value-laden features of the maternal role, as opposed to the negligible worth attached to the father's, was also apparent in conversations regarding the primary goals of infant care during the first year of life. Mothers and fathers were uniformly consistent in their perceptions of infants' needs. Three features of infant care were mentioned repeatedly as critical caretaking priorities; these were translated into highly regimented strategies, which were also commonly regarded as markers of good mothering: proper feeding, hygiene, and carefully controlled exposure to fresh air. Each mother acknowledged her sole responsibility for her child's consumption of nutritious foods, and many fathers specifically cited the preparation of infant meals as a task beyond their scope. Both parents typically agreed that "a child doesn't know when it's hungry; only a mother knows for sure."

In spite of the description of the father as playmate, no mention was made—by either parent—of the importance of play during the first year of life. Collectively, these interviews suggest that there were minimal expectations for the father's involvement during infancy, at least in part based on his supposed incompetency. What was expected of him, in terms of play, was not regarded as critical or even necessary to infant development.

Interviews with primiparous parents supported this interpretation, and they identified an additional factor which likely contributed to the general perception of fathers' contributions as insignificant. When fathers of firstborns were asked to describe the types of play activities they shared with their infants, some were able to describe specific routines (hide-and-seek, piggyback, playing in bed in the morning). There was little agreement between the parents, however, and in a number of cases neither the mother nor the father could easily describe the father's playtime activities. Parents also disagreed about the child's preferred mode of play, special toy(s), and favorite household objects. In contrast to the lack of shared recognition and appreciation of father-infant play, parents were in strong agreement regarding the infant's play partners outside the nuclear family. In a majority of cases, the grandparents were mentioned as favored and/or frequent playmates of the infants.

These characteristics of infant care—the emphasis on physical rather than psychological well-being, the rigid interpretation of the strategies for such care, and the frequent presence and involvement of extended family members—were repeatedly mentioned in conversations with fathers and mothers. They were also echoed throughout the home observations in each study.

The concern about infant appearance and hygiene was apparent in the careful monitoring of infant locomotor activity, the length and formal nature of bathing and grooming sessions, and the types of interactions with others permitted by the mother. Siblings were frequently warned not to get infants dirty, and some fathers were treated more as a hindrance than a help in mothers' caretaking endeavors. The extent to which infant care was assumed to require a highly specialized set of skills—beyond the reach of the average father—is apparent in the following vignette of a father and his 2-month-old firstborn infant. This scene (videotape transcription) was typical of those instances in which fathers attempted to assist in the physical care of their infants.

> The child is on the bed, after washing and before feeding. The mother is dressing it. The father is in a corner watching what the mother is doing. The observers are making a video-tape. The mother goes into another room. The father timidly approaches, observes the child, sees his bare feet, looks for his socks in a basket and puts them gently on the child with care and efficiency (the socks are of an old type, handmade with bows, and are very difficult to put on a child who moves). Reassured by his success, the father picks the child up and rocks him slowly and rhythmically, looking at him and trying to obtain eye contact while the child whimpers.
>
> The mother returns, glances at the child, takes him from the father, sits down and, before nursing undoes one of the bows (which cost the father such an effort) and ties it again, obtaining the same result as the father. She then begins nursing. The father observes the scene and appears "mortified." He returns to the marginal position he was occupying at the beginning. (Benigni et al., in press).

While the mother reaps praise and recognition as a consequence of the infant's appearance, this emphasis—and time spent—on aesthetic qualities of the infant's appearance left no room for the unexperienced father to take a more active role in infant care.

It is likely that such feelings of incompetency were also reinforced by the continual presence of other women in the infant care environment. It has already been noted that individuals in addition to the infant's immediate family were present during a vast majority of the home observations; they were also present during most of the parental interviews, even when appointments were made specifically for the mother and father. This level of social density was characteristic of families' daily routines, as verified in Daily Routine Interviews (regarding the previous 24-hour period) conducted at regular intervals through the study (Miller, New, & Richman, 1982). In short, while it was unusual to find the mother alone with the infant, it was highly unlikely that a father would be found in such a dyadic situation. Virtually 100% of his interactions with his infant were with an audience, one that frequently included individuals other than nuclear family members.

It is important to recognize that a majority of these individuals were intimately acquainted with the lives of the sample infants and their families. This familiarity not only facilitated interactions with the sample infants; it also served to increase the father's awareness of his amateur status. Given the highly regulated system of feeding, bathing, and dressing the infants, coupled with the frequent presence of not one, but *several* women (grandmothers, aunts, neighbor women)—all of whom were viewed as more competent at childcare tasks, it is no wonder that most of the fathers kept a distance between themselves and their infants.

The strength of these environmental and attitudinal variables was further highlighted in an analysis of individual differences in the frequency and patterning of paternal involvement.

Individual Differences in Paternal Behavior

Characteristics of the infant care environment, the mother, and the infant were all associated with individual differences in paternal behavior as observed in a subset of the home observations.[1]

In spite of the relative homogeneity of sample families in terms of family size, extended family availability, and socioeconomic characteristics, there were variations within the sample in the social density of the infant care environments. Social density factors (including the presence of other adults, children, and overall social density) were associated with individual differences in patterns of

---

[1]Observations at the 10-month-age point have been subjected to the most extensive data analyses to date (New, 1984).

mother-infant interactions as well as maternal strategies of infant care (New, 1984, 1986). Social characteristics of the infant care environment were therefore considered relative to paternal behavior, and results confirm the necessity of including the context in which fathers must perform in any examination of their behavior.

Room density (a measurement of the average number of people present during the observation) had no impact on the frequency of paternal involvement with the infant. It did, however, influence the quality of his interaction. High room density was negatively related to embellished paternal interactions (characterized by play, talking, affectionate and expressive gesturing) and positively associated with a more routine style of father-infant interactions (physical interactions without any social embellishment).

A second environmental variable took into account not only the number of people present but also the extent to which they were involved with the infant, potentially competing with the father for the attention of the infant. In cases of high interaction density (measured by the number of individuals per 5-second interval who directed behaviors to the infant), fathers did little more than hold their infants; they were significantly more routine in their behaviors (physical with few embellishments).

While there were no significant differences in the behavior of infant males and females, both mothers and fathers showed a tendency to respond to their infants in stereotypic fashion. Mothers of males were more likely to stimulate and respond to their infants with physical behavior than were mothers of females. Fathers of females were significantly more embellished in their infant interactions than were fathers of males.

Fathers were influenced by the mothers' styles of infant care and interaction. Infants receiving more embellished interactions from their mothers were less likely to participate in only routine types of interaction with their fathers.

Other differences in paternal involvement in infant care were associated with maternal education—even though there was great variability in paternal education (one father had only 3 years of elementary school, while another had completed medical school). Out of 20 women, 14 had only completed 5 years of schooling. Of the 6 remaining women, 4 had graduated from high school; 3 of these had attended college for at least 1 year.

Husbands of the more educated women in the sample were more active participants in infant care both in terms of the overall frequency of their infant interactions as well as their actual involvement in physical care tasks such as dressing and feeding the infant. These differences were reflected in paternal attitudes as well as behaviors, and two of these men were able to articulate some of the reasons behind their behavior. One father explained that it wasn't fair for his wife to have to do all of the work associated with childcare. Another declared that the father should "be involved in everything about the baby, because it is fundamental for the infant to sense the father's presence." He went on to explain that there "should not be a difference between the roles of the mother and the father; I can do everything except prepare the baby food." Each expressed the belief that their contributions were significant, and their wives agreed. These two wives were the most educated mothers in the sample; both were employed as schoolteachers. They were unique in declaring their husbands to be capable of doing what they did in terms of infant care. The wife of the father who exempted himself from planning the infant's meals explained that it was not a matter of skill; he simply did not understand what the infant liked. While this couple agreed to let the mother be in charge of the menu, this father was frequently observed feeding and dressing his infant, without interruption or criticism from the mother. She, in turn, acknowledged the unusual nature of his involvement, noting that "in Naples, this would be a revolution."

This family was atypical among other families in this sample in several respects, including the number of years of the mother's schooling (she was the only woman with a college degree) and the degree of paternal involvement in infant care. It was also the single nuclear family unit that functioned without reliance on extended family members. Both sets of grandparents and most other relatives lived in Naples, more than a day's drive away. The absence of such extended family members was apparent in the infant care environment; other differences were noted as well. Strategies for infant care were characterized by increased opportunities for infant autonomy and exploration. The infant in this family was the only one observed, at 10 months, feeding herself small portions of food which were cut up and displayed on her high-chair tray. This infant also had a specially designated drawer in the kitchen for her toys, to which she had frequent access.

While this single case hardly merits any conclusive interpretations, it is worth noting that increased participation on the part of the father was also associated with a marked deviation from other traditional characteristics of infant care in this community, such as the involvement of extended family members and the emphasis on physical care over other aspects of infant development. Without denigrating the father's role in implementing some of these changes, within the total sample maternal rather than paternal education was more predictive of such attitudinal, behavioral, and environmental differences.

DISCUSSION

Collectively, these findings suggest that (a) a majority of these Italian fathers saw their role in infancy as fundamentally minimal; (b) forces within the larger social and cultural context helped to maintain that attitude and discourage further involvement; and (c) variations in paternal behavior were associated with ideological differences as well as deviations from traditional Italian patterns and strategies of infant care.

Fathers' behavior with their infants varied in several ways from that reported in a number of Western studies. Observations of American primiparous fathers have described them as eagerly holding and interacting with their newborn infants (Parke, 1981). In this Italian sample, fathers had to be prompted by the mothers to do more than merely approach the infant. Their subsequent patterning of physically vigorous interactions was more typical of the "paternal style" described by other Western investigators (Belsky, 1979; Lamb, 1977, 1981). In this sample, however, that style was shared with a variety of non-maternal females, including aunts, grandmothers, and next-door neighbors. On the average, these women did as much (if not more) talking, holding, physical stimulation, and play with objects as did fathers.

Such results are congruent with other research on fathers, including the empirically based finding that the presence of the extended family within the caretaking environment is associated with less contact between fathers and children (Whiting & Whiting, 1975). Relatives appeared, in several instances, to overwhelm the father in his attempts to interact with his infant and virtually crowd him out of the situation. Such effects have previously been noted in examinations of father-infant interactions in triadic settings (e.g., Clarke-Stewart, 1978; Pedersen, 1981). The presence of other adults—particularly women—also likely contributed to the fathers' feelings of incompetence; such negative self-esteem has been associated with fathers' reduced involvement in infant care (Gamble & Belsky, 1982).

It remains rare for fathers to be questioned regarding their values or perceptions of their child care roles (Eisikovits, 1983), and ideological variation within a sample is not often acknowledged. Yet attitudinal differences are frequently associated with variations in other measures (Blurton-Jones, Woodson, & Chisholm, 1979). Maternal education is one independent variable that has been associated with paternal attitudes as well as behavior (Russell & Radin, 1983). One hypothesis concerning the influence of maternal education on child development which derives support from this study is that women who are more educated select husbands who share similar goals regarding childrearing (LeVine, 1980). Not only was there generally strong agreement between educated mothers and the involved fathers in this sample regarding infant care strategies; the more educated mothers also structured the infant care environment in ways that had consequences for their own behavior as well as that of their infants and their husbands (New, 1984).

Within this sample, most mothers deviated from the national trend of Italian women—who are becoming less likely to interrupt working activities because of marriage or childbirth (Battistoni, 1985). Yet their behavior was in conformity with previous studies noting that parenthood has a conservative impact on gender roles (Lamb, 1978). Of those women who returned to work, the two with the greatest amount of education were also the two who were most willing to share their domestic responsibilities with their husbands. These findings support the observation that women's education has a unique potential to affect the seemingly inflexible nature of the relationship between Italian women and their families. It has been suggested that *only* when a woman sees a role for herself outside of the family can she afford to share the parenting role with the father (Berkowitz, 1984). Given the growing practice in Italy for women to continue their schooling to a level equal to if not greater than their husbands, it seems reasonable to hypothesize that increased maternal education may be one of the strongest predictors of, and factors influencing, paternal involvement in childcare.

In conclusion, three features of family life and infant care in this community, evident in both samples, contributed to the diminutive role which fathers played in the care of their infants. Two of these features were discussed in the introductory section on Italian families: the extensive involvement of extended family members in the activities of the nuclear family; and the culturally prescribed gender roles for men and women with respect to child care. The third factor which hampered these fathers' efforts to take a more active role in infant care was the rigidly interpreted and monitored norms of infant care, in which physical aspects of the infant's well-being were of issue. In the case of Italian parenting, "everyone knows that a mother's responsibility may not be shared" (Moss & Campanini, 1960, p. 30). Among this sample, this belief was reflected in gender role assignments and perceptions of competency. Only the mother was considered capable of understanding the idiosyncracies of the developing infant; the father, regardless of whether he was willing, was simply deemed not able.

Our primary goal in this chapter has not been merely to identify the extent to which this small town reflects the patterns of family life and the paternal role attributed to greater Italy. Instead, we have hoped to reveal the *process* through which these factors influence fathers' perceptions, attitudes and behaviors in infant care and development.

In this sample, the paternal role was inextricably bound with other aspects of the culture, including family relationships, gender roles, and priorities of infant care. These cultural values, frequently cited as severely restrictive of Italian women, can also be seen as limiting a father's options with his children. Changes in the direction of increased paternal involvement in Italian infant care are not likely to take place without concommitant changes in these other domains.

ACKNOWLEDGMENTS

Each of the studies reported in this chapter was made possible through the cooperation of the Istituto di Psicologia del Consiglio Nazionale d elle Ricerche, Rome, Italy. Financial support was provided to the first author by a Sinclair Kennedy Traveling Grant from Harvard University; support was also provided via grants to Robert A. LeVine from the Population Council, the John D. and Catherine T. MacArthur Foundation, and the Spencer Foundation.

REFERENCES

Acquaviva, S. S., & Santuccio, M. (1976). *Social structure in Italy: Crisis of a system.* Boulder, CO: Westview Press.

Ardigò, A., & Donati, P. (1976). *Famiglia e industrializzazione.* [Family and industrialization.] Milan: Franco Angeli.

Avanzini, B. Barbero, A. & Lanzetti, C. (Eds.). (1980). *Problemi e modelli di vita familiare—a study in the urban environment.* [Problems and models of family life. A study in the urban environment.] Milan: Vita e Pensiero.

Bagnasco, A. (1977). *Tre Italie: La problematica territoriale dello sviluppo italiano.* [Three Italies: Territorial debate on the development of Italy.] Bologna: Il Mulino.

Balbo, L. & May M. P. (1975-76). Woman's condition: The case of postwar Italy. *International journal of sociology,* Vol. V (4), 79–102.

Balbo, L. (1978). La doppia presenza. [The double presence.] *Inchiesta,* 32, 7–11.

Banfield, E. C. (1958). *The moral basis of a backward society.* Glencoe, IL: Free Press.

Barbagli, M. (1984). *Sotto lo stesso tetto.* [Under the same roof.] Bologna: Il Mulino.

Barzini, L. *The Italians.* (1964). New York: Atheneum.

Battistoni, L. (1985). Female work trends. Report to the conference on "The family in Italy," Rome, 29–30, October. ISTAT—National Population Committee, Preliminary Draft.

Belsky, J. (1979). Mother-father-infant interaction: A naturalistic observational study. *Developmental Psychology,* 15(6), 601–607.

Benigni, L., Giorgetti, A., & Sasso, S. (in press). The ecology of fathering in a small Italian town. To appear in J. Valsiner (Ed.), *Cultural context and child development.* New York: Ablex.

Berkowitz, S. G. (1984). Familism, kinship and sex roles in Southern Italy: Contradictory ideals and real contradictions. *Anthropological Quarterly,* April, Vol. 57:2, 83–91.

Bianchi, M. (1982). La produzione femminile: famiglia e settore dei servizi. [Female production: Family and social services.] In L. Balbo & M. Bianchi (Eds.), *Ricomposizioni.* Milano: Franco Angeli.

Blurton-Jones, N., Woodson, R. H., & Chisholm, J. S. (1979). Cross-cultural perspectives on the significance of social relationships in infancy. In H. R. Schaffer & J. Dunn (Eds.), *The first year of life.* London: Wiley & Sons.

CENSIS—Ministry of the Interior. (1984). The condition of childhood between family and institutions. Rome: Ufficio Studi Ministero dell'Interno.

Clarke-Stewart, K. A. (1978). And daddy makes three: The father's impact on mother and young child. *Child Development, 49,* 466–478.

Cornelisen, A. (1976). *Women of the shadows.* Boston: Little, Brown, & Co.

De Masi, D. (1976). Arretratezza del Mezzogiorno e analisi sociologica. [Backwardness of the South and sociological analyses.] In E. C. Banfield (Ed.), *The moral basis of a backward society.* Glencoe, Ill.: Free Press.

Donati, P. (1985). Paper read at the conference "The paternal image in the new family dynamics." Milan, Universitá Cattolica, 17 October.

Donati, P., & Cipolla, C. (1978). *La donna nella terza Italia.* Roma: Editrice A. V. E., 1978.

Douglass, W. A. (1980). The South Italian family: A critique. *Journal of Family History, 5*(4), Winter, 338–359.

Eisikovits, R. (1983). Paternal child care as a policy relevant social phenomenon and research topic: The question of values. In M. E. Lamb and A. Sagi (Eds.), *Fatherhood and family policy.* Hillsdale, NJ: Lawrence Erlbaum Associates.

Fraser, J. (1981). *Italy: Society in crisis; Society in transformation.* London: Routledge & Kegan Paul Ltd.

Gabaccia, D. R. (1984). *From Sicily to Elizabeth Street: Housing and social change among Italian immigrants, 1880-1930.* New York: State University of New York.

Gamble, W. C., & Belsky, J. (1982). *The determinants of parenting within a family context: A preliminary analysis.* Paper presented at International Conference of Infant Studies, Austin, TX.

Giovannini, M. J. (1981). Woman: A dominant symbol within the cultural system of a Sicilian town. *Man, 16,* 408–26.

Goldthwaite, R. A. (1968). *Private wealth in Renaissance Florence: A study of four families.* Princeton, NJ: Princeton University Press.

Herlihy, D., & Klapisch-Zuber, C. (1978). *Tuscans and their families: A study of the Florentine catasto of 1427.* New Haven: Yale University Press.

ISTAT. (1981). General census of the population 25 October 1981, 2. Data on the structural characteristics of the population and the dwelling places. Tome 1. Dossier for the province of Viterbo.

ISTAT. (1983). Population and movement of population in the communes from 1964 to 1980. *Yearbook of demographic statistics 1982 and 1983.*

Kertzer, D. I. (1984). *Family life in central Italy, 1880–1910.* New Jersey: Rutgers University Press.

Klapisch-Zuber, C. (1985). *Women, family, and ritual in Renaissance Italy.* Chicago: University of Chicago Press.

Lamb, M. E. (1977). Father-infant and mother-infant interaction in the first year of life. *Child Development, 48,* 167–181.

Lamb, M. E. (1978). Influence of the child on marital quality and family interaction during the prenatal, perinatal, and infancy periods. In R. Lerner & G. Spanier (Eds.), *Child influences on marital and family interaction: A life-span perspective.* New York: Academic Press.

Lamb, M. E. (Ed.). (1981). *The role of the father in child development.* Rev. 2nd ed. New York: Wiley.

LeVine, R. A. (1980). Influence of women's schooling in maternal behavior in the Third World. *Comparative and International Education Society.*

Lewis, M., & Weinraub, M. (1976). The father's role in the infant's social network. In M. E. Lamb (Ed.), *The role of the father in child development.* New York: Wiley.

Littlewood, B. (1978). South Italian couples. In M. Corbin (Ed.), *The couple.* Harmondsworth: Penguin Books.

Livi Bacci, M. (1977). *History of Italian fertility during the last two centuries.* Princeton, NJ: Princeton University Press.

Mabilia, M. (1980). Family structure and the use of nicknames in a community of upper Padua. *Rassegna Italiana di Sociologia, 21*(4), Oct–Dec, 585–605.

Maraspini, A. L. (1968). *The study of an Italian village.* Paris: Mouton & Co.

Miller, P., New, R., & Richman, A. (1982). *Social ecology of infant development in Italy and America.* Paper presented at International Conference on Infant Studies, Austin, TX, March.

Moss, L. W. (1981). The South Italian family revisited. *Central Issues in Anthropology, 3*(1), 1–16.

Moss, L. W., & Cappannari, S. C. (1960). Patterns of kinship, comparaggio, and community in a South Italian village. *Anthropological Quarterly, 33,* 24–32.

New, R. (1984). *Italian mothers and infants: Patterns of care and social development.* Unpublished doctoral dissertation. Harvard University, Cambridge, MA.

New, R. (1986). *Social density factors and Italian infant care.* Paper presented at International Conference of Infant Studies, Los Angeles, CA. April.

New, R. (in preparation). Socialization of the Italian infant: Family and friends together.

Nordio, S., Piazza, G., & Stefanini, P. (1983). *Diventar padri.* Milan: Franco Angeli.

Paci, M. (1982). *La struttura sociale italiana.* Bologna: Il Mulino.

Parke, R. D. (1981). *Fathers.* Cambridge: Harvard University Press.

Parsons, A. (1970). Is the Oedipus complex universal? In W. Muensterberger (Ed.). *Man and his culture: Psychoanalytical anthropology after totem and taboo.* New York: Taplinger Publishing Co.

Pedersen, F. A. (1981). Father influences viewed in a family context. In M. E. Lamb (Ed.), *The role of the father in child development*. Rev. 2nd. ed. New York: Wiley & Sons.

Peristiany, J. G. (Ed). (1977). *Mediterranean family structures*. Cambridge: Cambridge University Press.

Rogers, S. C. (1975). Female form of power and the myth of male dominance: A model of female-male interaction in peasant society. *American Ethnologist, 2,* 727–756.

Rolle, A. (1980). The Italian Americans: Troubled Roots. New York: The Free Press.

Ronfani, P. (1983). Sociologia del diritto di famiglia. [Sociology of family law.] *Ressegna delle Ricerche sulla famiglia italiana, 1.* Milano: Vita e Pensiero.

Russell, G. & Radin. (1983). Increased paternal participation: The fathers' perspective. In M. E. Lamb and A. Sagi (Eds.), *Fatherhood and family policy*. Hillsdale, NJ: Lawrence Erlbaum Associates.

Saraceno, C. (1975). The vicious circle of the contemporary family: The family makes the mother, the mother makes the family. *La Critica Sociologica, 35,* Autumn, 8–18.

Saraceno, C. (Ed.). (1976). *Anatomia della famiglia*. [Anatomy of the family.] Bari: De Donato.

Saraceno, C. (Ed.). (1980). *Il lavoro mal diviso?* [work poorly divided.] Bari: De Donato.

Saraceno, C. (1981). Family models. In Aa. Vv. *Ritratto di famiglia degli anni '80.* Bari; Laterza.

Saraceno, C. (1984). Shifts in public and private boundaries: Women as mothers and service workers in Italian daycare. *Feminist Studies, 10*(1), Spring, 7–29.

Saunders, G. R. (1979). Social change and psychocultural continuity in Alpine Italian family life. *Ethos, 7*(3), Fall, 206–231.

Schreiber, J. M. (1977). Birth, the family, and the community: A South Italian example. *Birth and the Family, 4,* 153–157.

Siebert, R. (1984). *Le ali di un elefante*. [The wings of an elephant.] Milan: Franco Angeli.

Shorter, E. (1980). La transformazione del corteggiamento. [The transformation of courtship.] In M. Buonanno (Ed.), *Le funzioni sociali del matrimonio*. Milano: Edizioni di comunità.

Silverman, S. (1975). *Three bells of civilization: The life on an Italian hill town*. New York: Columbia University Press.

Sirey, A. R., & Valerio, A. M. (1982). Italian-American women: Women in transition. *Ethnic Groups, 4,* 177–189.

Valsiner, J., & Benigni, L. (in press). Naturalistic research and ecological thinking in the study of child development. *Developmental Review*.

West, M. M., & Konner, M. J. (1976). The role of the father: An anthropological perspective. In M. E. Lamb (Ed.), *The role of the father in child development*. New York: Wiley.

Whiting, B. B., & Whiting, J. W. M. (1975). *Children of six cultures: A psychocultural analysis*. Cambridge, MA: Harvard University Press.

7 The Father's Role in Early Irish Socialization: Historical and Empirical Perspectives

J. Kevin Nugent ´
University of Massachusetts at Amherst,
and
The Children's Hospital,
Harvard Medical School

INTRODUCTION

In efforts to develop an indigenous empirical tradition in the behavioral sciences, historical, literary, economic, and artistic sources can inform our scientific investigations of human behavior. The intuition, imagination, and feelings of the writer on the one hand, or the records of the historian on the other, can serve to illuminate aspects of behavior as convincingly as the scientist's measures can. The literature, poetry, and history of a culture become, therefore, a rich source of hypotheses which can suggest appropriate empirical investigations and can, in turn, sensitize the investigator to the complex history of the behavior or institution to be studied. This complementary focus is extremely helpful for the study of fathers and fatherhood within a particular culture, since the historical approach enables the investigator to trace the history of fatherhood in context as it emerged and developed over time. This, in turn, should contribute to a deeper appreciation of the role of different economic and cultural factors in shaping the nature of father-child relations over the course of history. Although the invariant aspects of fatherhood are biologically based, there is convincing evidence that the nature of fatherhood has been shaped and reshaped by cultural forces over time. Fatherhood is, as historian John Demos argues, a cultural invention (Demos, 1983). The style and quality of fathering is subject to the constraints, influences, and opportunities that each particular social-historical epoch presents. Applying an historical approach to the study of fatherhood in Ireland, this investigation attempts to describe and reconstruct the father's role in the evolution of parent-child relations in Irish society and then to examine the cultural and socially operative factors that may have contributed to its development. This approach is, however, fraught with difficulty because of the fragmentary and anecdotal nature of the sources. Moreover, many of these sources are largely the work of the upper class or aristocracy, so that the problem of representativeness is an inescapable methodological problem. The end product of such an endeavor may be a series of informed guesses, or what John Demos calls "a hypothetical history." A further limitation in applying an historical approach to this study is the reliance on secondary published sources. (A comprehensive historical study of father-child relations in Ireland remains to be done.) In this study of Irish fathers, the historical-cultural analysis serves as the context for the generation of hypotheses which were then tested out in an empirical study of Irish fathers and their children.

FATHERS IN EARLY IRISH HISTORY

Even up to the first half of the fifteenth century, the island of Hibernia (Ireland) was thought to be the boundary of the known world. It was this geographic isolation, situated as it was "at the remote corner of the farthest borders of the world," which led Giraldus Cambrensis (Gerald of Wales) to Ireland in 1184, to examine its customs and its people, in order "to explore the primitive origin of its race" (Gerald of Wales, p. 31, 1982). Ireland alone of all the Western European nations did not fall under Roman domination, so that its location at the far edge of the European continent and the absence of a Roman tradition distinguished its social and political organization from that of England or continental European societies of the period.

Within Ireland itself the very shape of the island made for unity of culture, since the central plains and lakelands offered no formidable barrier to the spread of new ideas once they had become established in the country (dePaor & dePaor, 1978). From the beginning of recorded history, there was unity of culture and language in Ireland. The country had its own native legal system, the Brehon Laws, which provided an elaborate classification of what was forbidden or permitted.

The primary unit of early Irish society was not the individual citizen but the kinship group of four generations, known as the *Derphine,* comprising all those related to one another up to second cousins. Since there was no centralized authority, custom and tradition were the agencies of order and one's kindred was the enforcing authority. This complex system of kinship was accompanied necessarily by detailed descriptions of the obligations of parents toward their children and towards each other. We are fortunate in having a rich body of legal, genealogical and historical materials compiled by the *Aes Dana,* the special class of poets and jurists, which include descriptions of the social organization of early Irish society.

Under the Brehon Laws, women had extensive civil rights. The common form of marriage was known as *Lánamnas Comthinchuir*, in which both parties contributed jointly to the marriage goods. Both husband and wife retained the ultimate ownership of what each had contributed for the duration of the marriage. The law tract describes the woman as *Comthigerna*, "a woman of equal lordship," "a woman of joint dominion."

Children's rights were also protected. With few exceptions, children were regarded as legitimate and their rights recognized under the law. (It was only when the Brehon Laws were finally replaced by English Common Law in the seventeenth century that illegitimate children were referred to as "base children" and ruled ineligible to share in the family inheritance.) The obligations of fathers toward their children were described in the Brehon Laws. Both parents were bound to share the responsibilities and expenses of rearing the children, and if either partner became sick or died, then the full responsibility and expenses of childcare fell to the other partner. The father, therefore, was expected to take over all the parenting responsibilities in the absence of the mother (Ō'Corráin, 1979).

It is extremely difficult to reconstruct the emotional texture of father-child relations from these Brehon Laws, since they may merely reflect the egalitarian ideals of a sophisticated and learned class of jurists. On the other hand, given their status as being mainly descriptive, it could be that they represent the actual social conditions of family life in Ireland before the twelfth century.

FAMILY CHILD RELATIONS IN MEDIEVAL TIMES

In the medieval poem *Buile Suibhne*, composed between 1200 and 1500, we are able to go beyond the jurist-made Brehon Law to take a closer look at the emotional texture of the *Derphine* in general and the father-child relationship in particular. The poem has its origins in literary and historical sources dating back to the time of the battle of Moira in 637 A.D. In that year, a battle was fought on the plains of Moira in Ulster, where the king of Dal-Aire, Suibhne (Sweeney) was defeated. Cursed by St. Ronan, the king became insane and imagined himself transformed into a bird. Moving from tree to tree he spent the rest of his days wandering over the length and breadth of Ireland. Lynchseachán, Sweeney's foster brother, followed him and tried to coax him to return to his tuath and his kinfolk. In the following passage from Seamus Heaney's (1983) version, we see Lynchseachán appeal to Sweeney's deepest feelings as a kinsman and a father:

> "Have you any news for me about my country?"
> "I have indeed, said Lynchseachán, for your father is dead."
> "That is a seizure, he said."
> "Your mother is dead too, said the young man."

"There'll be pity from nobody now, he said."
"Your daughter is dead, said Lynchseachán"
"The heart's needle is an only daughter," said Sweeney.
"And your son who used to call you 'daddy'," said Lynchseachán.
"Indeed," he said, "that is the drop that fells me to the ground."

The poem continues:

> *Lynchseachán:*
> "This telling what I would keep back
> wounds me to the very quick!
> In Dal-Aire, everyone
> Mourns the death of your son.
>
> *Sweeney:*
> Ah! Now the gallows trap has opened
> that drops the strongest to the ground!
> A haunted father's memory
> of his small boy calling 'daddy!'
> This is a blow I cannot stand.
> This sorrow is the one command
> I must obey. His death fells me,
> defenseless, harmless, out of the tree."

Sweeney's deeply felt grief at the death of his children can be contrasted with the apparent absence of bereavement in the face of a child's death that characterized parents' attitudes toward children in medieval Europe at that time (Aries, 1962; de Mause, 1974; Shorter, 1977; Stone, 1979). In his historical review of parental attitudes towards children in Western Europe, Aries argues that the exploitation and abandonment of young children was commonplace up to the Middle Ages, while Shorter and Stone conclude that parental indifference to young children characterized both English and European society even up to the seventeenth century. Sweeney's tender expressions of grief for his children and the use of the title "daddy" by his son — hitherto considered to be a relatively recent, seventeenth century phenomenon (Aries, 1962) — may reflect the unique quality of parent-child relations under the Brehon Laws in Gaelic Ireland. While allowing for some variance within the society, it is likely that since the goals and underlying values of the society were held in common, the style and quality of Sweeney's relationship with his children may reflect the orientation of an integrated society, which Toynbee refers to as the "Far Western Christian Civilization" (Toynbee, 1954).

In describing family relations in twelfth century Ireland, Giraldus Cambrensis (Gerald of Wales, 1982) was uncompromising in his criticism of the influence of the pagan Brehon Laws on the lives of the people. Giraldus' anthropological descriptions of Irish customs include diet and sleeping arrangements, agricultural practices and musical instruments, hair fashion and childcare. As a reforming ecclesiastical visitor, he was particularly critical of parents for their failure to swaddle their infants, a custom which was normative in more "civilized" English and European societies.

> I have thought it not superfluous to say a few things about the nature of this people both in mind and body, that is to say, of their mental and physical characteristics.
>
> To begin with: when they are born, they are not carefully nursed as is usual. For apart from the nourishment with which they are sustained by their hard parents from dying altogether, they are for the most part abandoned to nature. They are not put in cradles, or swathed; nor are their tender limbs helped by frequent baths or firmed by any useful art. The midwives do not use hot water to raise the nose, or press down the face, or lengthen the legs. Unaided nature according to her own judgement arranges and disposes without the help of any art the limbs that she has produced.
>
> As if to prove what she can do by herself she continually shapes and moulds, until she finally forms and finishes them in their full strength with beautiful upright bodies and handsome and well-complexioned faces (Gerald of Wales, p. 100).

Since Ireland, Giraldus pointed out, was at the remote corner of the farthest border of the known world, it was this isolation that served to explain the idiosyncrasies of Irish customs and childcare patterns.

In the second half of the twelfth century, the cultural unity of Gaelic Ireland was broken by the Norman invasion. For the next four centuries after the Norman conquest and partial colonization, two traditions—Gaelic and Anglo-Irish—lived side by side, each with its own political and social structure (Nicholls, 1972). Within the Gaelic community, the Brehon Laws remained constant, while English Common Law created a new social structure in the colonized parts of the country (Ó 'Corráin, 1978). By the end of the sixteenth century, with the Elizabethan conquest of Ireland, the old Gaelic order had virtually disappeared. The influence of the Brehon Laws had declined and had been gradually replaced by English Common Law.

THE INFLUENCE OF ENGLISH COMMON LAW AFTER 1600

Under the influence of English Common Law, the *Fine* (the joint extended family), was slowly replaced by the nuclear family unit, so that the nuclear family began to emerge as the primary unit of society in Ireland. By the eighteenth century, visitors to peasants' cabins reported that at night:

> The floor is thickly strewn with fresh rushes, and stripping themselves entirely the whole family lie down at once and together, covering themselves with blankets if

they have them, if not, with their day clothing, but they lie down decently and in order, the eldest daughter next the wall farthest from the door, then all the sisters according to their ages, next the mother, father and sons in succession and then the strangers, whether the travelling pedlar or beggar; thus the strangers are kept aloof from the female part of the family, and if there is an apparent community, there is great propriety of conduct. (Quoted in MacLysaght, 1979, p. 66).

This passage reveals no evidence of any kin group; the family unit had become nuclear, consisting only of father, mother, and children. Under English Common Law, women were described primarily in domestic terms as both wife and mother. Men's sphere became exclusively identified with the world of commerce and work. Inevitably, parent-child relations were transformed, and these changes began to appear in Gaelic society. As early as 1690, an Irish work entitled *Parliament na Mban* ("the parliament of Women") describes women as "ag tréigion an uile gnótha agus maithis puiblíghe, ag fanamhain go cónaightheach annsa mbaile, ag tabhairt aire dár gcoigil is dár maidí sníghe" ("withdrawing from all public affairs, remaining always at home, attending to our distaffs and our spindles"). There is evidence to suggest that even among the cottier and laboring classes from the early eighteenth century on, the family was withdrawing from community life. Women were written about more and more in domestic roles as both wives and mothers.

In the dominant genre of Gaelic poetry during this period, the *aisling* or "dream poem," we have the very personification of an idealized, passive female, who waits for her male deliverer to free her from captivity. Aodhagán Ó Rathaille (1675–1729) describes her this way: "Clóite lag beigh sí gan preab go bhfillfidh Mac an Cheannaí." ("She will be weak, depressed and lifeless until her deliverer returns.") (O Tuama, 1981). However, as if to underscore the coexistence of contrasting attitudes towards women within Gaelic Irish society, Bryan Merryman (1749–1803) in his classic Irish poem *Cúirt an Mheán Oíche* ("The Midnight Court") calls for the reinstatement of women to their traditional role in Irish society, as independent and politically active (Ó' Tuathaigh, 1979).

FATHERS IN 19TH- AND EARLY 20TH-CENTURY IRELAND

The persistence of small-scale agriculture and the slow and uneven pace of urban and industrial expansion in Ireland in the succeeding centuries served to preserve the different modes of parent-child relations, which defied any single attempt at classification (Connolly, 1985). For those who lived in farm households, continuity with past traditions may have been more characteristic than discontinuity. In the writings of Tomás Ó Crohán and Peig Sayers in the Gaelic tradition, fathers are seen to retain an active, integrated, companionate orientation towards their children, in contrast to their secondary and evanescent role in the general body of Irish literature in English at the beginning of this century. Seán Ó Muiríosa's nineteenth century elegy for his daughter has all the marks of a folk poem and thus may be more reflective of actual father-child relations in rural Ireland in the second half of the nineteenth century (Ó Tuama, 1981). The lament of Pádraig Ó h-Eigeartaigh for his drowned son, *Ochón! A Donncha,* written in the first decade of this century, shows clear continuity both in style and in sentiment with Sweeney's medieval poem (Ó Tuama, 1981). On the other hand, in the Anglo-Irish writings of Joyce, Snyge and O'Casey, fathers are generally portrayed as emotionally distant yet controlling, having little contact with their children except as disciplinarians.

The common image of the Irish father in twentieth century Irish literature is characterized by a certain emotional inflexibility and by the absence of explicit expressions of tenderness or affection towards his children. Contemporary Irish playwright Brian Friel, in "Philadelphia Here I Come" portrays a father's poignant inability to communicate with his son. Writers such as Austin Clarke, Frank O'Connor, John McGahern, and Edna O'Brien present us with images of the father as distant and often withholding praise and affection as a conscious policy of social control. Although this unitary image has been given the aura of dogma even by social scientists (e.g., Scheper-Hughes, 1979; McGoldrick, 1982), it is merely one of many images. It is counterbalanced by a rich canon of modern Irish literature which portrays fathers in another light as warm and actively involved with their children. Examples of this include poet Desmond Egan's descriptions of a more mature, companionable father-son relationship in poems such as *My Father,* or Seamus Heaney's poems describing mutually rewarding father-son and father-daughter relations. What contemporary Irish literature contains is not a unitary father profile but a rich catalogue of contrasting father portraits, some of which show continuity with the past, while others may be more recent products of historically variable cultural changes.

TWENTIETH-CENTURY ANTHROPOLOGICAL SOURCES

Anthropological studies of family relations have contributed, unwittingly perhaps, to the development of the monolithic image of Irish fathers as emotionally inflexible and repressed, whose only role in the family system was that of disciplinarian. Arensberg and Kimball's study of rural Irish life in County Clare in the 1930s, Humphrey's study of Dublin families in the 1950s, Brody's and Messenger's work in the West of Ireland in the 1960s, as well as the work of Scheper-Hughes in the 1970s suggest that Irish fathers play a minimal role in the early socialization process. Kane (1979) states that, in certain modern rural Irish settings, only when the child is 10 or 12 years of age—and only if the child is a male—does the father have extended contact with him.

Recent empirical data suggest that the conventional view of Irish fathers as emotionally distant, punitive, and playing a minimal role in child nurturance and care, may be less universal than has been assumed. These results make a strong case for the reexamination of the father's role in Irish society and suggest that the traditional assumption based on stereotypes of Irish fathers proposed by many social scientists (e.g., McGoldrick, 1982; McGoldrick & Pearce, 1981; Messenger, 1969; Scheper-Hughes, 1979;) may not be applicable today. In fact, Kane (1979) suggests that much of the ethnography of Irish family life is outdated, while Blacking (1979) in his review of the existing data on Irish families, concludes that it is impossible to generalize about Irish family relations.

A study by McKenna (1979), which examined the attitudes of a sample of Irish mothers toward parenting, provided information on their husbands' contribution to child caretaking. Sixty-two percent of these Irish fathers helped in putting the baby to sleep, while 49% fed the baby regularly, 36% changed the baby's nappies regularly, and 29% helped with bathing the baby. Mackey and Day (1979) did not study Irish fathers *per se* but they compared male adult-child interaction patterns in five countries: Ireland, the United States, Spain, Japan, and Mexico. They observed interactions in 20 sites in Ireland: Dublin, Athlone, Tralee, Cashel, and Sligo. The results showed that Irish men were with their children in considerable numbers and interacted with children at levels consonant with female adult-child dyads, in the 0–4 age group. If the results can be extrapolated as measures of nurturance, then Irish men seem to be providing experiences comparable to the men from the other four cultural areas studied.

These findings suggest that there may be considerable variability in the father's role in the contemporary Irish family. These changes may be a function of the large movement of families from rural to urban areas and of the increasing number of working mothers in Irish society. This rural to urban shift, documented in West Germany by Devereux, Bronfenbrenner, and Suci (1962), was found to be associated with increased levels of father-child interaction and a change in the father's role in the family from a more authoritarian to a more flexible one. Recent work by Parke, Grossmann, and Tinsley (1981), comparing German and American families, confirms the direction of these changes and emphasizes the role of the cultural environment in shaping the father-child relationship. We may be observing the same phenomenon in contemporary Irish society.

Increasingly, empirical studies are changing traditional father stereotypes. Recent work by Mirande (1979) and Bronstein (1984) in Mexico contradict traditional assumptions of Mexican fathers as aloof and authoritarian. Bronstein found that both middle-class and working-class fathers demonstrated a distinct monoauthoritarian and companionable relationship with their children, presenting a knowledgeable and mastery-oriented image as male role models. Ho and Kang (1984) in an intergenerational study of Chinese fathers in Hong Kong found that although continuity with the past remains strong, younger fathers show a distinct departure from the traditional authoritarian mode of childrearing and are becoming more involved in childcare.

Today, Ireland is in a state of rapid social change due to the twin factors of industrialization and urbanization. Only 23% of the population is now engaged in agriculture, while industrial output has grown by about 4% annually during recent years. As a result, emigration has declined and the population is increasing for the first time since the Great Famine over 130 years ago (1981, census of population of Ireland report). The birthrate is considerably higher than in any other country in the European Economic Community; in fact, one-third of the population is under 15 years of age. There is much evidence to suggest that rapidly changing economic and social conditions within a society will have profound effects on childrearing practices in general and on the role of the father in the socialization process in particular (LeVine, 1977).

This study was designed to test the validity of the hypothesis derived from this historical-cultural review of fatherhood in Irish history, namely that the shape and quality of the father-child relationship may be a product of the interaction of various social, economic, and cultural factors as they interact with each other and in turn influence the family system. The data, therefore, describes the father's involvement in early socialization in a sample of Irish families and, secondly, examines the effects of this involvement on the child's development over the first three years of life.

AIMS AND RATIONALE

One aim of the present study was to document the degree of involvement of a sample of Irish fathers in early socialization in the first year of life in order to better understand the effects of cultural and social factors on paternal involvement in infancy and early childhood. The second aim was to examine the effects of paternal involvement in the newborn period on developmental outcome up to the third year of the child's life.

Theories of infant social development in the past have focused almost exclusively on the mother-infant relationship. Within the psychoanalytic tradition, the father was assumed to have little contribution to make to the infant's social development until the Oedipal period (Freud, 1923; Mächtlinger, 1976). Even the evolutionary-ethological analysis of early social development presented by Bowlby (1969) argues for the uniqueness and exclusiveness of the mother-infant relationship. In his comprehensive review of the literature on the role of fathers, Lamb (1976) was forced to conclude that fathers seem to be the forgotten contributors to child development.

Over the past ten years, empirical studies of the father-infant relationship have increased dramatically. Extensive reviews by Biller (1970), Yogman (1982), Gunsberg (1982), Howells (1969), Lamb (1976), McGreal (1981), Palkovitz

(1985), Parke (1979) and Yogman (1985) conclude that fathers play an important and distinctive role in the socialization of their infants. Phylogenetic, anthropological, and historical data underscore the diversity in male's infant-care-taking roles and suggest that the father's role in early socialization may be limited more by social-cultural factors than by biological factors (e.g., Aries, 1963; Stone, 1977; West & Konner, 1976). By studying the role of the father in early socialization in an Irish sample, we have an opportunity to learn more about the way social and cultural variables influence the level of paternal care of young children.

While current research suggests that infants do form attachments to their fathers as well as to their mothers (Lamb, 1976) and that fathers and mothers have different styles of interaction with their infants (Clarke-Stewart, 1978; Lamb, 1978; Parke, 1979; Yogman et al., 1976), little is known about the effects of the father's involvement on the later developmental status of the infant. We do know, however, that the opportunity for fathers to be present at the birth of their infants does seem to affect the father-infant relationship (Greenburg & Morris, 1974; Klaus et al., 1976; Palkovitz, 1984; Pedersen, Yarrow, Anderson, & Cain, 1979). Parke and his colleagues (1976, 1980) further concluded that, in the newborn period, fathers were just as nurturant with their infants as were mothers. Yet while these studies show how fathers interact with their infants from birth on, we still know little about how paternal involvement in caregiving influences later development. Concurrent predictive studies of younger infants by Pedersen, Rubinstein, and Yarrow (1978) and Clarke-Stewart (1978) suggest that fathers play an influential role in their infant's cognitive development. However, in order to examine the generalizability of these results, it is important to replicate them in another culture using a longitudinal design. The present study constitutes a step in this direction.

The major contemporary analyses of child development propose that development is a function of continuous organism-environment transactions (e.g., Bowlby, 1969; Brazelton, 1979; Sameroff & Chandler, 1975), so that in order to understand the process of infant development one must examine the contributions of both infant and environment as they interact with each other. This interactional approach to the study of development has serious implications for assessing the impact of the father on an infant's developmental status. It means that we must expand our model of prediction to include assessments of the newborn's behavioural repertoire as well as assessments of the father's role and other elements of the caregiving environment. The work of Clarke-Stewart (1978), Parke (1979) and Pedersen, Anderson and Cain (1980) suggests that, when examining the effects of the father's role, the contributions of both mothers and fathers should be studied together. It was therefore hypothesized that by combining neonatal behavioral assessments with information from the father's and mother's contribution to the caregiving environment, it would be possible to maximize prediction to later outcomes.

The Neonatal Behavioral Assessment Scale (NBAS) (Brazelton, 1984) was used to assess the infant's characteristics to examine how these might interact with environmental stimulation and contribute to later development. Several studies (Crockenberg, 1981; Horowitz, Linn, & Buddin, 1983; Osofsky & Danzer, 1974; Waters, Vaughn, & Egland, 1979) suggest that certain infant characteristics measured by the Brazelton scale have an influence on the developing mother-infant relationship. Vaughn, Taraldson, Crichton, and Egland (1980), in a study of lower SES mothers and their babies, conclude that individual differences assessed by the NBAS shortly after birth accounted for a significant proportion of infant behavior later in the first year of life. Findings by Lester and his colleagues (Lester, 1984; Lester, Hoffman, & Brazelton, 1984), in a study of the NBAS as a predictor to later mental and motor development, suggest that patterns of individual differences over repeated Brazelton examinations in the first month are significantly correlated with Bayley Mental scores at 18 months. Nugent, Greene, and Brazelton (1984) and Sepkoski (1986) also found correlations between patterns of newborn behavior as measured by the NBAS and IQ scores at three and five years respectively.

We therefore hypothesized that by combining serial assessments of newborn behavior using the Brazelton scale with assessments of the caregiving environment, we would maximize the prediction to later developmental outcome. In order to assess the contributions of developmental influences, specific paternal, maternal, and environmental elements were measured.

METHOD

Subjects

The sample consisted of 48 Irish infants and their parents, recruited at the National Maternity Hospital, Dublin. The infants were all full-term, appropriate for gestational age, with Apgar scores not less than 8 at 1 and 5 minutes; they were the products of uncomplicated pregnancies and spontaneous vaginal delivery, born to mothers who had received routine prenatal care. Forty-four percent of the mothers were primagravida, while 56% were multigravida.

All the infants came from two-parent families living in Dublin or the neighboring counties. The sample was made up of working-class and middle-class families. Fifty-two percent of the fathers in the sample were from working-class backgrounds (skilled and unskilled blue-collar occupations), and 48% were middle-class (white-collar occupations). Fifty-nine percent of the fathers had completed the Secondary School Leaving Certificate; of the mothers, 41% had attained Leaving Certificate level. Adapting the Hollingshead Index (Hollingshead & Redlich, 1958) to an Irish setting, socioeconomic status was computed by combining scores on the fathers' and mothers' educational and occupational levels to arrive at a single score for SES.

Procedures

Infants and mothers who met the criteria for obstetric conditions were selected not later than 36 hours after delivery. It was explained to the parents that the aim of the study was to learn more about the growth and development of normal, healthy Irish infants during the first years of life. All subjects who were approached agreed to participate; 87.5% of the original sample was still in the project at the end of the first year, as was 85% at the end of the third year. On the first and third days of life, the infants were examined with the NBAS in a quiet, dimly lit room near the newborn nursery by an examiner trained to reliability according to the criteria set by Brazelton (1984).

For data analysis, the 26 behavioral items and 16 neurological items of the NBAS were summarized into 7 clusters developed by Lester, Als, and Brazelton (1982). Principal-components analyses were then performed on these data. Two main factors emerged. The first factor described the infant's muscle tone and motor maturity and the orientation responses to animate and inanimate visual and auditory stimuli; it was labeled *motor-attention*. High scores indicate better motor organization and higher levels of alertness. The second factor, called *state regulation*, measured the infant's effort to modulate his or her own state and the range, peak, and lability of state changes. High scores on this factor indicate better state organization and regulation over the first 3 days. These two factors were retained for subsequent regression analysis. Between the third and fifth day after delivery, the mothers were interviewed about their experience of pregnancy, labor, and delivery, and their attitudes towards child-rearing. Fathers were interviewed about their degree of involvement prenatally and about their experiences of labor and delivery.

The Parental Goals Rating Scale (Nugent, 1980b) was filled out by the mother. This scale was designed to collect information on the mother's child-rearing goals, that is, what characteristics they would like their children to have (e.g., to be competitive, cooperative, ambitious, bright, assertive). Characteristics were rated on forty 7-point scales. Based on LeVine's (1977) notion of child-rearing as cultural adaptation, the scale was designed to document the individual character traits that parents believe will enable their child to adapt successfully in their own society. The items were selected based on hypotheses generated from anthropological and empirical studies and the author's clinical experience with infants and parents in Ireland. The Parental Goals Rating Scale was subjected to principal-components analysis, yielding the following four factors: 1. *social cooperative* factor emphasizes sensitivity to social needs and the need for social communicative skills; it accounts for 26% of the total variance, 2. The *goal-oriented* factor emphasizes characteristics such as achievement motivation, academic orientation, a deliberative, goal-directed style; it accounts for 11% of the total variance, 3. The *independent* factor emphasizes independence, self-reliance, and the ability to go one's own way, it accounts for 9% of the total variance, 4. The *docile* factor emphasizes the preference to be a follower; it accounts for 7% of the total variance.

These four dimensions represent a profile of the personality traits and characteristics desired for their children by this sample of Irish mothers. A higher score on any of these four factors would indicate that these mothers wanted their children to be cooperative, goal-oriented, independent, or docile, respectively.

At one month, mothers filled out the Infant Characteristics Questionnaire (Bates, Bennett-Freeland, & Lounsburg, 1979), which contains 27 items rated on a 7-point scale, with a rating of 1 describing an optimal temperament and a 7 referring to a difficult temperament. The items are summarized into four major headings: (a) fussy-difficult, (b) unadaptable, (c) dull, and (d) unpredictable.

At 1 month, the fathers were again interviewed concerning their perceptions of their roles as fathers, their attitudes towards their infants, their lifestyle changes since the infant was born, and the quality of their interactions with their infants. The fathers also filled out the Father Caretaking Inventory (Nugent, 1980a), which was adapted from Yogman's work (Yogman, 1982) and was designed to record the amount of father participation in 10 childcare tasks, such as feeding the baby, changing nappies, and playing with the baby over the first month of the infant's life. This was scored according to whether they performed the task regularly (i.e., at least 3–4 times per week), occasionally (1–2 times per week), or never. The Father Caretaking Inventory was administered at one month and at one year. The Paternal Investment Rating Scale (adapted from Yogman, 1982) is a summary score consisting of six prenatal and perinatal variables selected from the interview and the Father Caretaking Inventory. It includes: (a) attendance at prenatal classes, (b) presence at labor and delivery, (c) involvement in feeding over the first month, (d) involvement in nappy changing in the first month, (e) father's perception of his role, and (f) lifestyle changes, (Nugent, Yogman, Lester, Hoffman, & Brazelton, 1982).

At 1 year, the Bayley Mental (MDI) and Motor (PDI) Scales of Infant Development (Bayley, 1969) were administered to the infants, after which the Bayley Infant Behavior Record (IBR) was filled out by the examiner. Principal-components analysis of the variables from the Bayley IBR resulted in a 4-factor solution that accounted for 65% of the total variance. The first factor was referred to as *Goal-Directedness* and accounted for 35% of the variance. The second factor, *High Activity,* accounted for 14% of the variance. The third and fourth factors, *Passivity* and *Attentiveness,* accounted for 10% and 6% of the variance, respectively.

At 3 years, the Stanford Binet Intelligence Scale was administered by examiners blind to the hypotheses of the study.

RESULTS AND DISCUSSION

The historical-cultural analysis of fatherhood in Ireland suggests that, while the invariant aspects of fatherhood may be biological, different economic, social, and cultural influences have combined to shape and reshape the father's role over time. The historical record, fragmented though it is, reveals considerable variability in the father's role over the course of Irish history and suggests that the father's role is characterized as much by discontinuity as by continuity. In response to the cultural and economic constraints of different epochs, coexisting but often contrasting styles of fathering emerged.

This historical survey led to the hypothesis that, while there is evidence from sociological and anthropological sources describing the Irish father as emotionally distant from his children and minimally involved in their nurturance and care, this description may not be as universal as had been assumed. It was argued that in a time of major social and economic change in Ireland, where in an increasing number of families both parents are working, the father's role may be in a state of flux. Data from this study of the father's role in early socialization suggest that in this predominantly urban middle- and working-class sample, Irish fathers are substantially involved in the care of their young children in that first year of life (Tables 7.1 and 7.2). These results show a similar trend to that observed in English and United States samples (e.g., Kotelchuck, 1976; Rendina & Dickershied, 1976; Richards, Dunn, & Antonis, 1977). In a comparison with Yogman's (1985) U.S. sample, a slightly higher percentage of Irish fathers participate in equivalent childcare tasks (Table 7.3). The data also show a significant correlation between caregiving at one month and one year ($r = .47$, $p < .05$). These results suggest not only that Irish fathers were substantially involved in early childcare but also that there was considerable stability in the degree of fathers' participation in caregiving tasks over the first year of the infant's life.

TABLE 7.1
Amount of Time in Caretaking Activities of Irish Fathers in the Infant's
First Month of Life

Caretaking Activity	Never	Occasionally (1-2 Times/Wk)	Regularly (3-4 Times/Wk)
1. Getting the baby up in the morning	39%	46%	15%
2. Putting the baby to bed	29%	25%	46%
3. Dressing the baby in the morning	67%	30%	3%
4. Changing the baby's nappies	16%	36%	48%
5. Taking the baby for a walk	54%	42%	4%
6. Singing to the baby	22%	23%	53%
7. Talking and playing with the baby	0%	7%	93%
8. Feeding the baby	26%	18%	56%
9. Picking up the baby when he/she cries	0%	20%	80%
10. Soothing the baby if he/she cries at night	26%	41%	33%

TABLE 7.2
Amount of Time in Caretaking Activities of Irish Fathers
When Infant is 1 Year Old

Caretaking Activity	Never	Occasionally (1-2 Times/Wk)	Regularly (3-4 Times/Wk)
1. Getting the baby up in the morning	21%	53%	26%
2. Putting the baby to bed	35%	44%	21%
3. Dressing the baby in the morning	59%	41%	0%
4. Changing the baby's nappies	27%	38%	35%
5. Taking the baby for a walk	26%	59%	15%
6. Singing to the baby	30%	32%	38%
7. Talking and playing with the baby	0%	9%	91%
8. Feeding the baby	6%	50%	44%
9. Picking up the baby when he/she cries	3%	9%	88%
10. Soothing the baby if he/she cries at night	43%	33%	24%

In examining the father's participation in childcare tasks over the first month, it was found that younger fathers were more likely to be highly involved in child-care ($r = .74$, $p < .001$). One plausible explanation for this finding is that in contemporary Irish society, households where both parents are working tend to be headed by younger couples (Census, 1981). In such situations, the division of parental labor may have to be renegotiated and family roles redefined. Since sex roles are redefined after the birth of a child (Lamb, 1979), paternal role orientation is likely to influence the degree of paternal caregiving. In this sample, the data show that where the division of domestic labor did not follow traditional patterns, fathers were more likely to be highly involved in infant care at one month ($r = .87$, $p < .005$) and up to the end of the first year ($r = .46$, $p < .05$).

TABLE 7.3
Comparison of U.S. and Irish Fathers on Selected
Caregiving Tasks at 1 Month

Caregiving Tasks	Irish Fathers	U.S. Fathers
1. Gets baby up	61%	20%
2. Dresses baby	33%	40%
3. Changes nappies	84%	80%
4. Puts baby to bed	71%	60%
5. Comforts baby when frets	100%	100%
6. Comforts baby when cries at night	74%	60%

A complementary finding, which confirms the importance of role resolution in the adaptation to fatherhood, shows that the degree to which the fathers modified their work schedule was related to their high level of participation in care both at one month ($r = .54$, $p < .05$) and after 12 months ($r = .40$, $p < .05$). These findings corroborate Palkovitz's (1984) conclusion that the success with which fathers resolve their roles after the birth of their infant is positively related to their level of involvement in their interactions with their young infants. Since fathers' responses on the caregiving inventory may be compounded by social desirability, observations of behavior can give some assurance that fathers were actually involved at the level they reported. Thus, we also looked at the effects of fathers' attendance at the prenatal classes and their presence during labor and delivery. Fathers who attended pre-natal classes and fathers who were present at the birth of their child were more likely to be active participants in childcare after one year. This is similar to the finding of Pedersen et al. (1979) that father's positive birth experience was associated with greater levels of father-infant attachment at one year. They contended that the birth experience may act as a catalyst for promoting paternal nurturant behavior. In this study, the fact that attendance at prenatal classes was also highly correlated with the amount of caregiving at 1 year ($r = .7$) suggests, however, that these fathers may have had a predisposition towards paternal nurturance which in turn may have been enhanced by presence at labor and delivery and continuous interaction with the infant over the first year.

The finding that fathers reporting high levels of marital satisfaction were more likely to be involved in infant care ($r = .8$, $p < .001$) is similar to findings by Grossman, Eichler, and Winicoff (1980), Feldman et al. (1983), and Heinicke (1984), which indicated that good marital adjustment was related to paternal adaptation. Feldman et al. (1983) concluded that the best single predictor of paternal satisfaction with his relationship with his infant was marital happiness. These findings stress the potential influence of a positive marital relationship on the father's overall adaptation to parenthood in the first month of his child's life.

The second purpose of the study was to examine the effects of early paternal involvement on later developmental status at one year and at three years. Using stepwise multiple regression analysis, the one-year results show that by looking at the additive effects of newborn behavior, paternal involvement, mother's childrearing goals, temperament and SES, we were able to predict the 1-year outcome from the newborn data. This combination of variables accounted for 52% of the variance on the Bayley MDI at 1 year, 67% of the variance on the Goal-Directedness factor on the Bayley IBR at 1 year, 62% of the variance on the Passivity factor at one year, and 57% on the Attentiveness factor of the Bayley IBR at 1 year.

The prediction matrix that accounted for higher scores on the Bayley MDI at 1 year included both infant characteristics and caregiving variables. Infant characteristics were from the NBAS Motor-Attention and State Regulation factors, with higher MDI scores found in infants who are motorically robust and highly alert but who, although they have well defined states, are slightly unpredictable in their state behavior. On the one hand, they provide a great deal of positive feedback to their parents; on the other hand, they may elicit more attention and involvement from parents because of their unpredictability. This same group of infants was rated as unpredictable by mothers at 1 month. Their fathers were highly involved in their care and their mothers wanted them to be goal-oriented. They seemed to need — and, consequently, received — a great deal of parental involvement.

This suggests that a certain degree of unpredictability and variability in newborn state behavior (as long as this unpredictability is slight and comes along with a well-organized motor and attention system) elicits more paternal involvement in infant care and relates to higher mental scores at 1 year. Recent findings by Horowitz, Linn, and Buddin (1983) seem to confirm the notion that infants whose behavior is variable tend to receive more stimulation. It may be, as Emde et al. (1976) have pointed out, that variability in newborn behavior is more adaptive from an evolutionary standpoint in that it elicits more facilitating involvement from the caretaker and thus enhances the organism's species-specific cognitive and affective adaptation.

This finding demonstrates the importance of the contribution of the infant's behavioral repertoire in eliciting paternal nurturance from his environment. In this case, the infant's relative unpredictability in state organization may have served to elicit more paternal involvement, while the infant's social responsivity on the other hand is likely to have provided a rewarding, mutually reciprocated cycle of interaction for both caregiver and infant (Als, 1979; Heinicke, 1984). Within this transactional analysis, the behavior of the infant may be seen to act as the catalyst in eliciting the high degree of involvement from the father. In sum, it is this combination of infant behavioral variables and caregiving variables which were related to high mental scores on the Bayley Scales at 1 year.

The same contribution of newborn behavioral characteristics was part of the constellation of predictor variables that was significantly correlated with goal-directed behavior on the Bayley Scale at 1 year. Again, it seems that the robust and responsive but slightly unpredictable infant elicits active participation from the father. Paternal involvement scores are high again, while the mothers in this group want their children to grow up to be independent. Low SES is combined with these variables and, taken together, they show a correlation with the IBR Goal-Directed dimension. This suggests that in the newborn period in lower SES families where infants are alert and motorically robust but somewhat behaviorally variable, when mothers want their children to be independent, then at 1 year the infants are rated as goal-directed. The fact that these variables are associated with lower SES homes suggests that the active involvement of fathers in childcare not only may be a response to the characteristics of the infant but also may be related to economic stress. In an increasing number of lower SES families, both parents are working — so fathers may be taking more responsibility for the care of the young child. What emerges, again, is that it is the combination of behavioral and caregiving variables that improves predictive power from the newborn period.

The Paternal Investment Rating Score was not part of the prediction matrix that predicted the Passivity and Attentiveness factors on the Bayley IBR.

Preliminary analysis of the 3-year outcome data suggests that fathers play an influential role in the child's cognitive development. These findings corroborate and extend the findings of Pedersen et al. (1979) and Clarke-Stewart (1978). There was a significant correlation between the Paternal Investment Rating Scale and Stanford-Binet IQ scores at 3 years ($r = .38$, $p < .05$). While no causal relationship can be inferred, the data suggest that there is a relationship between the degree of paternal involvement in the prenatal and newborn period and the child's IQ scores at 3 years. Since the Paternal Investment Rating Scale combines both behavioral and attitudinal father characteristics, gathered both prenatally and over the first month, it serves as a global measure of paternal adaptation in the neonatal period. As such, it constitutes a robust index of early paternal prenatal and postnatal involvement.

Whatever the origins of this high level of paternal involvement and whatever the nature of the child's development from birth to 3 years, the data here suggest that infants who had fathers who were actively involved in caregiving in the neonatal period have highest scores on the Stanford-Binet at 3 years. As such, it is a promising relationship which should be examined within the framework of the more comprehensive model used for the 1-year follow-up data.

CONCLUSION

The aim of this study was to document the level of fathers' participation in caregiving in a sample of Irish fathers, from the newborn period up to the end of the first year of life. The second aim was to examine the effects of paternal involvement on developmental status at the end of the first and third years of the child's life. A limitation of the present study was the small sample size and the overreliance on self report inventories and interview data as measures of paternal involvement. Nevertheless, the data reported here reveal that the Irish fathers of this predominantly urban sample were actively involved in the care of their young infants over the first year of life. This finding is at odds with the traditional view of Irish fathers described in the anthropological and sociological literature. The data support Kane's (1979) contention that much of the ethnography of Irish family life may be outdated. The findings make a strong case for the reexamination of the father's role in Irish society and emphasize the importance of collecting normative data for a national sample.

The high level of involvement of Irish fathers is consistent with recent findings from other Western societies. Within the Irish cultural context, it was argued that the high level of participation of Irish fathers in caregiving may be related to the rapidly changing economic and social patterns in Irish society. The entry of married women into the work world outside the home inevitably requires a redefinition of paternal and maternal roles in the family system. This redefinition of the father's role seems to be contributing to a broadening of the range and depth of the early father-child experience in modern Ireland. The evidence here suggests that if, in the past, Irish fathers were less involved with the care of their young infants this involvement was limited more by sociocultural than by biological factors.

Secondly, the data suggest that fathers' involvement in caregiving in the prenatal and early postnatal period is related to the child's cognitive development at 1 and 3 years. It appears from the data that newborn behavior and cultural practices may act synergistically to predict developmental outcome. The data suggest, furthermore, that individual differences at birth may have an important influence on how fathers respond to their infants. By combining newborn behavioral assessments with information from the caregiving environment we were able to predict significant amounts of the variance in developmental outcome at 1 year of age. The results support a model of prediction based on a more complex multivariate theory of development, in which organism and environment variables are combined to predict developmental outcome.

ACKNOWLEDGEMENTS

I would like to especially thank Dr. Dermot W. McDonald, Master, National Maternity Hospital, Dublin, whose generous support and cooperation made this project possible; Dr. Sheila Green, Pauline Beegan, and Hannah McGee, Trinity College, Dublin; Drs. Barry Lester, Joel Hoffmann, Michael Yogman, and especially T. Berry Brazelton, Chief, Child Development Unit. Sincere thanks to Kate Neff and Terry DiGioia who helped prepare the manuscript. Above all, I would like to thank the families who have extended me the privilege of learning from them.

Finally, I would like to express my deep appreciation for the generosity and kindness of the late Carmel McNulty, National Maternity Hospital, Dublin, who helped me in the early stages of the research.

The research on which this study is based was supported in part by a grant from Boston University.

ADDITIONAL READING AND REFERENCES

Als, H. (1979). Social interaction: Dynamic matrix for developing behavioral organisation. In I. Uzgiris, (Ed.), *Social Interaction and Communication in Infancy: New Directions for Child Development, Vol 4*. San Francisco: Jossey-Bass.

Arensberg, C., & Kimball, S. (1940). *Family and community in Ireland*. Cambridge: Harvard University Press.

Aries, P. (1962). *Centuries of childhood*. Vintage.

Bates, J., Bennett-Freeland, C., & Lounsbury, M. (1979). Measurement of infant difficultness. *Child Development*, 794–803.

Bayley, N. (1969). *Manual for the Bayley scales of infant development*. New York: The Psychological Corporation.

Beckwith, L., & Cohen, S. E. (1980). Interactions of preterms with their caregivers. In T. Field (Ed.), *High risk infants and children: Adult and peer interactions*. New York: Academic Press.

Bell, R. Q. (1974). Contributions of human infants to caregiving and social interaction. In M. Lewis & L. Rosenblum (Eds.), *The effect of the infant on its caregiver*. New York: Wiley.

Biller, H. (1970). Father Absence and the Personality Development of the Male Child. *Developmental Psychology, 2*, 81.

Blacking, J. (1979). Introduction. *Journal of comparative family studies*, X, 2, i–viii.

Bowlby, J. (1969). *Attachment and loss* (Vol. I). New York: Basic Books.

Brazelton, T. B. (1984). *Neonatal behavioral assessment scale*, 2nd Edition. London: Spastics International Medical Publications; Philadelphia: J. B. Lippincott.

Brazelton, T. B., Nugent, J. K. & Lester, B. M. (1987). The Brazelton Neonatal Behavioral Assessment Scale. In J. Osofsky (Ed.), *Handbook for infant development*, New York: Wiley.

Brody, H. (1973). *Inishkillane. Change and decline in the west of Ireland*. Harmondsworth: Penguin.

Bronstein, P. (1984). Differences in mother's and father's behavior toward children: A Cross-Cultural Comparison. *Developmental Psychology*, 20, 6, 995–1003.

Braudel, F. (1981). *The structures of everyday life: Civilization and capitalism 15th–18th century, Volume 1*. New York: Harper and Row.

Carney, J. (Ed.) (1969). *Early Irish poetry*. Cork: Mercier.

Census of Population (1981). Dublin: Central Statistical Office.

Clarke-Stewart, A. (1978). And daddy makes three: The father's impact on mother and young child. *Child Development, 49*, 466–478.

Clarke-Stewart, A. (1980). The Father's contribution to children's cognitive and social development in early childhood. In F. A. Petersen (Ed.), *The father-infant relationship: Observational studies in the family setting*. New York: Praeger.

Connell, K. H. (1968). *Irish Peasant Society*. Oxford: Oxford University Press.

Connolly S. J. (1985). Marriage in pre-famine Ireland. In A. Cosgrove (Ed.), *Marriage in Ireland*. Dublin: College Press.

Cosgrove, A. (1981). *Late medieval Ireland, 1370–1541*. Dublin: Criterion Press.

Cosgrove, A. (Ed.) (1985). *Marriage in Ireland*. Dublin: College Press.

Crockenberg, S. (1981). Infant irritability, mother responsiveness and social support influences on the security of infant-mother attachment. *Child Development, 52, 3*, 857–865.

Cullen, L. M. (1979). *Life in Ireland*. London: Batsford.

de Mause, L. (1974). *The history of childhood*. New York: The Psychohistory Press.

Demos, J. (1983). The Changing Faces of Fatherhood: A New Exploration in Family History. In F. Kessell & A. W. Siegel (Eds.), *The child and other cultural inventions*. New York: Praeger.

de Paor, M., & de Paor, L. (1978). *Early christian Ireland*. London: Thames and Hudson.

Devereaux, E., Bronfenbrenner, U., & Suci, G. (1962). Patterns of Parent Behavior in the United States of America and the Federal Republic of Germany. *International social science journal, 14*, 488–506.

Egan, D. (1983). *Collected poems*. Orono, Maine: The National Poetry Foundation.

Emde, R., Gaensbauer, T. G., & Harmon, R. J. (1976). Emotional expression in infancy: a bio-behavioral study. *Psychological issues monograph*, Series 10, no. 37.

Feldman, S. S. & Aschenbrenner, B. (1983). Impact of parenthood on various aspects of masculinity and femininity: A short term longitudinal study. *Developmental psychology*, 19, 278–289.

Fitzpatrick, D. (1985). Marriage in post-famine Ireland. In A. Cosgrove (Ed.), *Marriage in Ireland*. Dublin: College Press.

Freud, S. (1923). *New introductory lectures on psychoanalysis*. New York: Norton.

Garcia-Coll, C., Kagan, J., & Reznick, S. (1984). Behavioral inhibition in young children. *Child Development*, 55, 1005–1019.

Gerald of Wales. (1982). *The history and topography of Ireland*. Harmondsward, Middlesex: Penguin.

Greenberg, M. & Morris, N. (1974). Engrossment: The Newborn's Impact Upon the Father. *American Journal of Orthopsychiatry*, 44, 520–528.

Grossman, F. K., Eichler, L. S. & Winicoff, S. A. (1980). *Pregnancy, birth and parenthood*. San Francisco: Jossey-Bass.

Gunsberg, L. (1982). Selected critical review of psychological investigations of the early father-infant relationship. In S. Cath, A. R. Gurwit, & J. M. Ross (Eds.), *Father and child*. Boston: Little Brown.

Heaney, S. (1983). *Sweeney astray*. Derry: Field Day.

Heinicke, C. (1984). Impact of prebirth parent personality and marital functioning on family development: A framework and suggestions for Further Study. *Developmental Psychology*, 20, 1044–1053.

Ho, D. Y. F., & Kang, T. K. (1984). Intergenerational comparisons of child rearing attitudes and practices in Hong Kong. *Developmental Psychology*, 20, 6, 1004–1016.

Hollingshead, A. B., & Redlich, F. C. (1958). *Social class and mental illness: A Community Study*. New York: Wiley.

Horowitz, F. S., Linn, P., & Buddin, B. (1983). Neonatal Assessment: Evaluating the potential for plasticity. In T. B. Brazelton & B. M. Lester, (Eds.), *New approaches to developmental screening of infants*. New York: Elsevier.

Howells, J. G. (1969). Fathering. In J. G. Howells, (Ed.) *Modern perspectives in international child psychiatry*. Edinburgh: Oliver and Boyd.

Humphreys, A. J. (1966). *New Dubliners*. London: Rutledge, & Kegan, Paul.

Joyce, J.(1964). A *Portrait of the artist as a young man*. Harmondsworth, Middlesex: Penguin.

Joyce, J. (1961). *Ulysses*. New York: Random House.

Kane, E. (1968). Man and kin in Donegal: A study of kinship functions in a rural Irish community and in an Irish-American community. *Ethnology*, 7, 245–258.

Kane, E. (1979). The changing role of the family in a rural Irish community. *Journal of Comparative Family Studies*, 2, 141–162.

Klaus, M. and Kennell, J. H. (1976). *Maternal-infant bonding*. St. Louis: Mosby Company.

Konner, M. (1979). Evolution of human behavior development. In P. H. Liederman, S. Tulkin, & A. Rosenthal (Eds.) *Culture and infancy*. New York: Academic Press.

Kotelchuk, M. (1976). The Infant's relationship to the father: experimental evidence. In M. Lamb (ed.) *The Role of the father in child development*. New York: Wiley.

Lamb, M. (1972). Fathers: Forgotten contributors to child development. *Human Development*, 18, 109–121.

Lamb, M. (1976). Effects of stress and cohort on mother- and father-Infant Interaction. *Developmental Psychology*, 12, 435–444.

Lamb, M. (Ed.) (1976). *The role of the father in child development*. New York: Wiley.

Lamb, M. (1977). The Development of mother-infant and father-infant attachments in the second year of life. *Developmental Psychology*, 13, 637.

Lamb, M. (1978). Influence of the child on marital quality and family interaction during the prenatal, perinatal, and infancy periods. In R. M. Lerner & G. B. Spanier (Eds.), *Child Influences on Marital and Family Interaction: A Lifespar Perspective*. New York: Academic Press.

Lamb, M. (1980). The development of parent-infant attachments in the first two years of life. In F. A. Pedersen (Ed.), *The father-infant relationship: observational studies in the family setting.* New York: Praeger.

Laslett, P. (1973). *The world we have lost.* New York: Scribner and Sons.

Lester, B. M. (1984). Data analysis and prediction. In T. B. Brazelton (Ed.), *Neonatal Behavioral Assessment Scale,* 2nd Edition, Philadelphia: J. B. Lippincott.

Lester, B. M., Als, H. & Brazelton, T. B. (1982). Regional obstetric anesthesia and newborn behavior: A reanalysis towards synergistic effects. *Child Development, 53,* 687–692.

Lester, B. M., & Brazelton, T. B. (1982). Cross-cultural assessment of newborn behavior. In D. Wagner & H. Stevenson (Eds.), *Cultural perspectives on child development.* San Francisco: W. H. Freeman. 1982.

Lester, B. M., Hoffman, J., & Brazelton, T. B. (1984). Computing individual profile curves and predicting to 18 month outcome in term and preterm infants. Presented at the Symposium, The Meaning and Measurement of Patterns of Change in Neonatal Behavior. International Conference on Infant Studies, New York.

LeVine, R. (1977). Child rearing as cultural adaptation. In P. H. Leiderman, S. Tulkin and A. Rosenthal (Eds.), *Culture and infancy.* New York: Academic Press.

Mächtlinger, V. (1976). Psychoanalytic theory: Preoedipal and oedipal phases with special reference to the father. In M. Lamb (Ed.), *The role of the father in child development.* New York: Wiley.

Mackey, W. & Day, R. (1979). Some indications of fathering behavior in the United States: A cross-cultural examination of adult male-child interaction. *Journal of Marriage and the Family, 43,* 187–199.

MacLysaght, E. (1979). *Irish life in the seventeenth century.* Dublin: Irish Academic Press.

McCall, R. B. (1979). The development of intellectual functioning in infancy and the prediction of later IQ. In J. Osofsky (Ed.), *Handbook of infant development.* New York: Wiley.

McCall, R. B. (1983). Predicting developmental outcome: resume and the redirection. In T. B. Brazelton & B. M. Lester (Eds.), *New approaches to developmental screening of infants.* New York: Elsevier.

McGahern, J. (1971). *The Dark.* London: Panther.

McGoldrick, M. (1982). Irish families. In M. McGoldrick, J. K. Pearce, & J. Giordano (Eds.), *Ethnicity and family therapy.* New York: Guilford.

McGoldrick, M. & Pearce, J. K. (1981). Family therapy with Irish Americans. *Family process,* 1981, 20, 2, 223–244.

McGreal, C. E. (1981). The Father's role in the socialization of his infant. *Infant Mental Health Journal, 2,* 4, 216–225.

McKenna, A. (1979). Attitudes of Irish mothers to child rearing. *Journal of Comparative Family Studies, 2,* 229–251.

Merryman, B. (1981). In B. Kennelly (Ed.) *The Penguin Book of Irish Verse.* Harmondsworth, Middlesex: Penguin.

Messenger, J. C. (1969). *Inis Beag.* New York: Holt, Rinehart and Winston.

Mirande, A. (1979). A reinterpretation of male dominance in the Chicano family. *The Family Coordinator,* 28, 473–479.

Nash, J. (1976). Historical and social changes in the perception of the role of the father. In M. Lamb (Ed.), *The Role of the Father in Child Development.* New York: Wiley.

Nicholls, K. (1972). *Gaelic and gaelicised Ireland in the middle ages.* Dublin: Gill and Macmillan.

Nugent, J. K. (1982). Family relations in a contemporary Irish setting: the role of the father in infant socialisation. In *Growing Up Irish: Working Papers in Irish Studies.* Boston: Northeastern University.

Nugent, J. K., Yogman, M., Lester, B. M., Hoffman, J., & Brazelton, T. B. (1982). The father's impact on infant development in the first year of life. Presented at the Tenth International Congress for Child and Adolescent Psychiatry, Dublin, Ireland.

Nugent, J. K. (1980a). Father caretaking inventory. Unpublished manuscript. Child Development Unit, The Children's Hospital, Boston, MA.

Nugent, J. K. (1980b). Parental Goals Rating Scale. Unpublished manuscript. Child Development Unit, The Children's Hospital, Boston, MA.

Nugent, J. K., Greene, S., & Brazelton, T. B. (1984). *Predicting 3 year IQ scores from patterns of change in newborn behavior.* Presented at the International Conference in Infant Studies. New York.

O'Brien, E. (1960). *Country girls.* Harmonsdworth, Middlesex: Penguin.

O'Casey, S. (1972). *Three plays.* London: Macmillan.

O'Connor, F. (1961). *An only child.* London: Macmillan.

O'Connor, F. (1968). *My father's son.* London: Macmillan.

Ō'Corráin, D. (1979). Women in early Irish society. In M. MacCurtain & D. Ō'Corráin (Eds.), *Women in Irish society: The historical dimension.* Dublin: Arlen House.

Ō Criomthāin, T. (1978). *The Islandman.* Oxford: Oxford University Press.

Ó'Crohán, T. (1978). *The Islandman.* Oxford: Oxford University Press.

Ō hĒigearthaigh, P. (1981). In S. Ō Tuama (Ed.), *An Dunaire 1600–1900: Poems of the dispossessed.* Portlaoise, Ireland: Dolmen Press.

Ō Muirīosa, S. (1981). In S. Ō Tuama (Ed.), *An Dunaire 1600–1900: Poems of the dispossessed.* Portlaoise, Ireland: Dolmen Press.

Ō Rathaille, A. (1981). In S. Ō Tuama (Ed.), *An Dunaire 1600–1900: Poems of the dispossessed.* Portlaoise, Ireland: Dolmen Press.

Ó Tuama (Ed.) (1981). *An Dunaire, 1600–1900: Poems of the dispossessed.* Dublin: Dolmen Press.

Ó'Tuathaigh, G. (1978). The role of women in Ireland under the new english order. In M. MacCurtain and D. Ō'Courráin (Eds.), *Women in Irish Society: The Historical Dimension.* Dublin: Arlen.

Osofsky, J. D. & Danzger, B. (1974). Relationships between neonatal characteristics and mother-infant interaction. *Developmental Psychology, 10,* 124–130.

Palkovitz, R. (1984). Paternal attitudes and fathers' interactions with their five-month-old infants. *Developmental Psychology. 20,* 1054–1060.

Palkovitz, R. (1985). Father's birth attendance, early contact, and extended contact with their newborns: A critical review. *Child Development, 56,* 392–406.

Parke, R. (1979). Perspectives on father-infant interaction. In J. D. Osofsky (Ed.), *Handbook of Infant Development.* New York: Wiley.

Parke, R., Grossmann, K., & Tinsley, B. (1981). Father-mother-infant interaction in the newborn period: A German-American comparison. In Field et al. (Eds.), *Culture and early interactions.* Hillsdale, NJ: Erlbaum.

Parke, R. & O'Leary, D. (1976). Father-mother-infant interaction in the newborn period. In K. Riegel & J. Meacham (Eds.), *The developing individual in a changing world* (Vol. 2). The Hague: Mouton.

Parke, R. & Sawin, D. (1980). The family in early infancy: Social interactional and attitudinal analyses. In F. Pedersen (Ed.), *The father-infant relationship: Observational studies in family context.* New York: Holt, Rinehart and Winston.

Parmelee, A. H., Beckwith, L., Cohen, S., & Sigman, M. (1983). Early intervention: experience with preterm infants. In T. B. Brazelton & B. M. Lester (Eds.), *New approaches to developmental screening of infants.* New York: Elsevier.

Pedersen, F. A. & Robson, K. S. (1969) Father participation in infancy. *American Journal of Orthopsychiatry, 39,* 466–474.

Pedersen, F., Rubinstein, J., & Yarrow, L. (1979). Infant development in father-absent families. *Journal of Genetic Psychology, 135,* 51–61.

Pedersen, F., Yarrow, L., Anderson, B. & Cain, R. L. (1979). Conceptualization of father influences in the infancy period. In M. Lewis & L. Rosenblum (Eds.), *Social network of the developing child.* New York: Plenum.

Pedersen, F., Anderson, B. J., & Cain, R. L. (1980). Parent-infant and husband-wife interactions observed at age five months. In F. A. Pedersen (Ed.), *The Father-Infant Relationship: Observational Studies in the Family Setting.* New York: Praeger.

Redican, W. K. (1976). Adult male-infant interactions in nonhuman primates. In M. Lamb (Ed.), *The role of the father in child development.* New York: Wiley.

Rendina, I., & Dickersheid, J. D. (1976). Father involvement with first-born infants. *Family Coordinator, 25,* 373–380.

Richards, M. P. M., Dunn, J. F. & Antonis, B. (1977). Caretaking in the first year of life: The role of fathers' and mothers' social isolation. *Child Care, Health and Development, 3,* 23.

Robson, K. L., & Moss, H. A. (1970). Patterns and determinants of maternal attachment. *Journal of Pediatrics, 77,* 976–985.

Russell, G. (1978). The father role and its relation to masculinity, feminity and androgeny. *Child Development, 49,* 1174–1181.

Sameroff, A. J., & Chandler, M. J. (1975). Reproductive risk and the continuum of caretaking casualty. In F. D. Horowitz (Ed.), *Review of Child Development Research,* (Vol. 4.) Chicago: University of Chicago Press.

Sayers, P. (1970). *Peig.* Āth Cliath: Comhlacht Oideachais na hĒireann, Tta.

Scheper-Hughes, N. (1979). *Saints, scholars and schizophrenics: Mental illness in rural Ireland.* Los Angeles: University of California Press.

Sepkoski, C., Coll, C., & Lester, B. M. (1982). Cumulative effects of obstetric risk variables on newborn behavior. *Infant Behavior and Development, 5,* 33–40.

Sepkoski, C. (1986). The Relationship between NBAS change profile scores and 5 year McCarthy scores. Presented at the International Conference in Infant Studies. Los Angeles.

Shorter, E. (1977). *The making of the modern family.* New York: Basic.

Sigman, M., & Parmelee, A. H. Longitudinal evaluation of the high risk infant. In T. M. Field, A. M. Sostek, S. Goldberg, & H. H. Shuman (Eds.), *Infants born at risk: Behavior and development.* Jamaica, NY: Bruner-Mazel.

Stone, L. (1979). *The family, sex and marriage in England 1500–1800.* New York: Harper and Row.

Synge, J. M. (1962–68). *Works.* (Volumes I, II, III, IV). Oxford: Oxford University Press.

Toynbee, A. (1954). *A study of history, Vol. IV,* Oxford: Oxford University Press.

Trethowan, W. H. (1972). The Couvade syndrome. In J. Howells (Ed.), *Modern perspectives in psychoobstetrics.* Edinburgh: Oliver and Boyd.

Trivers, R. L. (1972). Parental investment and sexual selection. In B. Campbell (Ed.), *Sexual selection and the descent of man 1875–1971.* Chicago: Aldine.

Vaughn, B., Taraldson, B., Crichton, L., & Egland, B. (1980). Relationships between neonatal behavioral organization and infant behavior during the first year of life. *Infant Behavior and Development, 3,* 47–66.

Waters, E., Vaughn, B. E., & Egland, B. R. (1979). Individual differences in infant-mother attachment relationships at age one: Antecedents in neonatal behavior in an urban, economically disadvantaged sample. *Child Development, 51,* 821–829.

West, M. M., & Konner, M. J. (1976). The role of the father: An anthropological perspective. In M. Lamb (Ed.), *The role of the father in child development.* New York: Wiley.

Wrigley, E. A. (1977). Reflections on the history of the family. *Daedalus, 106,* 71–86.

Yogman, M. (1982). Development of the father-infant relationship. In H. Fitzgerald, B. Lester & M. Yogman (Eds.), *Theory and research in behavioral pediatrics.* New York: Plenum.

Yogman, M. (1985). The father's role with preterm and full-term infants. In J. Call, E. Galenson, & R. L. Tyson (Eds.), *Frontiers in infant psychiatry*, (Vol. II.) New York: Basic.

Yogman, M., Dixon, S., Tronick, E., Adamson, L., Als, H., & Brazelton, T. B. (1976). Father-Infant Interaction. *Pediatric Research, 10,* 309.

III ASIA

8 Fathers in Israel

Abraham Sagi
Nina Koren
Mayah Weinberg
University of Haifa

The role of the father in the family and in child development has been widely studied in recent years and we have substantially advanced our understanding of various aspects of fatherhood. We will not attempt to elaborate these advances here; the reader is referred to major reviews (e.g., Lamb, 1981) as well as to the introductory chapter of this volume. Our purpose is rather to examine fatherhood in a specific cultural context, detailing some aspects of fathering in Israel which may contribute to the understanding of fatherhood processes as a universal phenomenon.

This chapter is organized in the following way: In the introductory section we will present some of the unique as well as the universal features of Israeli society, with an emphasis on correlates of the family. Then we will venture into Israeli projects associated, directly and indirectly, with topics of universal concern, such as: increased paternal involvement, early infant-father interaction, formation of infant-father attachment, father absence, effects of early education programs with fathers, fathers and children at risk, fathers and human service organizations—including aspects such as the labor force, public policy, paternal legal status, and fathers in the welfare system. Finally, Israeli research on fatherhood will be critically integrated in terms of its universal generalizability.

OVERVIEW OF THE ISRAELI FAMILY

The special relationship which exists between Israel and the United States and close personal communication between Americans and Israelis cause Israel, to a greater extent than comparable countries, to adopt many current American attitudes and daily life activities. Unique Israeli features are nevertheless preserved, and differences still exist.

Israel is a young country characterized by waves of mass immigration. Thus, many young Israelis today have been brought up with diverse values and ethnic and religious influences. Israel is, moreover, an urban society: 92% of its Jewish population dwells in cities or townships; 24% of its labor force is employed in industry, 70% in services, and 6% in agriculture. Over the past two decades there has been a substantial increase in the participation of women in the Israeli labor force, including married women and mothers of preschool as well as school children. Despite this increase, however, the rate of women's participation in the labor market (40%) is still lower than that found in other Western countries (e.g., U.S.A. and Sweden) (Peres & Katz, 1984). In order to keep the labor force small so as to maintain full employment, the rate of maternal employment has always been kept low by government policy. Also, it should be noted that the average income of working women is lower than that of men (21% less per hour), and hence maternal employment is conceived as more marginal. These data relate to the Jewish sector of the Israeli population, which is the focus of this chapter. We will not attempt here to address family issues pertaining to non-Jewish minority groups.

The Jewish population in Israel can be divided roughly into two ethnic groups: Those originating from Afro-Asia and Islamic countries (55%), known as Sephardim, and those originating from European, North and South American, and various English-speaking countries, all known as Ashkenazim. A major difference between the two groups centers on the maintenance of traditional and religious family values, as opposed to the acquisition of modern values. The Sephardim are typically more traditional, and the Ashkenazim more westernized. Sephardic Israelis have tended to adhere to patriarchal values, extended kinship networks, large families, and a clear role division between men and women, with husbands as the breadwinners and the final authority in important decisions concerning the family. The sole responsibility of mothers was to care for their children (Palgi, 1969).

Eisikovits (1983) has discussed patterns of fatherhood in the context of a country with supportive immigrant absorption policies. The initial philosophy of immigration in Israel was based on the melting-pot model which resulted in a considerable rate of family disintegration, especially during the waves of mass Sephardic immigration in the 1950s. The melting-pot model has gradually been replaced by the pluralistic approach which recognizes that immigrants have different cultures, different parenting styles, different perceptions of how labor in the home should be divided, and so forth. The pluralistic approach might lead one to expect a more heterogeneous family system, as in other immigrant societies. There is empirical evidence, however, suggesting that families in the course of immigration (e.g., in Canada and Australia) are open to change and are receptive to a more egalitarian division in labor in their homes (Siddque, 1977;

Phillips, 1975). Similarly, despite strong attempts to safeguard their traditional family structure, Jewish immigrants from Russia, Georgia, and the Caucasus (Eilam, 1980; Eisikovits & Adam, 1981) have been found to undergo changes in family roles, which have enhanced the status of women and children within the family. Also, there is recent evidence suggesting that Sephardic Israelis undergo an acculturation process whereby they adopt many of the values associated with Ashkenazi Israelis, such as more egalitarian role division, increased rates of maternal employment, and increased paternal involvement in childcare. As Greenbaum and Kugelmass (1980) and Hai-Am (1985) conclude, Sephardic Israelis are continuously becoming less traditional and adjusting to Western values which prevail in Israeli society. There is a growing number of mixed marriages from the two ethnic sections and, for a growing number of young parents in Israel, the Sephardic/Ashkenazic distinction may not be as central as it used to be in the past.

In sum, because the vast majority of young parents today are Israeli-born and -raised, it seems to us important to approach the study of fathers in Israel from a standpoint which conceives most of the young families as being neither Ashkenazic nor Sephardic, but rather as Israelis. This is in line with Peres and Katz who provide evidence indicating a general trend toward diminishing ethnic differentiation in family structure, and a growing uniformity in various components of the family.

Peres and Katz (1981) and Katz and Peres (in press) described the power structure in contemporary Israeli families. Responsibilities for such basics as nutrition, care, and education are still female territory, whereas breadwinning and management of financial matters are considered as primarily male territory. Katz and Peres further report that the increase in the resources available to Israeli women in the realm of education, income, and occupational opportunities entails a more active participation in the process of decision making at home.

Peres and Katz (1981) have shown beyond doubt that despite the modernization which Israel has undergone, and despite the fact that rapid modernization in Western countries coincides with a decline in the centrality of the family, such a decline has not occurred among young Israeli families. This phenomenon deserves further comment. A major feature of life in Israel is the continuous threat to national security. Every healthy male in Israel is required by law to do reserve duty up to 45 days per year until the age of 54. This yearly load can be increased under the special circumstances of an active war. Thus, it would be practically impossible for Israelis to disregard an external national threat—a fact which adds a unique dimension to Israeli life in general, and to male roles in the family, in particular. It has been suggested (Peres & Katz, 1981) that this may reinforce familistic behavior. These writers contend that (in terms of the need-affiliation hypothesis) anxiety and awareness of personal danger are likely to raise the individual need for intimate affiliation (e.g., Freedman, Carlsmith, & Sears, 1974) and for a home as a stable emotional base. Also, we maintain that this unique situation stimulates paternal behavior to the effect that a considerably larger number of fathers in Israel—as compared to other Western countries—make the effort to be more active in family life and in childrearing.

Although direct international comparisons have not been conducted, we have reason to believe that family centrality is still more strongly preserved in Israel than in many Western countries. This is indirectly supported by a number of central social and demographic indices (Katz & Peres, in press; Peres & Katz, 1981). First, marriage is almost an absolute norm in the Jewish population, that is, the rates of those who do not marry at all or who marry after the age of 40 are marginal (2%–4%). Although the absolute rate of those who marry has not changed, a moderate increase in the age at marriage has occurred. It is assumed that this change is related to improved education (especially among women) and more effective methods of birth control. Second, birthrate is still higher in Israel than in many other Western countries (60% of its population have 2–4 children). This is despite the fact that the cost of living has been continuously on the rise in recent years and the economy is characterized by exceptionally high rates of inflation.

Third, until the 1970s there was considerable stability in the divorce rates of the Jewish family in Israel. This was in contrast with other trends in the Western world where the pattern was different; namely, signs of instability began to emerge as early as the mid 1960s. Since 1975, there has been a moderate increase in divorce rates in Israel as well but, comparatively speaking, the Israeli family is still more stable.

Lastly, Peres and Katz have pointed out that the family has always played a central part in religious and communal Jewish life. In the traditional Jewish community, there has always been an interplay between religion and family, and the most powerful religious influence on family life is evident in the legal system. In addition to the regular civil courts, Israel has Rabbinical courts which have the jurisdiction over all marital issues. Jewish religious institutions thus contribute to the centrality of the family. While the religious impact is most pronounced in religious sectors, its effect is felt by the entire Jewish population.

Taken as a whole, there are similarities and differences between Israel and other countries in relation to the family, but there are sufficient unique features associated with Israeli society in general, and with the Israeli family in particular, to merit a close examination of fathers in Israel. Indeed, cross-cultural research on patterns of fathering has recently been advocated by a number of scholars (e.g., Eibl-Eibesfeldt, 1983; Eisikovits & Wolins, 1983).

Cross-cultural research on fatherhood can be carried out in two complementary ways (Eisikovits & Wolins, 1983). One approach, anthropological in nature, would emphasize a context-specific inquiry usually employing qualitative instruments such as ethnographies. The other approach is that of cross-cultural developmental psychology, entailing the cross-cultural validation of various instruments in a systematic attempt to compare developmental concepts among cultures. The latter approach predominates in our analysis. To what extent the repertoire of fathering patterns in Israel resembles those found in other Western countries is the subject of the following sections, in the hope of shedding more light on the universality of fathering patterns.

FATHERS IN ISRAEL

After almost a decade of intensive investigation, it is apparent that fatherhood research has been approached from a variety of different angles and several directions have emerged. Styles, correlates, antecedents and consequences of paternal involvement, interaction, availability, and competence have been studied, some of these topics within the context of single-parent families, and some in intact families (e.g., Lamb, 1983; Lamb, Pleck, Charnov, & Levine, 1987; Lamb, Pleck, & Levine, 1985; Parke & Tinsley, 1983; Sagi & Sharon, 1983). We know today that we cannot treat fathers as a homogeneous group, but that we need to take into account individual differences which are the result of a constellation of variables. With this in mind, our review of Israeli research will be organized around the topics just outlined.

Fathers During the Pre-, Peri-, and Postnatal Stages

The prenatal and perinatal periods are generally viewed as a stage of transition to parenthood. Most research has focused on fathers in the perinatal and postnatal stages.

Branhill, Rubenstein, and Rockin (1979) suggested that during the prenatal stage the father holds the status of a "peripheral person," all preparations for the delivery being designed for the mother. Accordingly, a group of fathers was exposed to an intervention in which they were reinforced to deal with subjective feelings of loneliness. Paternal coping was facilitated by providing these men with information about pregnancy, and an opportunity to share their concern with their wives. Lahav (1984) took a somewhat more sophisticated approach and, in addition to the effect of intervention, examined psychological aspects of men during their wives' pregnancy. He found that androgynous fathers (as measured by the Bem Scale) reported greater pre-parental involvement than did either masculine- or feminine-type fathers. The masculine-oriented fathers were the least involved in pre-parental activities. Pre-parental behavior was defined in terms of emotional involvement in the pregnancy and physical assistance provided to the expectant mother. Consistent with Branhill et al., Lahav also found that prenatal intervention with the fathers had positive effects on pre-parental behavior. It is unfortunate, however, that the interaction effect between intervention and paternal gender-orientation was not reported.

In another study which combined both the prenatal and perinatal stages, Blum (1984) tested three groups of Israeli fathers: one group planned to attend the birth and underwent a preparatory course (no elaboration as to the nature of this course), the second attended the birth without a preparatory course, and the third was not present at delivery (no indication as to whether they attended any preparatory course). No differences were found on a variety of measures, including reports of husband-wife relationships, father-infant relationships, and levels of pain experienced on important variables by the mother during parturition. Owing to a lack of information, Blum's experimental design is questionable and makes it difficult to assess whether the absence of significant differences is the result of a methodological drawback or a genuine finding. Whatever accounts for this result, it is consistent with Palkovitz's (1985) recent review suggesting that there is no evidence to support bonding as a result of the father's early involvement with his infant.

In another interventive study, Ginger (1983) exposed one group of fathers and mothers to a fairly extensive intervention during the last trimester of pregnancy, consisting of information about infants' capabilities and perceptions, methods of caring for infants, and discussion of parental feelings about pregnancy, birth, and parenthood. Intervention took the form of group discussions, written material, and audiovisual demonstrations. The control group was exposed to a routine preparation course (Lamaze). On most outcome measures, no significant differences were found between the experimental and control groups. This finding is again consistent with Palkovitz's (1985) conclusion concerning the formative significance of early fatherhood history.

One postnatal study involving fathers has been conducted in Israel. Brenner (1984) took a correlational approach and found a moderate relationship between what she termed paternal involvement and maternal and paternal satisfaction with marital life. There were, however, a number of severe flaws in this study: The instrumentation process was methodologically deficient, there were some sampling problems, reports of findings seemed to be selective, and measures of association were based on variables which are not independent (self-reports from the same subject). It is unfortunate that this is the only Israeli study (to the best knowledge of the authors) conducted during the postnatal period, an area which has received increasing attention in the international fatherhood literature in recent years (e.g., Parke & Tinsley, 1983).

To summarize, the Israeli studies on fathers during the pre-, peri-, and postnatal stages indicate that fathers form a heterogeneous group and that paternal behavior toward infants may not necessarily be the consequence of intervention, but could result from a priori individual differences among fathers. Moreover, the Israeli research does not seem to indicate that early intervention with fathers has any formative significance on later paternal bonding.

Attachment Research

Only three studies on attachment behavior have been conducted in Israel, all of them in the kibbutz.

When discussing data pertaining to the kibbutz, it should be kept in mind that kibbutz members constitute only a tiny proportion of the population (about 3%), but at the same time have been heavily studied because of the uniqueness of the kibbutz as a social system. Unfortunately, much of the research on attachment and on patterns of sex differences in parent-child interaction has focused on Israeli kibbutzim (plural of kibbutz) whereas little research is available on city children. A brief description of this setting therefore seems in order.

The kibbutz is no longer a new phenomenon in sociological and psychological research, and its use as a natural laboratory has been discussed by Beit-Hallahmi and Rabin (1977). Each kibbutz is a cooperative community with an average of about 100 families. Kibbutz members, both men and women, work in agriculture and industry belonging to the kibbutz. The profits belong to the kibbutz as a system, and members are provided on an equal basis with housing, food, clothing, and other necessary services. During the day, children are cared for, physically and educationally, by child caretakers (metapelet—singular; meta-plot—plural) and teachers. Some kibbutzim still maintain the traditional style of sleeping arrangements, where the children sleep in a children's house together with other children of their own age rather than with their parents. Other kibbutzim have been shifting to a familial arrangement, whereby children join their parents in the afternoon and stay with them overnight.

Tiger and Shepher (1975) noted that most of the time which children spend with their parents is devoted to nurturant interactions, whereas education and socialization are taken care of by the collective system. Moreover, because the children's center is located inside the kibbutz (i.e., the childrens' home environment), it makes the parents more accessible to their children during the day. Indeed, family life is of crucial importance in the kibbutz. Tiger and Shepher stressed that couples usually make sure to have their meals together in the central dining room and are involved in cultural activities together, take their vacations together, and in many cases serve together during the night shifts (baby-sitting, etc.). Also, family parties are important occasions and parents take any oppor-tunity—sabbaths, holidays, and other occasions—to be with their children. There is an emphasis on what Tiger and Shepher refer to as "familism." Tiger and Shepher's findings indicated that it was the women (70%) who more strongly support the familial sleeping arrangement, whereas about 50% of the men did so. This figure is sufficient to indicate that many fathers want more involvement in the family.

The two initial studies by Maccoby and Feldman (1972) and Fox (1977) involved attempts to determine whether infants in kibbutzim formed attachments to their mothers and metaplot. Maccoby and Feldman concluded that 2-, 3-, and

4-year-olds were attached to their mothers, from evidence that the children protested at separation from their mothers and used their mothers as secure bases from which to explore. Fox showed that 8- to 20-month-olds protested at separation from both mothers and metaplot. This led him to conclude that the kibbutz childrearing practices do not prevent infants from forming attachments to their mothers, they simply allow children to form other attachments as well. A third study (Sagi, Lamb, Lewkowicz, Shoham, Dvir, & Estes, 1985) was designed to extend the findings of Fox and of Maccoby and Feldman. First, fathers were included as well, and this is in line with the conclusions of Lamb, Pleck, and Levine (1985) that infants can form attachment to their fathers just as they do to their mothers. Furthermore, Sagi, Lamb, Lewkowicz, Shoham, Dvir, and Estes (1985) sought to assess the security or insecurity of these relationships, using the Strange Situation procedure. Compared with samples studied previously in the United States, we found in the kibbutz sample a somewhat greater number of infants classified as insecure with their mothers but not with their fathers.

In line with Ainsworth, Blehar, Waters and Wall (1978), Sagi, Lamb, Lewkowitz, Shoham, Dvir, and Estes (1985) and Sagi et al. (1982) searched for factors likely to influence the development of C-type relationships, some of which may specifically account for the difference in distributions across attachment categories between mothers and fathers. From qualitative information obtained in the infants' houses and the parents' homes, it became apparent that maternal caretaking behaviors varied between these two settings. Mothers thus provided their infants with inconsistent experiences. Since fathers were less frequent visitors at the infants' houses, inconsistencies in father-infant interaction were less likely to occur. This perhaps explains the higher number of insecure mother-infant relationships.

A related finding is that, in an analysis of intra-individual consistency in security of infant attachment, there was no significant similarity between the infant's relationship with the mother and his/her relationship with the father. These findings are compatible with those of other researchers (Grossmann, Grossmann, Huber, & Wartner, 1981; Lamb, 1978; Lamb, Hwang, Frodi, & Frodi, 1982; Main & Weston, 1981). It should be noted that most researchers view this as evidence that the quality of the infant-mother attachment and the quality of the infant-father attachment are independent of one another, and result from the specific relationship between the infant and each of the parents, rather than result from the infant's temperament or personality traits.

We believe that the study of infant-parent relationships in the kibbutz system may add important information necessary to understand the process of attachment formation in infants. The unique setting of the kibbutz, the way fathers and mothers divide their responsibility for childcare, and the fact that fathers and mothers behave independently of one another all seem to provide indirect support for the contentions of Ainsworth et al. (1978) concerning the association between specific infant-adult relationships and insecurity/security of attachment. One note of caution should be mentioned. Questions have been raised recently concerning the validity of the Strange Situation procedure used by Sagi et al. (1985) and in other research on attachment worldwide (Lamb, Thompson, Gardner, Charnov, & Estes, 1984; Sagi, Lamb, & Gardner, in press). Not until these questions are addressed, both cross-culturally and methodologically, can we make definite statements from the data.

Sex Differences in Patterns of Parent-Child Interaction

In the last decade, sex differences in patterns of parent-child interaction have been explored using various approaches. Some researchers have studied behavior differences between mothers and fathers (Clarke-Stewart, 1978; Lamb, 1977c; Parke & Tinsley, 1981; Yogman, 1982), while others have been concerned with the social behavior of boys and girls (e.g., Maccoby & Jacklin, 1974). Interactions between sex of parent and sex of child have also been examined (Lamb, 1977a; Parke & O'Leary, 1976; Parke & Sawin, 1980). A reasonably clear picture has emerged, suggesting the existence of gender differences in parental behavior and differential treatment of boys and girls. The generalizability of these trends is limited, however, because most evidence is drawn from studies conducted in the United States.

The exploration of cross-cultural variability and consistency is especially important in light of speculation that the consistent behavior/gender differences documented in the United States are accounted for by biogenetic factors and/or early and continuous differential treatment of boys and girls by their environment.

It should be noted that three major sources of influence on sex-role differentiation have been identified: biogenetic factors, differential sex-role socialization, and immediate concrete demands of the specific role assumed by the parent (Lamb et al., 1987). In most research these factors are confounded, and therefore it has not been possible to determine the individual contribution of each of these sources of influence.

In one Israeli study conducted on kibbutzim, the investigators (Sagi, Lamb, Shoham, Dvir & Lewkowicz, 1985) were concerned with sex differences in parental and infant behavior. We assumed that, because of the kibbutz setting, it would be possible to isolate at least one source of influence on the development of sex role, namely, the immediate concrete demands of the specific role assumed by the parents.

Although males and females in the kibbutz system undergo socialization into traditional male and female roles, neither mothers nor fathers assume primary responsibility for parenting, as pointed out in the previous description of the kibbutz. It is evident that kibbutz mothers typically are more involved in childcare in early infancy than fathers are. However, during the 3 to 4 hours that infants spend each afternoon with their parents, the focus is on social interaction.

The parents, free from other responsibilities, can make themselves available to their children, and both parents engage in interaction with the child.

One of the hypotheses was the following: if the same pattern of sex differences in parental behavior observed in the United States was found on Israeli kibbutzim, this source of influence (i.e., immediate concrete demands) would not explain why mothers and fathers engaged in different types of interaction with their children. Instead, it would suggest that the other two sources of influence (biogenetic and differential socialization factors), albeit still confounded, may account for differences observed.

In the same study, the investigators also examined the behavior of infants who, because of the kibbutz setting, have fewer opportunities to interact with their mothers but more opportunities to interact with their fathers, compared with city-raised children. Should this shift have any formative effects on infants' preferences, one would not expect the preferences shown by American infants for the primary-caretaker mothers (Lamb, 1978).

In order to test these questions, first-born kibbutz-reared infants and their parents were observed. Sex differences in parental behavior similar to those observed in the United States (e.g., Field, 1978; Lamb, 1977c; Yogman, 1982) and in Sweden (Lamb, Frodi, Frodi, & Hwang, 1982; Lamb, Frodi, Hwang, Frodi, & Steinberg, 1982) were found. As in these countries, kibbutz mothers were more likely to vocalize, laugh, display affection, hold, and engage in caretaking than fathers were. Thus, the findings suggest that the concrete demands of the parental roles are not crucial determinants of these differences and that they may be accounted for by the more general sex-role expectations and/or biological factors.

Whereas American infants (especially boys) develop preferences for the same-sex parent on attachment-behavior measures (Lamb, 1977a, 1977b, 1977c) and Swedish infants develop preferences for their mothers (Lamb, Frodi, Hwang, & Frodi, 1983), these kibbutz infants showed no preference for either parent. The absence of preferences among the kibbutz infants may be due to the fact that neither parent served as primary caretaker beyond the first few months of life. Although it certainly exists, the differential involvement of mothers and fathers is not sufficiently great in the kibbutz to yield preferential relationships. In contrast to the interpretation of the parental behavior observed, the findings concerning infants' behavior may be interpreted as supporting the hypothesis that the concrete demands on parents do influence infant behavior—in this case, in the direction of absence of differential preference for either parent.

It is worth noting that infant preferences on attachment behaviors found in the United States (Lamb, 1976a, 1976b) were elicited in stressful situations, whereas the kibbutz observations were made in a stress-free context, so we do not know what might have been the preference pattern under more stressful conditions. Such information is of major importance because it would help determine how great a difference in the extent or type of parental involvement (Lamb, Frodi, Hwang, & Frodi, 1983) is necessary to cause infants to exhibit a preference for one parent or the other.

In sum, the nontraditional aspects of kibbutz life in general and parental involvement in particular, together with the observed data which tend toward the traditional direction, jointly seem to support the contention that sex of parent may have a more formative influence on parental behavior than factors associated with the family setting.

In a project comparing kibbutz and city pre-adolescents' perceptions of their parents (Avgar, Bronfenbrenner & Henderson, 1977; Devereux et al., 1974), both groups perceived their parents as equally supportive (i.e., nurturant, close, and warm) but the latter perceived their parents more as disciplinarians.

Although children's perceptions of both fathers and mothers were obtained, no detailed data distinguishing between mothers and fathers were reported. Rather, the authors stated that mothers significantly exceeded fathers in reported readiness to help children when they had problems, in pushing them to do their best, in letting them know how they expect them to act, and in employing withdrawal of companionship as a control technique. Fathers exceeded mothers only in their willingness to help children with their schoolwork. These patterns of parental role differentiation were virtually the same in the kibbutz and city samples, and in fact, similar to patterns observed in other countries (Devereux, Bronfenbrenner, & Suci, 1962; Devereux, Bronfenbrenner, & Rodgers, 1969). Interestingly, kibbutz settings had no effect on the way children perceived their fathers and mothers, despite the fact that social interaction between fathers and children in the kibbutz is more intense than that observed in the city.

Avgar et al. (1977) reported that, as in other cultures, both kibbutz and city boys saw their fathers as being more active with them than did girls. This greater involvement of fathers with boys occurred in the areas of both support and discipline. In contrast, girls in both samples saw their fathers as somewhat more indulgent. In both settings, mothers were seen as distributing their attentions more evenly between boys and girls on all supportive variables, while being somewhat more strict and punitive with boys than with girls.

It is unfortunate that these statements were not substantiated with statistical evidence. For some reason, despite reported differences between fathers and mothers, the authors decided to combine the data to yield a more general "parental" profile. Apparently, the authors were primarily interested in testing differences between settings. It should be recalled that the study was conducted more than a decade ago, when great excitement was generated by studies comparing kibbutzim with cities. Researchers were more concerned with main effects such as setting, paid less attention to interactions, and were also less aware of possible differences between fathers and mothers—all of which may explain why data on fathers and mothers were not presented separately. If we can regard the reported findings as real, one can see traditional patterns in both kibbutz and city in terms of parent-child interaction; the kibbutz setting did not make a difference.

The findings of Sagi, Lamb, Shoham, Dvir, and Lewkowicz (1985), Devereux et al. (1974) and Avgar et al. (1977) are consistent with studies conducted in the United States and another culture, namely, Sweden (Parke & Tinsley, 1983; Lamb, Frodi, Frodi, & Hwang, 1982). More specifically, American data reviewed by Parke and Tinsley (1983) suggest that both mothers and fathers may exhibit distinctive play styles, even when variations in maternal and paternal roles modify the amount of interaction. In Sweden, varying degrees of paternal involvement in infant care did not have a differential effect on parental behavior, a finding which led the investigators to conclude that sex of parent has more impact on parental behavior than family arrangements with regard to the concrete demands on mothers and fathers. Thus, the Israeli study is significantly informative for the understanding of universal early infant-parent interaction. Questions still remain about sex of parent as an important influence, and we do not know whether this is due to biogenetic factors, socialization factors, or both.

Varying Degrees of Paternal Involvement
and Child Outcome Measures

In a summary of key issues in the empirical literature concerning the role of the father in child development, Lamb (1983) has made a distinction between paternal involvement within traditional families (mother as caretaker, father as breadwinner) and families where fathers share equally in or are primarily responsible for childcare. He has presented evidence showing that within traditional families high paternal involvement is beneficial to children, whereas low paternal involvement can be detrimental to children.

The potentially positive contribution of paternal involvement within traditional families was not recognized until relatively recently, because researchers tended to assume that traditional families were normative and thus adaptive (and vice versa for deviations from the norm, e.g., father absence), and research questions were formulated accordingly. Increased paternal involvement in ways which deviate from the norm have only lately begun to receive attention (e.g., in the context of maternal employment) and negative assumptions were initially associated with this form of nontraditionality. Lamb (1983) and Lamb et al. (1987) indicate, however, that in families where fathers share equally in childcare or where they are the primary caretakers, the benefits seem to be extensive. These include cognitive competence, moral development, empathy, achievement motivation, sex role development, and adjustment. Lamb (1983) further suggests that paternal involvement per se may not necessarily be the direct cause of these effects. Rather, they may result from a combination of factors such as: two highly involved parents, high compatibility between family needs and employment arrangements, high congruence between maternal and paternal values concerning childrearing, and low marital conflict. In sum, what Lamb suggests is that children do best when there is a congruence between parents' values, preferences, and socioeconomic circumstances, and the way they divide their parental responsibilities.

Because we have Israeli data available from both traditional and nontraditional family settings, this distinction will be used as an organizational framework in reviewing these data. In a search for studies involving fathers in Israel, the following have been identified: two studies concerning moral and prosocial development, and another on the effects of paternal involvement on child autonomy, aggression, and adaptation—all within the traditional family. There are also two studies conducted within nontraditional settings, including the following outcome measures in children: development of empathy, sex role, locus of control, achievement motivation, and perceptions of parents.

Traditional Families

Moral and prosocial development.   Eisikovits and Sagi (1982) tested whether M. L. Hoffman's (1977) conceptualizations of the relationship between disciplinary techniques and moral development can account for findings that delinquents score lower than nondelinquents on various measures of moral development. Induction (i.e., reasoning) was found to be used less by fathers of delinquents than of nondelinquents, and fathers' use of induction was positively related to most moral measures. Sex of child was also found to be associated with use of disciplinary techniques by fathers; that is, fathers used induction with females more than with males. This is consistent with reports (Lamb, 1981) that fathers are more likely than mothers to behave more nurturantly with their daughters than with their sons, which may account for the finding that females are exposed to more induction by their fathers. Although the Eisikovits and Sagi study was not designed to focus directly on fathers (mothers were examined too, but these findings are beyond the scope of the present discussion), a number of implications seem to derive from the findings. First, we can see positive effects of fathers on their children, as reflected by the association between the use of induction and moral development. Second, negative paternal effects are evidenced as well. In normative terms, delinquency is seen as deviant, and hence as negative, and fathers' impact on delinquent behavior in children was demonstrated by the differential use of induction with delinquent and nondelinquent youths. Lastly, the differential use of induction with boys and girls is consistent with the stereotypic view of the ways fathers should treat their daughters and sons.

In another study, Bar-tal, Nadler, and Blechman (1980) explored, in preadolescent boys and girls, the association between their helping behavior and their perception of their fathers as being more or less inductive and power-assertive. A positive relationship was found, for boys, between helping behavior and the father's use of induction, and a negative relationship, for both boys and girls, between helping behavior and the use of power assertion. Furthermore, a positive relationship was reported between helping behavior in girls and their perception of their fathers as being supportive and as providing instrumental companionship. The findings of Bar-tal et al. are consistent with the general literature on socialization according to which identification with the same sex parent is an important socialization factor for boys, whereas girls more often identify with both parents. It is not surprising, therefore, that helping behavior in boys was found to be associated more with supportive paternal behavior than with maternal behavior, while helping behavior in girls was found to be associated with supportive behavior of both fathers and mothers.

In sum, both studies, one on moral development and the second on helping behavior, show that Israeli fathers and mothers activate socialization techniques which result in both negative and positive consequences consistent with the general literature in this area.

Autonomy, aggression, and adaptation.   In a study focusing primarily on father absence (to be reported in a later section), Levy-Shiff (1982) also reported data on patterns of fatherhood and their association with child outcome measures in intact families with three-year-old children. Extent, quality, and styles of involvement were assessed, yielding two total paternal involvement indices, one defined as caretaking involvement and the second as general (i.e., instrumental) involvement. Child outcome measures, including autonomy, aggression, and adaptation, were obtained independently of paternal measures. Levy-Shiff reported significant relationships between both indices of paternal involvement and child measures. More specifically, when the father was involved in both caretaking and instrumental behavior, the child was more autonomous, less aggressive, and more adaptive to his/her environment. Very little information is provided, however, on various important background variables in these families. For example, we do not know how many of the mothers participated in the labor force or what the division of labor in the home was, so it is far from clear which background and antecedent variables were associated with the group of more involved fathers. Were the involved fathers from a more traditional or nontraditional family setting? This is impossible to determine from the available data. One is reminded, however, that the data for this project were collected at a very early stage of fatherhood research (mid to late 70s), before definitions of traditionality and nontraditionality had been clearly stated. Moreover, there was a lack of sensitivity at that time among researchers in defining paternal involvement so as to take into consideration a variety of antecedent and other important variables, which only in later years were found to be of critical importance.

Despite this deficiency in Levy-Shiff's study, there was sufficient variability in paternal involvement in these families to indicate an association with important child measures. Thus, we have additional support from the Israeli context for the general conclusion that increased paternal involvement is associated with better psychosocial adjustment (Lamb, 1983).

Nontraditional Families

Increased paternal involvement. A more recent Israeli study in which greater attention was paid to the definition of nontraditionality was conducted by Sagi (1982). Sample selection was intended to ensure maximum variation in paternal styles and levels of involvement. Child measures included empathy, locus of control, sex-role orientation, and perception of the father in terms of dominance, nurturance, and punitiveness. As expected, greater paternal involvement was found to be associated with a higher level of empathy and an internal locus of control, and with perception of the father as more nurturant, more dominant, and less punitive. There was also a relationship between increased paternal involvement and a more masculine orientation in children. It should be noted that, although this pattern also applied to girls, their gender scores were nevertheless within the feminine range. The masculine orientation increased in girls, but their femininity score remained dominant. These findings show that a higher level of paternal involvement is associated with increased levels of both expressiveness (empathy) and instrumentality (internal locus of control), as well as with a broader perspective in gender orientation.

As suggested by Radin and Sagi (1982) and Sagi (1982), increasing paternal involvement can be conceived as an adoption of a new family role which, according to Aldous (1974), demands from men a high level of self-esteem, independence, interpersonal sensitivity, and control of the situation. Because such "role makers" can perform competently in diverse areas (e.g., in a conventional male occupation as well as in childcare), their sphere of influence in the family expands, and the entire system of family dynamics is affected. It is possible, therefore, that fathers who exhibit more nurturance than their traditional role permits do not reinforce in their children the stereotyped concepts concerning gender role. Instead, they may convey an attractive combination of both masculine and feminine traits. As Lamb and Frodi (1980) observed, there is no inherent contradiction between interpersonal warmth and masculinity.

Contrary to the "role making" hypothesis, Strauss, Gottesdiener, Fogel, and Tamari (1983) in another Israeli study attempted to support the Parsonian model (Parsons & Bales, 1955), claiming that their data indicated the dominant influence of mothers on children, whereas that of fathers was negligible. The study suffered from severe methodological problems, unclear instruments, confusion in items reflecting the instrumental and expressive concepts as presented by Parsons and Bales (1955), and selective presentation of significant correlations. Thus, the Sagi (1982) study remains the only valid Israeli study addressing this important aspect of fatherhood. The possible processes that may account for increased paternal involvement are still unclear, however, and there has not been as yet a thorough exploration of the motives for paternal involvement, or the reasons why some fathers play a greater role in childrearing than others do. These questions await further research. Also, the data of the Sagi study do not indicate whether paternal involvement has direct or only mediating effects on child development (e.g., compatible paternal employment context). A higher level of paternal nurturance may mediate such variables as sex-role orientation, independence, achievement, and locus of control. But it may also have a direct effect if, for example, more empathic fathers are imitated by their children, as Russell (1980) observed. These possibilities require further investigation.

Some limitations in generalizing from the Sagi (1982) study and a related study in the United States (Radin, 1982; Radin & Sagi, 1982) have been pointed out by Lamb (1982). An important reason for caution is that these data permit us merely to speculate about the effects of paternal involvement on children. Only correlational evidence is available about the relationship between paternal involvement and child measures, and the direction of this relationship is thus indeterminate. As with the Levy-Shiff (1982) study, we do not know whether additional characteristics—apart from paternal involvement—might contribute to the differences observed in the Sagi (1982) Israeli study. As Lamb suggests, only carefully designed longitudinal studies in which all of these important variables are taken into account will allow us to determine whether differences observed in child measures are caused by increases in paternal involvement. Furthermore, as a wide range of father-related variables is added to our research repertoire, clear-cut conclusions become even more elusive.

Moreover, Lamb et al. (1985), in summarizing the available research on the effects of increased paternal involvement, have shown that it promises both advantages and disadvantages in the family. Radin and Russell (1983) have called our attention to the fathers' perspective on increased paternal participation as an important variable to study, and they have presented some evidence suggesting that effects of increased paternal involvement on the father himself may be positive or negative. Similarly, L. W. Hoffman (1983) has focused on the effects of increased fathering on mothers, again presenting positive and negative aspects. Neither the Israeli study nor related studies in other cultures have examined these aspects in the depth proposed by these scholars, and this should be undertaken in future research on fathers. The Israeli study, with whatever limitations, contributes important data for those who are theoretically inclined to determine which aspects of parental behaviors are related to aspects of child development. Also, this research, together with other important studies (Lamb, Frodi, Hwang, & Frodi, 1982; Radin, 1982; Russell, 1982) have heightened interest in defining and studying nontraditional family forms, especially families in which fathers take a major role in childcare beyond that assumed by traditional fathers.

Father Absence

It is interesting to note that much of the research on the relationship between paternal involvement and psychological adjustment has been concerned with families where fathers are absent, and most findings show that father absence is associated with psychological maladjustment (for a review, see Biller, 1981). Questions have recently been raised about interpreting the results as effects of father absence per se. Rutter (1979), for example, has shown that marital discord, which (in cases of divorce, etc.) often precedes the absence itself, is perhaps the most significant variable directly associated with psychological maladjustment in children.

With regard to Israel, we are aware of only three studies related to the topic. In one study (Rosenfeld, Rosenstein, & Raab, 1973), the nature and effects of father absence in sailors' families were examined. The study employed qualitative methods of data collection without quantitative consideration. The authors reported behavior problems, maladjustment symptoms, and depression in children who were studied. The findings are consistent with those obtained by other investigators (Gronseth and Tiller, as cited in Rosenfeld et al., 1973).

There are two studies focusing on father absence due to death. Lifshitz (1976) compared children aged 9–14 in intact families with children whose fathers were killed in military service about 3–6 years before the study. Lifshitz reports various father-loss effects, but if the loss occurred before the age of 7, it had more adverse effects on cognitive development and child behavior than if it happened at a later age.

In the second study, Levy-Shiff (1978) investigated a group of three-year-olds who did not know their fathers at all. Some of the fathers were killed in the Yom Kippur War and some died because of illness. Unfortunately, Levy-Shiff treated all these children as a single group, although she suggested that "at least in the case of war orphans it is recognized that the father lost his life as a hero, a fact which may alleviate the feelings of the mother and cause the construction of a positive image" (p. 85). Levy-Shiff reported that father absence, more than the presence of a father was significantly associated with greater dependency, separation anxiety, difficulty in interaction with unfamiliar adults, and general emotional maladjustment. Because she assessed patterns of paternal involvement in all fathers, she was able to make a distinction between more involved fathers and less involved fathers in the intact families observed. She compared absence of "good" fathers and "bad" fathers and found that children without "good" fathers were not affected on various cognitive and behavioral measures as much as were children who had rejecting, restricting, and/or punitive fathers.

In sum, the fact that age of child interacted with loss of father in the Lifshitz study, and the fact that father absence was not the only influential factor in the Levy-Shiff study, are consistent with the general trend in the literature. As suggested above, other factors—more directly related to patterns of father-hood—are important and leave father absence per se with only a mediating role.

Fathers of Children at Risk

In recent years, researchers have drawn our attention to the fact that patterns of fatherhood can be further elaborated by looking at families with infants who are at a potential developmental risk. Since we now have one Israeli study address-ing fatherhood issues in this context, some consideration will be given to the issue.

In their review of the literature, Parke and Tinsley (1983) have shown that for a number of reasons the premature birth of a baby may increase the father's role in early caregiving. They presented evidence that paternal support in families with pre-term infants continues beyond the hospital period.

The only study with Israeli infants at risk was conducted by Levy-Shiff (1984), investigating fathers' involvement in spontaneous stimulation of devel-opmentally disabled young children. Levy-Shiff found that mothers verbalized, responded, paid attention, played with toys, and engaged in physical contact more frequently with their infants than did fathers.

However, because the amount of maternal interaction with developmentally disabled children decreased, differences between mothers and fathers were smaller than between parents of normally developed children. Unfortunately, because we do not know about the nature of maternal and paternal interaction in earlier stages of the infant's life, it is impossible to assess whether shifts had taken place in maternal and paternal behavior. These findings, therefore, cannot be compared with other reports on early paternal behavior with infants at risk younger than those studied by Levy-Shiff.

Maternal Employment

Another central variable related to paternal involvement is maternal em-ployment. There has been substantial controversy about whether or not maternal employment leads to increased paternal participation in household chores and childcare (L. W. Hoffman, 1983; Pleck, 1983). Hoffman claims that it does promote increased paternal participation, whereas Pleck contends that it depends to a great extent on the way we operationally define certain variables. Most scholars in the field (Lamb et al., 1987; Parke & Tinsley, 1983; Pleck, 1983) agree that fathers indeed increase the *proportion* of time which they devote to the total family work load when mothers participate in the labor force. However, it is suggested that this relative increase in paternal involvement occurs because wives have to reduce the amount of time they devote to housework and childcare, and not because husbands increase the absolute amount of time devoted to traditional maternal tasks. The complexity of the relationship between maternal employment and paternal involvement in family work is further illustrated by Russell's (1982) Australian study, in which he found that paternal involvement was changed as a function of maternal employment only when the families had children younger than 3 years of age.

Patterns of maternal employment in Israeli society are similar to those observed in other Western countries. Peres and Katz (1984) and Katz and Peres (in press) have shown a substantial increase in the rate of participation of women in the labor force in recent years, especially mothers of young children (about 24% in the mid 1950s vs. about 51% in the early 1980s). Age of children is no longer an obstacle to maternal employment. Consistent with Pleck's (1983) findings, the work load of mothers who combine paid work and family work is higher (13 hours per day) than that of either husbands (12 hours) or nonworking mothers (9 hours). Furthermore, there has not been a significant increase in absolute paternal involvement, but only a relative change. Husbands in both groups (i.e., with employed and nonemployed mothers) spend no more than 12 hours in activities involving paid work and family work, with a similar breakdown in both groups. Interestingly, size of family, which is perhaps still larger in Israel (among the Jewish population) than in other Western countries, was not found to be associated with any increase in paternal involvement in family work except when the number of children was more than 6, and this family size is not characteristic of Israeli society. Peres and Katz's (1984) study is the only large-scale survey on maternal employment in Israel and the patterns seem to be quite consistent with other findings.

In the Sagi (1982) study on various degrees of paternal involvement, maternal employment was of secondary concern, but some important findings may shed light on the issue. It was found that a large number of fathers highly involved in childcare had working wives. Moreover, of the families with highly involved fathers, most mothers had full-time employment, while in families with less involved fathers, most mothers had part-time jobs. As noted, however, the study was not designed to address directly the issue of maternal employment, and it is not clear to what extent the relationship between maternal employment and paternal involvement is associated with circumstantial or motivational factors.

As Lamb et al. (1987) note in their summary of the issue, because we do not have longitudinal data available, it is impossible to determine the direction of the relationship. We do not know whether maternal employment is an antecedent of increased paternal involvement, or whether maternal employment is made possible by increased paternal participation, or whether a third variable mediates between the two.

In sum, the Israeli data seem to contribute as much as findings in other national studies on the association between maternal employment and paternal involvement, and they, too, demonstrate the need to deepen the scope of inquiry in order to take into consideration the complexity of other variables.

Fathers in Human Service Organizations

The foregoing discussion has been concerned with various aspects of fatherhood without necessarily addressing their wider implications. This is the purpose of the present section, to examine human service organizations that are or should be concerned with fathers.

We will focus on two organizations for which empirical data are available, the child welfare system and the labor force.

The Child Welfare System

An examination of welfare services provided for children and families suggests that helping professionals (physicians, public health nurses, social workers, etc.) are not prepared ideologically, practically, or organizationally to encourage increased paternal involvement in the family (Jaffe, 1983; Lamb, Russell, & Sagi, 1983). Many child and family guidance clinics, for example, emphasize the importance of considering the entire family in the intervention process, yet it seems that they do little to involve all members of the family equally in treatment.

Lamb (1975) was the first to remind us that fathers are "forgotten contributors to child development." Jaffe (1983) draws our attention to the fact that fathers are "forgotten clients" in child welfare services. Jaffe examined all articles published in *Society and Welfare,* the Israeli quarterly journal of social work, since its inception in 1957. He noted that not a single article was found mentioning fathers as welfare clients, and this despite social workers' claim to acknowledge the importance of the father in social work intervention. Wolins (1983), on the basis of his extensive experience in the child welfare system, refers to the father as an "irrelevant" figure at best and as a "problem" at worst. Soliman and Mayseless (1982), working in an Israeli child, youth, and family clinic, took a more positive perspective. They examined the association between fathers' relationships with their children and psychotherapists' judgment of the children's problems. It was found that when the father's relationship with his child was good, the psychotherapist judged the problems to be less severe. Unfortunately, however, it is unclear whether both variables were assessed by the same workers, so that measurement interdependence may be a problem. Nevertheless, the study is important because it highlights the role of the father in the child welfare system. Approaching the issue from a different angle, Gilbert (1981) discussed the importance of psychological androgyny and has called our attention to the fact that flexibility and awareness of mental health service providers must be developed to deal with the concept of androgyny.

The issues just reviewed here have served as an impetus for two related studies in the Israeli child welfare system: (a) child welfare workers' perception of the role of fathers in the family and child welfare system; and (b) custody disputes as perceived by Israeli social work students and more experienced social workers.

Fathers in the child welfare system.   Sagi and Goldenberg (in preparation) assessed the attitudes of child welfare workers (all females) concerning the potential of males and females for successful childrearing, provision of nurturance, contribution to gender identity, and other related activities within the family. The findings showed child welfare workers to be very stereotypic in their outlook. They were maternally oriented, that is, they believed that mothers are better equipped than fathers with the tendencies and skills needed for successful parenthood. This view is inconsistent with recent research suggesting that fathers can be very capable parents (e.g., see review by Lamb, 1981). Furthermore, the same workers admitted that they involved significantly more mothers in treatment than any other group or combination of groups (e.g., mothers with children, fathers, fathers with children, parents and children). The study supported Jaffe's (1983) description of the father as a "forgotten client" in the child welfare system.

Custody Disputes.   We turn now to another important area in which current practices relating to fathers may not be consistent with the relevant research evidence, namely, custody disputes as perceived by Israeli social workers. As in most states in the United States, the doctrine of "the best interests of the child" (Goldstein, Freud, & Solnit, 1973) guides the work of the Israeli court system in child custody disputes. According to this principle, courts and affiliated professionals should strive to find the optimal arrangement for the child; decisions should be based on the quality of both past and future care provided by either parent, regardless of sex. In practice, such a consideration seems to ensure that (in most cases) mothers rather than fathers are awarded custody, because even in our changing society mothers still assume more responsibility for childcare than fathers do. However, contemporary changes in paternal involvement mean that an increasing number of fathers may qualify for custody. Despite these changes, judges still adhere to a maternal presumption and tend to prefer mothers over fathers, even when the father qualifies for custody. In their study, Settle and Lowery (1982) concluded that substantial discrepancies existed between the standard indicated by psychological research and those reported by judges.

Together with the general principle of the best interests of the child, the traditional assumption of the "tender years" doctrine (Thompson, 1983) guides the Israeli court system; namely, that a child under the age of 6, irrespective of gender, should be in the custody of its mother, except under special circum-stances (e.g., maternal unfitness) when fathers may be granted custody. Ben-or (1976) has suggested that to a great extent the interpretation of circumstances in relation to the concept of "best interests" is heavily influenced by the personal ideology of Israeli judges. It is not surprising, therefore, that a group of divorced fathers has recently formed a new "Association of Men for Fair Divorce."

Value bias may not be limited to judges. The expertise of helping profes-sionals and social workers working for the court has recently been challenged, and since experts in the helping professions are increasingly involved in custodial decisions, they may profoundly affect the outcome.

The study to be presented here (Sagi, in press; Sagi & Dvir, in preparation) is part of an ongoing project assessing the considerations used by professionals and judges in dealing with custody disputes. Inclusion of social workers in this type of study is becoming increasingly important, especially in view of recent data (Settle & Lowery, 1982) showing that many judges think that social workers or other professionals should be making decisions in custody cases, rather than the judges themselves. Because social workers provide recommendations for cus-tody arrangements to the Israeli courts, certified social workers constituted one group of experts questioned in this study. Social work students constituted an-other group. The students were considered important subjects because, as part of their training, they are continuously reminded to regard clients as unique indi-viduals, and to avoid imposing their own value system on their clients. Also, students are presumed to be exposed to the most up-to-date information and trends in social work and social science.

The subjects' recommendations in hypothetical custody disputes were as-sessed. Although the students and the workers used appropriate criteria (Thomp-son, 1983) in making their recommendations, custody was seldom awarded to fathers even when they qualified for it. There were indications that the subjects were value-biased in their judgments, even in cases in which both the best interest of the child and the knowledge now available to us suggest that custody should be awarded to the father.

Both studies (Sagi, in press; Sagi & Dvir, in preparation) invite the conclusion that social workers and social workers-to-be are not value-free. Despite profes-sional socialization emphasizing the essential need to detach professional judg-ments from personal values and social stereotypes, this does not seem to be the case. Perhaps the effectiveness of professional socialization should be recon-sidered. Meanwhile, social workers, at least in this context of inquiry, seem to continue to articulate the phenomenon of the father as a "forgotten client." It is not surprising that in Heyns's (1985) assessment of the organization and delivery of child services, she points out that the child welfare system in our society is in a relatively weak position compared to other human service organizations. This weakness might be associated with the fact that the child welfare system is female-oriented, and, as she suggests, female orientation in our society is still associated with a lack of political power.

The Labor Force

In order to better understand the role of the father in the family, we ought to consider the many ecological contexts in which people live (Bronfenbrenner, 1979). Accordingly, Sagi (in press) devised a study which was aimed at describing employers' attitudes toward family policy and the role of mothers and fathers in the family and workplace. Hwang, Elden, and Fransson (1983), in their Swedish study, suggest that the attitudes of employers and workmates may be a major factor which impedes the successful implementation of family policy in Sweden. This was the impetus for the Sagi study.

Personnel directors were interviewed concerning their attitudes toward parental roles in the family and their support for maternal policy and family policy programs. Most employers correctly observed that fathers are not as involved as mothers in childcare, and that the combined paid work and family work load is larger for mothers. This is consistent with data derived from systematic time-use analyses (Pleck, 1983). Employers also believed that males and females are equally concerned about their children and about their own possible contributions to childrearing and the quality of family life. Nevertheless, the personnel directors mainly supported maternal programs and were significantly less supportive of those family-oriented programs that may be needed to actualize or maximize paternal skills and contributions, thereby reducing the maternal workload.

Examples of maternally-oriented programs in Israel are maternity rather than parental leave, child sickness leave for mothers rather than for both parents, special tax credits for working mothers, preference given to working mothers in admitting children to day-care centers, and the like. As Sagi and Sharon (1983) suggested, although the various plans and benefits designed only for working mothers were well-intentioned, their effect may be to prevent a more equitable role allocation and, thus, to prolong the inequitable division of workloads between mothers and fathers.

In sum, the Sagi study suggests that although employers do not equally support programs for mothers and fathers, they have a positive attitude toward the family. Rather than expecting all employers to behave similarly, we have to develop strategies to approach employers more sensitively and effectively, acknowledging that there are individual differences in their perceptions. We may also need to develop educational programs for young children in order to change rigidly stereotyped perceptions of parental roles. Future generations should be made aware that the range of options among which parents may choose will be beneficial for employers, workers, families, and society-at-large.

Since Israel is a Westernized and industrialized nation, with a growing participation of women in the labor force, it is unlikely that the findings and issues discussed here are a purely local phenomenon. But clearly, further research on these issues should be carried out in additional cross-cultural contexts.

This is especially important in view of Cherlin's (1983) contentions that changes in corporate and government policy will not automatically bring about the desired changes in male and female roles. Evidence from Sweden and China suggests that state policy has not relieved the double burden of employed wives, and indicates that the ideology of male and female roles is resistant to change. Large-scale social and economic changes are required, however unpopular this view.

SUMMARY

The purpose of this chapter was to examine the repertoire of fathering patterns in Israel in relation to that found in other Western countries, and to assess the extent to which the Israeli findings can be generalized to other cultures.

We have chosen to review, in an Israeli context, as many topics as possible related to the issue of fathering. These included: components, antecedents, and consequences of paternal behavior; paternal competence; sex differences in parent-child interaction; traditional vs. nontraditional families; and policy-related aspects of fathering.

Taken as a whole, findings reviewed in this chapter are compatible with those reported in the general literature on fatherhood. The series of studies on fathers during the pre-, peri-, and post-natal stages are consistent with the claim that there is no evidence supporting the seemingly plausible hypothesis that the father's early history with his infant may have formative significance for the development of early paternal bonding.

Attachment research in Israel suggest that infants can form secure attachments to fathers as well as to mothers. The findings support, at least in part, Ainsworth et al.'s (1978) model of the relationship between a number of antecedent variables and attachment formation. The differentiation found between infant-father and infant-mother attachment further supports the notion of the importance of specific infant-adult relationships to the infant's own development. However, the Israeli study on attachment (Sagi, Lamb, Lewkowicz, Shoham, Dvir & Estes, 1985) suggests that cultural components may be associated with attachment behavior in the Strange Situation test, and that what we observed in this procedure was a culturally specific reaction of infants to strangers. The Israeli findings contribute to the general debate concerning measurement of attachment, as elaborated in a recent major review in the field (Lamb et al., 1984).

We have also been able to examine the nature and styles of parent-infant interaction in the unique setting of the kibbutz, in which we have shown that some patterns of parental involvement differ from those observed in most traditional Western societies. Despite the uniqueness of the setting observed, findings were in the traditional direction, supporting the conclusion of Lamb et al. (1985) that sex of parent may affect parent-child interaction more than changes in the setting in which the child is being raised, even when the nature of the setting minimizes the concrete demands that are on parents in most traditional societies. This finding is in line with the contention that early parent-infant interaction originates in either biogenetic factors or early socialization practices, and is not a function of the immediate concrete demands of the situation. As in other studies, the Israeli study still leaves biological and socialization variables confounded.

Considerable attention has been devoted to the series of studies examining the effects on children and parents of various degrees of paternal involvement in both traditional and nontraditional family arrangements, and also in the context of father absence and of families with infants at developmental risk. Again, consistent with most studies in other countries, paternal involvement was found to have both positive and negative aspects. This suggests that the shift from the "forgotten father" era has been an over-reaction, culminating in calls for the immediate institutionalization of increased paternal involvement in every aspect of life. The Israeli findings, together with other findings, show that, as in any other aspect of child development, there are individual differences in the nature and meaning of various degrees of paternal involvement, and these differences must be acknowledged both in future research and public policy considerations.

Lastly, we have reviewed fatherhood research from a policy perspective. All three studies examined indicate that professional workers in welfare agencies are stereotypically minded and regard fathers quite traditionally—despite the training of social workers for greater flexibility in their personal value system, and the emphasis on application of available knowledge concerning both fathers and mothers. The labor system is stereotypic as well, both at the attitudinal level of employers, and at the policy level concerning various aspects of parent-child interaction.

In all, the Israeli family is similar in many respects to the family in other countries, although there are some unique features associated with the implications of immigration, religion, economy, and national security. We have suggested that the unique Israeli situation can reinforce the striving on the part of men for a more active role in family life. However, these differences are apparently not sufficiently strong to be reflected in patterns of fatherhood as studied in the various contexts described in this chapter. As noted before, patterns of fatherhood in Israel and their impact on both parents and children are consistent with those documented in other countries. This traditional role division and its stereotypic connotations were succinctly expressed in a recent nationwide campaign organized by a highly influential women's organization in Israel (Na'amat) and heavily advertized by all means of mass communication (TV, radio, car stickers, etc.). Its principal slogan was "Be a man—give her a hand."

REFERENCES

Ainsworth, M. D. S., Blehar, M. C., Waters, E., & Wall, S. (1978). *Patterns of attachment.* Hillsdale, NJ: Lawrence Erlbaum Associates.
Aldous, J. (1974). The making of family roles and family change. *The Family Coordinator, 23,* 231–235.

Avgar, A., Bronfenbrenner, U., & Henderson, C. R. (1977). Socialization practices of parent, teachers, and peers in Israel: Kibbutz, moshav, and city. *Child Development, 48,* 1219–1227.

Bar-tal, D., Nadler, A., & Blechman, N. (1980). The relationship between Israeli children's helping behavior and their perception of parent's socialization practices. *The Journal of Social Psychology, 111,* 159–167.

Beit-Hallahmi, B., & Rabin, A. I. (1977). The kibbutz as a social experiment and as a child-rearing laboratory. *American Psychologist, 32,* 532–541.

Ben-or, Y. (1976). On the meaning of "the best interest of the child." *Hapraclit, 29,* 608–622.

Biller, H. B. (1981). Father absence, divorce, and personality development. In M. E. Lamb (Ed.), *The role of the father in child development.* (2nd ed.) New York: Wiley.

Blum, C. (1984). *The relationship between father's presence at delivery and the development of father-child, husband-wife relationship after childbirth.* Unpublished master's thesis, Bar-Ilan University, Tel Aviv.

Branhill, L., Rubenstein, G., & Rockin, N. (1979). From generation to generation: Fathers-to-be in transition. *The Family Coordinator, 28,* 229–235.

Brenner, M. (1984). *The relation between the amount of fathering and the satisfaction of the father and the mother with the marriage.* Unpublished master's thesis, Bar-Ilan University, Tel Aviv.

Bronfenbrenner, U. (1979). *The ecology of human development.* Cambridge, MA.: Harvard University Press.

Cherlin, A. (1983). Family policy: The conservative challenge and the progressive response. *Journal of Family Issues, 4,* 427–438.

Clarke-Stewart, K. A. (1978). And daddy makes three: The father's impact on mother and young child. *Child Development, 49,* 466–478.

Devereux, E. C., Bronfenbrenner, U., & Rodgers, R. R. (1969). Child-rearing in England and the United States: A cross-cultural comparison. *Journal of Marriage and the Family, 31,* 257–270.

Devereux, E. C., Bronfenbrenner, U., & Suci, G. (1962). Patterns of parent behavior in the United States of America and the Federal Republic of Germany: A cross-national comparison. *International Social Science Journal, 14,* 488–506.

Devereux, E. C., Shouval, R., Bronfenbrenner, U., Rodgers, R. R., Kav-Venaki, S., Kiely, E., & Karson, E. (1974). Socialization practices of parents, teachers, and peers in Israel: The kibbutz versus the city. *Child Development, 45,* 269–281.

Eibl-Eibesfeldt, I. (1983). Patterns of parent-child interaction in a cross-cultural perspective. In A. Oliverio & M. Zappella (Eds.), *The behavior of human infants.* New York: Plenum.

Eilam, Y. (1980). *The Georgians in Israel: Anthropologocal Perspective.* Jerusalem: Hebrew University.

Eisikovits, R. (1983). Paternal child care as a policy-relevant social phenomenon and research topic: The question of values. In M. E. Lamb & A. Sagi (Eds.), *Fatherhood and family policy.* Hillsdale, NJ: Lawrence Erlbaum Associates.

Eisikovits, R., & Adam, V. (1981). The social integration of new immigrant children from the Caucasus in Israeli schools. *Studies in Education, 31,* 77–84.

Eisikovits, R., & Wolins, M. (1983). Cross-cultural uses of research on fathering. In M. E. Lamb & A. Sagi (Eds.), *Fatherhood and family policy.* Hillsdale, NJ: Lawrence Erlbaum Associates.

Eisikovits, Z., & Sagi, A. (1982). Moral development and discipline encounter in delinquent and nondelinquent adolescents. *Journal of Youth and Adolescence, 11* 217–230.

Field, T. (1978). Interaction behaviors of primary versus secondary caretaker fathers. *Developmental Psychology, 14,* 183–184.

Fox, N. (1977). Attachment of kibbutz infants to mother and metapelet. *Child Development, 48,* 1228–1239.

Freedman, J. L., Carlsmith, J. M., & Sears, D. O. (1974). *Social Psychology,* Englewood Cliffs, NJ: Prentice Hall.

Gilbert, L. A. (1981). Toward mental health: The benefits of psychological androgyny. *Professional Psychology, 12,* 29–38.

Ginger, R. (1983). *Education for parenthood as a means of increasing fathers' competence in their babies' upbringing.* Unpublished master's thesis, Haifa University, Haifa.

Goldstein, J., Freud, A., & Solnit, A. (1973). *Beyond the best interests of the child.* New York: Macmillan.

Greenbaum, C. W., & Kugelmass, S. (1980). In N. Warner (Ed.), *Studies in cross-cultural psychology: Vol. 2.* New York: Academic Press.

Grossmann, K. E., Grossmann, K., Huber, F., & Wartner, W. (1981). German children's behavior toward their mothers at 12 months and their fathers at 18 months in Ainsworth's Strange Situation. *International Journal of Behavioral Development, 4,* 157–181.

Hai-Am, S. (1985). *Attitudes toward parental role during infancy amongst Israeli fathers and mothers of North African origin.* Unpublished master's thesis, The Hebrew University, Jerusalem.

Heyns, B. (1985). *The mandarins of childhood: The organization and delivery of child services.* Paper presented at a colloquium at the Department of Sociology, Haifa University, Haifa.

Hoffman, L. W. (1983). Increased fathering: Effects on the mother. In M. E. Lamb & A. Sagi (Eds.), *Fatherhood and family policy.* Hillsdale, NJ: Lawrence Erlbaum Associates.

Hoffman, M. L. (1977). Moral internalization: Current theory and research. In L. Berkowitz (Ed.), *Advances in experimental social psychology:* (Vol. 10.) New York: Academic Press.

Hwang, C-P., Elden, G., & Fransson, C. (1983). Arbetsgivares och arbetskamraters attityder till pappaledigheid. Unpublished manuscript, the University of Goteborg, Sweden.

Jaffe, E. D. (1983). Fathers and child welfare services: The forgotten client? In M. E. Lamb & A. Sagi (Eds.), *Fatherhood and family policy.* Hillsdale, NJ: Lawrence Erlbaum Associates.

Katz, R., & Peres, Y. (in press). Trends in the Israeli family. *Megamot.* (in Hebrew).

Lahav, Y. (1984). *Psychological aspects of men during their wives' pregnancy.* Unpublished master's thesis, Tel Aviv University, Tel Aviv, Israel.

Lamb, M. E. (1975). Fathers: Forgotten contributors to child development. *Human Development, 4,* 245–266.

Lamb, M. E. (1976a). Effects of stress and cohort on mother- and father-infant interaction. *Developmental Psychology, 12,* 435–443.

Lamb, M. E. (1976b). Twelve-month-olds and their parents: Interaction in a laboratory playroom. *Developmental Psychology, 12,* 237–244.

Lamb, M. E. (1977a). The development of mother-infant and father-infant attachment in the second year of life. *Developmental Psychology, 13,* 637–648.

Lamb, M. E. (1977b). The development of parental preferences in the first two years of life. *Sex Roles, 3,* 495–497.

Lamb, M. E. (1977c). Father-infant and mother-infant interaction in the first year of life. *Child Development, 48,* 161–181.

Lamb, M. E. (1978). Qualitative aspects of mother- and father-infant attachment. *Infant Behavior and Development, 1,* 265–275.

Lamb, M. E. (1981). Fathers and child development: An integrative overview. In M. E. Lamb (Ed.), *The role of the father in child development.* NY: Wiley.

Lamb, M. E. (1982). Generalization and inferences about causality in research on nontraditional families: Some cautions. *Merrill-Palmer Quarterly, 29,* 157–161.

Lamb, M. E. (1983). *The role of the father in child development: A summary of key issues in the empirical literature.* Testimony prepared for presentation to the Select Committee on Children, Youth, and Families. Washington, D.C.: House of Representatives.

Lamb, M. E., & Frodi, A. M. (1980). The role of the father in child development. In R. R. Abidin (Ed.), *Handbook of parent education.* Springfield, Ill.: Charles C. Thomas.

Lamb, M. E., Frodi, A. M., Frodi, M., & Hwang, C. P. (1982). Characteristics of maternal and paternal behavior in traditional and nontraditional Swedish families. *International Journal of Behavioral Development, 5,* 131–141.

Lamb, M. E., Frodi, A. M., Hwang, C. P., & Frodi, M. (1982). Varying degrees of paternal involvement in infant care: Attitudinal and behavioral correlates. In M. E. Lamb (Ed.), *Nontraditional families: Parenting and child development.* Hillsdale, N.J.: Lawrence Erlbaum Associates.

Lamb, M. E., Frodi, A. M., Hwang, C. P., Frodi, M., & Steinberg, J. (1982). Mother- and father-infant interaction involving play and holding in traditional and nontraditional Swedish families. *Developmental Psychology, 18,* 215–221.

Lamb, M. E., Frodi, M., Hwang, C. P., & Frodi, A. M. (1983). Effects of paternal involvement on infant preferences for mothers and fathers. *Child Development, 54,* 450–458.

Lamb, M. E., Hwang, C. P., Frodi, A., & Frodi, M. (1982). Security of mother- and father-infant attachment and its relation to sociability with strangers in traditional and nontraditional Swedish families. *Infant Behavior and Development, 5,* 355–367.

Lamb, M. E., Pleck, J. H., Charnov, E. L., & Levine, J. A. (1977). A biosocial perspective on paternal behavior and involvement. In J. B. Lancaster, A. Rossi, J. Altmann & L. R. Sherrod (Eds.), *Parenting across the lifespan: Biosocial perspectives.* Chicago: Aldine.

Lamb, M. E., Pleck, J. H., & Levine, J. A. (1985). The role of the father in child development: The effects of increase of paternal involvement. In B. B. Lahey & A. E. Kazdin (Eds.), *Advances in clinical psychology:* (Vol. 8.) New York: Plenum.

Lamb, M. E., Russell, G., & Sagi, A. (1983). Summary and recommendations for public policy. In M. E. Lamb & A. Sagi (Eds.), *Fatherhood and family policy.* Hillsdale, NJ: Lawrence Erlbaum Associates.

Lamb, M. E., Thompson, R. A., Gardner, W., Charnov, E. L., & Estes. (1984). Security of attachment as assessed in the Strange Situation: Its study and biological interpretation. *Behavioral and Brain Science, 7,* 127–147.

Lifshitz, M. (1976). Long range effects of father's loss: The cognitive complexity of bereaved children and their school adjustment. *The British Journal of Medical Psychology, 49,* 187–189.

Levy-Shiff, R. (1978). *The father's role in infancy: The influence of patterns of fathering and of father absence on the child's early development.* Unpublished doctoral dissertation, The Hebrew University, Jerusalem.

Levy-Shiff, R. (1982). The effects of father absence on young children in mother-headed families. *Child Development, 53,* (5), 1400–1405.

Levy-Shiff, R. (1984). *Father's involvement in spontaneous stimulation of developmentally disabled young children: Implications for intervention program.* Manuscript submitted for publication.

Maccoby, E. E., & Feldman, S. S. (1972). Mother attachment and stranger reactions in the third year of life. *Monographs of the Society For Research in Child Development, 37,* (serial number 146).

Maccoby, E. E., & Jacklin, C. N. (1974). *The psychology of sex differences.* Stanford: Stanford University Press.

Main, M. B., & Weston, D. R. (1981). Security of attachment to mother and father: Related to conflict behavior and the readiness to establish new relationships. *Child Development, 52,* 932–940.

Palgi, P. (1969). Types of families in Israel: A multi-variate study of aculturation. In R. Bar-Yosef & A. Shelach (Eds.), *The Family in Israel,* Jerusalem: Acadomon.

Palkovitz, R. (1985). Father's birth attendance, early contact, and extended contact with their newborns: A critical review. *Child Development, 56,* 392–407.

Parke, R. D., & O'Leary, S. (1976). Father-mother-infant interaction in the newborn period: Some findings, some observations, and some unresolved issues. In K. F. Riegel & J. Meachan (Eds.), *The developing individual in a changing world: Vol. 2 Social and environmental issues.* The Hague: Mouton.

Parke, R. D., & Sawin, D. B. (1980). The family in early infancy: Social interactional and attitudinal analyses. In F. A. Pedersen (Ed.), *The father-infant relationship: Observational studies in the family setting.* New York: Praeger Special Studies.

Parke, R. D., & Tinsley, B. R. (1981). The father's role in infancy: Determinants of involvement in caregiving and play. In M. E. Lamb (Ed.), *The role of the father in child development.* (2nd ed.), New York: Wiley.

Parke, R. D., & Tinsley, B. R. (1983). Fatherhood: Historical and contemporary perspectives. In K. A. McCluskey & H. W. Reese (Eds.), *Life span developmental psychology: Historical and cohort effects.* New York: Academic Press.

Parsons, T., & Bales, R. F. (1955). *Family, socialization and interaction process.* Glencoe, IL: Free Press.

Peres, Y., & Katz, R. (1981). Stability and centrality: The nuclear family in modern Israel. *Social Forces, 59,* 687–704.

Peres, Y., & Katz, R. (1984). *The working mother and her family: A demographic survey, social analysis, and policy considerations.* Tel-Aviv, Israel: Modi'im ezrachi Ltd. (in Hebrew).

Phillips, D. (1975). The effects of immigration on the family: The case of Italians in rural Australia. *British Journal of Sociology, 26,* 218–226.

Pleck, J. H. (1983). Husbands paid work and family roles: Current research issues. In H. Z. Lopata & J. H. Pleck (Eds.), *Research on the interweave of social roles: Families and jobs,* (Vol. 3). Greenwich, CT: JAI Press.

Radin, N. (1982). Primary caregiving and role-sharing fathers. In M. E. Lamb (Ed.), *Nontraditional families: Parenting and child development.* Hillsdale, NJ: Lawrence Erlbaum Associates.

Radin, N., & Russell, G. (1983). Increased paternal participation: The fathers' perspective. In M. E. Lamb & A. Sagi (Eds.), *Fatherhood and family policy.* Hillsdale, NJ: Lawrence Erlbaum Associates.

Radin, N., & Sagi, A. (1982). Childrearing fathers in intact families, II: Israel and the U.S.A. *Merrill Palmer Quarterly, 28,* 111–136.

Rosenfeld, J. M., Rosenstein, E., & Raab, M. (1973). Sailor families: The nature and effects of some kind of father absence. *Child Welfare, 52,* 33–44.

Russell, G. (1980). Fathers as caregivers: Possible antecedents and consequences. Paper presented at a study group on "The role of the father in child development: Theory, social policy and the law", sponsored by the Society for Research in Child Development, Haifa, Israel.

Russell, G. (1982). Shared-caregiving families: An Australian study. In M. E. Lamb (Ed.), *Nontraditional families: Parenting and child development.* Hillsdale, NJ: Lawrence Erlbaum Associates.

Rutter, M. (1979). Maternal deprivation, 1972–1978: New findings, new concepts, new approaches. *Child Development, 50,* 283–305.

Sagi, A. (1982). Antecedents and consequences of various degrees of paternal involvement in child rearing: The Israeli project. In M. E. Lamb (Ed.), *Nontraditional families: Parenting and child development.* Hillsdale, NJ: Lawrence Erlbaum Associates.

Sagi, A. (in press). Custody disputes as perceived by Israeli social work students. *Journal of Divorce.*

Sagi, A. (in press). Attitudes of employers toward family policy and increased paternal involvement in child care. *Child Care Quarterly.*

Sagi, A. & Dvir, R. (in preparation). *Custody disputes as perceived by Israeli social workers.*

Sagi, A., & Goldenberg, E. (in press). *Fathers as perceived by Israeli Social welfare workers.*

Sagi, A., Lamb, M. E., Estes, D., Shoham, R., Lewkowicz, K., & Dvir, R. (1982). *Security of infant-adult attachment among kibbutz-reared infants.* Paper presented to the International Conference on Infant Studies, Austin, Texas.

Sagi, A., Lamb, M. E., & Gardner, W. (in press). Relationships between Strange Situation behavior and stranger sociability among infants on Israeli kibbutzim. *Infant Behavior and Development.*

Sagi, A., Lamb, M. E., Lewkowitz, K. S., Shoham, R., Dvir, R., & Estes, D. (1985). Security of infant-mother, -father, and -metapelet attachments among kibbutz-reared children. In I. Bretherton and E. Waters (Eds.), *Growing points of attachment theory and research. Monographs of Society for Research in Child Development, 50,* Serial no. 209.

Sagi, A., Lamb, M. E., Shoham, R., Dvir, R., & Lewkowicz, K. (1985). Parent-infant interaction in families on Israeli kibbutzim. *International Journal of Behavioral Development, 8,* 273–284.

Sagi, A., & Sharon, N. (1983). Costs and benefits of increased paternal involvement in childrearing: The societal perspective. In M. E. Lamb & A. Sagi (Eds.), *Fatherhood and family policy.* Hillsdale, NJ: Lawrence Erlbaum Associates.

Settle, S. A., & Lowery, C. R. (1982). Child custody decision: Content analysis of a judicial survey. *Journal of Divorce, 5,* 125–138.

Siddque, C. M. (1977). On migrating to Canada: The first generation Indian and Pakistani families in the process of changing. *Sociological Bulletin, 26,* 203–226.

Soliman, P., & Mayseless, O. B. (1982). Correlates between mother's employment, father's involvement and child mental health. *Israeli Journal of Psychiatry and Related Sciences, 19,* 121–127.

Strauss, H., Gottesdiener, H., Fogel, R., & Tamari, D. (1983). On entering first grade: Note on impact of parents' attitudes on expectations of their children, an Israeli case. *Perceptual and Motor Skills, 56,* 362–370.

Thompson, R. A. (1983). The father's case in child custody disputes: The contributions of psychological research. In M. E. Lamb & A. Sagi (Eds.), *Fatherhood and family policy.* Hillsdale, NJ: Lawrence Erlbaum Associates.

Tiger, L., & Shepher, J. (1975). *Women in the Kibbutz.* New York: Harcourt Brace Jovanovich.

Wolins, N. (1983). The gender dilemma in social welfare: Who cares for children? In M. E. Lamb & A. Sagi (Eds.), *Fatherhood and family policy.* Hillsdale, NJ: Lawrence Erlbaum Associates.

Yogman, M. W. (1982). Development of the father-infant relationship. In H. Fitzgerald, B. Lester, & M. W. Yogman (Eds.), *Theory and research in behavioral pediatrics* (Vol. 1). New York: Plenum.

9 Fatherhood in Chinese Culture

David Y. F. Ho
University of Hong Kong

The study of fatherhood in Chinese culture is significant for a number of reasons. First, the simple fact of numerical superiority: Chinese fathers outnumber those of any other ethnic or national group. Second, it is a study of fatherhood in the culture with the longest unbroken history—one governed by the stringent ethic of Confucian filial piety. Third, the Chinese family has been undergoing transformation since the turn of the present century. One would ask: What concomitant changes in fatherhood have occurred?

In this chapter, I shall describe the pattern of fatherhood in traditional Chinese society, review relevant empirical studies from both Chinese– and English-language sources, and discuss the theoretical significance of the father's role in Chinese culture.

THE TRADITIONAL PATTERN

Given China's long history of unbroken cultural continuity and the Chinese reverence for tradition, a glimpse into the distant past is probably more meaningful and necessary for understanding the present than it would be in the case of any other culture. Specifically, for a full understanding of fatherhood in Chinese culture, a historical perspective is indispensable.

Confucianism and Filial Piety

The definition of fatherhood in traditional China was primarily a Confucian definition: Unquestionably, the father was the official head of the household.

227

Confucianism has been the dominant ethic for more than 2,000 years and was seriously challenged until the turn of the present century. It is, above all, an ethic for governing human relationships. The most important of these are the Five Cardinal Relationships: those between ruler and minister, father and son, husband and wife, elder and younger brothers, and friends. Of these five, the father-son relationship occupies the key position in the social fabric. And governing it are the precepts of filial piety, the cornerstone of Confucianism.

In traditional Chinese society, a son was expected to be obedient and respectful toward his parents, to provide for their material as well as mental well-being in their old age, and to perform ceremonial duties of ancestral worship after their death. Indeed, filial piety was the guiding principle in the traditional pattern of socialization (Ho, 1981a). It should be understood, at the same time, that fatherhood was governed no less by filial piety. To begin with, to father male heirs so as to ensure the continuation of the family line was a filial duty. For a boy to become a filial son was a greater imperative than it was for a girl to become a filial daughter. The reason was that the boy would become the head of a household, responsible for observing that filial duties are performed by its members. As a father, his primary concern would be to bring up his children as filial sons and daughters. Failure to do so would render himself an unfilial son in the eyes of his ancestors.

In short, fatherhood in Chinese culture cannot be understood without reference to Confucianism. In turn, Confucianism cannot be described without reference to filial piety.

Sex-Role Differentiation

The differentiation of parental roles was anchored in the cultural definition of sex roles, specifically, the stern male and the nurturant female. It would thus be instructive to trace the origin of sex-role differentiation in Chinese culture.

Since ancient times, sex roles have been sharply differentiated in China. In the *Record of Rituals,* a Confucian classic compiled in the second century B.C., we find a rigidly prescribed pattern of sex-role differentiation, particularly for the higher classes (see Legge, 1885, especially Books 1 and 10). The higher the sociopolitical status, the more rigid and stringent were the prescriptions. One of the most salient features of the prescribed pattern was the segregation of the sexes. A physical as well as psychological boundary was vigorously maintained between men and women, separating them into the "outside" world of men and the "inside" world of women. Communication between these two worlds was inhibited: Men were not to speak about what goes on inside the home, and women about the outside. As a matter of fact, among contemporary Chinese one can still witness the practice of referring to one's husband as the *waizi* (literally, the "exterior one") and one's wife as the *neizi* (the "interior one") or *neizhu* (the "interior" or "domestic assistant").

Social contact between the sexes, let alone sexual intimacy, was rigidly restricted. Close interaction between boys and girls came to an end at an early age: "At the age of seven, boys and girls did not occupy the same mat nor eat together" (Legge, 1885, Vol. 27, p. 478). At the age of 10, girls ceased to go out from the women's apartments. In principle, women were not to go outside of the house; if it was necessary for them to do so, their faces must be covered. The prescription for maintaining propriety was sometimes pushed to an extreme, as illustrated below:

When a married aunt, or sister, or daughter returns home (on a visit), no brother (of the family) should sit with her on the same mat or eat with her from the same dish. (Even) the father and daughter should not occupy the same mat. (ibid., p. 77)

The educational goals and preparation for adult roles were different for boys and girls. Boys were instructed to be bold and competent, and girls to be docile and submissive. Educational activities prescribed for boys encompassed much more than the three Rs: They learned music, the odes, ritual dances, archery, and chariot driving—in addition to the ceremonial, social, and filial duties. By contrast, nothing was mentioned to indicate that girls received any literary training. They were taught simply the household duties—which would also be their main duties in adult life.

Several salient features concerning sex-role differentiation in the *Record of Rituals* may be noted. First, the training of boys was based on the premise that the care of infants and young children, being a domestic duty, was outside of the male province. Second, to be educated was a male prerogative denied to females. And thus, it would be males who were to be held responsible for educating the young, because (presumably) only the educated could educate others. Third, the status distinction between boys and girls extended to the realm of moral education. As stated before, it was a greater imperative for boys to become filial sons than for girls to become filial daughters. Fourth, restrictions on close interaction between the sexes were extremely severe. In particular, the incest taboo appeared to be exceedingly strong. The combination of these four features exercised a powerful influence on the definition of fatherhood in Chinese culture in the centuries that followed.

These prescriptions for propriety in the *Record of Rituals* would probably strike the modern reader as being rather strange, extreme, and even unreasonable. As a matter of fact, that classic work is rarely read nowadays, even among highly educated Chinese. However, to students of Chinese society it can provide valuable insights not so readily gained elsewhere. Its emphasis on propriety, formality, and status hierarchy would put a great demand for impulse control on the individual, leaving little room for spontaneity or the unbridled expression of feelings. The extreme rigidity of prescriptions for proper conduct would tolerate no deviation from the norm and thus would inhibit the development of individuality. In particular, the socialization of males prescribed in the *Record of Rituals* would produce fathers who tended to view human conduct in terms of whether it meets or fails to meet some external moral or social criteria—and not in terms of individual needs, sentiments, or volition. That is, fathers would tend to be moralistic, rather than psychologically oriented.

Differentiation of Parental Roles

The sharp sex-role differentiation beginning in early childhood continued into adulthood and beyond, laying the foundation for the later differentiation between paternal and maternal roles. In brief, the paternal role was primarily that of an educator-disciplinarian, in addition to that of a provider; the maternal role was primarily that of a protective, nurturant agent (see Ho, 1981a). The father was expected to educate his children in addition to providing for their livelihood. As stated in the *Three-Character Classic,* a chief primer for beginners produced in the thirteenth century and memorized by millions of Chinese children until recent times: "Rearing without education is the fault of the father; teaching without strictness is the negligence of the teacher." This quotation embodies three important points. First, fatherhood entails the dual functions of rearing and education. Second, the responsibility for educating children rests on both the father and the teacher. This would be essentially a male responsibility, because in the past only men became teachers. Third, the teaching of children must be strict.

Of course, education and discipline were not exclusively a male responsibility. There are legendary examples of mothers who were credited for having provided the proper education for their sons, thus contributing to their superior moral character or achievement. Noted examples included the mothers of Mencius, the famed philosopher-educator, and Yue Fei, one of China's most celebrated national heros. Still, these were outstanding examples and were not representative of the ordinary situation.

On the other hand, nurturing the young was almost exclusively a female function. The father was not expected to have much to do with the care of infants or young children; that was within the province of the mother and other women. The reason was that infants and young children were not thought to be capable of learning very much or amenable to instruction (see Ho, 1986; cf. Ho & Kang, 1984). The role of the father became important only when the child was considered old enough to be instructed and disciplined.

Strict Father, Kind Mother

The perception of parental roles was succinctly captured in the popular expression, "Strict father, kind mother" (cf. Wilson, 1974, p. 73). The father was typically characterized as a stern disciplinarian, more concerned with the demands of propriety and necessity than with feelings, who was to be feared by the child; and the mother as affectionate, kind, protective, lenient, and even indulgent.

The notion of strict father and kind mother has ancient roots. To begin with, it is encoded in the written word. Etymologically, the Chinese character for father (*fu*) evolved from a primitive character representing the hand holding a cane, which is symbolic of authority. The character for mother (*mu*) evolved from one representing a woman with the breasts made prominent, which is symbolic of nurture; and the character for woman (*nu*) evolved from one representing a person in a kneeling or humble position, which is symbolic of submission.

As stated in the *Classic of Filial Piety* (Legge, 1879):

> Of all the actions of man there is none greater than filial piety. In filial piety there is nothing greater than the reverential awe of one's father. In the reverential awe shown to one's father there is nothing greater than the making him the correlate of Heaven. (p. 476)

Undoubtedly, the Confucian classics did not always associate fatherhood with reverential awe but made it clear, rather, that being a kind father was an ideal to be attained. As stated in the *Record of Rituals*, "Kindness on the part of the father, and filial duty on that of the son" were among "the things men consider right" (Legge, 1885, Vol. 27, p. 379; see also Legge, 1960b, p. 362). Nevertheless, in the mass culture, fatherhood came to be associated with reverential awe, rather than with kindness.

Confucian thought on education recognized that emotions could be antagonistic to the attainment of educational goals. For educational efforts to be effective, emotional detachment had to be maintained. More than anyone else, the educator—being a man of superior self-cultivation—must refrain from getting emotional. These beliefs led Mencius to advise against fathers teaching their own sons. The reason he gave was that the father might become angry when his son failed to act in accordance with what he had taught. If the father became angry, the son would say that the father himself had failed to act in accordance with his own teaching. The result would be that the father and son were offended with each other, contrary to what it should be. Thus, "the ancients exchanged sons, and one taught the son of another" (Legge, 1960a, p. 308). This has been interpreted by commentators on Confucian classics to mean that the ancients sent their sons away from home to be taught by masters—and not to mean that fathers as a rule did not teach their own sons. The practice of engaging someone other than the father to be the educator could circumvent the conflict arising from the necessity of educating one's children and the wish to avoid damage to the father-son relation which might result in the process. (Its modern analogue might be psychotherapists' avoidance of treating friends, close relatives, or members of their own family, based on the rationale that their own emotional involvement would be detrimental to the treatment.)

Now, if getting angry impeded the attainment of educational goals, so could too much love, it was commonly believed. The Chinese expression *niai* (literally, "drowning love") reflected the fear of parents that "loving a child too much" could interfere with discipline, and thereby result eventually in the child being spoiled ("drowned"). A popular saying states: "A kind (soft-hearted) mother brings up mostly rotten sons." Accordingly, parents must refrain from loving children too much for their own sake. A contradiction thus arose between the natural tendency of parents to love their children and the belief that parents had to refrain from loving them too much. The differentiation of parental roles into the strict father and the kind mother was one solution to this contradiction. The strict father played the role of the parent who, being the educational agent, had to observe that he and (especially) the mother did not drown the child with too much love.

To be sure, not all fathers were strict; nor were all mothers kind or indulgent. But the stereotypic view of strict father and kind mother has been strongly entrenched in the culture and has persisted to the present day. Furthermore, as we shall see, converging evidence from diverse sources suggests that it is not without a basis in reality. In point of fact, sometimes in formal language one still refers to one's father as *jiayan* (literally, the "strict one in one's family") and one's mother as *jiaci* (the "kind one in one's family"). It should also be added that none of what has been stated above implies that Chinese fathers did not love their children; what is implied is that they were culturally conditioned to inhibit displaying affection toward them openly (see Ho, 1972) and to avoid letting *niai* interfere with the goals of education.

REVIEW OF THE SOCIAL SCIENCE LITERATURE

Fatherhood in Chinese culture has not received the attention in research it deserves and empirical studies addressed specifically to this topic are virtually nonexistent. Nevertheless, some scattered data on parental roles and parent-child relationships are available. When pieced together, they point to a picture which is strikingly continuous with that of the distant past.

Socioeconomic Context

A knowledge of the pertinent socioeconomic context would enable one to understand better the parental roles in contemporary Chinese society. To begin with, more women are working outside the home than before. In 1981, 36.0% of the total number of employees in Mainland China were women (State Statistical Bureau, 1982). In the same year, women constituted 35.4% of the labor force aged 15 and over in Hong Kong (Census and Statistics Department, 1982; computed from Table II.1, p. 134); crude labor-force participation (economically active) rates of population aged 15 and over were 82.5% for men and 49.5% for women (Table 2.4, p. 31). Earlier data on the 1960s collected by Mitchell (1972a, p. 37) showed the following percentages of working married women in cities in five Southeast Asian territories: 32% for Bangkok, 31% for Hong Kong, 20% for Malaysia, 18% for Singapore, and 15% for Taipei. The Hong Kong data showed that the wife's income could be quite a substantial percentage (e.g., 50% or more) of the combined husband-wife income, especially when the husband's income was low (see Table 2.8, p. 38; cf. Hong Kong Young Women's Christian Association & Hong Kong Shue Yan College, 1982, Table 2.21, showing that the most frequent reason given for working by mothers was "to support family"). Also, as expected, mothers with young children were less likely to work (Mitchell, 1972a, Table, 2.10, p. 40).

An important factor that restricts how effectively parents can perform their parental duties is the length of their workday and workweek. In Mainland China, the basic system for employees is that of an 8-hour workday and a 6-day workweek; there are a total of 59 public holidays per year (52 Sundays plus 7 legally designated holidays). This system would apply to the majority of the labor force in urban settings. However, there is no formal system for rural workers or those who are engaged in individual labor (self-employed) in urban settings.

In Hong Kong, census data show that, most commonly, both male and female employees work 45 to 54 hours per week; the average hours of work per week for employees aged 15 and over in 1981 were 52.0 for males and 47.6 for females (Census and Statistics Department, 1982, Tables II 18–19, pp. 141–142). A comparison of the census data for 1976 and 1981 shows that the trend is toward a reduction in the number of hours of work per week. Earlier data reported by Mitchell (1972b, Tables 11.5, p. 325, 11.6, p. 327) showed that, in a descending order, the ranking of five Southeast Asian territories in terms of both the length of the workday (number of hours) and that of the workweek (number of days) was: Hong Kong, Taipei, Bangkok, Malaysia (six major cities), and Singapore. To give an indication of how hard many people in Hong Kong were working in the 1960s: 52% of employees (51% for men and 57% for women) worked 10 hours a day or more, and 58% (60% for men and 54% for women) worked 7 days a week!

Mitchell's (1972b) data also showed that for women in Southeast Asian cities the length of the workday and workweek approached, and in some cases exceeded, that of men from the same territory and ethnic background. Interethnic comparisons within territories indicated that Chinese had longer workdays and longer workweeks than other ethnic groups (Thai, Indian, and Malay), with the exception of Singapore Indians. Furthermore, this held true for both men and women.

Parental Roles — See changes in the father's role

Even in the present age, childcare duties are still performed mainly by the mother (The Boys' and Girls' Clubs Association, 1980; Solomon, 1971, p. 56; Su,

1968; but see Ho & Kang, 1984, for signs of change). This is so even for employed mothers (Hong Kong Young Women's Christian Association & Hong Kong Shue Yan College, 1982).

Su (1968) studied the perception of parental roles, using a questionnaire distributed to 708 fourth, fifth, and sixth graders in Taiwan. In general, there was a clear differentiation of perceived parental roles: The father was more likely to be the educator, and the mother the nurturant agent. The father was more likely to be regarded as the knowledgeable parent to whom the child would turn for help in doing homework, answering questions, and solving problems. (See, however, Hong Kong Young Women's Christian Association & Hong Kong Shue Yan College, 1982, Table 3.13k, showing that homework coaching was done far more frequently by the mother than by the father; also Mitchell, 1972a, Table 13.6, p. 306, showing higher percentages of mothers than fathers whom Form 5 [equivalent to Grade 11] pupils in Hong Kong said helped them with their homework, irrespective of the level of parents' education.) According to Su, the mother was more likely to be regarded as the caring parent to whom the child would turn for emotional support, physical needs, and help in dealing with problems of daily life.

Su reported that the majority of parents participated in play or recreational activities with their children. However, the amount or frequency of participation appeared to be rather limited: Only a minority of fathers and mothers spent time with their children on a daily basis. Responses to a question concerning frequency of participation were: "weekends" (39.8% for fathers, 30.8% for mothers), "occasionally" (29.8% for fathers, 25.9% for mothers), "seldom" (15.8% for fathers, 19.2% for mothers), and "a little time every day" (12.2% for fathers, 20.2% for mothers). Either the father (25.4%) or the mother (26.8%) could function as the main disciplinarian. In a majority of cases, the father was perceived to be the authority figure (66.8%) and the harsher disciplinarian (65.5%) in the home, and was the parent who was more feared by the child (61.2%). In contrast, the mother was more likely than the father to be perceived as the more forgiving parent (52.8% vs. 39.6%) and to be better liked by the child (35.0% vs. 22.6%). Thus, the data suggest that there is a direct association between the amount and severity of discipline and affectional distance, and that father-child affectional distance is greater than that between the child and the mother. The contrasting pattern of paternal and maternal roles bears a remarkable resemblance to that of rural Kwangtung on Mainland China, as described by Parish and Whyte (1978).

Similar results were obtained in a Hong Kong study (The Boys' and Girls' Clubs Association, 1980), using a modified version of Su's questionnaire given to 494 children. In particular, it was found that most parents typically do not spend time playing together with their children—not too surprising in the case of working parents who devote an excessive proportion of their time to work. Considerable parent-child distance in communication is suggested by the finding that as many as 56.1% of the *many* children kept unhappy feelings to themselves. Similarly, in a survey of 3,694 Form 5 secondary pupils in Hong Kong, Mitchell (1972c, chap. 9) reported that 68% responded that they "only occasionally" tell their parents what has happened or that they "hardly tell them anything" (p. 149); 27% of the boys and 33% of the girls responded that "nobody understands" them (p. 163). Corroborative data were also obtained in Mitchell (1972a, chap. 13): 34% of parents with children aged 18 or under at home stated that their children never tell them "their worries and problems," and 24% stated that their children never tell them "things that happened to them at work or at school."

That Chinese fathers are heavily involved in the discipline of their children, especially sons, can be seen in some cross-cultural data reported by Niem and Collard (1972): Chinese boys were disciplined by their fathers almost twice as often as American boys were. However, there is some evidence to suggest that mothers, at least those from nuclear families, are assuming a more important role as the authority figure in the home. Yuan (1972) reported that in Taiwan a clear majority (82.1%) of the primary schoolchildren who served as subjects mentioned both the father and the mother as persons "whose instructions must be obeyed." Among secondary schoolchildren, 30.4% mentioned the father, 43.7% mentioned the mother, and 26.0% mentioned both parents; furthermore, there was a tendency for the father to be perceived as more lenient than the mother. To the extent that these results represent a departure from the traditional pattern, they are symptomatic of the social changes that are taking place in Taiwan.

Paradoxically, the notion of "strict father, kind mother" receives reinforcement in a study of juvenile delinquents in Taipei (Rin, 1981). Fathers were found to predominate in cases involving overly strict and authoritarian parenting or excessive corporal punishment; mothers and grandmothers predominated in those marked by overprotection by family members. But it is clearly not true that only "soft-hearted mothers" bring up "rotten sons."

Affectional Distance

The overall picture that emerges from a review of the social science literature is that father-child relations tend to be marked by affectional distance, perhaps even tension and antagonism, in contrast to warm and close mother-child (especially mother-son) relations. This difference is revealed in children's perception of their parents (The Boys' and Girls' Clubs Association, 1980; Chan, 1981, Table 3; Mitchell, 1972c, chap. 9; Su, 1968), in children's stories (J. Hsu, 1972; Mead & Wolfstein, 1955, chap. on "Monkey"; Tseng & J. Hsu, 1972) and other reading materials (see Wilson, 1974, p. 73), in stories and novels (Heyer, 1953), in classic opera (J. Hsu & Tseng, 1974), in dreams (Eberhard, 1968, 1969), and in interviews with informants (Parish & Whyte, 1978; Solomon, 1971, chap. 3).

Further evidence for the difference in affectional distance is provided by a survey of historical stories of filial piety (Wang, 1950, cited in Heyer, 1953, p.

228), showing that a son's piety to his mother is the subject of over three times as many stories as is that to his father. Wang concluded that, in Chinese literature, sons show very little emotion toward their fathers but very intense emotion toward their mothers. This conclusion corroborates that derived from the analysis of a series of Thematic Apperception Test responses collected from 10 Cantonese village men between the ages of 25 and 45 (see Heyer, 1953, p. 228; consult also the analysis of Chinese Rorschach responses by Abel, 1950).

The only study I have found which is not entirely consistent with the overall picture is that of Tsai (1966). For both male and female secondary school students in Taiwan, the mother is the person with whom they are most closely related; father-daughter relations are clearly not as close as mother-daughter relations, but father-son relations are nearly equal to mother-son relations in closeness. (Cf. Mitchell, 1972c, Table 9.1, p. 152, showing no appreciable difference in closeness between same-sex and opposite-sex parent-child relations among secondary school students in Hong Kong.) Still, the weight of the evidence, it must be concluded, points to a difference in affectional distance between father-child and mother-child relations.

Changes in the Father's Role

Changes in the father's role in Chinese society are inseparable from the radical transformation of the Chinese family which has taken place since the turn of the twentieth century. Confucian values became the target of concerted attacks by intellectuals during the May Fourth period of the 1920s and 1930s, the period of intellectual revolution in modern China. Paternal authority came to symbolize the oppressiveness of the Confucian family system. The values of father-son solidarity were denounced in the literature of the May Fourth period and were replaced by the values of individual development and personal independence (see Chin, 1979).

One major aspect of change is the redistribution of authority within the family, which results in a decline of absolutistic paternal authority (see Ho, 1972, 1973). Data presented by Yuan (1972) suggest that mothers in Taiwan are sharing authority with fathers and are assuming a more important role as disciplinary agents in the home. This will probably have far-reaching significance for the entire pattern of familial relationships, particularly in helping to reduce or even eliminate the difference in affectional distance between the father's and the mother's relationship with the child.

More direct evidence for changes that have taken place is found in an intergenerational study by Ho and Kang (1984), showing greater departures from tradition among fathers than their own fathers (i.e., grandfathers) in Hong Kong. By comparison, the present generation of fathers subscribe less to the precepts of filial piety and to traditional ideas about child training. They put less emphasis on the child's respect for elderly people, and more emphasis on the child's expression of opinions, independence, self-mastery, creativity, self-respect, and all-round development. Younger fathers appear to be more aware of the young child's potential for learning. There is also some suggestion that they are becoming more involved in childcare, reflecting a weakening of the traditional parent-role differentiation between fathers and mothers. Undoubtedly, this has been made necessary because more and more mothers are employed (cf. Chu, 1970).

Father Absence

Paradoxically, the psychological significance of fatherhood is perhaps most dramatically, though indirectly, revealed when the father is absent during the child's formative years. Two questions for research concerning father absence are: First, how prevalent are father-absent families, and to what extent is the father absent from home in intact families? Second, what are the psychological effects of father absence on the family and, specifically, on the development of children? Unfortunately, available data on these questions are extremely limited.

Prevalence.   A screening questionnaire about the family situation was distributed to a total of 3,554 schoolchildren (Primary 4 to Secondary 2) from 5 primary and 4 secondary schools in Hong Kong (Kang, 1985). Of these, 264 appeared to come from single-parent families: 181 indicated that their father, and 83 indicated that their mother, was not living at home. A detailed questionnaire was then distributed to these 264 children. Confirmation of single-parent status was obtained from 234 (or 88.6%). This amounted to 6.6% of the total sample surveyed, inclusive of 3.4% due to death, 2.6% due to marital breakdown (divorce, separation, or desertion), and 0.6% due to other reasons. (Probably this was a conservative estimate, because there might be some single-parent families undetected.) There were approximately twice as many children from father-absent families (4.5%) than from mother-absent families (2.1%). Death (2.7%) was the reason most frequently given for father absence, approximately twice as frequent as marital breakdown (1.4%). For mother absence, however, the relative frequencies of these two reasons were reversed (0.7% for death and 1.2% for marital breakdown). This means that, in single-parent families resulting from the death of a parent, nearly four times as many children are affected by father absence than by mother absence. However, in single-parent families resulting from marital breakdown, the proportion of children affected by father absence is approximately equal to those affected by mother absence.

This last result contrasts sharply with the situation in the United States reported by Glick (1979, Table 1), who showed a special preponderance of father absence in the case of single parenthood due to marital breakdown. Three reasons may account for the Hong Kong result. First, very likely older female relatives would be present to help take care of the children in mother-absent families. Second, Chinese women traditionally did not have equal rights to family property and child custody in cases of divorce, remarriage, or death. Third, because of their lack of financial resources, mothers might be deterred from having custody over their children.

Cross-national comparisons point to some other interesting differences, although they have to be, of course, interpreted with caution. As compared with those for Britain (see Essen & Lambert, 1977) and the United States (see Glick, 1979), for instance, the Hong Kong data show that: (a) The overall percentage of single families is lower; (b) marital breakdown is less frequent as a cause of single parenthood; and (c) in single-parent families, the difference in relative frequencies between father absence and mother absence is smaller. By contrast, in Western societies women typically outnumber men several times as heads of single-parent households. For example, in Britain only about 1 in 6 single-parent families is headed by the father (O'Brien, 1980; cf. Essen & Lambert, 1977, Table 1); in France, only about 1 in 5 (Lefaucheur, 1980); and in the United States, only about 1 in 11 (calculated from Glick, 1979, Table 1, figures for 1978).

Psychological effects.   Negative effects of broken homes are described in Rin's (1981) study of 494 juvenile delinquents in Taipei. The overall rate of broken homes was 28.4%, which the author said seemed to be quite high when compared with other samples of school students and clinical patients he had previously studied. Father absence was found in 13.3% of the sample (9.4% due to death and 3.9% due to separation), mother absence in 10.0% (5.9% due to death and 4.1% due to separation), and absence of both parents in 3.9%. These data may be interpreted against the official statistics on juvenile delinquency and reformatory cases tried by all district courts in Taiwan from 1977 to 1981: father deceased in 6.2%, mother deceased in 4.0%, both parents deceased in 0.6%, and parents separated in 1.7% (see Lin, 1983, Table 10). The percentage of cases with both parents alive was lower than that for the general school population. In both sets of data, it may be observed that the percentage of father absence due to death is higher than that of mother absence due to death; and the same is true of the data gathered by Kang (1985) on schoolchildren in Hong Kong. However, the specific effects of father absence, as distinct from broken homes, require further analysis.

In Kang's study, 38 children from father-absent families resulting from marital breakdown were matched with another 38 from intact families on the basis of the child's sex, age, school and grade, birth rank, educational level of the mother, and whether the mother was employed or not. Among the 38 children from father-absent families, 8 had weekly contact with their fathers, 9 had monthly contact, 4 had yearly contact, and 17 had no contact at all. No significant group differences were found on measures of the quality of mother-child relations. However, mothers from father-absent families were more demanding and relied more on direct-object punishment (non-love-oriented punishment, e.g., physical punishment, deprivation of privileges and material rewards) than those from intact families. Other significant group differences were: (a) A higher percentage of mothers from father-absent families than mothers from intact families reported that their children "looked liked mother" (rather than father), and preferred that their children "looked like mother"; and (b) in the case of intact families, more mothers preferred that their daughters resembled their fathers in character; but in the case of father-absent families, more mothers preferred that their daughters resembled them in character.

Responses from the children indicated that a higher percentage from father-absent families than from intact families preferred to look like their mothers and to resemble them in character. A lower percentage of children from father-absent families mentioned the father as the parent who loved them the most, and a lower percentage felt that they were their fathers' favorite child. In sum, the pattern of results suggests that, as expected, father-child identification is weaker and father-child relations are less close in father-absent families than in intact families.

Another study (M. Hsu, 1979) investigated the effects of long-term father absence on children in Keelung, a commercial center and the largest fishing port in Taiwan. The sample consisted of 82 eighth-grade schoolchildren, 40 of whom were from fishermen's homes. Mean durations of father absence, over a period of the past 2 years, were 11.5 months for the fishermen and 6.3 months for the nonfishermen. On the average, the father was absent from home for a considerable period of time: about one half of the time among the fishermen and, even among the nonfishermen, one fourth. The results indicated that, for boys but not for girls, duration of father absence was significantly and positively correlated with measures of masculinity and maladjustment.[1] However, the interpretation of these results is equivocal. Duration of father absence was confounded with another variable, father's occupation. It is not clear what the effects of father absence per se were, after the effects of father's occupation have been controlled. The confounding of these two variables may account for the positive correlation between boys' masculinity and duration of father absence, which is somewhat unexpected.

THEORETICAL ISSUES

Three related issues are to be discussed: first, the theoretical significance of the father-son relationship for behavioral patterns in Chinese culture; second, the dissociation between affect and role as a coping mechanism for dealing with negative or ambivalent feelings toward one's father—a problem not acknowledged in Confucianism; and third, the challenge to contemporary fathers and their children in adjusting to changing values and the redefinition of fatherhood.

---

[1] I have relied on only the bivariate correlations reported, because there were obvious computational errors in the multiple regression analyses.

Dominance of the Father-Son Relationship

Many students of Chinese society have regarded the father-son relationship as structurally the most important in its social system. F. L. K. Hsu (1967), a major theorist, asserts that what he terms *father-son identification* is "a feature which is at the core of the Chinese kinship system" (p. 303). He explains that "the father-son relationship cannot be described by anything short of the psychological term 'identification.' For whatever the one is, the other is; and whatever the one has, the other has" (p. 63). Father-son identification and the big-family ideal require that there shall be complete community of interests between the old and the young. These are two basic factors which give rise to differences in the socialization experience and hence the personality development of children, especially sons, from different socioeconomic backgrounds. For instance, children from poor families are encouraged to be frugal and hardworking; those from wealthy families are in danger of leading the life of wasteful parasites.

In *Clan, Caste, and Club*, F. L. K. Hsu (1963; see also 1965) states that the Chinese family system is characterized by the dominance of the father-son relationship—in contrast to the dominance of the mother-son relationship in the Hindu system and the dominance of the husband-wife relationship in the American system. These differences in the family system lie at the root of three worlds: the Chinese situation-centered world, the Hindu supernatural-centered world, and the American individual-centered world, respectively. The situation-centered world is "characterized by ties which permanently unite closely related human beings in the family and clan. Within this basic human constellation the individual is conditioned to seek mutual dependence" (Hsu, 1963, p. 1).

According to Hsu (1963), the most important attributes of the father-son relationship are continuity, inclusiveness, and mutual dependence. Continuity refers to the fact that "each father-son relationship is a link in an endless chain of father-son relationships" (p. 50). Inclusiveness "expresses itself vertically and horizontally. Vertically each father-son relationship is a necessary link in a chain connecting lineal descendants already born or yet to be born. Horizontally it is the model against which are measured attitudes, duties, and obligations toward all agnatic male kinsmen and their wives in the ascending or descending generations" (p. 51). Mutual dependence refers to the reciprocity of duties and obligations between any two generations. By contrast, dependence of the child upon the mother is complete and unilateral. Dominance of the father-son relationship would lead to greater reciprocity and greater restriction of dependence to well-defined channels and limits; dominance of the mother-son relationship to greater unilateral and all-embracing dependence.

In the Chinese system characterized by father-son dominance,

> mother-dependence is soon tempered by the authority of the father . . . and later drastically curbed by the individual's integration into a network of specific human relationships, with specific duties, responsibilities, and privileges" (Hsu, 1963, pp. 53–54). "The son comes into close and continuous contact with his father and

other adult males fairly soon; he early gains a measure of the realities of life—that feelings, goods, and services have a way of circulating instead of going in any one direction and that their circulation is governed by rules (p. 52).

Thus, father-son dominance sets the stage for the situation-centered orientation of mutual dependence.

Central to Hsu's argument is the assumption that there is a close link between the kinship pattern of a culture and the psychological disposition of individuals within that culture. However, his claim that father-son dominance would lead to greater reciprocity and greater restriction of dependence lacks supporting evidence. In the Chinese case, father-son dominance would presumably predispose individuals psychologically to situation-centeredness. Again, empirical support is lacking. As we have seen, furthermore, there is strong evidence that affectional distance is greater in father-child than in mother-child relations. It must thus be concluded that the empirical basis for Hsu's argument is rather weak.

The notion of dominance of the father-son relationship may have sociological validity—to the extent that it is structurally the most important of role relationships in a patrilineal social system. But its psychological validity is doubtful (cf. the discussion on this point by Wilson, 1981, pp. 122–123). In real life, Chinese fathers are not as closely involved as Chinese mothers are in the emotional life of their children. They are expected to function more as disciplinarians than as nurturant agents. They have much less contact than mothers have with their children during infancy and early childhood—a period of crucial importance to psychological development. And one might argue that often fathers' impact on children's psychological development is assessable in a negative sense, by examining the effects of the absence of a warm or significant father-child relationship.

Likewise, Hsu's use of the term father-son identification is unfortunate. His characterization of father-son identification is in actuality sociologically, not psychologically, oriented. It does not entail identity (or even similarity) of internal personality attributes between father and son. Rather, the reference point is externally located: It is the people around who ascribed "identity" to them, in their treatments of and expectations from both. Thus, if the father has face, so does the son; and vice versa.

The discussion above reveals that there is a basic contradiction to be addressed: Psychological distance rather than closeness has been found to characterize the very relationship that is structurally the most important, namely, the father-son relationship. One might say that this is, at rock bottom, a contradiction between cultural prescription and the psychological reaction to it.

Dissociation Between Affect and Role

According to the precepts of filial piety, children ought to be respectful, obedient, and devoted to their fathers. But in actuality, they may be distant from, fearful of, and even antagonistic toward them. A contradiction thus arises, between what is and what ought to be. This contradiction must have confronted countless Chinese fathers and their children since ancient times, and the psychological response to it holds an important key to understanding interpersonal relations in Chinese culture. Yet, until most recently, it has not been addressed, let alone recognized, in the culture. Filial piety itself acts to repress awareness of such a contradiction, and in this sense engenders cultural blindspots (cf. Ho, 1981b). The question asked in evaluating filial conduct is: Does one act in accordance with the precepts of filial piety, not with how one feels about one's parents? The question of how one would deal with negative or ambivalent feelings toward one's parents would not even arise. More generally, in a world as prescribed in the *Record of Rituals,* feelings are irrelevant; only proper conduct counts. In such a world, out of necessity affect and role behavior would be dissociated.

The mechanism of affect-role dissociation makes it possible for children to remain filial sons and daughters, while their acts of filiality are performed with emotional detachment. Outwardly, they may act according to the role prescriptions for filial sons and daughters; inwardly, they may be, in fact, quite emotionally distant from their fathers. Thus, they may arrange for an elaborate funeral (including the hiring of professional mourners) for their deceased father toward whom they have little love.

Contemporary Problems

The appearance of new problems associated with changes in fatherhood demands attention—particularly problems in father-child relationships in the face of rapid social change and conflicting cultural values. In a study of family relations in modern Chinese fiction, Chin (1970) found that in Taiwan what stands out is the intensity of antagonistic feelings between father and son. This may seem to reflect the emergence of intergenerational problems as a consequence of the decline of filialism. However, it would be more accurate to say that contemporary literature, now freed from the ideology of filialism, is able to address head-on a problem which has long existed. (In traditional fiction, typically father-son conflicts are dealt with only indirectly or symbolically.)

Nevertheless, contemporary Chinese fathers do face additional difficulties. The decline of the old values of filial piety forces upon them the necessity to search for and establish new positive values (e.g., mutual respect), a process that may take generations. In the meantime, attempts to reimpose filialism are likely to be met with resentment and perhaps even open rebellion. Antagonistic feelings toward one's father can no longer be kept from coming into the open with the mechanism of affect-role dissociation. Fathers and their children must find new ways of resolving conflicts between them.

The decline of filialism also implies that father-child relationships will be fundamentally altered, with less emphasis put on obedience and filial obligations and more on emotional expression. Structurally weakened, these relationships will have to rely more on new cohesive bonds to preserve their integrity. In this context, a greater emphasis on paternal love may yet assume its rightful place in the redefinition of fatherhood in changing Chines society.

ACKNOWLEDGMENT

The author gratefully acknowledges the financial support he received from the Centre of Asian Studies of the University of Hong Kong in the preparation of this manuscript.

REFERENCES

Abel, T. M. (1950). *Columbia University research in contemporary cultures* (CH-610). Unpublished document, American Museum of Natural History, New York.

The Boys' and Girls' Clubs Association. (1980, February). [*A study of children's perception of parental roles*]. (Available from The Boys' and Girls' Clubs Association, 2 Lockhart Road, Hong Kong; published in Chinese.)

Census and Statistics Department, Hong Kong. (1982). *Hong Kong 1981 Census main report.* Hong Kong: Government Printer.

Chan, J. (1981). Correlates of parent-child interaction and certain psychological variables among adolescents in Hong Kong. In J. L. M. Binnie-Dawson, G. H. Blowers, & R. Hoosain (Eds.), *Perspectives in Asian cross-cultural psychology* (pp. 112–131). Lisse, The Netherlands: Swets & Zeitlinger.

Chin, A. L. S. (1970). Family relations in modern Chinese fiction. In M. Freedman (Ed.), *Family and kinship in Chinese society* (pp. 87–120). Stanford, CA: Stanford University Press.

Chu, C. P. (1970). A study of the effects of maternal employment for the preschool children in Taiwan. *Acta Psychological Taiwanica, 12,* 80–100.

Eberhard, W. (1968). Social interaction and social values in Chinese dreams. *Journal of Sociology* (National Taiwan University), No. 4, 21–43.

Eberhard, W. (1969). Social interaction and social values in Chinese dreams. *Journal of Sociology* (National Taiwan University), No. 5, 61–106.

Essen, J., & Lambert, L. (1977). Living in one-parent families: Relationships and attitudes of 16-year-olds. *Child: Care, Health and Development, 3,* 301–318.

Glick, P. C. (1979). Children of divorced parents in demographic perspective. *Journal of Social Issues, 35,* 170–182.

Heyer, V. (1953). Relations between men and women in Chinese stories. In M. Mead & R. Metraux (Eds.), *The study of culture at a distance* (pp. 221–234). Chicago: The University of Chicago Press.

Ho, D. Y. F. (1972). The affectional function in contemporary Chinese families. In *Mental health and urbanization: Proceedings of the 24th Annual Meeting of the World Federation for Mental Health* (pp. 131–137). Hong Kong: Mental Association of Hong Kong.

Ho, D. Y. F. (1973). Changing interpersonal relations in Chinese families. In H. E. White (Ed.), *An anthology of Seminar papers: The changing family, East and West* (pp. 103–118). Hong Kong: Baptist College.

Ho, D. Y. F. (1981a). Traditional patterns of socialization in Chinese society. *Acta Psychologica Taiwanica, 23,* 81–95.

Ho, D. Y. F. (1981b). Childhood psychopathology: A dialogue with special reference to Chinese and American cultures. In A. Kleinman & L. Y. Lin (Eds.), *Normal and abnormal behavior in Chinese culture* (pp. 137–155). Dordrecht, Holland: Reidel.

Ho, D. Y. F. (1986). Chinese patterns of socialization: A critical review. In M. Bond (Ed.), *The psychology of the Chinese people*. Hong Kong: Oxford University Press.

Ho, D. Y. F., & Kang, T. K. (1984). Intergenerational comparisons of child-rearing attitudes and practices in Hong Kong. *Developmental Psychology, 20,* 1004–1016.

Hong Kong Young Women's Christian Association & Hong Kong Shue Yan College. (1982).*Report on working mothers in family functioning*. Hong Kong: Author.

Hsu, F. L. K. (1963). *Clan, caste, and club*. New York: Van Nostrand/Reinhold.

Hsu, F. L. K. (1965). The effect of dominant kinship relationship on kin and non-kin behavior: A hypothesis. *American Anthropologist, 67,* 638–661.

Hsu, F. L. K. (1967). *Under the ancestors' shadow: Kinship, personality, and social mobility in village China* (rev. and exp. ed.). New York: Doubleday.

Hsu, J. (1972). [Chinese parent-child relationships as revealed in popular stories for children]. In Y. Y. Li & K. S. Yang (Eds.), *[The character of the Chinese: An interdisciplinary approach]* (Monograph Series B, No. 4, pp. 201–218). Taipei: Academia Sinica, Institute of Ethnology. (Published in Chinese)

Hsu, J., & Tseng, W. S. (1974). Family relations in classic Chinese opera. *The International Journal of Social Psychiatry, 20,* 159–172.

Hsu, M. (1979). Father absence, son's masculinity, and behavioral adjustment: A new evidence from modern Taiwan. *Bulletin of the Institute of Ethnology* (Academia Sinica), No. 48, 79–88.

Kang, T. K. (1985). *Mother-child relations in single-parent families*. Unpublished master's thesis. University of Hong Kong, Hong Kong.

Lefaucheur, N. (1980). Single-parenthood and illegitimacy in France. *Journal of Comparative Family Studies, 11,* 31–48.

Legge, J. (Trans.). (1879). *The Hsiao Ching* [Classic of filial piety]. In F. Max Muller (Ed.), *The sacred books of the East* (Vol. 3, pp. 465–488). Oxford: Clarendon Press.

Legge, J. (Trans.). (1885). *The Li Ki* [Record of rituals]. In F. Max Muller (Ed.), *The sacred books of the East* (Vols. 27–28). Oxford: Clarendon Press.

Legge, J. (1960a). *The Chinese classics: Vol. 2. The works of Mencius*. Hong Kong: Hong Kong University Press.

Legge, J. (1960b). The great learning. In *The Chinese classics* (Vol. 1, pp. 355–381). Hong Kong: Hong Kong University Press.

Lin, R. Y. (1983). General situation of juvenile delinquency in Taiwan, the Republic of China, and national programs for its prevention and treatment. In *Proceedings of the Second Asian-Pacific Conference on Juvenile Delinquency* (pp. 70–95). Seoul, Korea: Cultural and Social Centre for the Asia and Pacific Region.

Mead, M., & Wolfenstein, M. (Eds.). (1955). *Childhood in contemporary cultures*. Chicago: The University of Chicago Press.

Mitchell, R. E. (1972a). *Family life in urban Hong Kong*. Taipei: Oriental Cultural Services.

Mitchell, R. E. (1972b). *Levels of emotional strain in Southeast Asian cities: A study of individual responses to the stresses of urbanization and industrialization*. Taipei: Oriental Cultural Services.

Mitchell, R. E. (1972c). *Pupil, parent, and school: A Hong Kong study*. Taipei: Oriental Cultural Services.

Niem, T. I. C., & Collard, R. R. (1972). Parental discipline of aggressive behaviors in four-year-old Chinese and American children. *Proceedings of the 80th Annual Convention of the American Psychological Association, 7,* 95–96.

O'Brien, M. (1980). Lone fathers: Transition from married to separated state. *Journal of Comparative Family Studies, 11,* 115–127.

Parish, W. L., & Whyte, M. K. (1978). *Village and family in contemporary China*. Chicago: University of Chicago Press.

Rin, H. (1981). The effect of family pathology on Taipei's juvenile delinquents. In A. Kleinman & T. Y. Lin (Eds.), *Normal and abnormal behavior in Chinese culture* (pp. 213–229). Dordrecht, Holland: Reidel.

Solomon, R. H. (1971). *Mao's revolution and the Chinese political culture*. Berkeley, CA: University of California Press.

State Statistical Bureau, People's Republic of China. (1982). *Statistical yearbook of China—1981* (English ed). Hong Kong: Economic Information and Agency.

Su, C. W. (1968). [The child's perception of parent's role]. *Psychology and Education, 2*, 87–109. (Published in Chinese, with an English abstract)

Tsai, W. F. (1966). [A study of interpersonal relationships in the family]. *Thought and Word, 4*(2), 25–27. (Published in Chinese)

Tseng, W. S., & Hsu, J. (1972). The Chinese attitude toward parental authority as expressed in Chinese children's stories. *Archives of General Psychiatry, 26*, 28–34.

Wang, Y. C. (1950). *Columbia University Research in Contemporary Cultures* (CH-179). Unpublished document, American Museum of Natural History, New York.

Wilson, R. W. (1974). *The moral state: A study of the political socialization of Chinese and American children*. New York: The Free Press.

Wilson, R. W. (1981). Conformity and deviance regarding moral rules in Chinese society: A socialization perspective. In A. Kleinman & T. Y. Lin (Eds.), *Normal and abnormal behavior in Chinese culture* (pp. 117–136). Dordrecht, Holland: Reidel.

Yuan, S. S. (1972). [Family authority patterns, rearing practices and children's sense of political efficacy]. *Thought and Word, 10*(4), 35–55. (Published in Chinese)

10 The Modern Japanese Father: Roles and Problems in a Changing Society

David W. Shwalb
University of Utah

Nobuto Imaizumi
Hiroshima University

Jun Nakazawa
Chiba University

> *In pre-war days it was said that one should fear "earthquakes, thunder, fire and fathers," but since the war we have seen democracy combined with an overall feminization of society. In contemporary Japan, the father has forfeited his authority. . . . Accordingly, the comic in which "dumb dads" are bringing about the ruin of our schools seems to have become true. So [in December, 1981] the Society of Thunderous Fathers was formed. The founders included a famous actor, a cartoonist, an explorer, a member of the national Diet, and former sumo and boxing champions.*
> *(Ohgiya, 1983, p. 960).*

Although its leaders offered no serious means of improving the situation, the existence of a group such as the Thunderous Fathers may reflect more than an idle curiosity among the Japanese toward fatherhood. While overstating the weakness of the contemporary father, this group rightly notes the confused and controversial nature of the paternal role in modern Japanese culture. The Society's message is that various ills have resulted from the postwar behavior of fathers. And while few would support their call for the reemergence of tyrannical fathering, most Japanese would agree that fathers must redefine their role in child development. Mothering is universally accepted as a virtuous and valuable enterprise, but *the role of the Japanese father is ill-defined, devalued, and in a state of flux.*

Following the rapid expansion of father research in the West (Lamb, 1981), Japanese psychologists, sociologists, and psychiatrists have begun to write extensively about fathering in the past few years. The first symposium on fathering at the meetings of the Japanese Association of Educational Psychology was convened in 1980 (*Kyoiku Shinri Nenpo,* 1981), following by 20 years the first comparable American (APA) symposium. In 1984, the first comprehensive review of research on Japanese fathering appeared in the Japanese-language *Annual Review of Japanese Child Psychology* (H. Saitoh, 1984). In addition, several national government surveys have recently focused on the paternal role, and fathers are constantly discussed in the mass media.

In this chapter, we will integrate these divergent perspectives on fathers and document those issues and social trends currently most relevant to fathering and families in the Japanese context.

THE CHANGING CONTEXTS OF FAMILY AND SOCIETY

The father role is evolving in response to historical currents, the changing structure of the family, and changes in social and economic conditions. The following describes several contextual factors which may influence the Japanese paternal role.

Historical Setting

As the "earthquakes, thunder, fire and fathers" proverb suggests, the traditional definition of the father was as an awe-inspiring authority figure. As head (*kacho*) of the stem family (*ie*), the father was the legal, social, moral, and economic leader of the family. The eldest son was usually designated as successor and could take over as head early in adulthood if his father proved incompetent. One of the most important functions of the traditional Japanese father, therefore, was to train his successor in occupational, monetary, and moral matters. Yamazaki (1979) notes that this authority began to slip in the late 1800s as compulsory education was instituted and schools took over the educational function of the traditional father.

In terms of the legal definitions of fathers and families, the most significant transition took place at the conclusion of World War II. Prior to and during the war, the father exercised control over his wife and children (Ebihara, 1972). In return for taking responsibility for everyone, the father could expect absolute obedience and respect (Befu, 1971). With Japan's defeat, however, paternal dominance and the overall family system were viewed by occupying Americans as based on Confucianistic thought and as obstacles to the democratization of Japanese society (Kawai, 1960). Under the "New Civil Law," the Japanese father was reduced to a position of equal status with his wife and grown children.

It is generally assumed that this resulted in his significant loss of status within the family.

Wagatsuma (1977) downplays the stereotypical comparison of the prewar Confucianistic vs. the postwar "shadowy" father. He points out the absence of evidence concerning the actual behavior of prewar men and also criticizes the subjectivity of self-reports on which many generalizations regarding the modern father are based. Wagatsuma concludes that the personalities of fathers in both eras probably combine aspects of both images— tyrant and friend—and are distorted in self-reports by the social norms of each era.

In spite of the confusion over actual behavior, however, it is quite plausible that the dramatic changes in definitions and norms in the aftermath of the war have had significant impact on how modern fathers behave, since many now would prefer to act in a socially desirable manner. In the postwar era, it is desirable for the father to be democratic rather than autocratic.

Nuclearization of the Family

In the 40 years since World War II, fathering has changed in response to demographic trends toward a more aged, urban, and densely populated society (*Japanese Statistical Yearbook,* 1984). During this period, Japanese families have evolved continuously toward a typically nuclear form. The proportion of Japanese families described as nuclear was 60% in 1920, 63% in 1955, and 75% in both 1970 and 1980. Shinohara (1981) describes the present age as the "nuclearization era."

Yamane (1976) points to several effects of the transformation from a linear extended family to an isolated nuclear family. First, individual development is now emphasized more than family lineage, so that the father's interests are separated from those of his wife or children. This trend was confirmed by a recent national survey (*Asahi Shinbun* [Newspaper], July 28, 1984). The article describing this study was accompanied by a cartoon of a young father watching baseball on television by himself, while his wife danced to a radio exercise show and their lone child sat in bed talking to her doll.

The second of Yamane's hypotheses is that, in a self-contained family unit, a husband-wife partnership is more fitting than dominance by men. This would tend to weaken paternal authority. Third, he notes that the modern father must strive to finance his own house instead of inheriting an ancestral home. Indeed, many fathers have become isolated from their families at work, and mothers have been forced to seek a second income, struggling to meet the costs of a new home. If these three environmental effects on the postwar father are indeed true, he should be individualistic, share decision making with his wife, and be overworked.

Even in the age of the nuclear family, the Japanese retain aspects of the stem-family system. For instance, many parents live with their eldest sons in retirement. At least one grandparent lives in the home of 27.6% of Japanese families, compared with 14.1% in [South] Korea and under 3% in the United States and England (Sorifu [Prime Minister's Office], 1982a). In the four Western cultures represented in this international survey, about 90% of the families were nuclear. The sudden and very rapid conversion to the nuclear family was especially noteworthy in the case of the Japanese.

Population Trends

The Japanese father typically lives in a small family. In 1982, the size of the average Japanese family (3.3 members) was slightly larger than that in the United States (2.7) or Western Europe, but smaller than those in Korea (4.5), the Philippines (5.9), or Brazil (4.2 members) (Sorifu, 1985). By 1985, Japanese households averaged under three members (*Asahi Shinbun,* January 16, 1985). A report of the National Association of Mayors attributes this shrinking figure to increases in childlessness, divorce, and people living alone, as well as to declining birthrates.

The Japanese birthrate has declined steadily for several years, and in 1984—for only the second time since 1905—under 1.5 million babies were born (*Asahi Shinbun,* January 1, 1985). Known as the "baby bust," the birthrate dipped to 12.5 per 1000 population. As a result of having fewer children at home, it is possible that the bonds between mother and child may increase in intensity, and that there would be less need for fathers to help at home (e.g., as disciplinarians).

Another demographic factor related to fathering is the growing divorce rate. Relative to Western standards, the rate is small (1.9% of Japanese families and 9.4% of American families are of divorcees), but the numbers in both cultures are growing (Sorifu, 1982a). This trend, along with the trend toward more single-parent families, should have implications for child development, given the literature on father absence (Biller, 1974).

Standard of Living

Japan has become a very affluent society (Vogel, 1977) and, like other modernized nations, has an overwhelmingly middle-class consciousness (Vogel, 1965). The percentage of men and women in Japan who classified themselves as middle class was 94.4%—compared to 89.7% in the United States, 76.1% in Korea, and 98.0% in England (Sorifu, 1982a). There has been a steady increase in Japanese material possessions since the mid 1960s, and by 1981 almost 100% of families reported owning a color television and over 50% owned automobiles and stereo systems (Sorifu, 1983). Educational attainment in the present generation of Japanese fathers is roughly equivalent to that in the United States: About 20% of the fathers in both cultures had graduated from at least a four-year college (Sorifu, 1982a).

Overall, the average Japanese father is better educated, more middle-class, and materially better off than was his own father. A possible implication of this affluence and education is suggested by another national survey (Sorifu, 1980b). In this sample, younger, urban, and more prosperous adults valued their own lives more than that of their children, a tendency which contrasts with the past Japanese norm of child-centeredness. Japanese families traditionally have emphasized responsibility to children over the relationship of the couple or personal development (Sorifu, 1982a), but recent international comparisons indicate infrequent sharing of activities between fathers and children, or between husbands and wives. There is a danger for some fathers that this growing self-centeredness could be at the expense of relations with their children.

Schoolism and Japanese Society

Competition for social and occupational status is based on the prestige of one's academic degrees, so much so that the term "schoolism" (*gakureki-shugi*) has been coined to describe this emphasis on educational attainment. Entrance examinations for admission to lower and upper secondary schools and to college determine many people's prestige level and life course. Particularly for those aspiring to the managerial class, Japanese adult society is perhaps equally as stressful as the school environment (or more so) because workers must compete for limited promotions within their companies (Plath, 1983).

These forms of competition profoundly influence parenting, child development, and family dynamics. The mother is generally responsible for children's school performance, and the term "education mom" (*kyoiku mama*) is a popular depiction of her dominance in this domain (Reischauer, 1977). Meanwhile, fathers work long hours and frequent 6-day weeks, and many consequently have minimal contact with their families. Their efforts are most intense when they are being considered for promotions, or when the financial sacrifice required to pay for chidren's entrance examination preparations or tuition is greatest. (According to Sorifu, 1982a, 78.9% of Japanese parents pay for all their children's college costs.)

The lives of children are often centered around studies rather than human relationships. In a national poll of teenagers (Sorifu, 1983), "grades and studies" were the greatest worries of youth listed by 36.4% of the sample, while personal issues were much less frequently mentioned (e.g. "misunderstood by parents" was cited by only 3.8%).

Although men occupy an overwhelmingly superior position in the broader social context (Reischauer, 1977), the social pressure of schoolism reinforces maternal dominance and paternal weakness at home. Fathers may be the models of success under the schoolism system, and may share their wives' aspirations for the children. But they are often absent, insignificant figures in daily home life and may overindulge their children in order to have any sense of involvement

(Saitoh, 1972). As such, fathers are very successful as the dominant figures in Japan's "economic miracle" (Vogel, 1977), but their intense involvement at work often results in shallow interpersonal lives at home.

Summary

The Japanese father lives in an era which has seen the following trends in social context: (a) a democratic family system with traces of a past paternalistic system; (b) a small and predominantly nuclear family with remnants of the traditional stem family; (c) an increasingly materialistic, affluent, and individualistic society; and (d) an achievement-oriented society which places intense pressure on men as workers, women as mothers, and children as students.

PSYCHOLOGICAL STUDIES OF THE JAPANESE FATHER

In light of the supposedly shadowy existence of the contemporary Japanese father, scholars have attempted to identify his actual role. Many researchers have therefore sought to define the paternal role in studies of the father image. The father is obviously the second parent and performs his role in a society whose mentality is dominated by "mother fixation" (Lebra, 1976). This has led to several studies on division of labor, that is, on how fathers behave in relationship to the maternal role. In addition, clinically oriented scholars have detected an aspect of the father role which is neglected by research psychologists: his role in the etiology of child psychopathology. These three issues (images of the father, the paternal role, and the role of fathers in child psychopathology) are discussed next.

Children's Images of Fathers

Self-reports by children indicate that the image of the Japanese father varies between the ideal and the real, and also differs according to the child's age and sex. A recent survey of adolescents and college students indicated both similarities and differences between the images of mothers and fathers (Sorifu, 1981a). As shown in Table 10.1, the ideal maternal disciplinary style selected by most youth emphasizes understanding, while the authoritative style as most often idealized for fathers. However, when the same youth described the actual behavior of their fathers and mothers, the categorization for both parents were quite similar. Also evident in Table 10.1 is the difference between idealized and actual fathering.

The data in Table 10.1 suggest that the thunderous and weak fathers (the stereotypes cited earlier for pre- and postwar fathers respectively) are in the minority, but that they are more common than children would desire. In addition,

TABLE 10.1
Adolescents' Reports of Ideal and Actual Disciplinary Styles

	Father		Mother	
	Ideal	Real	Ideal	Real
Authoritarian	2.1	13.6	1.0	8.2
Authoritative	55.3	31.8	39.8	39.4
Understanding	35.3	28.9	49.4	32.8
Permissive	6.9	17.7	9.5	17.2
Not Present	0.4	7.2	0.3	1.8

Note. The values represent percentages of adolescents reporting each disciplinary style.
Note. From "Today's Youth: A Comparison with Those Ten Years Ago" by Sorifu, 1981, Tokyo: Prime Minister's Office.

these authoritarian and permissive fathers were reported with equal frequency. While fathers ideally are a bit stricter than mothers and are portrayed in the popular media as weaklings, they are actually described by this sample as mostly authoritative and understanding (i.e., similar to mothers).

Age trends.   Analyses of self-reports by 3rd- through 9th-grade pupils (Haraoka, 1972) showed that, with age, the image of the father becomes gradually less positive. This was seen both in pupils' ratings of shared activities with fathers and in their images of fathers as material providers. Similar findings of increasingly critical evaluations of fathers' personality (with age) were noted comparing 6th and 9th grades (M. Fukaya & K. Fukaya, 1975), and in general relations between fathers and 5th to 11th graders (Sorifu, 1983).

Along with the decline in ratings of the father with age were trends toward dissatisfaction with fathers. In a national sampling of students (Sorifu, 1983), the percentage responding that relations with one's father were "very good" declined from 55.6% of 5th graders, to 37.5% of 8th graders, and only 15.4% of 11th graders.

Comparing images of fathers among elementary and middle school pupils, Haraoka (1972) found that the young children were most concerned with what the father gives them or does for them. Young adolescents focused on how fathers relate to them as individuals, and the kind of role models fathers provide. By adolescence, a negative view of the father had developed, centering around his (perceived) lack of respect for the child and his interference with the child's growing sense of independence.

In another cross-sectional survey, Yoneda (1975) studied perceptions of fathers by fourth graders through college-age youth. He collected free-responses of qualities children "liked" and "disliked" about their fathers. As in Haraoka's study, younger children focused on the father as a provider, and adolescents on the father as a separate individual. The definition of a good father combined masculine ("responsible" or "active") and genteel (e.g., "kind" or "considerate") characteristics, consistently across age groups.

Sex differences.   Perceptions of the father also vary by children's gender. The Fukayas (1975) found that boys respect fathers mainly for their occupational roles (e.g., "makes money") while girls rated aspects of the father's personality (e.g., "understands me") more positively than did boys.

The Fukayas also devised an index combining children's ratings of their parents' activities concerning sports, studies, sociability, and popularity, and compared ratings of mothers vs. fathers among fourth, sixth, and ninth graders. In fourth grade, mothers were rated as more important than fathers by both boys and girls, particularly in their involvement with the child's education. Boys' ratings of both parents became less positive with age. The decline concerning the mother figure was most notable following the transition to middle school, at which point boys rated their fathers with higher respect than they rated their mothers. Ratings of fathers by their daughters were constant across age groups and were always lower than those for the mother. In sum, the father becomes (relatively) more important and is rated less favorably by older boys, and he remains the "second parent" for daughters of all ages.

The Paternal Role

Several researchers have tried to pinpoint the functions of the father. From these studies it appears that he exercises a weak secondary role in the home, that his role changes according to the child's developmental level, and that only his economic function has remained strong in the wake of postwar social change.

Division of labor.   Table 10.2 (adapted from Sorifu, 1982a) compares the division of labor in budgeting and disciplinary matters between Japanese, United States, and Korean families. As the figures indicate, the Japanese wife is usually the dominant force in decisions regarding daily financial expenditures (although the father has a strong voice in the case of major purchases). In the United States the responsibility is most often shared by the couple, while in Korea there is no clear tendency towards one arrangement.

In disciplinary matters, the majority of the Japanese reported, as did parents in the other two cultures sampled, that decisions are shared. However, a higher proportion of Japanese reported that the mother is dominant in disciplinary matters. So, while sharing is most common across cultures, Japanese wives (and Korean husbands) are more influential than their spouses and their counterparts in the other cultures.

TABLE 10.2
Division of Labor:
Budgeting and Discipline

	Husband mainly	Shared	Wife mainly
	Budgeting		
Japan	9.2	16.3	73.9
U.S.	23.6	56.4	19.7
Korea	26.2	31.0	42.4
	Discipline		
Japan	8.7	58.7	31.7
U.S.	11.2	81.9	6.0
Korea	24.8	62.3	11.7

Note. The values represent percentages of families' division of labor.
Note. Adapted from "International Survey on Youth and Their Environment" by Sorifu, 1982, Tokyo: Prime Minister's Office.

In other areas—including decisions about travel, choices of housing, what school the child will attend, and the number of children—Japanese are not mother-dominated. Yet overall, the authors of the government report describe Japan (along with France and West Germany) as "mother-dominant," the United States and England as "couple-shared," and Korea as "father-dominant" in decision-making patterns.

Mothers are more involved with children's personal problems than are fathers, according to a 1978 survey of Japanese adolescents (Sorifu, 1981b). Among high school youth, 25.8% listed the mother as the one whom they talked to about their troubles, but only 6.9% listed the father. It is notable that friends were most frequently listed (by 64.9%), and that fathers were cited less than were siblings (14.2%) and even "nobody" (20.0%). As with his role in budgetary matters, the Japanese father appears to have a minor role as a parent.

Intracultural variations.   The paternal role in Japan appears to differ according to the age of the child and the social status of the family, although the handful of studies in this area paint an incomplete picture of the variation in the paternal role. They suggest the need for more comprehensive research on fathers, particularly as related to various personal characteristics of both father and child.

Many scholars have found that fathers' behavior depends on the child's age. For instance, Takeuchi, Uehara, and Suzuki (1982) surveyed 123 fathers of preschoolers about relations with their children in the first five years of life.

These fathers recalled being active in caretaking and in discussions with their wives about childrearing in the infancy and toddler years, but also reported a significant decline in their involvement during the later preschool years. Shinohara (1981) reports that many Japanese fathers are involved with their infants (as a result of the democratized nuclear family system), but that such "childcare papas" become distant as responsibilities increase in their workplace. As anthropologist Sofue (1981) concludes, it is characteristic of the Japanese that, after the earliest years of childhood, care of the children is given over completely to the mother.

H. Yamada (1979) also found a decrease in paternal involvement with children between infancy and preschool years. She hypothesized that age 3 is the point at which fathers generally separate themselves from their children's lives. The most common activities reported by her sample, and that of preschoolers studied by J. Kida (1980), were bathing and taking the child (ages 3–5) for walks.

Tabuchi and Tanaka (1978) surveyed 300 fathers of preschoolers (ages 4–6) about their experiences with infants and found that one third reported (in retrospect) being involved with infants, while another third of the sample were completely uninvolved. These fathers' roles were mainly limited to that of playmate. It should be noted that no objective data or maternal reports were provided in any of the survey studies reported here to corroborate fathers' estimates of involvement.

Investigating variations in the paternal role as related to *social position,* Isogai (1972) compared samples of farmers, white-collar workers, and blue-collar laborers. He found that middle school pupils of suburban, white-collar "salarymen" had the most contacts with their fathers and had fewer complaints against them than did children of farming or working-class fathers. Wagatsuma (1977) speculates that the reason for such a trend is that, in better educated and urban families, women's roles and norms of democracy are strongest. Across occupational groups, however, contacts with fathers were limited. For instance, the salarymen ate dinner with their families on only half of the weeknights, and blue-collar workers were usually absent from their homes on weeknights. Isogai reported that even in rural Japan few sons work alongside their fathers. Evidently, postwar farmers in his sample are not occupational role models, as had traditionally been the case.

Worker, friend, and authority.   Among the functions of the contemporary father, the role of breadwinner is clearest. Ideally, Japanese children tend to prefer that the father value his family more than his work. In surveys between 1970 and 1980 (Sorifu, 1981a), teenagers divided evenly between preferences for home-oriented and work-oriented fathers, although a distinct trend toward home orientation was found (from 47.1% in 1970 preferring home-centeredness to 58.9% in 1980).

In reports of actual behavior, however, fathers are perceived as strongly work-oriented. For instance, high school students in Hiroshima indicated by a margin of 92% to 7% that their fathers were "mainly workers" (*hataraki-mono*). In this sample, 65% stated they would prefer that their mothers not work outside the home (*Chugoku Shinbun*, November 22, 1984). Since the large majority of men's jobs are away from home, the distinction between the male workplace and the female-dominated home remains clear in these data.

Children and adolescents in two samples (M. Fukaya, 1978; Kashiwaguma, 1981) gave very positive ratings to their fathers' behavior as workers. In addition, 7th to 12th graders in the latter sample gave strong positive ratings to fathers for their thinking about politics and social issues, and for their sense of right and wrong. These ratings indicate that besides a worker, the father is seen as a man of society and a model of moral judgment. The role of the father, according to M. Fukaya, is to direct their children to the outside world and show the child the sacrifices one must make as a worker, as a role model.

Although they respect their fathers' work, children seem to have a weak understanding of this work (M. Fukaya, 1978) and do not want to pursue the same occupation as their fathers' (M. Fukaya & K. Fukaya, 1975). As noted earlier, a comparison of sixth and ninth graders' ratings of fathers' occupation-related characteristics revealed that children became somewhat less positive with increasing age. The Fukayas concluded that, as children gain an increasingly realistic perception of their once-idealized fathers' activities outside the home, their evaluations become more critical.

Japanese fathers apparently want to be like friends to their children. Along with equalizing the power of husbands and wives, an important effect of the postwar constitution was to replace formal, hierarchical parent-child relations (superior vs. inferior) with a relationship based on egalitarianism and mutual assistance. Under this arrangement the father no longer occupies a position of superiority with respect to his children (Ebihara, 1972). However, consciousness of inequality between parent and child may still be strong within the family, despite the surface advocacy of democratic relations (Harano, 1981). Objective data are required to determine whether equality is merely a legalistic facade.

Isolated from his children at work, many Japanese fathers became weak and insignificant figures at home. These men often resort to becoming chums with their children when they become dispensable as authorities. In place of the distant and formal father recalled by adults in a 1977 survey (NHK, 1977), the ideal father has become a friendly man who plays with his children and takes them on weekend outings. According to one international survey of adolescents (Sorifu, 1984), the ideal father is, above all, a friend.

M. Fukaya (1978) found that, for fifth- and sixth-grade children, a combination of toughness at work and kindness at home is desirable in fathers. This duality of "hard" and "soft" fathering is similar to the above-mentioned finding that adolescents idealize fathers as both understanding and authoritative (Sorifu,

1981a). It may be that the Japanese ideal is a father who is expressive at home and instrumental at work (Parsons & Bales, 1955).

Vogel (1965) surveyed middle-class urban homes and found that Japanese mothers build up an artificial image of the absent father as an authority figure. These mothers then invoke this ideal image to gain compliance from their children. Fathers he studied seldom exercised much direct authority. Indeed, the following recent surveys of fathers, mothers, and children indicate that fathers are neither disciplinarians nor strict.

When a sample of fathers was asked who is responsible for discipline in the home (Sorifu, 1981a), 60.5% named the mother, 22.2% said it was the mother and father equally, and only 5.6% named the father. These same men were also asked how strict or easygoing they were with their children. The response "just average" was received more often (53.1%) than "strict" (32.5%) or "easy" (13.9%).

Reports by children also indicate that fathers as authorities are not strict. Among adolescents in 11 cultures, the Japanese father was rated lowest for his degree of self-confidence, and for having the least frequent dialogues with children (Sorifu, 1985). In another cross-national comparison, 10- to 15-year-olds rated Japanese fathers as less strict, less respected, and less idealized than did Korean or American youth (Sorifu, 1980a).

There are, of course, individual differences in strictness, as is seen in data from both fathers and mothers. A recent survey of mothers was reported under the title "Are the Lords of Tokyo Papier-Mache Tyrants?"—suggesting the superficiality of paternal authority (*Asahi Shinbun*, November 10, 1984). Mothers in this sample were split evenly between views of their husbands as weak vs. powerful. Finally, one half of the fathers in another Tokyo sample (*Asahi Shinbun*, April 22, 1984) expect to be "lion types" and one third "kittens" in future relations with their 1-year-old children.

Summary.   The three functions of the Japanese father are as (a) the main wage earner for his family, (b) a friend to his children, and (c) a somewhat dubious authority figure. His personality is generally perceived as more warm than tough, and he is respected for his work as breadwinner.

Fathers and Psychopathology of Youth

If some fathers are as ineffectual as many claim, one inadvertent aspect of the Japanese paternal role may be in contributing to psychological disorders in children. Despite the generally superior academic achievements of Japanese youth as a population (H. Kida, D. W. Shwalb, & B. J. Shwalb, 1985), a visible minority of children are plagued by behavioral problems. There has been much speculation, based on analyses of case-study materials, that fathers may be in part responsible for these ailments.

Consideration of delinquency, family violence, school refusal (a morbid fear of attending school), apathy, and student rebellion all suggest the need for close attention to the father's impact. Of course, the vast majority of Japanese children suffer from no such ailments. In addition, most children respect the father as a breadwinner, however secondary his parenting role may be. But these disorders are increasing in incidence (Yamazaki, 1979) and are of concern to all Japanese parents.

Ineffectual fathers and dominant mothers.   The child's home environment is the most often discussed origin of child psychopathology. For instance, in summarizing 200 case studies of problem behavior among preschool children, Naijo (1981) notes that mothers frequently describe the father as one source of the problems. However, paternal personality generally has been ignored in treatment of these cases. Okado (1981) has also observed that many of today's weak or absent fathers were themselves raised by "dumb dads." To Okado, children of fathers who are physically present but psychologically absent, or who are cruel and rejecting, are more at risk than fatherless children.

In a roundtable discussion of the paternal role, Maruki and others (*Jidoshinri*, 1976) speculated about the "*femininity*" and "weakness" of the modern father. As a result of inadequate contacts with children, such fathers may overcompensate by spoiling them. Many fathers also lack confidence about dealings with their children as a result of this lack of contact.

A father may transmit his weakness to the child. Nishihira (1981) reports that due to the lack of masculine models, sons have often been found to exhibit inappropriate social behavior. And in the cases of school refusal (Hanta, 1976) and delinquency (Uryu, 1984), many boys appear to have shared femininity, immaturity, dependency, and weak standards with their fathers.

Hanta also relates several behavioral disorders to the syndrome of "maternal dominance." In many households, the mother is the leader because the father is absent, the mother is dominant in power relations over the father and children, and/or the father has personality problems. Hanta's study of the children in mother-dominant families indicated a high incidence of disobedience, self-consciousness, and asociality among sons. A smaller study of his revealed that, in 9 of 16 cases of school refusal, the families were identified as mother-dominated.

Violence in the home.   Family violence has been described as the "greatest problem for the Japanese family" (*Heibonsha's* World Encyclopedia 1982). First reported in the media around 1977, a growing number of children (80% of whom are boys) have been identified as committing violent acts within their homes. The targets of these acts are most often mothers (in 85% of cases), fathers (24%), or grandmothers (7%). According to a government study of 1051 cases of family violence (Sorifu, 1980c), the average age of such violent youth is about 15 or 16 years old.

This same survey also shed light on the possible origins of the violence and its association with other behavior. The three phenomena most often coinciding with family violence are overexpectations of parents (in 21% of cases), a powerless father (18%), and an overprotective mother (17%). Such family dynamics are encouraged by the societal conditions associated with industrialization and schoolism. As mentioned earlier, many parents pressure their children strongly to perform academically—at the expense of other aspects of their development. This is illustrated in a case study of a violent son who screamed "Give me back my youth! Give me back my life!" as he victimized his parent (Shinsaku, 1982b). It has been hypothesized also that this pressure is greatest in families with highly educated parents or with older siblings who have been very successful academically, thus setting an unreachable standard (*Asahi Shinbun*, January 25, 1984).

Case-study analyses also indicate that violence-prone families tend to exclude the outside world, and that both parents have minimal contacts outside their homes (Shinsaku, 1982a). By shutting the doors of their homes to the world, parents may intensify the conflicts within the home. Inamura (1980) also discovered a correlation between family violence and discord between husbands and wives over childrearing matters. He describes a syndrome of over-involved mothers who are highly dependent on their children's achievement for vicarious satisfaction, combined with father absence or a shadowy paternal presence. Such parental characteristics are hypothesized to be correlated with low impulse control and a weak sense of self among children.

School refusal.   K. Fukaya (1980) depicts family dynamics similar to those associated with family violence in describing the origins of school refusal. Overexpectations, however, do not appear to be a major factor in the school refusal syndrome. Studied in Japan for over two decades school refusal has most often been noted among elementary school children (Tamai, 1965). Although fathers of school-refusal children often appear assertive at first, they reportedly yield to maternal dominance under pressure and are characterized commonly as passive, dependent, feminine, and asocial (Yamazaki, 1979).

Apathy and rebellion.   In late adolescence, two other forms of psychological problems have been linked to family dynamics: a cold, apathetic emotional state, and violent rebellion by students against authority. Here, two seemingly opposite states (one passive and one overactive) are both associated with schoolism and with fathering.

In evaluating 49 case studies of male undergraduates at the elite Tokyo University, K. Yamada (1984) depicts the syndrome of "apathy," calling it the greatest mental health problem among college students in the past decade. In such cases, despite their superior ability, students withdraw from studies and become passive, unmotivated, and lethargic. Unlike the consistent paternal weakness associated with school refusal and family violence, however, there were several cases of apathy with either weak or dominant father figures. Yamada views apathy and withdrawal as a form of revenge by these young men against their fathers. The fathers are portrayed either as inadequate role models or as professionals who overemphasize the importance of school grades and entrance examinations as the sole purpose of adolescent life. The apathetic students had withstood the pressures of both parents and succeeded in entering a famous university, but found that their success was meaningless. In despair, they apparently refused to perform any further.

Another psychiatrist, Doi (1973), first described Japanese society as "fatherless" and wrote that Japanese youth are in search of values because they receive no moral training from their fathers. Doi claims that Japanese student rebels of the 1960s did not internalize social norms because they lacked a strong figure to help them repress their impulses (Wagatsuma, 1977). In Doi's controversial view, a powerful father would be more helpful to such youth than improved communication between generations. This is because friendship is available from friends and is not needed from the father, who can provide discipline and an adult model not available from peers.

Overall, a family dynamics view of deviance in childhood and adolescence is apparent in the pscyhiatric and clinical literature. It is the consistent view that— weak, strong, or absent—some Japanese fathers may adversely affect their children's personality development and social adjustment. Most often it is claimed that a weak father, a dominant mother, and unrealistic expectations of children combine to facilitate maladaptive behavior.

CURRENT ISSUES IN FATHERING

The role of the father as breadwinner has driven a wedge between men and their families. Recent developments in Japanese society bear on this work role and the degree of paternal involvement with children. First is the growing tendency for companies to isolate middle-aged men even further from their families. Secondly, the stress of men's lives at work is seen to impact negatively on their mental health. Thirdly, the position of women in Japanese society is becoming somewhat stronger. And finally, the government has begun to take small steps toward encouraging paternal involvement.

Transfer Isolates

A new social phenomenon impacting on fathering is the increasing tendency for middle-aged company men to live in isolation from their families, after being transferred out of town by their companies (*Heibonsha's World Encyclopedia*, 1983). About 19% of white-collar salarymen who are transferred are now reportedly forced to live in such isolation. The reasons given for their situations include children's schooling (in 46.6% of such cases) and ownership of a house (in 39.7% of the cases) (Ohgiya, 1985).

In many instances, families are hesitant to move their children to a new school district, due to the great urgency associated with academic success and children's reluctance to leave their lifetime friends. In addition, it is very difficult in Japan to resell one's home, as both the builder and purchaser of a house are often deeply in debt. This makes it impractical to acquire a second home when one is transferred out of town. As a result, many company men leave their families behind and move to the new location alone.

There is already evidence that problems occur often in families with the husband transferred away. According to surveys of such fathers (*Asahi Shinbun*, September 30, 1984), 28% of these fathers are very irritated by the effects of their transfers on the family situation. In addition, 42% of fathers and 32% of mothers felt that father-child relations had been adversely affected (*Asahi Shinbun*, May 5, 1985). Smaller proportions—22% of the men and 20% of their wives—felt that husband-wife relations were also harmed. In a third survey, 85% of the fathers polled reported some discomfort with the effects of transfer isolation on children's education, communication within the family, and so forth. Yet 60% of these same men reported a new sense of "freedom" in the arrangement, and one in five had not returned home in the past year (*Asahi Shinbun*, February 19, 1985). In-depth research is required to reveal the true effects of such transfers on the development of both children and men.

Stress and Suicide

Fathers undergo a great deal of stress at the workplace. One startling outgrowth of this stress has been seen in recent nationwide statistics on suicide (*Asahi Shinbun*, May 12, 1985). In the years 1983 and 1984, the number of deaths by suicide (two thirds of which were men) were the highest since World War II. The largest increases were among men in their 40s and 50s, for whom threefold increases in suicides were reported between 1974 and 1984 (*Asahi Shinbun*, June 12, 1984). Among occupational groups, company managers appear to be especially affected by these trends.

The most frequently noted problem among these suicide victims was "worries concerning one's job." The *Asahi* article related this problem among company men to the stress associated with transfers, sacrificing of one's family life, difficulties in keeping up with changing technology, a sense of hopelessness in a society which discourages job changes, and the upheaval that has taken place in the Japanese value system since World War II.

Changes in Women's Status

Fathering is also changing in response to changes in the status of Japanese women. The idea that the woman's place is in the home is declining in popularity

(*Asahi Shinbun*, February 25, 1985), and maternal employment is becoming increasingly common. In a 1976 national survey of women, 49% agreed with the statement "Men belong at work and women at home"; only 36% agreed in 1984. This trend in public consciousness might lead to inroads by women in the traditionally male-dominated workplace, which could alter fathers' present-day isolation from the home. In comparative studies, a plurality of Japanese adults felt that a woman should take on a job only after her children have grown up and a plurality of Koreans felt a woman should never work outside the home while married, while in the United States a majority favored work at any point in the lifespan (Sorifu, 1982a).

Public school socialization and curricula have traditionally reinforced the separation of the sexes into home and work domains. For instance, home economics was until recently a required course in high school for females only. Boys learned implicitly that skills in home management and childrearing are irrelevant to men, and have avoided the sophisticated and practical training provided in the home economics courses. The Japanese Educational Ministry (*Nihon Keizai Shinbun*, December 20, 1984) has begun revising the curriculum to require boys (probably beginning in the 1990s) to take such coursework as well. This movement, if implemented seriously, could have the effect of training the next generation of fathers to work more effectively in the home, and implant in students the norm of shared parenting rather than sharp division of labor.

In another instance of national policy, the Diet (Japan's national legislative body) recently passed its first comprehensive law concerning equality of the sexes (*Ann Arbor News*, July 7, 1985). Although many women's groups consider the bill as superficial, the legislation's passage indicates that equality has become socially desirable. The growing power of women is shown in a 1984 survey in which 78% of adults reported that the position of women in public society had improved in the preceding decade (*Asahi Shinbun*, January 21, 1985). All of the above trends should lead to at least some narrowing in the gap between the status of Japanese men and women.

Outside the home, the sexual power-balance remains strongly male-dominated (relative to many Western societies). The norm remains firm that men are workers first, fathers second, and husbands third, while women are mothers first, wives second, and are not to have careers (Schooler & Smith, 1979). Therefore, while women are often the dominant force domestically, their progress toward equal status in the public domain has been small and late in coming.

Increases in Paternal Involvement

Recent actions taken by the Japanese government indicate some concern with father absence as well as interest in increasing men's involvement with their children.

Both fathering and participation in homemaking have seldom been encouraged previously, but in April 1985 the city of Tanashi (a Tokyo suburb) enacted a policy of giving childcare leave to its male employees (*Asahi Shinbun,* February 8, 1985). If they so wish, these municipal employees may now relieve their wives of some responsibilities for childcare, for instance to take children to and from day-care centers. Initiated by legislators of progressive minority political parties, this law is the first such instance in Japan of paternity leave.

In another case of local government action, the Hiroshima Board of Education (*Chugoku Shinbun,* August 10, 1984) recently initiated programs to educate fathers about their importance as parents. Through televised lectures, programs of "shared study projects" for fathers and their elementary school children, and community lecture series throughout the prefecture, the government is attempting to increase paternal involvement in children's education.

On the national level, the Education Ministry has published a new "Guidebook of Family Education" (*Asahi Shinbun,* January 31, 1985). In it the family is described as a major root of delinquency and problem behavior. This guidebook, which has drawn considerable media attention, advocates and explains how fathers can take an active role. They are advised to contribute from the child's infancy, as both a support for the mother and through direct nurturant contact.

Finally, national legislation is being developed which would make it possible for fathers to witness their children's elementary and middle school classes (*Sankei Shinbun,* March 17, 1985; *Yomiuri Shinbun,* December 13, 1984). In every Japanese school, several days are designated annually as "visitation days," on which parents may observe classes and discuss matters personally with teachers. Since these weekday events fall on men's working days, their participation has been difficult. Therefore laws are being formulated to allow fathers days off to attend visitation days and become more knowledgeable about their children's education. In some localities, visitation days have been moved to Saturdays to facilitate fathers' participation.

Summary

Four phenomena have received widespread attention recently in the Japanese press. First, large numbers of company workers are being forced by job transfers to live apart from their families. Second, occupational stress seems to be taking a toll on middle-aged men, who are increasingly prone to suicide. Third, while the woman's place is still "in the home," opinion surveys and preliminary actions by the government suggest some increase in the power of women in Japanese society. Finally, the local and national governments are taking small steps to strengthen the role of the father in the family.

PROSPECTS FOR FATHER RESEARCH

In light of the immediacy of the issues raised above, research on Japanese fathers in their changing social context is indeed timely. Much has already been written on fathers, and many empirical reports of research have been reviewed by H.

Saitoh (1984) and in this chapter. The following observations concerning the literature on fathering to date are intended to suggest directions for subsequent research:

1. There have been few experimental or observational studies of Japanese fathers. Instead, the literature consists almost entirely of correlational survey research. We can thus conclude little about cause-and-effect relations from the Japanese data base on fathers and children. While direct observations of Japanese fathers would (potentially) be subject to serious observer effects, correlational research alone is clearly insufficient.

2. Most researchers have relied on verbal reports by children about their fathers. Data have seldom been collected directly from fathers about either parenting or family life, and multiple sources of data have rarely been tapped.

3. The Japanese literature on mother-infant relations has centered on attachment and includes extensive observational data (e.g., Takahashi, 1982). In contrast, the role of the father during infancy has seldom been studied, and we know very little about father-infant attachment. Given the undisputed importance of this developmental period and the suggestion by some research that "childrearing papas" are involved with their infants (e.g., Takeuchi et al., 1982), the study of Japanese father-infant relations deserves increased attention.

4. There have been almost no psychological studies on sex roles in Japanese society. Despite the social change mentioned earlier, sexual division of labor remains stringent. The psychological effects of family and societal structure on father is one important avenue for future research.

5. The clinical and psychiatric literature, as well as the mass media, have paid more attention to issues relevant to real-life fathering than have research psychologists. The widespread discussion of a link between weak fathering and pscyhopathology, and of stress, transfer isolates, and so forth indicates that the general public and scholarly community are deeply interested in fathering. An important contribution of Japanese psychologists would be to study psychological issues of concern in their own culture, going beyond their initial descriptive and replicative bases. Research should consider how their society is changing and whether or not Japanese fathers can adapt to such change.

6. The case-study method has proven useful in highlighting the correlation of childhood pathologies with paternal behavior and personality. This type of research would be enhanced by supplementing case studies with observations of families as they actually interact and by psychological assessments of each family member. Within the family-dynamics framework, the study of husband-wife relations would seem particularly useful in Japan, given the strong influence of mothers on the paternal role.

7. Two additional weaknesses in the Japanese father literature are important to note: (a) It is often an extension of research on children or mothers, and (b) the study of the father is more often the study of father-child relations. How men themselves develop and how their relations with their wives and children change over time are completely neglected in the Japanese literature.

We have seen that the Japanese father has intrigued the public as well as psychologists, sociologists, psychiatrists, educators, and government leaders. There are available for the cause of father research a large number of scholars who have extensive knowledge of Western theory and research and are highly trained in research methodology. As researchers turning specific psychological issues of important the Japanese public and undertake multidisciplinary, multimethodological investigations, we may identify how fathers in such a rapidly evolving social context can best serve the interests of their society, children, wives, and selves.

SUMMARY

The image of the postwar father in the Japanese popular media is one of a hardworking breadwinner who has minimal psychological involvement with his wife and children. On the whole, the thesis that Japanese fathers are increasingly weak and ineffectual is only partially supported by the evidence reviewed here.

The father must be evaluated in light of the recent rapid and significant changes in Japanese society. Historical and legal trends appear to have diminished his authority as leader of the household and as teacher of his children. Several recent trends in family life have also redefined the paternal role. First, the unusually rapid nuclearization of the family has been associated with a clear separation of occupational and family life, distinct male/female division of labor, and an individualistic mentality. Second, demographic trends—including lower birthrates and higher divorce rates—have led to smaller families. Third, in the context of growing affluence, expectations have been raised for fathers to financially support materialistic aspirations. Finally, pressure has mounted on Japanese fathers to lead Japan's "economic miracle" and to support children's competition in an environment where success at school is equated with success in life.

Psychological studies of Japanese fathering have focused on images and definitions of the paternal role, fathers' degree of involvement in childrearing and household affairs, and the involvement of some fathers in child psychopathology. Empirical research (mainly self-reports from a single source) indicates that the popular image of weak fathers may be exaggerated, that actual and ideal paternal images differ, and that perceptions of fathers may vary according to the age and gender of the child. The father appears to be a breadwinner and a friendly authority figure, but in childrearing and household matters he is clearly the "second parent." Although most fathers are respected, in some families the father has been implicated as one source of ailments including school refusal, violence within the family, delinquency, apathy, and rebellion.

A set of recent developments in Japanese society bear on the importance of the changing paternal role. These phenomena include: (a) the increasing numbers of company managers forced by transfers to live away from their children, (b) the mushrooming suicide rate among middle-aged men, (c) the growing influence of women in the public (non-family) domain, and (d) the first governmental measures which appear to be aimed at increasing the father's influence at home.

Weaknesses in the psychological literature on Japanese fathering include a lack of objective research methods and the tendency to focus on replications of Western research studies. It was suggested that the strong public interest in Japanese fathering should encourage scientists to probe the important question of how men, as fathers, respond to the rapid social changes which characterize Japanese society today.

REFERENCES

Befu, H. (1971). *Japan: An anthropological introduction*. San Francisco: Chandler.

Biller, H. B. (1974). *Paternal deprivation: Family, school, sexuality and society*. Lexington, MA: Lexington.

Doi, T. (1973). *The anatomy of dependence*. Tokyo: Kodansha International.

Ebihara, N. (1972). The position of the father in modern society. *Jidoshinri, 26*(3), 1–10.

Fukaya, K. (1980). School refusal children and parent-child relations. In T. Takuma & H. Inamura (Eds.), *School refusal*. Tokyo: Yuhikaku.

Fukaya, M. (1978). *The life of today's children*. Tokyo: Dai-ichi Hoki Shuppan.

Fukaya, M., & Fukaya, K. (1975). *Theory of modern childhood*. Tokyo: Yuhikaku.

Hanta, S. (1976). Children in the maternally-dominated home. *Jidoshinri, 30*,(10), 85–90.

Harano, K. (1981). Can fathers gain the friendship of their children? In H. Katsura (Ed.), *The paternal role*. Volume 5. Tokyo: Kaneko Shobo.

Haraoka, H. (1972). Changes in the ideal father image and children's developmental level. *Jidoshinri, 26*(3), 21–30.

Heibonsha's World Encyclopedia. (1982). Tokyo: Heibonsha.

Heibonsha's World Encyclopedia. (1983). Tokyo: Heibonsha.

Inamura, H. (1980). Violence in the family: The sickness of Japanese-style parent-child relations. Tokyo: Shinyosha.

Isogai, Y. (1972). Differences in social class and images of the father. *Jidoshinri, 26*(3), 21–30.

Japanese Statistical Yearbook (1984). Tokyo: Statistics Bureau, Management and Coordination Agency.

Jidoshinri (1972). The role of the father: A roundtable discussion in search of a new paternal role. *Jidoshinri, 26*(3), 56–72.

Kashiwaguma, Z. (1981). The father in relation to the mother. In H. Katsura (Ed.). *The paternal role*. Volume 5, "Home Education Series". Tokyo: Kaneko Shobo.

Kawai, K. (1960). *Japan's American interlude*. Chicago: University of Chicago Press.

Kida, H., Shwalb, D. W., & Shwalb, B. J. (1985). School achievement and socialization in Japan: Implications for educators. *Evaluation in Education: An International Review Series, 9*(3), 217–300.

Kida, J. (1980). Childrearing behavior of fathers in dual-occupation families. *Bulletin of the Shiga University Faculty of Education, 30*, 116–135.

Kyoiku Shinri Nenpo (1981). Symposium 1: The role of fathering in the development of infants and young children. *Annual Review of Educational Psychology, 20*, 93–95.

Lamb, M. E. (1981). *The role of the father in child development* (2nd Edition). NY: Wiley.

Lebra, T. S. (1976). *Japanese patterns of behavior*. Honolulu: University Press of Hawaii.

Naijo, Y. (1981). Examples of father participation in infants'/children's lives and in the child-rearing locale. *Annual Review of Educational Psychology, 20,* 95.

NHK [Japan Broadcasting Corporation] (1977). The family and education. *Gekkan Yoron Chosa, 9*(1), 33–53.

Nishihira, N. (1981). The formation and breakdown of paternal authority. In H. Katsura (Ed.), *The paternal role.* Volume 5, Tokyo: Kaneko Shobo.

Ohgiya, S. (1983). The Society of Thunderous Fathers. In *Basic information on current expressions.* Tokyo: Jukokuminsha.

Ohgiya, S. (1985). The transfer isolate express train. In *Basic information on current expressions.* Tokyo: Jukokuminsha.

Okado, T. (1981). The psychology and guidance of the fatherless child. In H. Katsura (Ed.), *The paternal role.* Tokyo: Kaneko Shobo.

Parsons, T., & Bales, R. F. (1955). *Family, socialization, and interaction process.* Glencoe, IL: Free Press.

Plath, D. W., (Ed.) (1983). *Work and lifecourse in Japan.* Albany: State University of New York Press.

Reischauer, E. O. (1977). *The Japanese.* Cambridge, MA: Harvard University Press.

Saitoh, H. (1984). The role and influence of the father. In *Annual review of Japanese child psychology.* Tokyo: Kaneko Shobo.

Saitoh, K. (1972). Fathers and the subject of "amae". *Jidoshinri, 3,* 94–99.

Schooler, C., & Smith, K. (1979). And a Japanese wife . . . *Sex Roles, 4*(1), 23–39.

Shinohara, T. (1981). The role of the father in the era of the nuclear family. In H. Katsura (Ed.), *The paternal role.* Volume 5, Tokyo: Kaneko Shobo.

Shinsaku, Y. (1982a). Changes in family structure. In *Basic information on current expressions.* Tokyo: Jukokuminsha.

Shinsaku, Y. (1982b). Schooling-oriented society. In *Basic information on current expressions.* Tokyo: Jukokuminsha.

Sofue, T. (1981). A cultural-anthropological examination of the father. In H. Katsura (Ed.), *The paternal role.* Volume 5, Tokyo: Kaneko Shobo.

Sorifu (1980a). Japanese mothers and children: An international comparison. *Gekkan Yoron Chosa, 12*(5), 50–57.

Sorifu (1980b). The improvement of the family foundation. *Gekkan Yoron Chosa, 12*(2), 65–73.

Sorifu (1980c). A survey on violence in the family. *Gekkan Yoron Chosa, 12*(12), 67–68.

Sorifu (1981a). *Today's youth: A comparison with those ten years ago.* Tokyo: Prime Minister's Office.

Sorifu (1981b). *White paper on youth.* Tokyo: Prime Minister's Office.

Sorifu (1982a). *International survey on youth and their environment.* Tokyo: Prime Minister's Office.

Sorifu (1983). *White paper on youth.* Tokyo: Prime Minister's Office.

Sorifu (1984). Wives. *Gekkan Yoron Chosa, 7,* 2–32.

Sorifu (1985). *White paper on youth.* Tokyo: Prime Minister's Office.

Tabuchi, S., & Tanaka, K. (1978). Analysis of fathers' child-rearing behavior. *Proceedings of the 20th meetings of the Japanese Association of Educational Psychology,* 506–507.

Takahashi, K. (1982). Attachment behavior to a female stranger. *Journal of Genetic Psychology, 26,* 299–307.

Takeuchi, K., Uehara, A., & Suzuki, H. (1982). A study of fathers' child-rearing consciousness. *Proceedings of the 24th meetings of the Japanese Association of Educational Psychology,* 302–303.

Tamai, S. (1965). Research on so-called school phobia. *Seishin Eisei Kenkyu, 13.*

Uryu, T. (1984). The recent problem of fatherlessness and juvenile delinquency. *Japanese Journal of Psychotherapy, 10,* 137–142.

Vogel, E. (1965). *Japan's new middle class: The salaryman and his family in a Tokyo suburb.* Berkeley: University of California Press.

Vogel, E. (1977). *Japan as number one.* Cambridge, MA: Harvard University Press.

Wagatsuma, H. (1977). Some aspects of the contemporary Japanese family: Once Confucian, now fatherless? *Daedalus, 106*(2), 181–210.

Yamada, H. (1979). Fathers and childrearing: The state of such relations and related issues. *Research Reports of the Yamanashi University Faculty of Education, 30,* 151–162.

Yamada, K. (1984). Apathy and fathering. *Japanese Journal of Psychotherapy, 10,* 149–154.

Yamane, T. (1976). Changes in the Japanese family. In K. Morioka & T. Yamane (Eds.), *"Ie" and the contemporary family.* Tokyo: Baifukan.

Yamazaki, K. (1979). Transition of the father's role in the Japanese family. *Annual Report of the RCCCD, Hokkaido University Faculty of Education,* 43–53.

Yoneda, H. (1975). Perceptions of the father in childhood and adolescence. *Bulletin of the Hiroshima University Faculty of Education, 23,* 375–381.

IV AFRICA

11 A West African Perspective

Augustine B. Nsamenang
Social Sciences Research Centre,
Yaounde, Cameroon

INTRODUCTION

West Africa is one part of the world that has not yet experienced the full consequences of the industrial revolution. However, it has had brought to it from outside some of the modern techniques of production and communication in vogue in the industrial world (Mair, 1974).

In West Africa, people are still preoccupied with getting a living, not mastering the environment. People are still greatly dependent on the food they grow themselves and the animals they herd rather than on the goods they manufacture. They rely much more on the mutual support and assistance of their kin than on organized welfare services. In consequence, their most significant relationships and alliances are with their kin. Kinship is, therefore, what orders the social structure.

The principal effect of the West African pattern of life on the individual is lineage cleavage or a centripetal tendency among kinsmen to remain within the family or kin group and, when outside it, to keep within the boundaries of its immediate direct extension—the clan—and not stray much farther beyond. This kind of social organization makes possible the development of a broad system of extended family networks which typify West African societies.

In south-central Cameroon, the village, "centred on a minimal patrilineage and grouped around a polygamous headman" was, according to Guyer (1980), "the most important social unit." The village system with a predominant pattern of patri-virilocal residence is the social pattern of most West African societies.

Because of the predominance of patrilineal over matrilineal societies in West Africa and the importance accorded men in West African cultures, scientific neglect and scholarly disregard of the role of men and of the father is rather surprising.

The primary purpose of this chapter, then, is to present a West African perspective on the father's role. But before we delve into this we shall examine, albeit briefly, the West African background and the peoples and their ways of living. Next, the chapter focuses on the family and then on marriage. These are two core institutions in West Africa in which the father is the culturally designated principal actor. The fifth section examines the image of the father presented in West African cultures, while the discussion in the sixth part of the chapter shifts to an empirical illustration of the effects of fathering (or lack of it) on children. The chapter terminates with a consideration of emerging trends in family life and parenting.

THE WEST AFRICAN BACKGROUND

West Africa is one of the major geographical regions of the continent of Africa. It is bounded in the south and west by the Atlantic Ocean and in the east by Lake Chad and the Cameroon Adamawa Highlands. The northern boundaries of Mauritania, Mali, and Niger constitute its northern limit. Politically, West Africa consists of all those states that lie south of Morocco, Algeria, and Libya and west of Cameroon.

The total area of West Africa is some 6.2 million square kilometers—about two thirds the size of the United States of America. This land area is shared by 16 countries whose total population in 1974 was about 121 million, of which over 71 million lived in Nigeria alone (Udo, 1978).

Physiographically, West Africa is a vast, low tableland characterized by a narrow continental shelf, a narrow coastal plain, several interior surfaces, and undulating landscapes. The main highland areas are the Bamenda and Adamawa Highlands in Cameroon, the Jos and Mambila Plateaus in Nigeria, and the Futa Jalon Highlands in Guinea. Mount Cameroon, 4,100 m above sea level, is the highest peak in the region. It had a volcanic eruption in 1983.

Lake Chad (an inland drainage), the Sanaga, the Benue, the Cross River, the Niger, the Volta, and the Gambia are the major waterways in the region which facilitate movement.

There are three main ecological belts in West Africa, each of which is characterized by distinctive agricultural activities and cultural practices. The equatorial rain forest along the coast gives way in the hinterland to shrubs, thornbushes, and savanna and, eventually, on the fringes of the Sahara Desert to the Sahelian Belt, characterized by an absence of rainfall and permanent vegetation. The heavy rainfall along the coast drops off very quickly as one approaches the Sahelian zone, and some areas may be bone-dry for long periods. Countries like Niger, Burkina Faso, Mali, Mauritania, and the northern parts of Senegal and Cameroon are currently being devastated by the worst drought in living memory.

The continent of Africa encountered a bitter colonial experience in the hands of European imperialists, beginning in the fifteenth century and climaxing in November 1884 at the Berlin Conference. Here every nation of Europe except Switzerland (14 nations in all) partitioned the continent of Africa amongst themselves (see July, 1974). In West Africa, where Europe came early and remained late, the Western impact was strongest. This European influence wrought irreversible changes in the demographic, cultural, social, economic, and political structure of the region. One unfortunate consequence of this colonization, the Slave Trade, resulted in the forceful transfer of some 15-20 million Africans, mainly West Africans, as slaves to European plantations in the Americas (Oyebola, 1976). Despite this massive physical transfer of West Africans, West Africa today is still Black Africa's most populous region.

THE PEOPLE AND THEIR WAYS OF LIVING

The 121 million people of West Africa belong to several ethnic stocks, each of which speaks a different language. Cameroon alone—with more than 239 ethnic languages (Che, 1985)—is a veritable babel of tongues which clearly exemplifies the rich diversity in the region.

West African peoples fall into two broad groups: the northern peoples who came into West Africa from across the Sahara Desert (i.e., they are of Arab descent); and the southern peoples who are Negroes, Sudanic-speaking blacks "whose languages and customs suggest a common ancestry far into the remote past" (July, 1974).

The northern people are nomadic herders who migrate from one place to another in search of pasture and water for their livestock. For some, the whole population has to move in the dry season to the few sources of permanent water and back in the wet season to their homes. Others can leave women and old people in permanent homes where there is water for humans but must send their young men away with the herds in search of water and pasture.

Many of these nomadic herders have settled down to practice elementary forms of farming. Most of them live in large towns and farming villages and are organized into large political units ruled by very influential and powerful traditional kings or sultans. The majority of the northern people profess the Muslim faith. Their typical mud huts with grass thatch or flat roofs present a sharp contrast to the makeshift tents of nomadic herders.

Oyebola (1976) has outlined the identity marks of Negroes as "their dark or dark-brown skin, short frizzy or spiralled hair, a flat broad nose, a measure of projecting jaws and thick lips that are often everted." Political organization among the Negroes ranges from the extensive forest kingdoms of Ashanti, Benin, Dahomey, and Yoruba through the *Fondoms* ("chiefdoms") of the Bamenda Grassfields to the largely fragmented groupings of the hinterland where the village group is the largest unit. The *Fon* ("king") was entirely independent in the administration of his village kingdom which he sought to enlarge and enrich through marriage (Guyer, 1980). The advent of the colonial administration saw the gradual breakdown of this structure. But nowhere has it led to the total social disintegration of indigenous structures. The local rulers are jealous of their sovereignty and guard it tenaciously. They are religious as well as temporal leaders of their people, and have no enthusiasm for any limitation on their authority as heads of virile states.

The predominant religion amongst the Negroes is traditional religion, the core of which is ancestral worship. Christianity and Islam nevertheless coexist but without excluding a lively faith in ancestral spirits and the supernatural. What people cannot understand or themselves control they ascribe to the supernatural, usually personalized in the ancestors whose goodwill they must seek to secure in order to live and prosper (Mair, 1974). Furthermore, they believe that people—if they know the right potion and substances—can obtain power beyond the natural to help or harm others. Hence, illness or failure in an endeavor is frequently attributed to the evil forces or ill wishes being called in against a person from enemies. Barrenness in a woman, for example, is sometimes blamed on some fault of hers or a transgression of some taboo, on account of which ancestral spirits are neither willing to "insert" a soul in her womb nor willing to be incarnated in her.

Because the lines between the living and the dead are rather blurred, "the ancestors are conceived of as continuing spiritual presences watching over and admonishing their descendants" (Ellis, 1978). The belief in ancestral spirits is so strong that many West Africans "have shrines of their ancestors" to which they go "to ask for the blessing of their ancestors in any important projects they want to undertake" (Tetteh, 1967).

Because West Africans live at the fringes of traditional and Western cultures, contemporary West Africans are at a dilemma of "deciding how to maintain the traditional values and yet adapt to and benefit from the 'modernizing' influence of Western cultures" (Stapleton, 1978). The cultural amalgam is indeed complex. But West Africans are basically traditional with only a "thin layer of modern sophistication concealing" the central core of "traditional beliefs and feelings" (Obiechina, 1975). This is particularly true of beliefs and practices regarding childrearing; these are not amenable to easy changes since they are tenaciously held with beliefs about life itself (Uka, 1966). The challenge is, therefore, how to make the technologies of the Western world accessible to traditional West Africans without destroying their indigenous cultures.

The basic economy of West Africa rests upon agriculture, which is practiced by over 80% of the population (WHO, 1976). The family farm constitutes its basic building block. Farming decisions are affected by the farmer's access to the labor of the opposite sex (Guyer, 1980). Consequently, "a farmer should be conceived of as neither an individual male or (sic) female but as a husband and wife who work in a symbiotic relationship" (Hill, 1978). They typically live in a farming village of mutually supportive kinsfolk who cooperate in all spheres of peasant life and sometimes engage in the same productive activities. Male and female workers are recruited by kin, and to a lesser extent, non-kin ties.

Their agricultural practices vary from zone to zone and include farming, fishing, herding, and crafts. Agricultural crops vary from the desert date-palms and savanna cereals to the rain-forest crops like cocoa, palms, bananas, cassava, and coffee.

These crops are usually raised on small family farms with the aid of the iron hoe and the machete. New fields are cleared through traditional slash-and-burn techniques (July, 1974). The vagaries of the weather are a constant threat of harvest failure and famine. Even with normal conditions, the chronic insufficiency of energy intake threatens farming effectiveness; this is especially acute during the growing season when people frequently face labor-intensive activity in the fields with exhausted granaries and empty stomachs. This sets up a vicious cycle of inadequate productivity, low incomes, and a low standard of living.

Farming responsibilities are based on sexual division of tasks, crops, and rights to mobilize resources. Male and female tasks are primarily defined in terms of the tools to do the work. Men generally use the axe and the long-handled digging stick while women do most of the work requiring the short-handled iron hoe. In some communities, the women assume the important work of weeding and transplanting; in others, this is the job of men, who are also charged with the heavy work of clearing new land or preparing fields for the first seeding (July, 1974). Women have prime responsibility for horticultural activities and day-to-day work in the field; cash crops are principally male crops but the yam field requires the collaboration of men and women as their tasks alternate over the growing season. Harvesting is a community affair shared by all—men, women, and children—in a headlong rush to bring in the crops before they are damaged by the attacks of predatory birds, monkeys, and insects.

On the whole, both men and women "in their separate and overlapping, symmetrical and complementary tasks and activities" (Clark, 1980) contribute to the traditional political economy.

But male labor in the traditional food production chain began to be diverted towards the cash sector with the introduction of cash crops, which were associated with tax payment. The men could not, unfortunately, afford to buy a substantial proportion of the family diet from their cash-crops incomes (Henn, 1978). As long as this remains true, rural women will continue to maintain the full variety of subsistence patterns of farming. The female share of the traditional food system has thus remained the basis of subsistence in today's West Africa.

In the past, men and women worked together for family subsistence without either having recourse to the money economy. The change from a purely subsistence economy to a largely cash economy was necessitated by the need for cash to pay taxes and school fees—two practices unknown prior to the advent of the colonial administration. The cultivation of cash crops consequently opened the floodgates of the cash economy. And today, the urban demand for food, which has offered women a way of making regular cash income from the marketing of food crops—together with the production and sale of cash crops, the insatiable desire to buy consumer goods, and the need to pay taxes and school fees—have all contributed to launch West African societies into a market economy, though not without vestiges of subsistence.

Local transactions take place in periodic markets; these serve not only for trade but also for social and cultural exchanges. Elders and kinsmen meet together on the market day to consort and discuss matters of the traditional government. Young men and women customarily use market days for courtship. The people of the Bamenda grassfields in Cameroon use the markets to make public announcements, admonish criminals, assign public tasks, or make arrangements for a community project (Chilver, 1962; Ritzenthaler, 1962). Markets are put into similar uses throughout the region.

Only very small numbers of people in West Africa still live by the oldest means of survival—hunting and gathering wild food. Even the Pygmies of the southeastern Cameroon forests are attached in a serf-like relationship to settled populations on the borders of their hunting groups. Through government resettlement programs, the hunting bands are very slowly but constantly losing individual members to the new settlements or neighboring villages, where they are encouraged to learn to be farmers and only part-time hunters. They are also encouraged to benefit from educational, health, and other social services, though this has met with minimal success so far.

THE FAMILY

The family is the most basic structural unit of every society. It ensures the supply and maintenance of new members without which the society would disappear. While a nuclear family consists of a man, his wife, and their offspring, a joint family is made up of the heads of two or three lineally related kinsfolk of the same sex, their spouses, and offspring—all of whom occupy a single homestead and are jointly subject to the same authority and single head (Ayisi, 1979).

The basic structural unit of West African societies is the extended family. The extended family consists of a number of joint families who are "bound by ties of mutual obligation" (Green, 1974). Mutual obligation amongst kin relates to cooperation in the upbringing of children through kinship fostering and in economic activities and matters of defense and security. The extended family forms the raison d'être of all social cooperation and responsibility. It acts as a social security for members of the lineage group and knits together kin, facilitating the feeling of rendering mutual support in all important matters in the interest and welfare of the entire group.

In traditional African thinking, in other words, the interests and welfare of the group supersede those of the individual because individuals come and go but the group persists. Asserting the interests or welfare of the individual above those of the group is, consequently, considered deviant behavior. People who attempt to assert their independence and personal interests and try to disengage themselves from communal life do so at the expense of their peace of mind and at great risk of losing the psychological comfort of a feeling of belonging. To feel that one does not belong to one's kin is, according to Esen (1972), "comparable to some kind of death," and most West Africans tend to avoid it.

Obiechina (1975), a commentator on the West African novel, vividly portrays this relationship between the individual and his community as follows:

> The West African novel tends to show the individual characters not through their private psychological experiences, but through community and social life and activities of collective and general nature with individual sentiments and actions deriving force and logic from those of the community.

A fundamental reason for this deep-rooted sense of community spirit is that, from early in life, the child is made aware of the overriding importance of kinsfolk and is taught all the things he or she needs to know to function as a member of the group. In order to reinforce the spirit of communal life, West Africans emphasize reconciliation in handling disputes and domestic conflicts. Reconciliation is a valuable African attribute which is a central principle in the Charter of the Organization for African Unity (OAU). In this regard, Busia (1967) rightly observed that whenever a council of lineage representatives "met to discuss matters affecting the whole community, it had always to grapple with the problem of reconciling sectional and common interests" and "had to talk things over" till "unanimity" was reached. The readiness and ease with which the victims of the Nigerian political crisis and civil war were accepted and integrated into families clearly illustrates the importance and usefulness of our kind of social system.

African communalism is built on the kinship system. Kinship may involve ties of blood (biological kinship), descent (jural or legal kinship), or marriage (affiliation) (Peil, 1977). Kinship constitutes the primary basis for the individual's rights, duties, rules of residence, marriage, inheritance, and succession.

Most West Africans trace their descent unilineally, that is, through father to father's father, or mother to mother's mother, as far back as they can reckon (Mair, 1974). But among the Yoruba people of Western Nigeria (Fadipe, 1970) and the Nso of the Bamenda Grassfields of Cameroon, kinship extends to all those who can be traced by blood on both the paternal and maternal side, and kinship by marriage extends to the most distant kinsfolk of the spouse. The larger the circle of one's kin, the greater one's social and political importance (Fadipe, 1970). Persons linked to either mode of descent form lineages which constitute not only the source of rights of inheritance and succession but the source of duties, obligations, and the rules which regulate personal and communal life.

West Africans describe themselves by terms which are used only for near relatives; for example, a person uses "brother" for almost all male members of the group in the same generation (Ayisi, 1979). Similarly, the terms "father" or "mother" are used for people of one's father's or mother's generation. Hence, the child is taught early to regard his adult kin as his "other" fathers and mothers and their children as his brothers and sisters. They, in turn, treat him accordingly (Maquet, 1978). A man may, therefore, call not only his father's son "brother", but also the first or second cousins of his own generation.

A group of people who regard themselves as related in this way do so because they have descended from the same ancestor or ancestress. If descent is traced to a common ancestor through the male line, as in most of West Africa, the society so formed is called a patrilineal society. If, on the other hand, descent is traced through the female line, as among the Kom of Cameroon and the Ashanti of Ghana, then the society is matrilineal.

The division of societies into these discrete categories is important because in West Africa a distinction is made between sociological paternity (pater) and biological paternity (genitor). In matrilineal societies, one's mother's people are more important than one's father's people because the individual derives all his jural rights from his mother's people. Children also belong to the mother's lineage. But the father still has a special ritual link with his children with corresponding obligations on either side. For example, the father has to name his children, arrange marriages for his sons, and provide them with a gun, bow and arrow, fishing net, or a trade. In modern times, most fathers give their children an education. The children, too, have to perform certain services such as mortuary rites, which in many societies include the provision of their deceased father's coffin. In fact, most fathers expect a befitting burial from their children, especially their sons.

A striking feature of West African societies is the extent to which traditional political relations are almost coterminous with kinship relations. The traditional political structure and kinship organizations are completely fused—which is, perhaps, why national politics in West Africa today continues to be bedevilled by ethnicity.

Bonds among kin are emphasized and strengthened by the practice of kinship fostering. A kinsman (or occasionally a non-kinsman) assumes the rights and duties of parenthood often until the child's marriage, but without the biological parents surrendering their full rights as they would in adoption (Schildkrout, 1973). The child, in turn, looks to the foster parents rather than his biological parents for assistance and gives them the obedience and services which are expected from a child. The biological parents delegate rights to others as a means of unifying the kin group which may have become separated in space or to provide childhood help in a household that otherwise has no children.

Kinsmen foster the children of other relatives in order to demonstrate their concern and regard for "these relatives" of the family. In this sense, fostering is seen to be an African way of rearing children "within the context of the extended family" (Ware, 1975). Children may also be fostered for advantage: to receive an education, to be taught a trade, or to be disciplined more carefully (since it is believed that the child's biological parents are too attached emotionally to their offspring to give him or her a good upbringing). Hense, the preference is to have children reared by relations or friends who will not "spare the rod and spoil the child." One primary motivation for fostering children today is the degree to which the child's family is incapacitated by poverty. In such cases, the preferred placement is the home of a more affluent relation or friend who will pay for the child's education or at least guarantee food and lodging in exchange for work in the house (Laosebikan & Filani, 1981).

Within the network of kinship relationships, the growing African child is rapidly integrated into the community by introducing him or her to the interactions, social roles and skills, disciplines, and aspirations necessary for group membership. When they are quite young, children begin their activities in the family production line as part of their training in housework, agriculture, or a trade. Children in eastern Nigeria, for example, "take active and important part in the work of the compound and village" (Uchendu, 1965). And in Ghanaian homes, "children participate in the work of the house from a very early age" (Kaye, 1962). As children grow older, their sphere of activity increases and they begin to cooperate with their parents in the production and distribution of family resources until their time of marriage (Keyatta, 1938). While girls help their mothers, boys work alongside their fathers, paying attention for the essential reason that their fathers' business may be theirs one day.

In addition to learning the necessary roles and skills for living, West African children also internalize the aspirations of their society. Consequently, children grow up to see the prestige attached to parenthood and learn that this is a worthy aspiration. This encourages them to model their parents in the hope that one day they will achieve the same status and prestige. West Africans grow up to regard marriage and eventually parenthood as a primary goal in life, and the risk that sufficient parenthood may not be attained makes people very anxious (Wober, 1975).

MARRIAGE

Marriage is an ubiquitous institution in all human societies. Few institutions dramatize any culture's view of male roles so clearly as the institution of marriage. It is one of the most powerful means of maintaining cohesion in West African societies and of enforcing conformity to the kinship system and to ethnic and social organizations, without which social life would be difficult.

Peil (1977) sees marriage as a publicly recognized, more or less permanent union between a man and a woman—the conjugal pair. Marriage is, therefore, a socially approved means by which a man and a woman come together to form a union for the purpose of procreation. West African marriages are expressly effected for this purpose.

For every marriage to be legal, certain requirements have to be fulfilled. The ceremony should be preceded by certain customary observances, for example, the payment of a bridewealth. Bridewealth is a payment or service to a woman's kin in compensation for the loss of a member. It cements and legalizes the marriage contract and establishes paternity rights. A man who has not made the bride payment on a woman may forfeit his claim to any children who may be born. When a divorce occurs, the bridewealth must be refunded by the kinsmen of the divorced woman before she can legally remarry. If this condition is not satisfied, any children born out of wedlock belong to the original husband.

The amount of bridewealth payable on a girl differs form one area to another and also varies within the same area according to circumstances (e.g., the girl's education). Because children belong to their mother's descent group, bride-wealth payable in matrilineal societies is usually much smaller than in patrilineal societies, where children belong to the father's kin.

Through the marriage ceremony, a man acquires the sole access to sexual intercourse with his wife, the sole purpose of which is procreation and not merely the gratification of a bodily desire (Kenyatta, 1938). Parenthood, then, becomes the central purpose of marriage; the desire for children, a passion.

The desire for children is deep-rooted in the hearts of both men and women, and on entering marriage they regard procreation as their first and most sacred duty. The young couple is therefore expected to have children as soon after the marriage ceremony as possible. Parents become anxious when their daughter does not become pregnant within the first year of marriage (Uka, 1966). Pregnancy of a newlywed woman brings joy to the family of both the man and (more especially) the woman. A woman who sees the signs of pregnancy after marriage becomes elated and announces the news with a sense of self-fulfillment (Ayisi, 1979). Pregnancy, therefore, seems to have some cathartic effects on African women—and men too. It not only confirms the fecundity of both the man and his wife but, in a way, consummates the marriage. It is also a sign that the ancestral spirits are sending a representative, through the couple, into the community.

The fact that a couple has no children is interpreted as sufficient proof that they are bad people and their badness is being punished with childlessness by the ancestors. Consequently, childlessness is felt by both men and women as "the greatest of all personal tragedies and humiliations" (Fortes, 1950). Childlessness is a frequent cause of divorce or recourse to polygyny.

A childless marriage is practically a failure and ceases to be meaningful in the West African context for the simple reason that children bring joy not only to parents but to the clan as a whole. In West Africa as in Kenya, the social position of a married man or woman who has children "is of greater importance and dignity than that of a bachelor or spinster" (Kenyatta, 1938). After the birth of their first child, the parents become the object of higher regard than they were prior to the birth of their child. The naming of the child marks a further change in the status of the parents, who ccme to be known and addressed not in their personal names but as someone's father or mother. Within the traditional milieu, for instance, this writer is rarely addressed by his personal name, he is called "Kila's father" because his first child is named Kila.

The payment made for marriage confers rights and duties on the partners of the union. These are personal rights and duties which are reciprocal obligations of the husband and wife in the performance of certain duties. Thus, in addition to the legal status established between an African husband and has wife, each partner has to perform specific duties to the other as well as to members of each other's kin group, who have by the marriage become affines. These rights and duties then form the legal basis for all customarily recognized marriages.

The implication here is that marriage is not simply between a man and a woman (i.e., the immediate partners) as in Western societies where it ideally follows the love and free personal choice of individuals, but between families or even communities. This being the case, the kinsmen of both parties have a lively interest and role in the union. They often choose the mate or at least manifest their approval of the choice and participate in the *rite de passage* which constitutes the marriage. Today, prospective partners who want to make an independent choice and can pay their way without family backing can do so even if their family disapproves; but the majority still seek family consent for their choice. This reinforces the fact that marriage in this part of the world is as much a family affair as it is an individual affair. The material, moral, and spiritual support of the family for the ceremony and during marriage (and for women especially should the marriage break down) makes it important that their approval be gained. The family would feel reluctant to refund the bridewealth in an event of divorce if it did not approve the marriage in the first place.

In West Africa, the number of marriageable women outnumber the number of marriageable men, and polygyny is commonplace in this society where it is the norm to marry and bear children. In contrast to polyandry (a form of marriage in which a woman marries more than one husband), polygyny is a marriage practice wherein a man marries more than one wife. Polyandry is not known to be in practice in any West African community today. There is, however, another form of marriage known as *levirate,* by which a man inherits his brother's widow. Sometimes a woman may "marry" the widow of a deceased brother and then permit a member of her lineage or family to cohabit with the woman (Ayisi, 1979). Children of such a union belong to the woman who is the "husband" of the widow. This is consistent with the dogma of African paternity which distinguishes between sociological paternity (pater) and biological paternity (genitor). Levirate is very rare today.

Despite Christian influence which encourages monogamy, polygyny continues to thrive even among Christians. Among the Creoles of Sierra Leone (Harrell-Bond, 1975) and the Yoruba of Nigeria (LeVine, Klein, & Owen, 1967), missionary influence has led to great emphasis being placed on monogamous religious marriage, but men's great desire for many children leads to an extensive pattern of the so-called outside wives whose children are readily accepted and integrated into their family. A similar pattern can be observed in much of West Africa where even polygamous men still have several children with outside wives. Polygyny facilitates the mobilization of female labor for their husbands (Guyer, 1980) since "another wife" means an additional pair of hands on the farm and in the house. Wives are, therefore, both the sign of wealth and the main means (labor) for generating it. Their daughters bring bridewealth and new marriage alliances to the village; their sons increase the size, importance, and military strength of the group; and their agricultural work produces surpluses for feasting and exchanges (Guyer, 1980).

In polygamous families, each wife has her own hut or room within the family compound. She is responsible for the care of her own children and shares duties with co-wives in relation to her husband (Boserup, 1970) and family provisioning. She endeavors to give her children the best opportunity and training so that they may not be relegated in future to a subordinate position among other children of the extended family (Mabogunje, 1975). Mabogunje further provides an insight into the conflict (sometimes feud) that exists in polygamous households in Nigeria and elsewhere, when he reports that "it is rare to find the wives in a polygamous home acting in unison all the time. There is always rivalry among them as to who would be the husband's darling" and whose children would derive maximum benefit from the father's supportive attention.

Marriage includes parenthood, the most crucial aspect of the union to the West African. Parenthood presumes responsibility for the offspring. The sexual division of parental responsibilities allocates different roles to men and women. In this regard, women have prime responsibility for the procreation, nurturance, and care of children. Women's nurturing role extends to horticultural activities, food processing, and food distribution. In contrast, men defend the family, village, and property against external attack. But both men and women in their separate and joint activities contribute to family welfare and subsistence.

THE FATHER IN WEST AFRICAN CULTURES

There is a palpable lack of scholarly interest in fathering among researchers in West Africa. A few scholars—such as Bekombo (1981) in Cameroon, Hake (1972) and Uka (1966) in Nigeria, Lombard (1978) in Ivory Coast, and Kaye (1962) in Ghana—merely mention the father in their separate discussions of childrearing as if he were an insignificant entity in the lives of his children. This scientific neglect or devaluation of the father as a primary agent of socialization gives the impression that, in spite of the high esteem accorded the father in West African cultures, he remains only a peripheral figure in the lives of his children.

West African customs put women in a subordinate position to men. Nevertheless, in some areas of social life, men and women are eligible for the same kinds of positions, as in prophecy, divining, and traditional healing. But many women's decisions affect only women and the resources they control, whereas men's decisions bind the whole group (both men and women).

The traditional principle is that all wealth produced by a man's wife is for the benefit of her husband. He is expected to control what happens within the family, even to the extent of deciding whether or not his wife should undertake any activity outside the domestic sphere. Any deviation threatens the man's very identity. The social class and lifestyle of a family are determined mainly by the husband's position in the community, and his success both in business and in social life confers on his wife and children their main source of status and prestige.

The father can thus be seen to be the most esteemed member of the West African family. He is, in most societies, the governing helm of the family and its central authority. As the family's principal lifeline to the world outside the home, the father is not only the person who brings into the family the mores, values, and expectations of the society but also the one who sets and enforces standards of behavior and controls family decision making, even filial marital choices. He assumes a crucial role in problem solving and protection of the family by exercising a moderating influence on the family's interactions with the external world and by being called upon to intervene and resolve any problem that may arise between the family and the society. Should there be any individual in the family in open challenge to the father's authority, such a case is regarded and treated as an insurrection.

The primary responsibility of a man's wife is to bear his children—especially males, who represent the continuation of his lineage in order that his name not become extinct. West Africans prefer to die in poverty and leave children than to die childless but rich (Nsamenang & Loasebikan, 1981). "To leave no heirs behind is the worst evil that can befall a man" (Jahn, 1961). The belief that if a man dies childless he has either wasted his life or lived in vain makes the anxiety for parenthood very intense.

Not only is there a great desire for fatherhood but a great wish for many children, probably to offset the infant mortality rate, which is perhaps the highest in the world. The desire for many children is tempered somehow nowadays by considerations of the economic strains of bringing up and educating children. Today large families are possible mainly in the rural areas, where about 80% of the population lives and where children's contribution to the family economy is still substantial.

West Africans value children for the prestige and respect they bring, the help and assistance they offer, and the support and companionship they provide, particularly in old age. The feeling that children should satisfy their parents and compensate them for the disappointments and shortcomings of their own lives is widespread. Consequently, parents (fathers, in particular) want their children to work harder than they themselves did in order to escape poverty and the humiliation of being unable to read and write in a world where these skills have become almost the minimum requirement for active and successful citizenship (Okedara, 1980).

A West African father is a central figure in the life of his family. His power and control of family members is enormous. Because culture backs his authority, he literally dominates the personalities of the members of his family and wields virtually unlimited control over family resources. He is expected to be the first person to be consulted or informed of any trouble or major change in the child's life. He can, and often does, call on his children for assistance at any time and can even intervene, without being considered as intruding, in the affairs of a married child, particularly his son. In theory, the father's authority lasts as long as he is alive, but it is not uncommon for the injunctions of a father to continue to haunt and influence his children long after his death.

The objective of the father's authority is not, however, to indulge in personal whims but to promote the best interests of his family and children, although ignorance sometimes thwarts some of his best intentioned behaviors.

The father plays a critical role in the process of launching the child into the social world of which his kin are of strategic importance. The importance of the kin group is reflected in the conceptualization of the child as a plant growing up in the middle of a field (his lineage group). As the principal explorer of the world outside the home, the father is the one who filters the beliefs, attitudes, and practices of the society in general and their kinsfolk in particular. He attempts to instruct the child on what to do to become a functional and acceptable member of the group.

In line with societal expectations, fathers raise their children to be respectful and obedient. In order to achieve this objective, they are rather stern and strict. Like Ghanaian parents, they justify the severity of their training with the belief that "If a person is trained strictly then that person becomes a good person; if you would not train them strictly he or she (sic) would be a bad girl or boy" (Ellis, 1978). This comment captures the essence of the indigenous thinking about human nature. It acknowledges an innate human tendency toward evil. The severity of traditional upbringing, then, is needed to curb the child's evil or destructive tendencies. It is believed in Northern Nigeria (Hake, 1972), as elsewhere in the region, that if one is too lenient in training a child, he or she would bring disgrace to self and family. In consequence, punishment is judiciously used as an aspect of caring and a necessary component of parenthood.

The main thrust of child training is on negative sanctions rather than on positive reinforcement of socially desirable behaviors. For example, Ga fathers in Ghana punish children to be "good," insult them when they are "bad," but neither praise nor reward them when they are good (Ellis, 1968). Other methods that parents adopt to teach morality and acceptable behavior to their children are Biblical and Koranic injunctions and cultural taboos.

Mothers tend to handle children's disciplinary problems more often than fathers because mothers are traditionally more accessible to children than fathers. In addition, in many societies of the region, taboos prevent fathers from frequent contacts with infants and very young children. Men hardly ever come in close contact with infants and very young children except in occasional ritual events or in unusual circumstances, such as when the mother has to perform a pressing domestic chore with only the father around to help. Rare is a West African father who shows tenderness and nurturance toward children. Such a father is regarded as effeminate or otherwise behaving inappropriately. The typical role of the West African father does not emphasize involvement in the routine care of children, rather it stresses his paternalistic, material, spiritual, emotional, and social support of the family. Most fathers do not come into intimate relationship with their children until they begin to toddle or talk, during which time they can sit around the fireplace in the evening and tell their children folktales.

If a crisis erupts or the mother's disciplinary efforts fail, the father is usually called in to handle the situation—a practice which gives the father the image of a stern parent and the mother, the "kind one." Compassionate mothers tend to shield erring children from stern fathers.

The above sketch represents a perspective on fathering in the largely traditional society of the past, in which the father participated in childrearing—at least in some of its social aspects, such as telling folktales to children and acting as a male model for children. Because men and women participated in subsistence activities together and family members kept close to home, children were able to learn from their father's interactions with his wife (their mother) that men exist as well as women and how to become a husband/father or wife/mother.

But the sociocultural flux initiated by the influence of Western values on African philosophies and modes of life has wrought significant shifts in the role of the father. These changes have imposed demanding social and economic priorities on contemporary fathers, especially the urban fathers, who now feel so wrapped up in business that they enjoy pursuing success. They do not spend time with their children—not because they do not love them but because they are uncertain how to father. These priorities are now preventing most fathers from doing the things they had been expected to do as guides, companions, and models for their children. Bronfenbrenner (1974) has called this reversal of paternal priorities "a betrayal of our children."

The main repercussions of this betrayal are twofold. First, many West African children are seemingly growing up with only remote ideas of what a father really is. Second, there is an increasing incidence of psychoemotional disturbances in children attributed to faulty or inadequate fathering. These are beginning to become manifested clinically.

WEST AFRICAN FATHERS: SOME CLINICAL EVIDENCE

Preliminary clinical evidence from Nigeria and Cameroon concerning paternal influence on children indicates that fathering is an aspect of parenting that should no longer be neglected nor undermined.

Our clinical experience in the Psychology Clinic at the University of Ibadan, Nigeria (Nsamenang; 1983; Nsamenang and Laosebikan, 1981) involved psychotherapy with emotionally disturbed and/or underachieving children. It was soon discovered that children's psychological disorders were due to pathogenic patterns of fathering. The main purpose of therapy was to interest and co-opt the fathers of these disturbed children in their treatment regimen and to foster cordial and humane father-child interactions.

A majority of the children whose fathers participated in their therapy showed more remarkable improvement than the children of nonparticipating fathers. Some of the participating fathers even wished they could relate more intimately to their children.

The discovery that relations between fathers and their children were far from satisfactory and that they could be improved by clinical intervention gave rise to an experimental study of the quality of the fathering experienced by a group of adolescents in Bamenda, Cameroon (Nsamenang, 1983). This study utilized a stratified random sample of 24 male and 24 female adolescents (and their literate fathers) from four randomly selected secondary schools in Bamenda town. Subjects were divided into an experimental group and a control group, matched for number of father's children and level of father's education. The experimental group of fathers then undertook the experimental treatment—Father Involvement Training (FIT). This three-hour weekly workshop (held for five consecutive weeks) was designed to sensitize fathers to their role, to teach techniques for the control and discipline of children, and to foster parent-child relations. The overall results indicated that participating in the FIT program significantly improved the quality of fathering and generated concomitant improvement in adolescent emotional adjustment.

Further evidence of psychological breakdown in children resulting from a seeming absence of fathering or from pathogenic fathering comes from two cases this writer handled in the General Hospital in Bamenda, Cameroon, between April and August, 1984.

The first case involved a 17-year-old named Alen, who was in the fourth year of secondary school. His predicament started soon after birth when a bitter quarrel over his paternity led to the separation of his parents. Alen was to realize as he grew older that he did not really resemble his elder siblings physically, a realization which seemed to prove the veracity of the paternity dispute. When he insisted on knowing his biological father, his uncompromising mother instead tried to coax him into adopting his maternal grandfather's name. Of course, this was incongruous to his self-concept and therefore unacceptable.

Because his mother remained adamant and did not disclose his paternity, he progressively became restless and insomniac and suffered persistent bouts of headache, heat and fullness in the head, and intermittent mental blackouts— symptoms which grossly marred his educational progress. He ultimately broke down and had to discontinue schooling at the time he was required to establish a permanent record of his name in preparation for the certificate examination.

The second case involves a 19-year-old boy, Yuri, who spent his infancy and early childhood with only his mother because his father had abandoned his mother when she was pregnant with him. His father later married two other wives and took Yuri in his middle childhood to stay with him and his two wives and their children. Yuri was the odd one in the house, performing odd tasks and enjoying fewer privileges than the other children. His mother, still an abandoned mother of very meager means, has had eight other children (not with his father). Yuri, to the displeasure of his father, occasionally visited them.

Yuri had expected that his position as the first child in the family and his brilliant academic record would, at least, earn him some respect in the family. Instead he was openly discriminated against. He complained about the naked discrimination and his father's neglect of his mother. He became quite prayerful and in the terminal years of secondary education began to experience trancelike states. In the first semester of high school, he became greatly agitated and very talkative and claimed to be an outstanding mathematician.

Throughout the years, Yuri had developed very hostile but repressed emotions against his father but, like every African child, could not muster the courage to confront his father to vent his bitterness. His father's failure to supply what he described as his "basic high school requirements," unlike most fathers of his socioeconomic status, was a trauma far beyond his threshold level to tolerate. Yuri went into an emotional crisis under the weight of this trauma.

EMERGING TRENDS IN FAMILY LIFE AND PARENTING

Because our conception of the family is shaped as part of our primary socialization and because it is so fundamental to the continuance of society, family institutions are highly resistant to change. Nevertheless, they do undergo gradual change as a result of changes in the social, cultural, economic, and political spheres of society.

In certain respects, the present family system in the rural areas is the same as in the past, whereas it has changed considerably in the urban areas. Both the continuities and changes are related to the ways in which West Africans are coping with family life and social demands, often at variance with deep-rooted customs, in a society in transition.

Prior to the colonial rule there was no system of political organization or government above the village or kingdom, but today the national government supersedes all others.

Although the large extended family still thrives, distant kin are less often part of the household today than they were previously. But contact is still maintained with a fairly wide circle of kin, and complete isolation of nuclear families with no contact whatsoever is very rare indeed. Even "the urbanite still has strong loyalties to his extended family and keeps contact with its members" (Tetteh, 1967).

Matrilineal societies, such as the Kom of Cameroon and the Akan of Ghana, are under considerable pressure to reverse their rules of inheritance. The custom that children inherit from their mother's brother rather than from their father makes relatively little difference when there is not much to inherit, but it can be much more problematic and hurtful if the children's father spent his lifetime building up a fortune, whereas their uncle was barely able to support himself. Furthermore, as the children argue: "Everyone has a father but not everyone has a mother's brother." They see no reason to work hard on their father's farm or business if the result will go to others.

In the marriage scene, the number of monogamous households, the number of people remaining single throughout their lives, and the divorce rate are increasing. People now have greater freedom to choose their marriage partners and make other personal decisions than in the past.

Within the family, the father has began to become simply one of the family instead of its undoubted head and central authority. Father's authority is still considerable but his despotic powers are gradually eroding, and other members of the family are gaining in strength and independence at his expense. This is perhaps so because the prestige of family members today depends more on their individual achievements than on reflected glory from the father. In addition, today's children are more knowledgeable in matters of modern living than their parents. And the contemporary father may find it unreasonable to instruct his family on how to behave in the social world because today each family member tends to sort out what is acceptable behavior in his or her own social circle.

In the struggle between the generations and sexes, the tides disfavor the father. As far as the law and politics were concerned, all the fathers together, responsible for their family units, were the state. If the father's rights were upheld, then justice was done or was seen to have been done. But today, the law is concerned with the rights of individuals—men, women, and children—not the rights of fathers alone. Should the family split up, the courts will try to decide the custody of the children in accordance with the children's interests and welfare, not merely in favor of the father. In the past, a father could forbid his erring wife "ever to see his children again" (Green, 1976).

The father's salary is no longer the sole family income. As increasing numbers of women are assuming economic responsibilities outside the homes, some women even earn higher incomes than their husbands. Women farmers also provide a major source of family income, combining food production with trading in farm products and handicrafts. Boserup's (1970) small sample from Bamenda, Cameroon, indicates that indigenous women contribute some 44% of the family's gross income. The ever-increasing desire for consumer goods and the spiralling inflation have made two incomes a necessity for most families.

Female participation in the labor force varies considerably between the nations and ethnic groups of the region. Women in the southern areas of Ghana, Nigeria, and Cameroon, for instance, have a rate of economic activity which is very high by world standards (Peil, 1974) and have considerably greater authority and public status than women of the hinterland who have been less active economically and politically. Women appear to have higher prestige and power in societies where they participate more fully in economic and political activities.

The role of the man as protector has also declined because if a woman is threatened or attacked today she may call in the police rather than depend on her husband who is more likely today than previously to be the aggressor.

As women are combining economic and career responsibilities with their roles as wife and mother, an increasing number of men (especially young husbands) can be observed to be helping out in such matters as baby's baths and feedings, laundry, shopping, accompanying children to hospital or clinic, and cooking. But basic questions remain about father's role: Is such helping father's essential role or is there something different a father can do that a mother cannot? What exactly can a father do to give his children the benefit of a good father? What are the conditions under which fathers experience satisfaction by increasing their share of parenting? What are the impediments? What are the implications and repercussions on the parents, children, family, and society? How well are women combining their roles as wife and mother with their economic and career responsibilities? These are salient questions which can serve as springboards for useful family-life and parenting research.

Our contemporary families seem to be in trouble not so much because of the problems of poverty, ignorance, and disease but because the inherited conception of the family is rather tenacious and inadequate for coping with the requirements for living in a society in a critical stage of transition. From the perspective of parents, the central issue is how to parent in a changing society with conflicting demands. Traditional and modern directives regarding parenting are not only scarce but often conflicting—and parents are literally waging an endless struggle to reconcile these contradictions. The outcome is parental confusion and inadequately parented children.

What parents require is a recognition of the complexity of contemporary issues, a readiness to accept that there are likely to be different ways of dealing with them, and a cultivation of the capacity to resolve problems of parenting in today's West Africa.

The challenge facing parents and society, in the face of an ever-increasing number of women spending a sizeable portion of their time and energy away from home and children, is to forge new conceptions of the family and of family life. This may be facilitated, not impaired, by a revision of the sexual division of parental responsibilities to reflect the realities of the contemporary West African situation.

REFERENCES

Ayisi, E. O. (1979). *An introduction to the study of African cultures* 2nd Ed. Ibadan: Heinemann.
Bekombo, M. (1981). The child in Africa: Socialization, education and work. In G. Rodgers & G. Standing (Eds.), *Child Work, Poverty and Underdevelopment.* Geneva: ILO.
Boserup, E. (1970). *Women's role in economic development.* London: George Allen & Unwin.
Bronfenbrenner, U. (1974). Children, families and social policy: *An American perspective. In the family in society: dimensions of parenthood.* London: DHSS, HMSC.
Busia, K. A. (1967). *Africa in search of democracy.* London: Routledge and Kegan Paul.
Che, M.   Seminar on languages: Proposes 'Fulfulde, Beti, Duala' for Cameroon. *Cameroon Tribune,* N°587, Wednesday, Sept. 18, 1985, p.4.
Chilver, E. M. (1962). Nineteenth century trade in the Bamenda grassfields. *Afrika Und Ubersee,* Vol. XLV/4, 223–250.
Clark, C. M. (1980). Land and food, women and power, in Nineteenth Century Kikuyu. *Africa,* 50(4), 335–450.
Ellis, J. (1968). Child-training in Ghana, with particular reference to the Ga tribe, M. A. thesis, University of Ghana.
Ellis, J. (1978). The child in West African society. In J. Ellis, *West African Families in Britain.* London: Routledge and Kegan Paul.
Esen, A. (1972). A view of guidance from Africa. *Personnel and Guidance Journal,* 50(10), 792–798.
Fadipe, N. A. (1970). *Sociology of the Yoruba.* Ibadan: Ibadan University Press.
Fortes, M. (1950). Kinship and marriage among the Ashanti. In A. R. Radcliffe-Brown & D. Forde (Eds.), *African Systems of Kinship and Marriage.* London: Oxford University Press.
Green, M. (1974). Land tenure in an Ibo village. In E. I. Nwogugu, *Family Law in Nigeria.* Ibadan: Heinemann.
Green, M. (1976). *Goodbye father.* London: Routledge and Kegan Paul.
Guyer, J. I. (1980). Female farming and the evaluation of food production patterns amongst the Beti of south-central Cameroon. *Africa,* 50(4), 335–450.
Hake, J. M. (1972). *Child rearing practices in northern Nigeria.* Ibadan: Ibadan University Press.
Harrell-Bond, B. E. (1975). *Modern marriage in Sierra Leone.* The Hague: Mouton.
Henn, J. K. (1978). *Peasants, Workers, and Capital: The political economy of rural incomes in Cameroon.* Ph. D. Dissertation, Harvard University.
Hill, P. (1978). Food farming and migration from Fante villages, *Africa,* 43(3), 220–230.
Jahn, J. (1961). *Muntu.* London: Faber & Faber.
July, R. W. (1974). *A history of the African people.* 2nd Ed. New York: Charles Scribner's Sons.
Kaye, B. (1962). *Bringing up children in Ghana.* London: Allen & Unwin.
Keyatta, J. (1938). *Facing Mount Kenya.* London: Heinemann.
Laosebikan, S., & Filani, T. (April, 1981). Another view of the African custom of rearing children outside the homes of their biological parents. Revised version of the paper, *Clinical experience with fostered children at Ibadan,* presented at the Nigerian Psychological Society Conference, Jos, Nigeria.
LeVine, R. A., Klein, N. H., & Owen, C. R. (1967). Father-child relationships and changing lifestyles in Ibadan, Nigeria. In H. Miner (Ed.), *The City in Modern Africa.* London: Pall Mall Press.
Lombard, C. (1978). *Les jouets des enfants boule.* Paris: Quatre-Vents.
Mabogunje, T. (1975). The legal status of women in Africa. Commonwealth Students' Children Society, Report of Ibadan Seminar on the African child in Great Britain.
Mair, L. (1974). *African societies.* Cambridge: Cambridge University Press.
Maquet, J. (1978). *Africanity: The cultural unity.* New York: Oxford University Press.
Nsamenang, A. B., & Laosebikan, S. (April, 1981). Father-Child relationships and the development of psychopathology: Two clinical examples. A paper presented at the Nigerian Psychological Society Conference, Jos, Nigeria.

Nsamenang, A. B. (1983). *Experimental improvement of the quality of fathering among a group of Cameroonians*. Ph.D. Thesis, University of Ibadan, Nigeria.

Obiechina, E. N. (1975). *Culture, tradition and society in the West African novel*. Cambridge: Cambridge University Press.

Okedara, J. T. (1980). Qualitative impact of literary education: a case study. Studies in Literacy Education, N°7, Department of Adult Education, University of Ibadan, Nigeria.

Oyebola, A. (1976). *Black man's dilemma*. Ibadan: Board Publications.

Peil, M. (1977). *Consensus and conflict in African societies*. London: Longman.

Ritzenthaler, R. (1962). Cameroons village: An ethnography of the Bafut. Publications in Anthropology, N°8. Milwaukee Public Museum (Wisconsin).

Schildkrout, E. (1973). The fostering of children in urban Ghana: problems of ethnographic analyses in a multi-cultural context, *Urban Anthropology*, 2, 48–73.

Tetteh, P. A. (1967). Marriage, Family and Household. In W. Birmingham *et al* (Eds.), *A Study of Contemporary Ghana*, Vol. 2. London: Allen & Unwin.

Stapleton, P. (1978). The West African background. In J. Ellis (Ed.), *West African families in Britain*. London: Routledge and Kegan Paul.

Uchendu, U. C. (1965). *The Ibo of Southeast Nigeria*. New York: Holt, Rinehart & Winston.

Udo, R. K. (1978). *A comprehensive geography of West Africa*. Ibadan: Heinemann.

Uka, N. (1966). *Growing up in Nigerian culture*. Ibadan: Ibadan University Press.

Ware, H. (1975). The changing African family in West Africa, Commonwealth Students' Children Society, Report of Ibadan Seminar on the A African Child in Great Britain.

WHO, (1976). The African region of WHO. *WHO Chronicle*, Vol.30(1), 2–48.

Wober, M. (1975). *Psychology in Africa*. London: International African Institute.

12

Intimate Fathers: Patterns of Paternal Holding Among Aka Pygmies

Barry S. Hewlett
Department of Sociology and Anthropology
Southern Oregon State College

Despite the steady accumulation of systematic studies of infant and child development in non-Western populations (Draper, 1976; Konner, 1977; Leiderman, Tulkin, & Rosenfeld, 1977; Monroe & Monroe, 1971; Whiting & Whiting, 1975) there are few detailed ethnographic data on the father-infant relationship in these populations. Given the paucity of systematic research in non-Western societies on father-infant interactions and on the father's roles in all stages of the child's development, it is ironic that this variable (i.e., the degree of father vs. mother involvement with children) should be so consistently invoked as an explanatory factor in the literature. It is hypothesized to be related, for example, to universal sexual asymmetry (Rosaldo & Lamphere, 1974); variations in sexual dimorphism (Wilson, 1975); the origins of the human family (Lancaster, 1975); contemporary patterns of gender-activity differentiation; (Brown, 1970; Burton, Brudner, & White 1977); the association of males with culture and females with nature (Ortner, 1974); smooth functioning of the family (Zelditch, 1955); and proper moral development (Hoffman, 1981).

This chapter seeks to partially remedy this shortcoming by examining the father-infant relationship among an extant population of hunter-gatherers of the Central African Republic, the Aka pygmies. One feature of the father-infant relationship will be emphasized—holding (see Fig. 12.1). Holding is selected as a focal topic because it is a direct form of paternal investment, an observable and, consequently, a measurable behavior essential to the survival of the Aka infant. Studies of American fathers indicate that the father's interaction while holding his infant is quite distinctive from the mother's holding of the infant.

Extensive observational research on the American father-infant relationship has consistently demonstrated that fathers are more likely than mothers to engage

FIG. 12.1 Aka father with his infant in the village fields searching for palm wine.

in vigorous play with the infant (Arco, 1983; Belsky, 1979; Clarke-Stewart, 1978; Crawley & Sherrod, 1984; Field, 1978; Lamb, 1976, 1977a, 1985; Parke & O'Leary, 1976; Yogman, 1982; but see Pederson, Anderson, & Cain, 1980, for an exception). American fathers' vigorous play with the infant is evident at three days after birth and continues throughout infancy. The American data have been so consistent that some researchers have indicated a biological origin (Clarke-Stewart, 1980). The function of father's physically stimulating play with the infant is suggested to be the critical means by which father-infant attachment is established and the initial means by which the infant learns social competence (Lamb, 1981). Mother-infant attachment develops as a consequence of the frequency and intensity of the relationship, while the infant's attachment to the father occurs as a result of the highly stimulating interaction. Because mothers and fathers represent different styles of interaction, infants are likely to develop differential expectations of them, which in turn increases the infant's awareness of different social styles. Later in childhood, it is suggested, it is primarily the father who introduces the child into the public sphere. These functional differences in parenting style are suggested as support of the expressive/instrumental role theory first introduced by Durkheim (1933) and elaborated by Parsons and Bales (1955). According to this conceptualization, the male role is primarily "instrumental": oriented to the external world and responsible for helping the child establish ties with this world (i.e., social competence). In contrast, the female role is "expressive": responsible for the emotional and affective climate of the home, the nurturance of the young, and domestic tasks.

The few observational studies conducted in industrialized nations outside of the United States have questioned the universality of the American data. Swedish fathers play slightly more with their infants than do mothers, yet the distinctive physical style of American fathers does not exist (Lamb, Frodi, Frodi, & Hwang 1982). Swedish infants demonstrated significantly more attachment behaviors toward mothers than toward fathers (Lamb, Frodi, Hwang, & Frodi, 1983), whereas American infants exhibited no such preference (Lamb, 1976, 1977b). This fits the theoretical model mentioned above—if Swedish fathers do not provide distinctive playfulness they will not become as affectively salient as the primary caretaking mothers. German fathers observed with their newborns in the mothers' hospital rooms also did not exhibit this stimulating playfulness with their newborns (Parke, Grossmann, & Tinsley, 1981). Although the American studies of fathers are remarkably consistent, the few European studies suggest that more extensive crosscultural research is essential to understanding the father's role in infant development. One consistency exists in the American and European studies: mothers are more likely to be the caregivers.

This study extends our understanding of parenting styles by examining parent-infant interactions among a human population that subsists primarily by hunting and gathering. The subsistence pattern is of significance because it characterized 99% of human history; until approximately 12,000 years ago, hunting and gathering was the universal subsistence mode. The Aka pygmies are one of the last remaining hunting and gathering populations whose daily lives are available to direct observation. Since the Aka lifestyle is more consistent with our past, possibly we may better understand some of the selective conditions under which the father-infant relationship emerged.

Why focus on holding? As mentioned above, differences in mothers' and fathers' parenting style might be observed while parents hold their infant. But recent ethological studies have also indicated that holding is a significant factor for infant survival in populations, such as the Aka pygmies, where infant mortality rates are high (Babchuk, Hames, & Thompson, in press; LeVine, 1977; Konner, 1977; Neuwelt-Truntzer, 1981). Low infant mortality is a relatively recent phenomenon in industrialized populations. While infant mortality in highly industrialized nations ranges from 3 to 6% (Babchuk, Hames, & Thompson, in press), Pygmy infant mortality rates range from 15 to 33% (Neuwelt-Truntzer, 1981; Weiss, 1973). Holding purportedly provides psychological comfort (Altman, 1980) as well as protection from environmental factors such as predators, temperature changes, intraspecific aggression, and accidents (Bowlby, 1969; Freedman 1974). It may also be a mechanism permitting the transmission of information from mothers to infants (Konner, 1977). A limitation of these studies is that generally only mother-infant contact is considered. We know that compared to mothers, fathers in most nonindustrialized populations only infrequently hold infants, assist in childcare, or even stay around infants (Babchuk, Hames, & Thompson, in press; Whiting & Whiting 1975; and see Tables 12.7 and 12.8). Yet little is known about the social and environmental conditions under which fathers hold or carry the infant, or the differences and similarities between mothers' and fathers' caretaking style.

Although at times specific hypotheses such as those mentioned above will be examined, the primary intention is to provide a quantitative description of the context, frequency, and styles of Aka father-infant holding.

METHODS

The Study Population

The Aka pygmies are foragers of the tropical forest regions of the southern Central African Republic and northern Congo-Brazzaville. The Aka in this study are associated with the Bokoka section of Bagandou village (Central African Republic). There are approximately 300 foraging Aka associated with Bokoka, and 769 farmers, primarily Ngandu peoples, who live in the village.

Over the course of a year, the Aka spend about 56% of their time in hunting, 27% of their time in gathering, and 17% of their time in village work for the Ngandu (Bahuchet, in press). The relative importance of hunting and gathering activities fluctuates from season to season. It is estimated, for example, that the Aka spend up to 90% of their time in net hunting in the drier season (January to May), while during part of the rainy season (August to September) 60% of their time is spent collecting foods, especially caterpillars (Bahuchet, in press). Much of the vegetable food in the Aka diet is obtained through trading meat to farmers for manioc and other cultigens. Although the Aka net-hunt in the forest the majority of the year and spend little or no time in the cultivation of plant foods, they are transitional foragers in the sense that a large proportion of their diet comes from these domesticated village products. Seldom does a day go by without some of this food being eaten. While residing part of the year near the Ngandu village, Aka provide labor to their village *nkomu* (patron) for which they receive access to the farmers' fields. The Aka come to the village three or four months a year to assist in the clearing of the fields.

As with the Mbuti pygmies of Zaire (Hart, 1978; Turnbull, 1965), most camp members—male and female, young and old—participate in the net hunt. From the time Aka leave the village and return to the forest (February-March) until caterpillar season (July-August), they often net hunt 6 days a week, 4 to 9 hours per day. Net hunts decrease in frequency during the caterpillar season and the major rainy season (August-October); individual and small-group foraging techniques (e.g., spears, crossbows, traps) are utilized more frequently during these seasons. Most Aka associated with Bokoka are in the village from late November until mid-February.

The Aka are patrilineal, having shallow patriclans, and are generally patrilocal except for a few years after marriage when the male provides bride service in the camp of his wife's family. Aka kinship terms are basically generational; for instance, *tao* refers not only to the natural father but to all of the fathers' brothers, all grandparents are called *koko*, all offspring called *mona* and all brothers and sisters called *kadi*. As has been described for other hunting-gathering populations, the marriage and kinship rules are flexible and adaptive to situational constraints (Lee & DeVore, 1968; Turnbull, 1965, Woodburn, 1968).

There are four important demographic units: the nuclear family, the camp, the patriclan, and the band. The camp (*lango*) consists of 1 to 15 nuclear families, but averages around 25 to 35 individuals. The core of the camp usually consists of adult males belonging to the same patriclan (*dibanda*)—that is, individuals tracing their ancestry patrilineally to a mythical plant or animal. Their clan name is the same as their Ngandu trading partner. Aka members of the Bodikala clan, for instance, usually trade with Ngandu farmers of the Bodikala clan. Consequently, Aka and Ngandu children grow up with their future trading partners. The final demographic unit, the band, is a more elusive entity as the Aka do not have a native term for it. Essentially, it is a group of 60 to 100 individuals who hunt and gather in the same vicinity. Its core usually consists of 2 to 3 clans. During the various seasons, the band goes through periods of concentration and dispersal within the hunting-collecting territory.

There are few Aka status positions. There is no headman in the sense of a person commanding ultimate authority in certain situations, yet there is the *kombeti*, who is generally more influential in subsistence and camp movement discussions. He is often the liaison person with the Ngandu farmers. The farmers show deference to the Aka *kombeti* (e.g., saying hello to him first, giving him more cigarettes), yet the Aka themelves do not show any such behavior towards him (intergenerational inequality is minimal). The *nganga* is the traditional healer and provides a wide range of services to the community—such as divination on hunts, curing of witchcraft, and herbal healing. The *ntuma* is the great elephant hunter who has often killed several elephants on his own. He leads important hunting and seasonal rituals and organizes the training of young boys in the men's secret society. These status positions are usually held by males.

Sharing, cooperation, and autonomy are but a few of the Aka core values. The community cooperates daily on the net hunt, all food hunted is shared with members of the camp, and decision making is the reserved prerogative of the individual; if one is not content with living conditions, for instance, one moves to another camp. As a result, camp composition changes daily.

The Sample

The sample consisted of 15 Aka families with infants between 1 and 18 months of age. Eight of the infants were female and 7 were male, 6 between 1 and 4 months of age (2 males, 4 females), 5 between 8 and 12 months of age (3 males, 2 females) and 4 between 13 and 18 months of age (2 females, 2 males). Six families resided near the Ngandu village while observations were undertaken (2 infants from each age category, one of each sex) while 9 families lived in the forest (4 infants in the 1-4 month age category (3 female, 1 male)), 3 infants in the 8-12 month category (2 male, 1 female), and 2 infants in the last age category (one of each sex). Seven of the infants were firstborns to the couple (some from each age group), while 8 of the families had other children (usually one other child). In 3 of the 15 families, the father was polygynous (one father in each age group).

The sample size was quite modest, especially by comparison to standards of Western psychological family observational studies. Since the mobile Aka live in small (25-35 individuals), sparsely distributed camps it was necessary to travel 75 km on foot to establish this admittedly scant sample.

Sampling Techniques

Three types of focal sampling (Altman, 1974) were utilized: father focal all day (6 A.M. to 6 P.M.), infant focal all day, and infant focal for 2 morning hours. Father focal observations were conducted with each of the 15 fathers on randomly selected days. Every 15 minutes the father's activity, the people he was interacting with, the people touching him, the people within 1 m, nearest neighbor to him, his availability to his infant, and the location and activity of the mother were noted. Modifications of Johnson's (1975) time-allocation activity codes were utilized to code mothers' and fathers' activities. Any direct interaction (e.g., holding) with his infant was noted minute by minute—what the father did with the infant (caretaking, playing, soothing, etc.), what other activities he engaged in while holding, and the mother's activity. Condition of receiving the infant and conditions for terminating the hold were also noted. A condition for beginning a father focal observation was that the mother be residing in the camp; she need not be present but she had to be living in the same camp as the father. Occasionally it was difficult or intrusive to keep the father within view (especially on a net hunt); consequently, observations were temporarily terminated during this time. The mean length of the 15 father observations was 689.5 minutes (about 11.5 hours).

Father focal observations have not been conducted in previous cross-cultural child development studies for the simple reason that fathers usually have infrequent contact with children; father focal observations would take considerable time and energy to gain relatively little data on father-infant relations. Consequently, infant and mother focal observational techniques have dominated previous studies. Father observations were attempted in this study because fathers were known to do considerable caretaking. A secondary purpose of this study was to determine what fathers do while they are not investing time with their infants.

All-day infant focal observations were conducted with 6 infants (2 from each age group)'residing in forest camps. This limitation was due to the fact that in the forest the primary subsistence activity was the net hunt in which almost everyone participated. Following the infant while being held by the mother was not a problem because other adult males were nearby. In the village, on the other hand, female activity outside of the camp was often solitary or with a few other females, so a male observer could be intrusive (if not threatening) to both males and females. For this reason, no all-day observations were attempted in that setting. To help compensate for the fewer infant focal hours, 2 hours of infant focal observation were conducted on each of the 15 infants. During infant focal observations, activity of infant, infant proximity to others, and availability of mother and father were coded every 15 minutes. Types of behaviors coded (regardless of time) included: number and length of nursing bouts, types of play with others, types of play alone, attachment behaviors (e.g., reaching for, crying for, crawling to, touching), quality of caretaking (intensive or perfunctory), caretaker exchanges, and conditions under which exchanges occurred. A condition for beginning an infant focal observation was that the mother and father be residing in the camp (but not necessarily present) at the time of the observation. The average length of the all-day infant focal observations was 648.5 minutes (about 10.5 hours), while the average length of the morning two-hour infant focal observations was 115.9 minutes (about 1.9 hours).

All-day father and infant observations in the forest were undertaken only on days in which a net hunt was performed. Net hunts were almost daily during much of the study period. There were days when it rained and people rested or searched for fruits or honey. Due to the limited number of total observations possible during the short study period, it was decided to limit forest observations to days when a net hunt occured.

In total, this study is based on 264 hours of focal observation: 172 hours focusing on fathers and 92 hours focusing on the infant. Spot observations were also conducted by a trained research assistant, but those results will not be reported here. Structured questionnaires were also administered to 20 adults and 16 adolescents to solicit their views, feelings and expectations of their mothers, fathers and significant others in their childhood.

RESULTS

Frequency and Context of Father Holding and Availability

Over the 264 hours of observation, Aka fathers held their infants 8.7% of the time, or about 1 hour of father holding during a 12 hour (6 A.M. to 6 P.M.) observation period. Table 12.1 demonstrates that when one controls for age and

TABLE 12.1
Mean Percentage of Time Fathers Held Their Infants
during Daylight Hours in Forest and Village Settings
(from All-Day Observations)

Age of infants	Forest			Village		
	n^a	M	SD	n	M	SD
1-4 months	4	8.8	5.0	2	10.2	6.4
8-12 months	3	7.7	7.0	2	10.8	7.5
13-18 months	2	4.8	1.8	2	4.1	3.0
overall	9	7.6	5.0	6	8.4	5.7

^{a}n = number of father-infant dyads

general setting (forest versus village), one finds a gradual decrease in father holding with age, which one would expect since the infant is held less as he/she grows older. Table 12.1 also demonstrates that there were no significant differences in how often fathers held infants in the village and forest contexts.

Significant differences were found when specific settings within each of the two general contexts were examined. Fig. 12.2 indicates that fathers were much more likely to be holding their infant while in the camp than on the net hunt or out in the village fields. Table 12.2 indicates that there was no overall difference between father holding in the village and forest, yet Fig. 12.2 suggests that fathers in the two forest contexts held their infant more than fathers in the two comparable village contexts. The inconsistency is a consequence of forest fathers spending a smaller percentage of their day in camp when father holding is greatest. Fathers in the forest spent 29% of their day (6 A.M. to 6 P.M.) in the

TABLE 12.2
Mean Percentage of Time Mother, Father, and Others Held Focal
Infant During Daylight Hours in Two Forest Contexts: in Camp
and on the Net Hunt

Age of infant (months)	Mother	Father	Others	Total
	Forest camp			
1-4	51.0	22.0	27.0	100.0
8-12	45.3	11.2	2.3	58.8
13-18	31.8	14.3	9.4	55.5
	Net hunt			
1-4	87.3	6.5	6.2	100.0
8-12	87.8	5.9	0.0	93.7
13-18	88.9	2.4	1.1	92.4

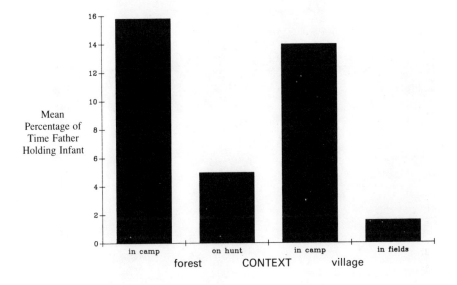

FIG. 12.2.   Mean percentage of time father held infant in four contexts.

camp and 71% of their time on the hunt, while fathers in the village spent on average 52% of their time in the camp and 48% of their time outside of the camp. Figure 12.2 does not take into account the total time fathers spent in each of the contexts.

Table 12.2 breaks down the two forest settings—in camp and on the net hunt—by age and compares father holding to mother holding and holding by others. In considering age and setting, fathers spent the most time holding 1-to-4-month-old infants in the forest camp. On the net hunt, mothers were the main caretakers; fathers and others infrequently held the infant in this setting. The 1- to 4-month-olds were held essentially all the time in both settings, while older infants were held about half the time in the camp and more than 90% of the time on the net hunt. This lends support to the notion that holding is performed to protect the infant from predators, snakes, and accidents. These potential dangers are more likely to be encountered or happen in remote forest locations on the hunt rather than in the camp clearing, and as a result infant holding is almost constant during this time.

Occasionally, it was difficult to tell if the parent was more interested in the protection of the infant or capturing game. Several instances were recorded where the mother holding the infant placed the infant alone on the ground and ran to capture the animal. The infant was left alone about 10 m from the parent, often crying, until the parent killed the animal. In instances where large (25-75 kg), potentially dangerous game were captured, it made sense to leave the infant at some distance, but usually the game weighed less than 6 kg. Instead of bringing

FIG. 12.3.   Most paternal holding occurs in camp. This father watches his two children in camp while his spouse leaves camp to get water.

the infant close to the net where the capture took place and where it would be possible to see the infant, the mothers said they preferred to be unencumbered so they could run faster to make sure the game did not get away.

Table 12.2 also demonstrates the relative consistency in father holding. Regardless of the infant's age, he held the infant about 20% of the overall time the infant was held in the camp and about 6% of the total time the infant was held on the net hunt (e.g., the 8 to 12 month infants were held 58.8% of the time while in the forest camp, and the fathers held the infants about one-fifth of this time (11.2% of the time)).

Holding is a direct form of father investment while availability or proximity maintenance is a type of indirect investment. Is there a relationship between the two? If fathers are near their infants more frequently do they hold their infants more often? Tables 12.3 through 12.5 summarize the father availability data. In comparing the general village versus forest contexts (Table 12.3), fathers residing in the forest were much more available to their infants than were village fathers: While residing in the forest, fathers were within earshot 85% of the day, while a movement to the village meant he would not be near his infant 54% of the day. In comparing the availability and holding data, one finds that being near his infant more often does not mean that he will hold him/her more often. Fathers in the forest were available more often than fathers in the village, yet held their

TABLE 12.3
Comparison of Father's Availability in Forest and Village Settings

Setting	Within visual range					Within hearing range (but not within visual range)					Out of area				
	n^a	M^b	SD	SE	t	n	M	SD	SE	t	n	M	SD	SE	t
Forest	15	63.6	15.2	4.1	3.3**	15	21.9	7.2	1.9	8.4**	15	14.5	10.4	2.8	6.9**
Village	6	42.9	10.3	4.7		6	3.4	2.8	1.3		6	53.7	11.0	5.0	

[a] n = number of all-day observations.
[b] Mean scores are the average percentages of time fathers are available during daylight hours (6 A.M. to 6 P.M.)
**$p<.005$ (19 df)

TABLE 12.4
Fathers' Availability to Their Infants in Four Settings

Setting	Within visual range					Within hearing range					Out of area				
	n^a	M^b	SD	SE	t	n	M	SD	SE	t	n	M	SD	SE	t
Forest Camp	15	88.5	16.5	4.4		15	6.0	11.4	3.0		15	5.5	10.5	2.8	
					5.5*					6.2*					2.7*
Forest Hunt	15	53.3	17.3	4.6		15	28.1	7.1	1.9		15	17.6	12.7	3.4	
Village Camp	6	78.3	11.8	5.3		6	4.7	5.4	2.4		6	17.0	12.9	5.8	
					9.4*					0.9					9.6*
Village Fields	6	9.3	11.2	5.0		6	2.1	3.3	1.5		6	88.6	10.6	4.7	

[a] n = number of all-day observations

[b] Mean scores are the average percentages of time fathers are available during daylight hours.

*$p < .005$ (28 df, 10 df)

TABLE 12.5
Comparison of Father and Mother Availability in Forest Setting

Parent	Within visual range				Within hearing range (but not within visual range)					Out of area			
	n^a	M^b	SD	SE	t	n	M	SD	SE	t	n	M	SD	SE	t
Mother	6	92.7	8.0	3.6	5.3**	6	2.0	3.9	0.9	4.5**	6	5.2	7.4	3.3	2.2*
Father	15	63.6	15.2	4.1		15	21.9	7.2	1.9		15	14.5	10.4	2.8	

*$p<.025$ (19 df)
**$p<.005$ (19 df)
[a]n = number of all-day observations
[b]Mean scores are the average percentages of time fathers or mothers are available during daylight hours (6 A.M. to 6 P.M.)

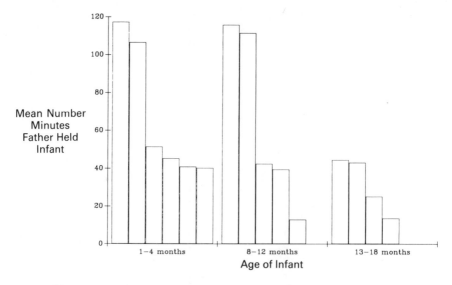

FIG. 12.4. Individual variability in Aka father holding. Each column represents the mean number of minutes one focal father spent holding his infant during daylight hours.

infants just as frequently as fathers in the village. Table 12.4 shows more specifically that fathers in the forest on the net hunt were near their infants (i.e., within view or hearing distance) 80% of the time on the hunt, yet they infrequently held the infant in this setting. By comparison, fathers living in the village and working outside of the camp, were near their infant only 12% of the time. The significant differences in father availability in the forest versus the village setting were a consequence of different subsistence activities undertaken while residing in the forest or village. Net hunting enabled fathers to be near their infants as the mother, who usually transported the infant, assisted with the family net. In the village, Aka obtained vegetable foods by providing labor to the farming Ngandu. Ngandu male and female subsistence activities seldom overlap and Aka males help Ngandu males and Aka females help Ngandu females. As a result of the divergent activities, fathers were less available to their infants. Also, while in the village, Aka males often left the camp at the first sign of dawn to search for palm wine that accumulated in special trees during the night. Small groups of men often did not return to camp until mid-morning, thus decreasing even more their availability to their infants.

Table 12.5 compares fathers availability in the forest context with that of mother. Although Aka fathers are very available to their infants, mothers are essentially always available.

Fig. 12.4 demonstrates the individual variation within the Aka community. One Aka father averaged 13 minutes holding his infant during the day, while another father with an infant of similar age averaged spending almost 2 hours

(116 minutes) holding his infant. While the number of hours of systematic observation per father were few, the individual patterns that did emerge were consistent with the more numerous daily casual observations. Some fathers regularly provided assistance in holding the infant, while others, although intimate and affectionate with their infants, provided markedly less direct care. What factors might account for such variation? Table 12.6 statistically examines some factors which have been identified in previous studies as contributing to intracultural variation in paternal childcare. Fathers favored holding firstborns, infants under 12 months, and infants in households where mother, father, and infant were coresidents. Younger fathers tended to hold infants more than older fathers. Only two factors were statistically significant—marriage type and the number of brothers of the father. The number of brothers is potentially a more pervasive factor than polygynous marriage because a man would usually have two brothers before the polygynous marriage would take place.

TABLE 12.6
Father Holding and Some Demographic
and Life-Cycle Variables

Variable	n^a	M^b	SD	SE	t
Marriage type					
Monogamy	12	68.4	36.0	10.8	
Polygyny	3	26.0	21.6	15.1	2.1**
No. of father's brothers					
None	4	97.0	36.3	21.0	
Two	4	37.3	16.8	9.7	2.6**
One (or half brother)	7	44.7	29.5	13.2	0.4
Infant birth order					
Firstborn	7	71.1	40.2	16.6	
Later born	8	44.1	30.6	11.5	1.3
Household composition					
Parents & infant only	7	73.4	37.4	15.8	
Parents, infant, & sibling(s)	8	41.8	31.0	11.5	1.6
Father's age					
Under 30	7	72.0	39.2	16.1	
Over 30	8	43.2	30.4	11.5	1.4
Sex of infant					
Female	8	58.7	33.8	13.0	
Male	7	54.7	42.5	17.3	0.08
Age of infant (months)					
1-4	6	67.0	35.3	15.8	
8-12	5	64.8	46.1	23.0	0.08
12-18	4	31.7	15.1	8.6	1.3

[a]n = number of fathers
[b]Mean scores are the average number of minutes fathers spent holding their infant during daylight hours (6 A.M. to 6 P.M.)
**$p<.01$

The factors extracted for analysis often overlapped. Younger fathers were also likely to have a firstborn and to have a household composition of parent and infant. Two of the three polygynous fathers also had two brothers.

Who did more caretaking when the father contributed less? Comparing the 4 fathers with no brothers to the 4 fathers with 2 brothers, other caretakers held the infant of a father with two brothers twice as frequently as they held the infant of a father with no brothers (11.7% vs. 5.0%). The wives of husbands with two brothers also did slightly more holding than wives of husbands with no brothers.

Another factor that might contribute to great individual variation in father holding is the means by which infant and childcare tasks were culturally transmitted. An investigation into how Aka communicated and acquired subsistence and childcare skills (Hewlett & Cavalli-Sforza, in press) demonstrated that almost 90% of the child care skills were transmitted from parent-to-child. Generally, boys acquired childcare skills from their father or mother, while girls acquired the skills from their mother. Seldom did Aka learn from a "teacher" (e.g., from a specialist during initiation) or from simply watching other adults in the community. A cultural transmission model developed by Cavalli-Sforza and Feldman (1981) predicts that traits transmitted parent-to-child generate variation between individuals within a population in comparison to the one-to-many transmission type (e.g., teacher-to-pupils or media-to-audience) or the many-to-one type (e.g., older member of a social group to younger members of the social group), where uniformity is generated. The model predicts precisely what is found: tremendous individual variation in childcare patterns. Aka parents are unquestionably very influential in transmitting parenting skills, but at this time longitudinal data do not exist that might help to distinguish whether the mode of

TABLE 12.7
Comparison of Father Holding in Selected
Hunting-Gathering Populations

Population	Age of infants (mos.)	Father holding (% of time)	Source
Gidjingalia[a]	0-6	3.4	Hamilton (1981)
	6-18	3.1	
!Kung[b]	0-6	1.9	West & Konner (1976)
	6-24	4.0	
Efe pygmies[c]	1-4	4.0	Winn (1985)
Aka pygmies	1-4	22.0	This chapter
	8-18	14.0	

Note. All observations were made in a camp setting.
[a]The Gidjingali are Australian aboriginies.
[b]!Kung are foragers of the Kalahari Desert (Botswana and Namibia)
[c]The Efe pygmies are bow and arrow hunters of NE Zaire.

TABLE 12.8
Comparison of Father Presence with Infants or Children Among Selected
Hunting-Gathering and Subsistence Farming Populations.

Population	% of time father is present or within view during observations	Primary setting of observations	Source
Gusii	10	house/yard & garden	1
Mixteca	9	house/yard	1
Ilocano	14	house/yard	1
Okinawan	3	public places & house/yard	1
Rajput	3	house/yard	1
!Kung	30	camp	2
Aka pygmies	88	forest camp	3

Sources:
1. Whiting & Whiting (1975)
2. West & Konner (1976)

transmission is more or less influential in predicting an individual's childcare patterns than the demographic variables mentioned earlier.

Tables 12.7 and 12.8 compare father holding and availability in some band and tribal societies for which quantitative data exist. By comparison to the Aka, the fathers in the other populations seldom hold or are in the presence of their infants. For instance, Aka fathers hold their 1- to 4-month-old infants on the net hunt more than any of the other hunting-gathering fathers hold their infants in camp. Aka fathers are probably more directly involved and available to their infants than any band or tribal population known in the literature. That is why they are characterized as "intimate" in the title this chapter.

Characteristics of Father Holding

The Aka father data do not support the contention that fathers are the vigorous, rough-and-tumble playmates of their infants. Only one episode of physical play by a father was recorded during all 264 hours of observation. In examining all infant focal observations (92 hours of observation) where mothers', fathers', and others' play could be directly compared, it was found that fathers never engaged in vigorous play, mothers played vigorously 3 times and others played roughly with the infant 9 times. Although the data are obviously meager, data regarding other caretakers are striking given the relative infrequency with which they hold infants. Who are the "others" engaging in physical play with infants? Eight of

FIG. 12.5. Aka father soothing his infant in the middle of the night.
The father sings quietly as he dances and plays the rattle.

the 9 cases were performed by older (3- to 12-year-old) brothers and sisters of the
infants. This is especially significant as brothers and sisters account for only 12%
of the total time "others" held the infant.

Table 12.9 examines the frequency of various activities which mothers and
fathers engaged in while holding the infant. Father's activity data are based on all
day father and infant focal observations (about 235 hours of observation), while

TABLE 12.9
Father's and Mother's Activity While Holding Infant

Activity	Relative frequency		Frequency per hour while holding	
	Father	Mother	Father	Mother
Feed/Nurse	.063	.422	0.62	2.80
Clean	.152	.116	1.50	0.77
Soothe	.178	.050	1.76	0.33
Affection	.272	.040	2.70	0.26
Transport	.089	.228	0.88	1.51
Play	.230	.132	2.28	0.88
Other	.016	.012	0.16	0.08
Totals	1.000	1.000	9.90	6.63

mother's data are based on all-day infant focal observations only (63 hours of observation). The data measure the frequency with which certain activities occurred while the parent held the infant; each episode was marked only once whether it lasted a few seconds or hours (e.g., with transporting). With these limitations in mind, the data do indicate different qualities of mother and father holding. Mothers were more likely to be the providers of nourishment and the transporters of the infant while the fathers were more likely to hug and kiss or play with the infant as they were holding. Fathers also provided more episodes of activity while holding than did mothers. On the average, fathers held their infant a shorter time than did mothers: Over 102 father holds were reported ($M=11.1$ minutes) compared to over 111 mother holds ($M=23.3$ minutes). Fathers were more likely to invest in relatively brief and intense episodes of activity, such as play or affection. Mothers, on the other hand, were more inclined to invest in

FIG. 12.6. Fathers play more frequently while holding their infant than mothers, but physical play such as this is rare.

FIG. 12.7. An Aka family returning to camp after the net hunt. The mother's basket is loaded with meat and food collected on the hunt. When mother's workload is excessive, fathers are more likely to help in infant care.

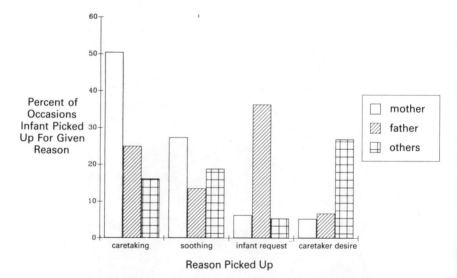

FIG. 12.8. Reasons mothers, fathers, and others initiated picking up the infant.

TABLE 12.10
Father's Activity While Holding Infant

Father's activity	Relative frequency engaged in this activity while holding
Primary caretaking—no other activity and devotes near full attention to infant	.26
Talking with others adult males	.25
Talking with others besides adult males	.12
Economic activity (making string, net-hunting)	.06
Transporting infant from net hunt	.05
Idle	.15
Eating or drinking	.08
Other (preparing meal)	.03

longer, more energetically demanding activities, such as transporting and nursing.

Tables 12.10 and 12.11 list the activities fathers and mothers engaged in while the father held his infant. The data are derived from 102 father holds that took place during the all-day father and infant focal observations. Following each father hold, father's and mother's primary activity during the hold was noted. Again, these are frequency measures rather than durational. For instance, father and mother were usually "idle" during part of every hold, yet it was coded as such only if it was the primary activity.

Aka fathers provided "quality time" to their infants since in over one fourth of the holds the father did not engage in any other activity and devoted his attention almost entirely to the infant. During most holds, the father participated in other activities. Although women are often characterized as being talkative, fathers in over one third of the episodes engaged in conversation with others, especially adult males, while holding the infant. With the exception of transporting the infant back from the net hunt, father was much less likely to hold the infant while engaged in economic activity than in social activity. This reinforces the earlier finding that fathers primarily held their infant while in the camp—not while in the forest or in the fields, when they are usually engaged in economic activity. The father often held the infant while the mother was busy collecting firewood, preparing a meal, or net hunting (see Table 12.11). This reflects the Aka conception of a good father—one who assists with infant care when the mother's workload becomes excessive.

Another method of delineating fathers' and mothers' caretaking styles has been utilized by Lamb (1977), and was attempted in this study. Lamb found that American mothers and fathers picked up their infants for different reasons— mothers were more likely to pick up the infant for caretaking purposes and

TABLE 12.11
What Mother Is Doing While Father Holds Infant

Mother's activity	Relative frequency engaged in this activity
Left camp to collect firewood or water	.24
Food preparation	.32
House maintenance (making and repairing)	.07
Net hunting	.18
Idle	.12
Other (talking to other, eating)	.08

fathers for playing. In this study, each time an Aka parent voluntarily picked up his/her infant (i.e., when the parent initiated action) a purpose for picking up the infant was coded (caretaking, control, play, affection, infant request, caretaker desire, soothe, other). In a short time it was obvious that the results would be limited as the Aka seldom voluntarily pick up the infant: One usually gets the infant from someone else or the infant initiates and completes the action by climbing onto the parent's lap. Only 176 instances of clearly parent initiated holding were recorded. Fig. 12.8 compares four reasons why parents and others picked up their infants. (Only those purposes in which there were at least 25 cases are shown; for instance, in only 3 cases was an infant picked up to play with, so that reason was not included in Figure 12.8). There were a number of significant differences. Most frequently, mothers picked up the infant for care-taking (mother-father $\chi^2(1, N = 139) = 8.02$, $p<.005$); fathers picked up the infant because the infant made some gesture or call to be picked up (mother-father $\chi^2(1, N = 139) = 20.38$, $p < .005$); while others picked up the infant simply because they wanted to (other-father $\chi^2(1, N = 81) = 6.10$, $p<.025$).

In the American studies, "play" has been an important behavior for differentiating mothers' and fathers' caretaking styles. Researchers have demonstrated that fathers may not play with the infant any more than mothers do, but fathers' style of play is characteristically more physical, rough-and-tumble, and unpredictable while mothers' play is more conventional (e.g., pat-a-cake, peek-a-boo) and toy-mediated. All instances of Aka infant-caretaker play were coded into one of four categories of play: major physical (rough-and-tumble, total body movement, chase), minor physical (tickling, nibbling, slight bouncing in lap); object-mediated (3 subtypes: parallel, stimulus, and tease); and face-to-face. Each episode of face-to-face play with infants 1 to 4 months of age was further coded with 1 to 3 descriptive codes from a list of 6 (proximal, distal, verbal, physical, visual, tactile).

Most Aka infant play occurred in early infancy and was primarily of the face-to-face type. Of the 238 instances of play observed in the infant focal observations (102 hours of observation), 72% occurred in the 1- to 4-month age group, 15% in the 8- to 12-month age group, and 13% in the 13- to 18-month age group. Sixty-five percent of the 1- to 4-month-olds play was of the face-to-face type. Since the number of play episodes among the older infants was so few, only 1- to 4-month-old infants' play episodes will be examined in detail.

Fig. 12.9 summarizes mothers', fathers' and others' types of play with 1- to 4-month-old infants. Physical rough-and-tumble play was rare, and no differences existed between mother, father, and others with respect to this play type. Minor physical play—especially bouncing the infant lightly on the lap and nibbling at his/her stomach—was engaged in more often by fathers than by mothers ($\chi^2(1, N = 106 = 9.43, p<.005$). There were no differences in the frequency with which mother, father, and others engaged in object-mediated or face-to-face types of play with the infant. Significance tests based on data from Tables 12.12 and 12.13 indicated that there were no significant differences between the types of face-to-face play that male and female infants received or between the types that mothers, fathers, and others provided.

It was demonstrated previously that fathers were more likely to engage in play while holding than were mothers (see Table 12.10). Yet, if one takes all 92 hours of infant focal observations (all-day and the next morning) and compares fathers', mothers' and others' frequency of play while holding, fathers still played with infants more frequently than did mothers (mothers played 1.2 times per hour; fathers 3.0 times per hour). However, others played more frequently with

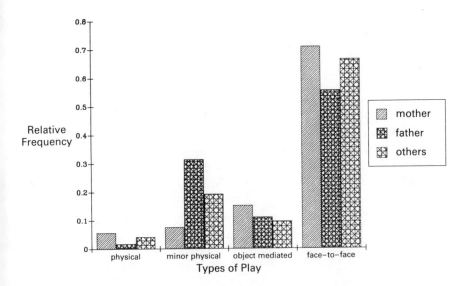

FIG. 12.9. Mothers', fathers' and others' types of play with 1- to 4-month-old infants.

TABLE 12.12
Types of Face-to-Face Play 1- to 4-Month Old Infants
Receive from Caretakers Holding or Within Proximity
of the Infant

| Type of play | Relative frequency | |
	Male infants	Female infants
Proximal	.24	.20
Distal	.09	.15
Verbal	.19	.22
Physical	.13	.11
Visual	.09	.16
Tactile	.25	.16

Note. No significant differences were found ($p < .01$).

the infant than mother and father combined—13.41 times per hour. Mothers'
and fathers' frequency of play are slightly higher in these calculations than those
in Table 12.8 because the morning observations, which always took place in
camp where play was more frequent, have been added here. This suggests that
others, in comparison to fathers and mothers, might be more aptly characterized
as the infant's playmates.

DISCUSSION

Although based on a limited data set (few individuals, few observations, over a
short 6-month period), several patterns of Aka paternal infant-holding emerge.

TABLE 12.13
Types of Face-to-Face Play Mothers, Fathers, and
Others Provide Their 1- to 4-Month-Old Infants

| Type of play | Relative Frequency | | |
	Mothers	Fathers	Others
Proximal	.25	.20	.21
Distal	.09	.14	.13
Verbal	.21	.20	.21
Physical	.10	.14	.13
Visual	.10	.18	.11
Tactile	.24	.16	.21

Note. No significant differences were found ($p < .01$).

First, Aka father holding of their infants is often context-specific—it generally occurs during leisure time, while sitting down in camp talking with other males. Second, vigorous play is not characteristic of the Aka father's interaction with his infant; it is more likely to be an older brother or sister who provide this style of interaction while holding. Aka fathers are more likely than mothers to engage in minor physical play with their infant (e.g., tickling, slight bouncing) while holding. The quality of father holding, by comparison to mother holding, is more brief and intensive in activities and requires relatively little energy investment (soothe, affection, play). Third, Aka fathers who contribute the most care are those with the fewest brothers. And, fourth, Aka fathers do more infant caretaking than fathers in any other band or tribal population studied.

These data need further explanation. How do these father-infant behaviors fit within the broader context of Aka society? Why do Aka fathers do less infant holding in economic settings? Why don't they play vigorously like American fathers? Why is the number of fathers' brothers important for predicting Aka father-infant interactions? And why do Aka fathers hold their infants more than fathers of any other foraging population?

While residing in the village, Aka fathers do not assist in infant care while engaged in economic activity outside of the camp because male and female subsistence activities do not overlap; father cannot take care of the infant because he is not near the infant. (The infant goes with the mother because of the frequent nursing.) While residing in the forest, however, fathers do have opportunities to assist in infant holding since male and female subsistence activities overlap, but seldom do they help out. They were most likely to help out by transporting the infant back to camp after the completion of the net hunt. Aka frequently gave two explanations for the lack of father holding on the hunt: (a) Holding an infant made it more difficult to run after game, and (b) men were faster runners than women. One parent had to carry the infant on the net hunt while the other parent had to be available to chase game. Since men were faster runners they should be free to run after game with the spear. Neither men nor women mentioned nursing the infant as a constraint. Aka women did not appear to be that slow; they were always faster than I. But, as mentioned earlier, women next to the net often put their infant down on the ground to run after game; a clear indication that infant holding constrained their running and consequently, their hunting ability.

An ultimate explanation might also be suggested. Economic activity may be a time of male intrasexual competition. A better hunter or provider may attract available females and help keep existing spouses from leaving. If an Aka father can spend a minimal amount of time assisting in the physical care of the infant while engaged in economic activity, even if the infant is nearby, he might do so to become a more successful hunter. If Aka fathers spend more time in economic activity and assist less frequently in infant holding, then they should be more successful hunters and have greater reproductive success. The cornerstone of this suggestion is that women would prefer (select) men who spend time hunting rather than helping with infant care. Unfortunately, data do not exist to test this hypothesis.

The Aka father data do not support the contention that fathers are the vigorous, rough-and-tumble playmate of the infants (as the American father data indicate). They do suggest that, in comparison to mothers, fathers are slightly more playful: Fathers are more likely to engage in minor physical play with their 1- to 4-month-old infants than are mothers, and fathers play more frequently with infants while holding than mothers do. But characterizing the Aka father as the infant's playmate would be misleading. Other caretakers holding the infant engage in play with the infant much more frequently than fathers or mothers, and mothers have more episodes of play over the course of a day than fathers or other caretakers because they hold the infant most of the time. The Aka father-infant relationship might be better characterized by its intimate and affective nature. It has already been mentioned that Aka fathers hold their infants more than any other human population known to the literature. Fathers also show affection more frequently while holding than do mothers (Table 12.9) and infants seem to regularly seek father holding, possibly because of its affective nature (Figure 12.8).

So how can vigorous play be a significant feature in American studies of father-infant attachment, but not among the Aka? Four factors appear to be important for understanding Aka infant play and attachment: familiarity with the infant; knowledge of caretaking practices (e.g., how to hold an infant, how to soothe an infant); the degree of relatedness to the infant; and cultural values and parental goals.

First, due to the frequent father holding and availability, Aka fathers know their infants intimately. Fathers know the early signs of infant hunger, fatigue, and illness—as well as the limits in their ability to soothe the infant. They also know how to stimulate responses from the infant without being vigorous. Unlike American fathers, Aka wait for infants to initiate interactions. The Aka mother is even more familiar with the infant's cues than the father is; other caretakers are least familiar with them. As indicated earlier, these other caretakers play more frequently with the infant while holding than mothers or fathers do and are the most physical in their play—thus suggesting a possible relationship between intimate knowledge of the infants' cues and the frequency of play while holding.

Second, knowledge of infant caretaking practices also seems to play a role in determining how much play is exhibited in caretaker-infant interactions. Child caretakers were the most physical and loud (singing) in their handling of the infant. Children were not restricted from holding infants, but they were closely watched by parents. While "other" caretakers were more playful than mothers or fathers, possibly because of the reason mentioned above, younger "other" caretakers were more physical than older ones because they probably did not know how to handle and care for infants as well as adult caretakers.

A third factor to consider is the degree of relatedness of the caretaker to the infant. If vigorous play can assist in developing attachment, more closely related

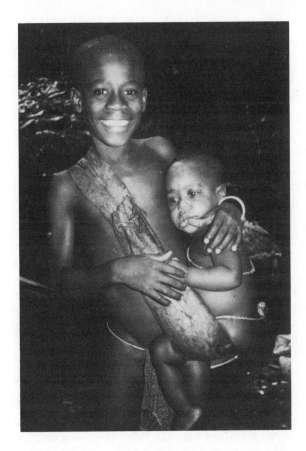

FIG. 12.10.   An Aka boy transports his sister across camp.

individuals may have a greater vested interest in establishing this bond than distantly related individuals. Attachment not only enhances the survival of the infant, but can potentially increase related caretakers genetic fitness (i.e., if the infant survives to reproductive age, the related caretaker will perpetuate some of his/her own genetic composition (this is called inclusive fitness by evolutionary biologists)). Aka mothers and fathers establish attachment by their frequent caretaking; vigorous play is not necessary to establish affective saliency. Brothers and sisters on the other hand, might establish this bond through physical play. Aka brothers and sisters, in fact, provided essentially all of the physical play the focal infants received; cousins and unrelated children were more likely to engage in face-to-face play with the infant instead of physical play.

Finally, the general social context of infant development should also be considered. American culture encourages individualistic aggressive competition; Aka culture values cooperation, non-aggression and prestige avoidance (i.e., one does not draw attention to oneself even, for instance, is one kills an elephant). Apparently, Americans tolerate—if not actually encourage—aggressive rough-and-tumble type of play with infants. Also, due to the Aka high infant mortality rate, the primary parental goal for Aka infants is survival. The constant holding and immediate attention to fussing reflect this goal. In the United States, infant mortality rates are markedly lower and, as a result, parental concern for survival may not be as great. The Aka infant is taken away from a caretaker who plays roughly with the infant, in part, because it could be seen as aggressive behavior, but also because the pervasive aim of infant care practices is survival of the infant, and rough-and-tumble play could risk the infant's safety.

Tentatively, these factors help clarify why Aka fathers do not engage in vigorous play like American fathers, but do participate in more minor physical play than Aka mothers (but not more than other caretakers). American fathers seldom participate directly in infant care and consequently are not as familiar with infant cues. To stimulate interaction and (possibly) attachment, they engage in physical play. Aka fathers on the other hand, are more likely to engage in minor physical play rather than in vigorous play since they, by comparison to American fathers, are more familiar with their infants, but not as familiar with them as mothers. The American father's playful relationship with his infant appears to be similar to the play Aka brothers/sisters-infant play relationship. But, from my experience in both cultures, Aka brothers and sisters are much less physical in their play with infants than American fathers (e.g., Aka never tossed infants in the air or swung them by their arms), a possible consequence of Americans' greater tolerance of roughhousing. These four factors are obviously speculative and need further empirical study.

The number of brothers that an Aka father has is an influential factor in predicting the amount of time an Aka father spends holding his infant. If one compares the Aka fathers who have two brothers and do little direct caretaking to the Aka fathers with no brothers and do a substantial amount of caretaking, other social and economic distinctions emerge. A general profile of the high-invest-ment father includes: no brothers, very few relatives in general, married rela-tively late in life, monogamous, and his wife is from a distant clan. He has a small hunting net, relies more on individual hunting techniques (e.g., small traps), has a close relationship with Ngandu villagers, and is of relatively low status (he seldom holds any of the status positions of *kimbeti, ntuma, nganga*). Fathers with low direct investment often have the opposite characteristics: two or three brothers, more likely to have two wives, wife (or wives) is from a nearby clan, large hunting net, and so forth.

There is an explanation why an Aka male with more brothers is likely to have the other above-mentioned characteristics of low investment fathers. The pa-triclan forms the core of the hunting-collecting group, so a male with a few brothers is more likely to have a reliable economic support group than a male with no brothers. Females prefer to marry into a more economically reliable group and seek males with more resources (i.e., brothers). Consequently, males with a few brothers do not have to travel as far to find a spouse and can marry earlier as more females are attracted to them. This in turn also means that the family of the wife is nearby to help if problems arise. Since the high investment father does not have a group of reliable brothers, he establishes a more variable strategy; he builds alliances with related clans to net hunt, places greater emphasis on individual hunting techniques and establishes closer ties to the Ngandu farmers.

What does an Aka father with more resources do if he spends less time in infant caretaking? He has more related family members to help out with child-care, but does he have more leisure time? As we have seen, most father caretaking occurs in the camp, so the father who has more resources is most likely to have more time available in camp for other activities than the father with few resources. It appears that these fathers spend more time in what might be called "status maintenance." They visit other nearby camps and spend considerable time talking with other males. Fathers at both ends of the continuum are following their best reproductive strategy. A father with few kin to rely upon, is unlikely to obtain high status; his best reproductive strategy is to invest time with existing offspring to ensure their survival (the mother would also need more help as there are fewer kin to assist in childcare). High status fathers, on the other hand, have a reliable kinship base and, can consequently, spend time maintaining and trying to improve their status. Less child caretaking time does not translate into more leisure time: Fathers who do less caretaking spend more time in maintaining their status. Although status differentiations among Aka are minimal, some status increase for Aka fathers (e.g., *kombeti*) is likely to lead to greater reproductive success (Hewlett, in press).

A somewhat analogous situation can be seen with American fathers. It has been demonstrated that blue collar fathers spend more time with their children than professional fathers (Mortimer & London, 1984). The work schedule of the blue-collar workers allows more time with the family. The professionals' high motivation and potential for career advancement often draws men (and women) away from their families. The professional could keep the same or similar hours as the blue collar worker, but the competition to maintain and potentially improve status makes it worthwhile to spend time engaged in work and extracurricular activities instead of spending time with the children.

Finally, why do Aka fathers provide so much infant caretaking? Two features of Aka society are quite distinctive from other foraging populations: male and female overlapping subsistence patterns, and the great distances traveled by women while engaged in subsistence activities. These features may help explain why Aka fathers are the secondary infant and child caretakers, while among most other band and tribal populations the older female sibling is preferred (Weisner & Gallimore, 1977). An older female sibling would be able to help the mother transport the infant relatively short distances—to the fields near the village or to collecting areas close to the camp—but would have difficulty carrying the infant for the long distances involved in the net hunt (8 to 25 km). An adult is needed, in this case the father, to transport the infant such distances. When Aka fathers do help out in transporting the infant on the net hunt, it is usually when they are returning to camp after the net hunt, and the mothers basket is loaded down with game meat and other items collected on the hunt.

Besides the great distances traveled, Aka life is unusual in that men and women generally work together or at least near each other while on the net hunt. The paternal intimacy demonstrated by Aka is also found among the Mbuti pygmies of Zaire (J. Hart & T. Hart, personal communication, 1985), the only other group known to use a similar hunting technique (i.e., net hunting) where male and female subsistence patterns overlap. Efe pygmy men (Zairian neighbors to the Mbuti) are bow-and-arrow hunters, a subsistence activity in which women do not participate. These fathers show no interest in childcare—especially of infants (Bailey, 1985; Winn, personal communication, 1985). Other Efe men are often more likely to hold the infant than the father (Bailey 1985). The precise mechanisms that make overlapping subsistence activities critical to predicting degree of paternal investment have not been determined.

Paradigms

The significance of the Aka father-infant relationship might better be appreciated if the Aka relationship is put into the context of two heuristic models that are cited in the father-infant literature. The Lamb (1985) and the Parsons and Bales (1955) models have been reiterated throughout this paper and will be discussed only briefly here. Attention will focus on the mother-father parenting dichotomies suggested by LaRossa and LaRossa (1981).

According to Lamb (1983, 1985) and others (Clarke-Stewart, 1980; Yogman, 1982), the father's vigorous play functions to develop attachment to the father and is the initial means of establishing social competence. Aka data tend to run counter to this prediction. Fathers do not engage in physical play with their infants, but there is little question that Aka infants by 8 months old are attached to their fathers. Fathers, for instance, were more likely than mothers to pick up the infant due to infant desire (an attachment behavior). Whether infants are more attached to their mothers than fathers is a difficult question. If one uses traditional behaviors to measure attachment (e.g., fuss for, approach) there is little doubt that mothers would be favored because infants demonstrate these behaviors to mothers frequently each hour in order to nurse. Also, Aka children appear to be socially competent, however one may measure it, even though fathers do not play vigorously with them.

The Parson and Bales paradigm suggests that fathers also foster social competence by being more punitive and restrictive. Interview data from American adolescents confirm their expectation (Bronfenbrenner, 1961; Kagan & Lempkin, 1960). Interviews with 16 Aka adolescents on the other hand, run counter to their expectation: Aka adolescents suggest it is the mother rather than the father who is more punitive. Twelve of the 16 said that it was their mother who most often hit them, usually for not doing something asked to do, while only 2 said their father. Ten of 16 said their mother yelled at them most often, while only 2 mentioned their father.

Aka data do tend to support the characterization of mothers as the infant caretakers (e.g., holding, feeding, cleaning)—mothers hold the infants more frequently and longer than fathers or other caretakers, and they are more likely to pick up the infant for caretaking purposes than fathers or others. Interview data also support this view. When asked who does one tell if one is hungry, 8 of the 16 adolescents said mother, 6 said paternal grandmother, and 2 said stepmother; nobody mentioned the father as the provider.

Contrary to the Parson and Bales model, there is no clear support either in the observational or in the interview data that mothers provide more nurturance or emotional support than fathers. Observational data indicates Aka fathers are affectionate and soothe the infant frequently. When questioned about times they were ill, 8 of the 16 adolescents said their mother was more sympathetic while they were ill, 5 said father, and 3 said both mother and father.

The Aka father-infant data are not consistent with the extensive American data, but this does not mean that the Lamb (1985) hypothesis should be rejected. These data are quite meager for any changes to be suggested, but they do indicate that—if fathers are active infant caretakers throughout infancy (not just a few months as in the Swedish studies (Lamb, Frodi, Hwang, & Frodi 1983)) and if fathers know from early experiences and training how to care for infants—vigorous play may not be necessary to establish attachment. Other family members besides the father may utilize playfulness as a means of establishing attachment. The notion that father's physical play also functions to initially establish social competence needs to be reevaluated. There is no support for this in the Aka material; theoretically in the Aka case it should be brothers and sisters who initially establish social competence, but I doubt strongly if this is the case.

LaRossa and LaRossa (1981) describe mother-father role dichotomies that they have found useful in distinguishing mothers' and fathers' parenting styles in their studies of American families with newborns. One distinction they make is role distance versus role embracement. Fathers are more likely to distance themselves from the parenting role while mothers are more likely to embrace the parenting role. American women generally "want" to remain in primary control of the children, while fathers may show interest in caretaking, they are more likely to keep some distance from caretaking while embracing their role as the breadwinner.

Another mother-father distinction deals with intrinsic and extrinsic values. LaRossa and LaRossa (1981) report the following:

The intrinsic value of something or someone is the amount of sheer pleasure or enjoyment that one gets from experiencing an object or person. The extrinsic value of something or someone is the amount of social rewards (eg. money, power, prestige) associated with having or being with that object or person (p.64).

They suggest that fathers generally have low intrinsic value and relatively high extrinsic value in childcare, while mothers have high intrinsic value and low extrinsic value in childcare. Fathers

> . . . will roughhouse with their toddlers on the living-room floor, and will blush when hugged or kissed by the one-year-olds, but when you really get down to it, they just do not have that much fun when they are with their children. If they had their druthers, they would be working at the office or drinking at the local pub . . . they commit themselves to their kids out of a sense of responsibility (ibid., p. 65).

These role dichotomies may be useful for understanding American mother-father parenting styles, but have limited value in characterizing Aka mother-father distinctions. Aka mothers and fathers embrace the parenting role. Generally, mothers and fathers want to hold the infant, and certainly both derive pleasure from interacting with the infant. As indicated earlier, fathers were in fact more likely to show affection while holding than were mothers. Fathers also: offered their nipple to the infant when the infant tried to nurse, often cleaned dirt from the infant's nose, chest, and hair as they held the infant; picked lice from their hair; cleaned mucus from their nose; and cleaned them after they urinated or defecated (often on the father). Fathers' caretaking did not appear any more or less perfunctory than mothers'. Aka fathers are not constrained by infant caretaking; if a father does not want to hold or care for the infant he gives the infant to another person. Intracultural variation exists in fathers' attitudes and feelings towards parenting, for instance, some fathers want to spend little time with their infants. But overall, Aka fathers embrace the parenting role just as much as they embrace their hunting role.

The intrinsic-extrinsic role dichotomy also does not fit well with Aka mother-father parenting styles. Again, both Aka mothers and fathers place great intrinsic value and little extrinsic value in parenting. The fathers' intrinsic value can be seen in the previous statements, but their lack of extrinsic value can best be demonstrated by comparing Aka fathers with Ngandu fathers. When an Ngandu father holds his infant in public he is "on stage." He goes out of his way to show his infant to those who pass by, and frequently tries to stimulate the infant while holding it. Aka, on the other hand, are matter-of-fact about their holding or transporting the infant in public places (e.g., while walking through the village). Aka fathers would visit me in my village house and I would be the one to draw attention to the fact that one of them was carrying his infant. Ngandu fathers would visit me holding their infants only if the infant was ill and needed some medicine. Aka fathers did not act differently in private and public places. Ngandu fathers showed a striking difference. Inside their house they did not show any interest in caring for their infants.

CONCLUSION

Aka fathers are intimate and affectionate with their infants. They are not the infant's vigorous playmate as has been found in American father-infant studies. Considering the Swedish and German studies along with the Aka material, American fathers appear to be unusual, if not deviant.

Almost constant holding in infancy is seen as an essential feature of Aka infant caretaking, possibly as a consequence of relatively high infant mortality, and fathers provide a substantial proportion of this caretaking. It was not possible to determine if the constant holding, in fact, did increase infant survival; no infants were held only occasionally.

Finally, the Aka father-infant relationship appears to be markedly different from the American father-infant relationship. Existing paradigms and hypotheses utilized to explain the role of father in child development are often generated from research with American families. The Aka data indicate that existing hypotheses, although insightful, need considerable modification if they are to be applicable cross-culturally.

ACKNOWLEDGEMENTS

Research for this chapter was supported by grants from the Wenner-Gren Foundation, University of California Humanities Fund, and the Swan Fund. I am indebted to P. Herbert Leiderman who initially raised my interest in fathers, and to the government of the Central African Republic, especially to Jean-Claude Kazagui, le Haut Commissaire de la Recherche Scientifique et Technologique, for facilitating the project. Etobe, Boseke, Samole, and Maman provided special insights into Aka fatherhood and Justin Mongosso assisted tremendously with logistical advice. I also wish to acknowledge the useful comments of P. Herbert Leiderman, Napoleon Chagnon, Donald Symons, and Michael Lamb on earlier drafts of the chapter.

REFERENCES

Altman, J. (1974). Observational study of behavior. *Behavior* 49, 227–267.
Altman, J. (1980). *Baboon mothers and infants*. Cambridge, Mass.: Harvard University Press.
Arco, C. M. B. (1983). Pacing of playful stimulation to young infants: Similarities and differences in maternal and paternal communication. *Infant Behavior and Development*, 6,223–228.

Babchuk, A., Hames, R. B., and Thompson, R. A. (in press). Sex differences in the recognition of infant facial expressions of emotion: the primary caretaker hypothesis. *Ethology and Sociobiology.*

Bahuchet, S. (in press). Food supply and uncertainty among Aka pygmies (Loybaye, Central African Republic). In I. de Garine & G. A. Harrison (Eds.), *Coping with uncertainty in food supply.* Cambridge: Cambridge University Press.

Bailey, R. C. (1985). *The socioecology of Efe pygmy men in the Ituri Forest, Zaire.* Unpublished Ph.D. dissertation. Harvard University.

Belsky, J. (1980). A family analysis of parental influence on infant exploratory competence. In F. A. Pedersen (Ed.), *The father-infant relationship: Observational studies in family settings.* New York: Praeger.

Bowlby, J. (1969). *Attachment and loss.* Vol. 1: *Attachment.* New York: Basic Books.

Bronfenbrenner, U. (1961). Some familial antecedents of responsibility and leadership in adolescents. In L. Petrullo & B. M. Bass (Eds.), *Leadership and interpersonal behavior.* New York: Holt Rinehart, and Winston.

Brown, J. K. (1970). A note on the division of labor by sex. *American Anthropologist,* 72, 1073–1078.

Burton, M. Brudner, L. A., & White D. R. (1977). A model for the sexual division of labor. *American Ethnologist,* 4, 227–252.

Cavalli-Sforza, L. L. & M. W. Feldman. (1981). *Cultural transmission and evolution: A quantitative approach.* Princeton, N.J.: Princeton University Press.

Clarke-Stewart, K. A. (1978). And daddy makes three: The father's impact on mother and young child. *Child Development,* 49, 466–478.

Clarke-Stewart, K. A. (1980). The father's contribution to children's cognitive and social development in early childhood. In F. A. Pedersen (Ed.), *The father-infant relationship.* New York: Praeger.

Crawley, S. B. & Sherrod, K. B. (1984). Parent-infant play during the first year of life. *Infant Behavior and Development,* 7, 65–75.

Draper, P. (1976). Social and economic constraints on child life among the !Kung. In R. B. Lee & I. DeVore (Eds.), *Kalahari hunter-gatherers.* Cambridge, Mass.: Harvard University Press.

Durkheim, E. (1933). *The division of labor in society.* (Trans. by George Simpson). New York: MacMillan Company.

Field, T. (1978). Interaction behaviors of primary versus secondary caretaker fathers. *Developmental Psychology,* 14, 183–184.

Freedman, D. G. (1974). *Human infancy: An evolutionary approach.* New York: Wiley.

Hart, J. (1977). From subsistence to market: A case study of the Mbuti net hunters. *Human Ecology,* 6, 325–353.

Hewlett, B. S. (in press). Sexual selection and paternal investment among Aka pygmies. In L. Betzig, P. Turke, & M. Borgerhoff-Mulder (Eds.), *Human reproductive behavior—A Darwinian perspective.* Cambridge, England: Cambridge University Press.

Hewlett, B. S. and Cavalli-Sforza, L. L. (in press). Cultural transmission among Aka pygmies. *American Anthropologist.*

Hoffman, M. L. (1981). The role of the father in moral internalization. In M. E. Lamb (Ed.), *The role of father in child development.* New York: John Wiley.

Johnson, A. (1975). Time allocation in a Machiguenga community. *Ethnology.* 14, 301–310.

Kagan, J. & Lemkin, J. (1960). The child's differential perception of parental attitudes. *Journal of Abnormal and Social Psychology,* 61, 440–447.

Konner, M. J. (1977). Infancy among the Kalahari desert San. In P. H. Leiderman et al. (Eds.), *Culture and infancy: variations in the human experience.* New York: Academic Press, 1977.

Lamb, M. E. (Ed.). (1976). *The role of father in child development.* New York: Wiley.

Lamb, M. E. (1977a). The development of mother-infant and father-infant attachments in the second year of life. *Developmental Psychology,* 13, 637–648.

Lamb, M. E. (1977b). Father-infant and mother-infant interaction in the first year of life. *Child Development*, 48, 167–181.

Lamb, M. E. (Ed.) (1981). *The role of the father in child development* (Rev. Edition). New York: Wiley.

Lamb, M. E., Frodi, A. M., Frodi, M., & Hwang, C. P. (1982). Characteristics of maternal and paternal behavior in traditional and non-traditional Swedish families. *International Journal of Behavior Development*, 5, 131–151.

Lamb, M. E., Frodi, M., Hwang, C. P., Frodi, A. M. (1983). Effects of paternal involvement on infant preferences for mothers and fathers. *Child Development*, 54, 450–458.

Lamb, M. E. (1985). Observational studies of father-child relationships in humans. In D. M. Taub (Ed.), *Primate paternalism*. New York: Van Nostrand Reinhold Company.

Lancaster, J. B. (1975). *Primate behavior and the emergence of human culture*. New York: Holt, Rinehart, and Winston.

LaRossa, R. & LaRossa, M. M. (1981). *Transition to parenthood: How infants change families*. Beverly Hills: Sage Publications.

Lee, R. B. & DeVore, I. (1968). *Man the hunter*. Chicago: Aldine.

Leiderman, H. P., Tulkin, S. R., & Rosefeld, A. (1977). *Culture and infancy: variations in the human experience*. New York: Academic Press.

LeVine, R. A. (1977). Child rearing as cultural adaptation. In P. H. Leiderman et al. (Eds.), *Culture and infancy: Variations in the human experience*. New York: Academic Press.

Monroe, R. H. & Monroe, R. L. (1971). Household density and infant care in an East African Society. *Journal of Social Psychology*, 83, 3–13.

Mortimer, J. T. and London, J. (1984). The varying linkages of work and family. In P. Voydanoff (Ed.), *Work and family: Changing roles of men and women*. Palo Alto, California: Mayfield.

Neuwelt-Truntzer, S. (1981). *Ecological influences on the physical, behavioral and cognitive development of pygmy children*. Unpublished Ph. D. dissertation, University of Chicago.

Ortner, S. B. (1974). Is female to male as nature is to culture? In M. Z. Rosaldo & L. Lamphere (Eds.), *Woman, culture and society*. Stanford, CA: Stanford University Press.

Parke, R. D., O'Leary, S. (1976). Family interaction in the newborn period: Some findings, some observations and some unresolved issues. In K. Riegan & J. Meacham (Eds.), *The developing individual in a changing world*. The Hague: Mouton.

Parke, R. D., Grossmann, K., & Tinsley, B. R. (1981). Father-mother-infant interaction in the newborn period: a German-American comparison. In T. M. Field, A. M. Sostek, P. Vietze, and P. H. Leiderman (Eds.), *Culture and early interactions*. Hillsdale, N.J.: Lawrence Erlbaum Associates.

Parsons, T. & Bales, R. F. (1955). *Family, socialization and interaction process*. Illinois: Free Press.

Pedersen, F. A., Anderson, B. J. & Cain, R. L. (1980). Parent-infant and husband-wife interactions observed at age five months. In Frank A. Pedersen (Ed.), *The father-infant relationship*. New York: Praeger.

Rosaldo, M. Z. & Lamphere, L. (1974). *Woman, culture and society*. Stanford, Ca.: Stanford University Press.

Turnbull, C. M. (1965). *Wayward servants: The two worlds of the African pygmies*. Garden City, N. Y.: Natural History Press.

Weisner, T. S. & Gallimore, R. (1977). My brother's keeper: Child and sibling caretaking. *Current Anthropology*, 18, 169–190.

West, M. M. and Konner, M. J. (1976). The role of father in anthropological perspective. In Michael E. Lamb (Ed.), *The role of father in child development*. New York: Wiley.

Weiss, K. (1973) Demographic models for anthropology. *Memoirs of the society for America Archaelogy, No. 27, American Antiquity*, 38(2).

Whiting, B. B. & Whiting, J. W. M. (1975). *Children of six cultures*, Cambridge, Mass.: Harvard University Press.

330   HEWLETT

Wilson, E. O. (1975). *Sociobiology: The new synthesis.* Cambridge, Mass.: Harvard University Press.

Yogman, M. W. (1982). Observations on the father-infant relationship. In H. M. Fitzgerald, B. Lester & M. W. Yogman (Eds.), *Theory and research in behavioral pediatrics.* New York: Plenum Press.

Woodburn, J. (1968). Introduction to Hadza ecology. In R. B. Lee and I. DeVore (Eds.), *Man the hunter.* Chicago: Aldine.

Zelditch, M. (1955). Role differentiation in the nuclear family. In T. Parsons & R. Bales (Eds.), *Family, Socialization and Interaction Process.* New York: Free Press.

V AUSTRALIA

13

Fatherhood in Australia

Graeme Russell
Macquarie University

Societal assumptions and research in Australia, as well as family and employment policies, present a mixture of perspectives about fatherhood. At one level, there is the constantly stated claim that Australian males (and presumably fathers too) are extremely chauvinistic, and that the Australian family is rigidly patriarchal (cf. Bryson, 1984). Stagoll (1983, p. 17), in reviewing family therapy in Australia, has argued that Australian men are "left out of family life, taking refuge in self-conscious masculinity around sport, 'ockerdom' (defined as boorish, uncouth chauvinistic Australianism) and alcohol as compensation." Consistent with this "chauvinistic" perspective is the Government's insistence that family allowances (a benefit given to those who have dependent children) can be paid *only* to the mother, even if it is the father who is the full-time caregiver. In contrast to these views, research indicates that there are few differences between Australian and other Western fathers regarding participation in childcare (Russell & Radin, 1983). This is true both for findings about modal patterns and about the incidence of highly involved, nurturant, and sensitive fathers (Harper, 1980; Russell, 1983a).

There is also a cultural diversity within Australia which restricts considerably generalizations that can be made about fatherhood. For one, there is the aboriginal population, which ranges from traditional tribal groupings in the north of Australia, to groups residing in small country towns, to those living in clearly defined areas in major cities. Although the largest single population group is of Anglo-Saxon origin (with the majority having been born in Australia), there has been a strong emphasis on immigration from non-Anglo-Saxon countries since the Second World War. The largest numbers have come from Italy, Greece,

333

Yugoslavia, Germany, and the Netherlands, although there have been reasonably high levels of immigration from 30 or more countries. In 1976 about 20% of the Australian population of 15 million were born overseas, with 25% of these immigrants coming from non-Anglo-Saxon countries (Storer, 1981). Few studies have examined differences between these cultural groups: therefore, the present review relies almost entirely on findings for Anglo-Australians.

Recently, there has been a small, but nevertheless highly noticeable increase in interest in fathers and their contribution to family life in Australia—in the media (especially in newspapers and magazines), in psychological and sociological research, and in policies and practices associated with the family. Several diverse social changes probably account for this. These include: (a) a social and medical emphasis on the desirability of fathers being present at the birth—indeed, the attendance of Australian fathers at childbirth is now almost so commonplace (about 80% attend) as to not warrant major attention, and their participation in antenatal classes is actively encouraged, (b) a trend towards dual employment in families with young children, resulting in increased social and individual family pressure on fathers to contribute more to childcare and housework; (c) changes in employment patterns for men (e.g., increased levels of unemployment), and perhaps a more questioning attitude by men towards their investment in work and career (cf. Bryson, 1974); (d) increased divorce rates and, combined with changes in policies and practices, a resultant increase in disputes between mothers and fathers about custody, access, and maintenance; (e) an increase in the numbers of single fathers and, especially, those who are not employed; (f) the general social questioning of the position of women and men in society; and (g) a broadening of research interest in families away from an exclusive emphasis on mothers towards the study of all family members (cf. Goodnow, Burns, & Russell, 1985).

Despite these changes, the contribution that male parents make to families is still not given anywhere near the same status as that given to the contribution that female parents make. This is very evident in recent parenting books (cf. Russell, 1983c), in approaches to parent education, and in the relative scarcity of research on fathers compared to that on mothers. This latter point is obvious from an examination of the proceedings of recent Australian research conferences on families (e.g., the 1983 Australian Family Research Conference) and child development (e.g., the 1980, 1982, and 1984 National Child Development Conferences).

While there is not a solid body of research which covers the range of issues associated with fathers, several themes and emerging trends are obvious. First, Australian family research has been characterized by a strong and continuing emphasis on divisions of labor. More recently, dual-employment families and families in which fathers either share or have the major responsibility for daily childcare have been studied. Of the emerging trends, one of the most obvious is the study of mother-father differences in beliefs about parental roles and parental influences over development. There have also been recent trends towards the study of issues associated with custody and access and the study of fathers in the context of family therapy and child behavior problems. Very few Australian studies have examined child development outcomes, and approaches have tended to be descriptive, with interview and self-report techniques being the most common methods.

The present review is divided into seven sections. The first examines beliefs about fatherhood, both from a general cultural perspective and from that of fathers themselves. The second and most substantive section examines divisions of labor for paid and unpaid work. The father-child relationship is the major topic covered in the next section, emphasizing the content and quality of fathers' social interactions with their children. Child development issues are examined in the fourth section, with particular attention being given to father-mother differences in beliefs and values about child development. Questions of whether or not levels of involvement are increasing are discussed in the fifth section. The sixth and seventh sections cover, in turn, single fathers and the family law issues of custody and access.

BELIEFS ABOUT FATHERHOOD

Cultural Stereotypes

Research findings on stereotypes about fatherhood tend to support the general assertions of Bryson (1984) and Stagoll (1983) noted above. Russell (1983a) asked a small sample of parents what they thought were the generally accepted societal expectations of fathers. Fathers and mothers both agreed that a father is expected to be the breadwinnner, head of the house, family protector, and disciplinarian (especially in more serious matters). He is expected to present a masculine model, and to spend time and play with his children when he can— especially with his sons (e.g., playing rough-and-tumble, football). In another study, Richards (1978) found parents described "the good father" in terms of disciplining, being the familial authority figure, and spending time being involved with older children. These findings are also consistent with Harper's (1980) analysis of the images of fathers, and with the "stereotyped" fathers described by Connell, Ashenden, Kessler, and Dowsett (1982).

Government policies and assumptions about the family (e.g., the recent abolishment of paternity leave for federal government employees) and general media images of fathers in Australia also present a stereotyped view. There is little evidence of fathers being portrayed in nurturant or caregiving roles. And, as has been argued by Russell (1983c), although recent parenting books pay more attention to fathers, they are commonly portrayed in very traditional ways. Green (1984), in his highly popular book for parents of toddlers, stated:

"Fathers are particularly suited to taking youngsters to run off energy in the park, or taking them outside to help in the garden or around the house." (p. 43)

"Picture, if you will, the husband snapping his fingers as he sits with his feet up, waiting for his wife to fetch him a can of beer, and the minor tantrum when it does not appear." (p. 4)

Stereotypes also exist about the relative contributions of fathers from different cultural groups. An argument often heard is that Anglo-Australian fathers, especially those born in Australia, are more crudely chauvinistic than fathers of Mediterranean descent (especially Italians and Greeks), and less expressive and openly demonstrative to their children. It is also argued that Mediterranean fathers are more involved with children because of their cultural emphasis on fathers presenting models of authority and discipline. It remains to be seen, however, whether there is any validity to these stereotyped images of different cultural groups.

Fathers' Perspectives

Russell (1983a) and Russell and Russell (1985b) asked fathers what they thought their role and responsibilities were. Findings were remarkably consistent across the two quite different samples (see below for a description of the samples). The most common response was breadwinning (59% in the first study; 60% in the second), with the next most common being a general response related to socialization/support for the development of the children (43% and 47%). In contrast, there were surprisingly few fathers who said that they should be: the disciplinarian (14% and 13%); the head of the house (12% and 20%); or the person who provides love and affection (18% and 12%). Although the majority of fathers therefore saw their most significant family contribution as breadwinning, it is obvious that few saw their role as being as restrictive as the stereotype might imply.

One of the strongest and most widely held beliefs is that mothers are by nature better suited to care for children—that they have a biological advantage over fathers and are more competent, sensitive, and patient with children, and perhaps above all, that children need their mothers (cf. Harper & Richards, 1979; Russell, 1983a). Parents were asked in the two Russell studies for their beliefs about women having a maternal instinct and being more sensitive to children, and whether fathers have the ability to care for children. Although the majority of fathers in both studies agreed that mothers had a biological advantage over fathers and were more sensitive to children (78% of the fathers in the first study and 58% in the second), a significant number also believed that fathers had the ability to be competent caregivers *if* the situation demanded it (49% in the first study; 73% in the second). Further, Russell (1983a) reports that fathers who were highly participant were strong in their views that fathers could be competent and sensitive caregivers. It may be that fathers need to have this experience before they will change their beliefs. But, as is evident from findings presented below, few Australian fathers have had the experience of being highly participant.

DIVISIONS OF LABOR

As has been noted by Bryson (1983), one of the positive aspects of Australian family research is that there has been an emphasis on divisions of labor for over 30 years. Nevertheless, there are limitations to making historical comparisons, especially given that there have been major differences in samples and methods of data collection. Two of the early studies were based on data collected from 12-year-old children, whereas recent studies have been based on interviews with both parents.

Family Financial Support and Management

With the current emphasis on father-participation in childcare, little attention has been given to the traditional role of fathers as breadwinners. Yet, as was described above, studies report that most fathers consider this to be their major role and responsibility. This view is supported by figures for participation in the paid work force.

Paid Work.   The most recent survey conducted of labor-force status and family characteristics (Australian Bureau of Statistics, 1983) showed that, of all two-parent families in which there were dependent children, 92.8% had fathers who were employed full-time, 2.5% who were employed part-time, and 4.6% who were not employed. As would be expected, participation rates for mothers were considerably lower. Of the mothers, 20% were employed full-time; 26% part-time; and 54% were not employed. Also, it was only in 19% of these families that both parents were employed full-time. When the children are very young, fathers have even greater responsibility for breadwinning. The corresponding employment figures when families had a child under 4 were: *full time:* fathers - 94.5%, mothers - 12%; *part-time:* fathers - 2.5%, mothers - 20%; *not employed:* fathers - 3%, mothers - 68%. Only 11.5% of this group had both parents employed full-time. It has also been suggested (e.g., Brennan, 1983) that immigrant families are overrepresented in this dual-employment group.

Family Management.   As was noted above, although the sterotyped father image includes being "the head of the house" and "the person who makes major decisions," very few fathers see themselves in this way. These perceptions are broadly consistent with the findings from early Australian family studies (see below for details) which have asked about actual family decision making. Both

Oeser and Hammond (1954) and Adler (1965) studied children's perceptions of decision-making patterns for a range of activities (e.g., household duties, childcare and control, family expenditures), and found that, overall, mothers made 50% of decisions. These findings led Adler to coin the term *matriduxy* to denote what he perceived to be the powerful leadership functions of mothers in Australian families. In contrast, Fallding (1957) reported that, in 55% of families, fathers were "in effective control"; in 34%, there was a "partnership in management"; and in only 11% was the mother "in effective control."

In a more recent study, Edwards (1981a, 1981b, 1982) examined financial management and control in 50 families with dependent children under 16 years of age. The sample included single- and dual-employment families, and high- and low-income groups. In 50% of families, mothers managed family finances (i.e., handled the money and made payments); this pattern was more prevalent in low-income families where the mother was not employed. In 14% of families, fathers were the managers; in 14%, management was joint; and in 22%, incomes and financial management were essentially separate. Control of finances (i.e., influence over decisions about purchases and patterns of spending), was found to be joint for half of the couples, whereas fathers had more control in 40% of families. Mothers who were employed had more say in decisions than those who were not employed. These latter findings are in line with the earlier findings of Fallding (1957), and are generally consistent with descriptions of the Australian family as being patriarchal in nature.

Childcare and Domestic Work

Early Research.   Bryson (1983) has provided a comprehensive review of 30 years of Australian research on divisions of labor. There were three major studies in the 1940–1960 period: Oeser and Hammond (1954; data collected between 1947 and 1950); Fallding (1957; data collected in the early 1950s); and Adler (1965; data collected in 1957 and 1958). The first and the last of these had 12-year-old children (Oeser & Hammond, n=85; Adler, n=1525) complete a "Day at Home" questionnaire (developed by Herbst, 1954), which asked them to indicate which parent performed and made decisions about a range of family activities. The study by Fallding is particularly noteworthy because of its intensive style, and because he interviewed each family member individually as well as the entire family group. Fallding recruited 38 families (20 professionals and 18 tradesmen) in which there were two children, one of whom was an adolescent.

As noted by Bryson (1983), findings were consistent across the three studies in showing that divisions of labor are very traditional, with mothers being more active than fathers in family decision making and dominating all tasks except for traditional male household tasks (e.g., household repairs, mowing lawns). Further, while all studies found that both parents participated in childcare activities, the overwhelming majority of mothers controlled these activities.

Recent Research.   There are several recent studies which have examined fathers' and mothers' perceptions of divisions of labor for childcare and domestic work. Harper and Richards (1979) studied 195 sets of Australian-born parents from three social-class groups: families in which the father was a low-income, blue-collar worker; those in which the father was a middle-income, white-collar worker; and families in which the mother was professionally trained. In 52 families, mothers were employed full-time; in 45, they were employed part-time; and, in 98, they were not employed outside the home. The subjects recruited had at least one child under 12 (62% had preschoolers). All mothers were interviewed, whereas 83% of their husbands completed and mailed back a questionnaire. The findings they present, however, rely almost entirely on information collected from mothers, and critical data about fathers (and even mothers' perceptions of fathers) are often missing.

Overall, Harper and Richards' findings confirm those of earlier studies in revealing traditional divisions of labor, especially when mothers were not employed outside the home. In these families, for example, 58% of the fathers did not do any household chores at all, whereas 92% of the mothers always washed the clothes, 85% always did the ironing, and 80% always cooked the meals. These researchers found more evidence of fathers sharing in childcare tasks (particularly feeding and putting the child to bed) than in housework. Having both parents employed full-time was associated with fathers doing *relatively* more housework and childcare. Harper and Richards (1979) also report that professional fathers perform more household chores than working-class fathers, especially when their spouses are employed full-time, but that social class factors have little impact on involvement in childcare.

Russell (1983a) conducted (from 1977 to 1979) a study of 309 two-parent families, nearly all of whom were either born in Australia or were Anglo immigrants. Four major types of families were studied, although it is only the first three that are relevant in this section—the fourth type, *shared caregiving,* is described below. The first three were defined by maternal employment status: mother not employed (n = 145); employed part-time (n = 47); and employed full-time (n = 46). Families were recruited in a quasi-random fashion from seven shopping centers in Sydney (selected to ensure a wide cross-section on social class variables) and two small country towns. All families were recruited such that they had at least one child under 10 years of age; nearly 70% had preschoolers.

In contrast to Harper and Richards (1979), this study was based on joint mother/father interviews, and emphasized divisions of labor for childcare in terms of time spent and frequency of task performance (unfortunately, questions about housework were not included). Fathers were found to be at home and available to their children (when they were awake) for an average of 33 hours a week (the comparable figure for mothers was 70 hours), and they spent an average of 2.5 hours a week on childcare tasks, which constituted 11% of this work. In relative terms, fathers were most likely to attend to their children at night, less likely to bathe and dress their children, and least likely to feed them or change their nappies (diapers). Thirty-five percent of fathers did not feed, dress, or bathe their children each week; 50% of those with infants did not regularly change nappies.

Few differences in father participation were found as a function of maternal employment status, except that fathers whose spouses were employed were more likely to spend time being the sole caregiver (4.7 hours/week, compared to 1.0 hour/week when mother not employed). There was also a nonsignificant trend for fathers to spend more time on childcare tasks when their spouses were employed and when they had young children. In agreement with Harper and Richards, fathers' occupational and educational status were not associated with levels of participation in childcare, although fathers were more involved when their spouses were more highly educated.

A subsequent study, also employing joint interviews with parents, was conducted in 1981 and 1982 by Russell and Russell (1985a, 1985b). It examined divisions of labor in mainly middle-class, well-educated families (n = 57) in which the eldest child was in first grade (mean age = 6.8 years). These fathers were at home and available to their eldest child for 33 hours/week (mothers = 55) and spent an average of 2 hours/week being the sole caregiver (mothers = 23). The percentages of fathers who regularly performed or had the sole or shared responsibility for a range of tasks were: child's dress, 6%; child's school needs, 3%; putting child to bed, 67%; washing/ironing, 5%; house cleaning, 12%; car/house repairs, 97%. Thus, these average figures confirm the above findings in showing a traditional pattern of divisions of labor for childcare and domestic work in Anglo-Australian families. Studies which have investigated divisions of labor in other cultural groups are reviewed next.

Cultural Perspectives

As was noted above, although Australian society contains a complex mix of cultural groups, very little research has been conducted on father-participation in non-Anglo groups. Bottomley (1979), in her study of the Greek-Australian community, cites anecdotal material which supports the view that Greek-Australian men (in comparison to Anglo-Australians) respond more positively to children and are more affectionate towards them. But she also argues (G. Bottomley, personal communication, February, 1985) that this does not necessarily mean that they will be more active participants in childcare. Indeed, her hypothesis is that Greek-Australian families have a very clearly defined division of labor, with fathers being dominant in family decisions. Some support is given to this by the study of Burns and Homel (1985).

Burns and Homel present self-report data on divisions of labor for 11 child-rearing tasks for families in which there were children aged 9–11 years. (In 50%

of the families, the information was reported by mothers; in 50%, by fathers.) Families were chosen to represent a wide range of socioeconomic classes and immigrant groups. They compared divisions of labor between Anglo- and non-Anglo-Australian fathers (61% were Greek or Cypriots; 20% were either Italian, Maltese or Yugoslav). Based on a review of the ethnographic literature, it was predicted that non-Anglo fathers would be more involved in public and authority childrearing activities (e.g., taking children on outings, disciplining children) and less involved in domestic activities (e.g., getting children's breakfast, organizing children's clothes). While strong support was not found for this hypothesis, it was found that Anglo fathers were more involved in "seeing children are clean and tidy when necessary," and non-Anglo fathers were more involved in "transporting children to sports activities/functions" and "buying books for children." The two groups did not differ, however, in total father involvement summed across the 11 items.

Little data are available on father-participation in childcare in Australia's aboriginal culture either. Further, making generalizations about this group is quite problematic given the diversity in aboriginal social and family grouping. There is a range from small traditional groups of 20 in Arnhem Land in the Northern Territory, to those who live in groups in Western-style houses in smaller family units in urban areas. Also, there is no uniformity of family patterns within traditional groups: some fathers have one wife, while others have up to eight; some have very young children when they are in their 30s, others when they are 60.

In a rare but highly original investigation, Hamilton (1981) conducted an indepth study of the Gidjingali tribe in North-Central Arnhem Land in 1968 and 1969. Although most of the people in this group had had contact with Europeans, Hamilton argued that this had had little effect on people's relationships with each other. This was a participant observation study, employing a detailed observational system, analyses of photographs, tape recordings, and interviews. Hamilton presented her data in terms of the child's age.

The major observations for the period from birth to 6 months were as follows. Although fathers may be given the baby to hold within a few hours after the birth and sometimes carry the infant around for a short time, they never go very far from the mother. Of the total number of observations made of adults carrying babies, fathers were involved in only 3.4% of them. Fathers are obviously pleased about having a baby and are warm and supportive, but somewhat distant. Fathers see that the mother attends to the infant's needs and "can berate the mother for not doing so" (p. 35).

The same style of interaction was common with 6- to 18-month-olds. Of all observations made of adults alone with children at this age, the father was involved in only 8% of them. Also, fathers criticised their children and commanded them to do things less often than mothers did, but they were more likely to provide information to their children. Although few sex-of-child differences were found for these age groups, fathers tended to respond differently to older (3–5 years) boys and girls. They interacted more with sons, and "criticised" their daughters more than they did their sons.

Apart from these latter findings about sex-of-child differences, Hamilton's (1981) findings are generally consistent with those noted above for other cultural groups in Australia. A common finding amongst all of the research reviewed is a very rigid pattern of divisions of labor for childcare. It should be kept in mind, however, that this represents the modal or average pattern, and that there is likely to be a considerable range in levels of involvement. Findings for the range of involvement are considered in a subsequent section.

FATHER-CHILD RELATIONSHIPS

The above review shows quite clearly that the majority of fathers make their most significant contribution to the family through their employment, and by performing traditional male household tasks. The evidence also indicates, however, that fathers are at home and available to their children for a considerable period of time each week. What then do fathers do with their children? What are the most common types of social interactions, and what is the nature or quality of their relationships with their children? The available evidence appears to be consistent with cultural stereotypes in showing that fathers' interactions with their children are much more likely to be associated with play (Harper & Richards, 1979; Russell, 1983a).

Play and Other Social Interactions

Both Russell (1983a) and Russell and Russell (1985a) have made detailed analyses of play and other social interactions. In the Russell (1983a) study, fathers reported that they spent an average of 9 hours/week "playing" with their children (where play was defined liberally to cover a range of social interactions including, for example, a child helping a father with gardening). Of the total amount of time fathers spent interacting with their children, 80% of it was play-oriented. Russell (1983a) also reported father-mother differences in the content of these social interactions. Compared to mothers, fathers engaged more frequently in outdoor and amusement/fun play, and less frequently in indoor/conventional play and story reading. Also, 45% of fathers (compared to 20% of mothers) did not regularly read a story to their children each week, whereas 9% of fathers (and 23% of mothers) did this every day. Additional analyses revealed that, in contrast to a prevalent finding in the recent literature, fathers did not interact preferentially with their sons.

In the second study, Russell and Russell (1985a) report data for ratings of frequency of father-child interactions for 6- to 7-year-olds for a variety of play and educational activities. In comparison with mothers, fathers engaged less in activities of the following general types: cognitive/educational (e.g., listen to child read, help with schoolwork); intimate activities (e.g., read a story, sit and talk about things), and inside activities (e.g., play with toys, help with craft/drawing), but engaged more in physical/outdoor play (e.g., ball games, rough-and-tumble play). Although there was a trend for fathers of sons to engage in more physical/outdoor play than fathers of daughters, this difference was not statistically significant.

Another study which focused on play was conducted by Elmslie (1981). This was a naturalistic observational study (parents were not aware that they were being observed) of 160 adult/child pairs (children aged from 1 to 8 years) conducted on weekends in a public park in Sydney. Findings were consistent with other observational and self-report studies in showing that mothers initiated more caretaking interactions than fathers did, and that fathers participated more in active play. Elmslie failed to find significant differences between parents, however, for the actual style of play; fathers did not engage in more physical or rough-and-tumble play. And, in agreement with the Russell and Russell (1985a) self-report data, she also failed to find that fathers interacted preferentially with sons.

Quality of Father-Child Relationships

Russell and Russell (1985a) and Elmslie (1981) have also assessed the quality of father-child relationships using observational techniques. Elmslie employed a range of parent-child relationship measures in her naturalistic study, and found a nonsignificant trend for fathers to spend more time in close proximity to older boys. Differences were not found between mothers and fathers for either personal distance or tactile contact, nor for the display of physical affection, control, or social verbalizations.

The Russell and Russell (1985a) study included a 2-hour home observation during the late afternoon/early evening. Parent-child interactions (for the 6- to 7-year-olds) were coded in terms of the frequency of occurrence of a set of 21 behaviors and the affective responses of those present. Mothers were found to be more likely to consult with their child, be dominant or assertive (e.g., direct or command the child to do something), and provide information, whereas fathers joked with and teased their children more. Children responded more positively to fathers' initiations of physical affection and to mothers' initiations of consulting, and more negatively to fathers' initiations of joking or teasing. Overall, however, the findings were more remarkable for the absence of differences in the ways in which children responded to their two parents.

There was a general trend for mothers to react more positively to child behaviors and for fathers to react with more neutral affect. Post-observation interview data suggested, however, that fathers felt inhibited in the expression of affect because of the presence of the observers (Russell, 1983b). These mother/father differences in affect were especially evident for the following child behaviors: the communication of feelings, the display of independence in decision making, and the requesting or providing of information. Fathers responded more positively than mothers did, however, to children's initiations of shared activities. In agreement with the self-report data, there were surprisingly few sex-of-parent by sex-of-child interaction effects, with very little indication of fathers interacting preferentially with sons or of fathers having closer or warmer relationships with their sons.

FATHERS AND CHILD DEVELOPMENT

As was mentioned above, there have been few studies of the specific effects that fathers have on child development. There are, however, several studies which have examined mother/father differences in cognitions about childrearing (values, beliefs about the nature of development, perceived influence). These studies are based on the theoretical argument that parental cognitions will vary as a function of parenting experiences, and that they will either mediate or determine parental socialization practices and child development outcomes. Studies have also been conducted on parental reports of childrearing practices, children's perceptions of their fathers, and fathers' contributions to the development of child behavior problems.

Childrearing Values.   Mother/father differences in childrearing values have been examined in four recent studies. Three of these have employed a similar set of items to investigate values in families with mainly preschoolers (Russell, 1983a), with 6- to 7-year-olds (Russell & Russell, 1985b), and with 11-year-olds (Russell & Russell, 1982). A consistent finding across the three studies was that fathers placed less value than mothers did on both interpersonal sensitivity and expressiveness, and personal well-being (e.g., having a positive self-image, being happy). Russell (1983a) also failed to find that the level of participation in day-to-day childcare had a major impact on father's values. Further, contrary to previous research and cultural stereotypes, fathers were not found to place more emphasis on children conforming to traditional sex-role norms.

Cashmore (1983) examined parental childrearing values (mainly values for cognitive/skills and control/obedience) for a group of 100 firstborn children (aged 12 to 14), half of whom were Anglo-Australian and half were of Italian-Australian background (all parents were born in Italy). Overall, few differences were found between mothers and fathers, except that fathers valued children having the ability to work out unusual problems more. While there was not a significant cultural group by sex-of-parent interaction, Italian-Australian parents (i.e., both fathers and mothers) placed more emphasis on obedience and being well-organized. Anglo-Australians placed more emphasis on items such as "having the ability to work out unusual problems," "being interested in how and why things happen," and "having a good imagination."

Perceived Influence.   Given the vast differences noted above both for time spent with children and for the content of parent-child interactions, mothers and fathers might hold very different beliefs about their potential to influence their children. Five studies have examined perceived parental influences, using vastly different methods and samples (Antill, 1984a, 1984b; Knight, 1983; Russell, 1983a; Russell & Russell, 1982, 1985b). Several findings consistently emerged. Fathers have been found to perceive that they have less influence over their children than mothers do (Knight, 1983; Russell & Russell, 1982), and they tend to place more emphasis on biological determinants of behavior (Antill, 1984a, 1984b).

Highly significant mother-father differences have also been found for the types of behavior that parents perceive they are able to influence (Russell, 1983a; Russell & Russell, 1982, 1985b). Fathers rated their influence less than mothers did in the following areas: getting along with others; sensitivity to others' feelings; attitudes and morals; expressiveness; manners and appearance; modesty; and health. In contrast, they rated their influence as being greater over: sense of humor; problem solving and trying hard at things; coping with rough-and-tumble play or fighting; independence; competitiveness; and being good at sport. These fathers' perceptions of their areas of influence, it might be noted, are clearly consistent with Australian reports of the major dimensions of masculinity (Antill, Cunningham, Russell, & Thompson, 1981). What is needed now is research which examines whether in fact fathers' influences are critical for the development of these child behaviors.

Child Outcomes.   Strong associations between father characteristics and reported childrearing practices have been found in a study which examined familial influences over the development of androgyny in adolescence (Teasdale, 1986). This study involved the independent assessment of sex-roles in a group of 147 adolescents with an average age of 15.7 years, and the self-report of parental characteristics and childrearing practices from their predominantly middle-class parents. The most striking finding was the dominance of father-variables over mother-variables in accounting for the differences between androgynous and sex-typed adolescent girls and boys. Androgyny was associated with: parental performance of cross-sex household tasks; fathers holding more egalitarian sex-role attitudes; fathers having a more child-centered, supportive, and democratic approach to childrearing, and being less demanding in sex-role and rule enforcement; and fathers encouraging cross-sex characteristics, independence, creativity, and intellectual curiosity. Although this study does not enable clear statements of cause and effect to be made, it does lend strong support to previous suggestions that fathers might be even more critical during adolescence. This hypothesis is given further support by the research reviewed next.

The Australian Institute of Family Studies (Ochiltree & Amato, 1984, 1985) studied 195 primary school children (from grades 3 or 4) and 207 secondary school children (from grades 10 and 11) from two- and one-parent families. One of the trends that they report is that secondary children who were defined as low in competence (using measures of reading skill, self-concept, and everyday skills), but who came from families in which resource levels were high (defined by a range of measures, including income, occupational status of parents, housing status, housing density) reported a lack of father-involvement. This lack of involvement was most often associated with their fathers having a high level of involvement in work. These authors conclude that more attention should be given to the influences that fathers have on development, and argue in particular for more emphasis on the study of the effects of work demands.

Children's perceptions.   Children's perceptions of and satisfactions with their parents (and their families) and the ways in which these perceptions mediate other outcomes (e.g., moral development) have been the subjects of three recent studies. Highly stereotyped perceptions of fathers, emphasizing his contribution to the family through his job, have been given by children in studies by Ochiltree and Amato (1984, 1985) and Riach (1982). Riach also found, however, that responses were less stereotyped when children had parents who shared childrearing tasks and responsibilities. Ochiltree and Amato (1984, 1985) also reported that children generally gave positive evaluations of their relationships with their fathers, although secondary school children made more negative evaluations of their fathers than of their mothers. The majority of children also reported being satisfied with the amount of time they spent with their fathers and with the degree of interest that their fathers showed in them, but a significant number (especially primary schoolers) also said that they would like to spend more time with their fathers. When asked why their fathers didn't spend more time with them, most said it was because he spent too much time working. They also said that if they had more time they would like to spend it playing with their fathers or going on outings with him (e.g., to the movies).

Children's evaluations of fathers' socialization behaviors (a "general" father, not their own) was the subject of a study by Siegal and Barclay (in press). They asked 240 working-class children (whose ages ranged from 6 to 17) to evaluate fathers' discipline techniques in a range of situations in which a child was described as having transgressed. In contrast to previous research into mothers' techniques, children evaluated the use of physical punishment more highly for fathers. It was also found that boys evaluated fathers more positively than girls did, and that boys were more approving of fathers using physical punishment, and girls were more approving of the use of induction (reasoning and pointing out the harmful consequences of transgressions). Finally, a positive relationship was found between ratings of induction and first-grade boys' self-reports of empathy, suggesting that fathers have a prominent role to play in boys' social development.

Child Behavior Problems. A major theme in the child development literature concerns the negative impact that fathers can have through their physical or psychological absence. While there have not been any major Australian studies which have linked a lack of father-involvement directly with child behavior problems, two studies present some suggestive findings. In the first, Howard (1979, 1981) examined links between perceived parental bonding (Parker, Tupling, & Brown, 1979) and depression in a group of 100 male offenders (modal age 17 years) who had been committed to State Training Schools. The main variables found to "explain" depression were a perceived lack of paternal care and, to a lesser extent, maternal overprotection. Further, Howard concludes that the absence of caring and involved fathers is highly critical in the development of delinquency.

In the second study, Detmering (1985) examined maternal and paternal self-held responsibility for the causes of disturbed behavior in a sample of 70 children (7 to 11 years old) who had been referred for psychiatric treatment. Only 14% of fathers (compared with 32% of mothers) took active responsibility for their children's behavior problems. It was also found that a significant number of fathers had increased their levels of responsibility after therapy, and that this increase in self-held responsibility was predictive of a successful outcome. Successful therapy was also associated with *all* family members rating the father-child relationship as having become closer. Further research is needed to follow up these suggestive findings, especially to clarify the specific role of fathers in relation both to child behavior problems, and to the outcome of family therapy (cf. Heubeck, Detmering, & Russell, 1986).

Conclusions. Although there has been very little Australian research on the effects that fathers have on child development, the above review indicates that there is a growing body of research into Anglo-Australians which addresses these issues in an indirect way. Fathers appear to hold different childrearing values than mothers and have different ideas about what aspects of child development they can have an impact on. Compared to mothers, they rate themselves as having less influence over child development and appear to place less value on children being expressive and having interpersonal sensitivity. Fathers were also found to believe that they are more able to influence the characteristics which are associated with traditional masculinity. Nevertheless, consistent with other findings reviewed above, fathers do not seem to be more orientated towards sons than to daughters.

CHANGES IN FATHER-PARTICIPATION

Are Fathers Becoming More Involved?

A frequent question currently being asked by Australian family researchers, social commentators, and the media alike is whether or not a change is occurring and fathers are becoming more involved. Given the wide range of methods used and the scarcity of studies which have collected data from fathers themselves, it is difficult to be certain whether there has been a trend over time towards greater father-participation in either housework or childcare (apart from the very obvious increase in father-participation in antenatal classes and childbirth). In 1976, Curthoys speculated that a "quiet revolution" was occurring within the Australian family, with men taking a greater role in childcare, especially during out-of-work hours. Some recent studies (cf. Glezer, 1983) suggest that, while there has been a significant shift toward egalitarianism in attitudes about divisions of labor for family work in the last 10 years, these "new" attitudes are not very evident in findings for the frequency of actual performance of household tasks. This is consistent with Bryson's (1983) conclusions after her comprehensive review of Australian research into divisions of labor:

> The more recent studies show that men are participating to a somewhat greater extent in certain household tasks which were previously carried out by their wives and possibly that they are taking a more active role in childrearing. However, men's participation in fathering has always been higher than in purely domestic chores. The research shows men's increased activity in household chores to be linked to women's greater participation in the work-force though this does not seem to be the case with fathering. The changes overall are not, however, great and, without some considerable alteration of women's subordinate position in the work-force and other spheres of power in the wider society, this could not be expected to have a significant effect on gender equality. (p. 125)

My own conclusion after examining the critical variables associated with father-participation in a shopping center sample was that there was evidence of "a slow but nevertheless significant shift in father participation" (Russell, 1983a, p. 74). This conclusion was based primarily on the outcome of a cross-sectional analysis which showed that father-participation was associated with couples having been married for fewer years. This was significant even when ages of children had been taken into account. Much more systematic research (e.g., using longitudinal designs) is needed now to examine this question in a direct way, using standard methodological techniques (e.g., time-use techniques or family observations) and samples which are comparable with those of earlier studies.

Fathers' Evaluations of Their Involvement

It is common for people to assert that fathers are basically happy with their relatively low level of involvement, and that in fact they are doing what they want to do and are not interested in change. However, this might not necessarily be the case, as the pressures within Australian society are very strong for fathers to conform to a traditional pattern of family involvement and to achieve their status in the community through their participation in paid work (Harper, 1980; Russell, 1983a). Recent research indicates that this may not be what fathers actually prefer.

Fathers were asked in the Russell (1983a) study what they enjoyed most about being a father, what they disliked about it, and, if they had a choice, what they would change in their life in order to improve their relationships with their children. (Data presented here come from the first three of the family types identified in the Russell (1983a) study reported above.) The things that fathers enjoyed most were: watching children grow and develop (27%), the status and achievement associated with being a parent (20%), the stimulation and fun (20%), having personal growth/learning experiences (18%), and the expression of love and affection (14%). In contrast, fathers rated the following as the aspects which they disliked most: the costs and anxieties (21%), the constancy and demands (19%), the loss of freedom (17%), and time conflicts (17%). There was also a group (19%) who said that they enjoyed everything about being a father.

Although 29% of fathers said that there wasn't anything that they would like to change in order to get on better with their children (with most of these saying that their relationship was currently very good), the majority (52%) said that they would like to spend more time with their children. Fathers, therefore, appear to share the view of the children in the Ochiltree and Amato (1985) study in emphasizing a desire to spend more time together. Nevertheless, only half of the fathers were specific about how they would spend the time (the most common activity mentioned was play). There was also another group of fathers who said that the way that they would like to change was to become more patient or tolerant with their children (26%). It is, of course, an open question as to whether or not these fathers would change their lives if more options were open to them. And, it remains to be seen if this would result in a change either in fathers' satisfaction or in the quality of the father-child relationship. Russell's (1982, 1983a) analyses of the experiences of extremely highly participant fathers provides some data which address these questions.

Highly Participant Fathers

Harper and Richards (1979) and Russell (1983a) have drawn attention to the wide variability in father-participation in childcare and domestic work. Harper and Richards describe it as "enormous variations" (1979, pp. 188, 190) and argue that it is independent of mother's work-force participation or other family characteristics. They also drew attention to two families in which fathers either shared or had the major responsibility for childcare, a family type which was researched further by Harper (1980).

Harper (1980) made an in-depth study of 15 fathers at home (8 were at home full-time and 7 were employed part-time), mainly recruited from personal contacts. Complete details of the sample were not given; however, from the information provided, several points are clear. First, although the sample tended to be middle-class and professional (14 of the 15 mothers had professional careers), it was quite diverse in terms of the fathers' occupation and the reasons why families adopted this pattern (some because of the fathers' rejection of career values, some for egalitarian beliefs, and some simply for pragmatic reasons). While this study is limited by the nature and size of the sample, it provides a wealth of data on the possible antecedents and consequences of adopting a nontraditional pattern, based on the accounts of fathers.

One of the major aims of the Russell (1983a) study was to focus on the *range* of father-participation, particularly in those families in which fathers were highly participant. In agreement with Harper and Richards, Russell also found considerable variability in patterns of participation for employed fathers. In families with infants, 3% of fathers shared all childcare tasks equally, and 2 "took over" when they returned from work. It was also noted that 14% of all fathers in this sample spent 7 or more hours each week on childcare tasks.

Russell (1983a) also studied 71 families in which fathers were highly participant (termed "shared caregiving families"), recruited by a variety of methods (but mainly from notices placed on boards and contacts made at preschools and playgroups). These fathers performed an average of 45% of childcare tasks, and spent 26 hours each week being the sole caregiver (the average for mothers was 16). Eighty-six percent of mothers were employed full-time, and 14% part-time, whereas 48% of the fathers were employed full-time, 30% part-time, and 22% were not employed at all. It is difficult to know how typical this or Harper's sample was of these nontraditional families, whether this pattern is increasing, how common it currently is, or what the antecedents of it are. My estimate (Russell, 1983a), based on the numbers recruited through the quasi-random shopping center approach, is that they constitute 1–2% of families with preschool aged children. This corresponds to 5–10,000 families, a figure which is broadly consistent with the Australian Bureau of Statistics estimate that, of the full-time housekeepers in 1979, approximately 2% (13,000) were male.

Four general types of explanations were given by these families for why they had adopted a shared caregiving pattern: (a) inability of fathers to gain employment; (b) need to increase family income; (c) career factors—mainly the strong desire of the mother to pursue a career; and (d) egalitarian beliefs about childcare responsibilities and sex roles. Those who gave the first two types of explanations (31) usually argued that the change was an economic necessity, whereas the others (40) saw their change as being a matter of choice.

Additional analyses (Russell, 1983a) suggest the following factors are associated with high father-participation in Anglo-Australian families: having fewer and older children; having a mother who is more highly educated and has a higher status job; having a father who had had more experience with children and who rejects traditional ideas about masculinity (cf. Russell, 1978); having mothers and fathers employed in jobs which permit some degree of flexibility in career structure and work times, and which have fewer demands to work long hours. Nevertheless, as was noted above, high father-participation is not simply associated with either maternal employment status nor professional middle-class couples. Nor is there a strong association with fathers' levels of education or occupational status. The above factors have only been found to be associated (or not associated) with high father-involvement; the research is not sufficiently advanced yet to allow us to make cause-and-effect statements.

Another factor to emerge was that fathers were changed by the experience of shared caregiving. Fathers in shared caregiving families, in contrast to fathers in traditional families (Russell, 1982), were more likely to say that they derived enjoyment from their children's expressions of love and affection and from watching their children develop. These fathers also said that, as a consequence of being more highly participant, they had become closer to their children and had developed a more sensitive relationship which was based on an improved understanding of their children. This change was rated by them as the most significant advantage of a shared caregiving lifestyle. Further, they argued that changes in the quality of relationships had not occurred as a result of simply spending more time with their children, but rather as a consequence of the type of time they spent—having the sole and extended day-to-day responsibility for their children.

Being a highly participant father, however, was not without its problems. When asked about the negative aspects, the most common responses from fathers were: loss of freedom (35%); problems of adjustment to being at home (45%); and the loss of status associated with their reduction in commitment to paid work (32%). A 2-year follow-up of 27 of the first 33 families recruited into the study, who could be located, revealed that 11 had reverted completely to traditional lifestyles (Russell, 1983a). Continuing as a highly participant father was made more difficult for some fathers because of a lack of general social support, combined with the absence of support from male friends and workmates.

These findings, together with those of Harper (1980), emphasize the need both to give more attention to social attitudes towards "full-time" fathers and to look for ways to provide them with additional community support. Both Harper (1980) and Russell (1983a, 1983c, 1984) also emphasize that if this lifestyle is to become a viable option then more flexibility must be introduced into employment policies in Australia (e.g., paternity leave, permanent part-time work, job-sharing, averaging incomes over the lifecycle).

SINGLE FATHERS

It is difficult to obtain accurate figures concerning the numbers and characteristics of the Australian single-father population. The Australian Bureau of Statistics (1983) estimates that there are 34,900 male-headed single-parent families with dependent children. This constitutes approximately 12% of the single-parent population. It is also estimated that, in 57% of these families there is one dependent child, in 36% there are two, and in 7% there are three or more. Australian Government policy is such that unemployed single fathers are entitled to a supporting parent's pension. In 1983, 77% of single fathers (and 53% of those with preschoolers) were employed full-time and 5% (13% with preschoolers) part-time, leaving 18% (34% with preschoolers) who were unemployed and potentially on the pension.

Two recent studies have examined issues associated with the difficulties experienced by single fathers. Katz (1979) used a self-completed questionnaire (returned by mail) to study a volunteer sample of 409 single fathers recruited through Parents Without Partners. This was quite a diverse sample which covered a range of social classes (e.g., 23.5% were tradesmen, 14.4% were process workers and laborers); family characteristics (e.g., 16% had preschoolers, 39% had children between 7 and 12); and causes of divorce or separation. A major focus was on the difficulties experienced by single fathers. The most significant difficulties noted were: feelings of loneliness, conflicts between work and the demands of childcare, financial difficulties (especially caused by having to employ others to care for children), and problems with children (mentioned as a major issue by 37% of fathers). Katz concludes that more attention needs to be given to the special issues associated with being a single father and advocates several policy initiatives. Currently, most attention in Australian society is given to issues associated with single mothers, with policymakers often discounting arguments about single fathers because of their low proportion relative to single mothers. But, with changing patterns of family court decisions (see below), policymakers might be forced to address this issue more seriously in the future.

The difficulties experienced by single fathers were also the focus of an interview study (using both a clinical approach and standard structured questions) of a middle-class sample (n = 20) conducted by Garnett (1980). The sample was recruited through advertisements and personal contacts. A major question of interest was whether fathers who had younger children (under 5 years) found the transition to single fatherhood more difficult than those who had older children (aged 6 to 12 years). Few differences were found between these two groups, indicating that fathers with very young children coped just as well as those with older children (both groups considered that they were coping well as single parents). It was also found that single fathers had less difficulty with becoming a single father than they did with becoming a separated person.

CUSTODY AND ACCESS

Issues associated with family law, custody, access, and maintenance have been very prominent in the media and in community, professional, and academic discussions during the past 10 years. One reason for this perhaps is the change which occurred in 1975 in Australian family law to a no-fault system with a major emphasis on conciliation through counsellors. Another reason is the increased divorce rate and, therefore, the increased number of people who have experienced court proceedings and the consequences of divorce and separation (e.g., poverty, problems with being a single parent, access and maintenance disputes). A final reason for attention being focused on these issues in Australia is the increased level of violence associated with the family court. A judge was killed recently, and the homes of two Family Court judges have been bombed.

Outcome of Cases.   Australia is fortunate in having an active research section associated with the family court. Their reports have provided valuable information about court processes and decisions associated with guardianship (defined in terms of legal responsibility for children), custody (defined in terms of day-to-day care and control), and access. Two major reports have recently been published on family court decisions. The first was primarily about uncontested cases (Horwill, 1979), and the second about defended cases (Horwill & Bordow, 1983). Only about 10% of cases in Australia are fully contested.

Horwill (1979) studied a representative national sample of 430 orders in the Family Court (424 were undefended cases). He found that the custody of all of children went to mothers in 78% of cases and to fathers in 14% of cases (the remainder mainly went to other relatives or into foster care). Horwill and Bordow (1983) present data for decisions for all orders in the Melbourne court in 1980, and for a randomly selected sample of 50 defended cases each from Melbourne and Sydney in the same year. Data for all orders were as follows: sole guardianship to mother, 70.3%; joint guardianship but custody to mother, 8.4%; sole guardianship to father, 13.1%; joint guardianship but custody to father, 5.1%.

In 54% of the defended cases all the children went with the mother whereas in 31% they went with the father. But, somewhat surprisingly, it was only in 20% of these cases that joint guardianship was awarded. Horwill and Bordow did not find that the sex, age, or position of the children in the family had much impact on decisions. Neither did ethnic background nor maternal employment status. Although the numbers were small, there was a trend for paternal employment status to be critical. A detailed analysis of sample characteristics showed that fathers with professional backgrounds were overrepresented in defended cases, and semiskilled and unskilled blue-collar workers were underrepresented. Further, nonprofessional employed white-collar fathers were more likely to be granted guardianship; nonprofessional self-employed fathers were the least likely.

Access and Continuing Father-child relationships.   A common view is that, even though many fathers are awarded quite liberal access by courts, the amount of contact that fathers actually have with their children after divorce is considerably reduced and, in a good number of cases, eventually ceases altogether. An argument often made in defense of fathers (cf. Jordan, 1985) is that they avoid seeing their children because they find it too hurtful or emotionally traumatic. Two recent studies provide a somewhat different perspective of fathers' behavior and feelings about access.

The Family Court has examined access patterns across a 3-year period (Weir, Silvestro, & Bennington, 1983). The sample (n = 70) included three groups: one in which access was completely determined by the parents, one in which it was agreed upon after consultation with court counsellors, and one in which it was decided by a judge. While the number of non-custodial parents (71% of whom were fathers) who had regular contact with the children dropped from 77% at 6 months to 66% at 3 years, two thirds still had fortnightly or greater contact after 3 years, and 60% maintained their regular pattern of access throughout. Clearly, these findings do not support the view that the majority of fathers are not interested in their children and, when given the opportunity, "fade out" or opt out of their responsibilities.

Fathers who were filing for divorce through the Sydney Family Court were the subject of a study by Gilmour (1983). This group (n = 24) did not have care and control of their children, and had been separated from them for between 12 and 24 months. They had an average of 2.1 children, whose ages ranged from 1 to 14 years, with a mean of 7.3 years. The average number of hours/week the fathers had access to their children was 12. It was found that 46% wanted greater contact, 88% were concerned that they were losing influence over their children, and 66% were concerned about conflicts with their ex-spouse over the children. Further, 71% of the fathers rated the loss of their children as the single most significant aspect of separation (the next most significant reported loss was financial). Problems of adjustment and separation distress were associated with feelings of low self-efficacy as a parent and dissatisfaction with relationships with children, and with access problems. Clearly, therefore, the maintenance of the father-child relationship is a critical aspect of fathers' adjustment to separation.

CONCLUSION

The above analysis provides a general picture of the patterns of involvement primarily for Anglo-Australian fathers. Findings indicate that the modal pattern is one of a traditional type, with fathers being much more involved in play than in childcare, and having the responsibility for family financial support and traditional male household tasks. There is nevertheless a wide range of paternal involvement, and a small group of extremely highly participant fathers have been identified. In agreement with my conclusion of 1981 (published as Russell (1983a)), the present review of research findings indicates that, although the future *will* likely see Australian fathers becoming more highly participant in childcare, this change is likely to be very slow indeed.

Despite the fact that there is a significant minority of fathers who are highly participant and who want greater options, the dominant ideology in Australia is much more consistent with the traditional pattern. And, as has been argued elsewhere (Russell, 1984), it is these traditional fathers who dominate positions of power, making it less likely that perspectives on fatherhood will be broadened or that the options for fathers will be increased through major changes in either employment or leave policies. The dominance of this traditional perspective is well illustrated both by the difficulties experienced by various employee groups (e.g., the N.S.W. Teachers' Federation) to obtain paid parental leave for fathers, and by the recent rejection by the Australian government of a proposal to ask *men* as well as women in the next census how many children they have parented. The major argument against this was that the question would be too sensitive for men!

Nevertheless, there is evidence of small but significant changes occurring at various levels which could ultimately influence policy decisions. In a recent paper co-authored by the president of the Australian Council of Trade Unions, it was stated that:

> Trade unions are now making a number of clear assertions: . . . They are recognising that both parents should be able to share the experience of childrearing. (Dolan & Forbath, 1983, p. 4)

My subjective impression too, primarily based on my observations and invitations to participate, talk, or contribute articles, is that more attention is being given to fatherhood in approaches to preparation for parenthood and in parent education. It is also my impression that more emphasis is being given to fathers in decisions about the provisions of services at the community level. From the research perspective too, it appears to be becoming easier to find a sample of fathers who are at home caring for their children (even if it is for a short period of time).

This review began by pointing out the diversity of the Australian culture, a diversity that has not been well represented in research to date. What is needed now is research which takes account of this diversity and explores differences in fatherhood between the various cultural groups. More attention also needs to be given to questions associated with the impact that fathers have on children, and to exploring the antecedents of their involvement. It is perhaps only after a better understanding is obtained of the antecedents and consequences of father participation (or lack of participation) that arguments for policy changes and for increasing the options for Australian fathers will have more impact on decision makers and on fathers themselves.

REFERENCES

Adler, D. (1965). Matriduxy in the Australian family. In A. F. Davies & S. Encel (Eds.), *Australian society: A sociological introduction*, Vol. 1. Melbourne: Longman Cheshire.

Antill, J. (1984a). Parental beliefs concerning sex differences, sex-role stereotyping and cross-sex interests and behaviour. Unpublished paper, Macquarie University.

Antill, J. (1984b). Parental sex-role related childrearing practices: The impact of background and sex-role characteristics and parental beliefs about sex-role development. Unpublished paper, Macquarie University.

Antill, J., Cunningham, J., Russell, G. & Thompson, N. (1981). An Australian Sex-Role Scale. *Australian Journal of Psychology, 33,* 169–184.

Australian Bureau of Statistics (1983). *Labour force status and other characteristics of families.* Australia, July 1983, Cat. No. 62240.

Bottomley, G. (1979). *After the Odyssey: A study of Greek Australians.* St. Lucia, Queensland: University of Queensland Press.

Brennan, D. (1983). *Towards a national child care policy.* Melbourne: Institute of Family Studies.

Bryson, L (1974). Men's work and women's work: Occupation and family orientation. *Search, 5,* 295–299.

Bryson, L. (1983). Thirty years of research on the division of labour in Australian families. *Australian Journal of Sex, Marriage & Family, 4,* 125–132.

Bryson, L. (1984). The Australian Patriarchal Family. In S. Encel, M. Berry, M. de Lepervanche & T. Rowse (Eds.), *Australian Society: Introductory Essays.* 4th Edition. Melbourne: Longman Cheshire.

Burns, A., & Homel, R. (1985). Sex-role satisfaction among Australian children: Some sex, age and cultural group comparisons. Unpublished paper, Macquarie University.

Cashmore, J. (1983). *Factors in parent-child agreement.* Unpublished Ph.D. thesis, Macquarie University.

Connell, R. W., Ashenden, D. J., Kessler, S. & Dowsett, G. W. (1982). *Making the difference: Schools, families and social divisions.* Sydney: George Allen & Unwin.

Curthoys, A. (1976). Men and childcare in the feminist utopia. *Refractory Girl, 10,* 3–5.

Detmering, J. (1985). *Parental beliefs about emotional disturbance and their relationship to the outcome of therapy.* Unpublished Ph.D. thesis, Macquarie University.

Dolan, C. & Forbath, B. (1983). Child care: The industrial issue. In *Papers of the National Association of Community Based Child Care Conference.* Sydney, 1983.

Edwards, M. (1981a). Financial arrangements within families: Empirical results and tax implications. Paper presented to a Conference on *Women and Taxation,* United Nations Association of Australia, Melbourne, June.

Edwards, M. (1981b). *Income distribution within families.* Paper presented to a workshop on Income Security, University of Melbourne, July.

Edwards, M. (1982). Financial arrangements made by husbands and wives: Findings of a survey. *Australian & New Zealand Journal of Sociology, 18,* 320–338.

Elmslie, A. (1981). *Adult interactions with children: An observational study in a park setting.* Unpublished Honours Thesis, Macquarie University.

Fallding, H. (1957). Inside the Australian family. In A. P. Elkin (Ed.), *Marriage and the family in Australia.* Sydney: Angus & Robertson.

Garnett, M. (1980). *The psychological affect of lone fathers during transition.* Unpublished Masters Thesis, Macquarie University.

Gilmour, L. (1983). Not happily ever after: The implications of marital separation for men. Unpublished Honours Thesis, Macquarie University.

Glezer, H. (1983). *Changes in marriage and sex-role attitudes among young married women: 1971–1982.* Paper presented to an Institute of Family Studies Conference, Canberra.

Goodnow, J. J., Burns, A. & Russell, G. (1985). The family context of development. In N. Feather (Ed.) *Australian Psychology: Review of Research.* Sydney: George Allen & Unwin.

Green, C. (1984). *Toddler Taming.* Sydney: Doubleday.

Hamilton, A. (1981). *Nature and Culture: Aboriginal child-rearing in North-Central Arnhem Land.* Canberra: Institute of Aboriginal Studies.

Harper, J. (1980). *Fathers at home.* Melbourne: Penguin.

Harper, J. & Richards, L. (1979). *Mothers and working mothers*. Melbourne: Penguin.

Herbst, P. G. (1954). Conceptual framework for studying the family. In O. A. Oeser & S. B. Hammond (Eds.), *Social structure and personality in a city*. London: Routledge & Kegan Paul.

Heubeck, B., Detmering, J. & Russell, G. (1986). Father involvement and responsibility in family therapy. In M. E. Lamb (Ed.), *The father's role: Applied Perspectives*. New York: Wiley.

Horwill, F. M. (1979). The outcome of custody cases in the Family Court of Australia. *Conciliation Courts Review, 17*, 31–40.

Horwill, F. M. & Bordow, S. (1983). *The outcome of defended custody cases in the Family Court of Australia*. Family Court of Australia, Research Report No: 4.

Howard, J. (1979). *Helplessness, depression and delinquency*. Unpublished Masters Thesis, Macquarie University.

Howard, J. (1981). The expression and possible origins of depression in male adolescent delinquents. *Australian & New Zealand Journal of Psychiatry, 15*, 311–318.

Jordan, P. (1985). *The effects of marital separation on men*. Family Court of Australia, Research Report No: 6.

Katz, A. J. (1979). Lone fathers: Perspectives and implications for family policy. *The Family Coordinator, 28*, 521–528.

Knight, R. (1983). *Parents' ideas about childhood and parenting: A constructivist approach*. Unpublished Ph.D. thesis, Macquarie University.

Ochiltree, G. & Amato, P. (1984). The child's use of family resources. Paper presented to the XXth International CFR Seminar on *Social Change and Family Policies*, Melbourne, Australia.

Ochiltree, G. & Amato, P. (1985). *The child's eye view of family life*. Melbourne: Institute of Family Studies.

Oeser, O. A. & Hammond, S. B. (eds.) (1954). *Social structure and personality in a city*. London: Routledge & Kegan Paul.

Parker, G., Tupling, H. & Brown, L. (1979). A parental bonding instrument. *British Journal of Medical Psychology, 52*, 1–10.

Riach, L. (1982). *A child's eye view: Children's descriptions of parents*. Paper presented to the Second National Child Development Conference, Melbourne.

Richards, L. (1978). *Having families: Marriage, parenthood and social pressure in Australia*. Melbourne: Penguin.

Russell, A. & Russell, G. (1982). Mother, father and child beliefs about child development. *Journal of Psychology, 110*, 297–306.

Russell, G. (1978). The father role and its relation to masculinity, femininity and androgyny. *Child Development, 49*, 1174–1181.

Russell, G. (1982). Highly participant Australian fathers: Some preliminary findings. *Merrill-Palmer Quarterly, 28*, 137–156.

Russell, G. (1983a). *The changing role of fathers?* St. Lucia, Queensland: University of Queensland Press.

Russell, G. (1983b). *A cognitive mediational approach to observing and understanding social interactions*. Paper presented to a symposium on "Observational methodology in the study of social interaction: Implications for Theory", International Society for the Study of Behavioral Development, Munich.

Russell, G. (1983c). *A practical guide for fathers*. Melbourne: Thomas Nelson Australia.

Russell, G. (1984). *Changing patterns of divisions of labour for paid work and child care*. Paper presented to the 1984 ISA-CFR International Seminar on Social Change and Family Policies, Melbourne.

Russell, G. & Radin, N. (1983). Increased paternal involvement: Fathers' perspectives. In M. E. Lamb & A. Sagi (Eds.), *Fatherhood and family policy*. Hillsdale, New Jersey: Lawrence Erlbaum.

Russell, G. & Russell, A. (1985a). *Mother-child and father-child relationships in middle childhood*. Paper presented to the Eighth Biennial Meeting of the International Society for the Study of Behavioural Development. Tours, France.

Russell, G. & Russell, A. (1985b). [Mother-child and father-child relationships in middle childhood.] Unpublished data.

Siegal, M. & Barclay, M. S. (in press). Children's evaluations of fathers' socialization behaviour. *Developmental Psychology*.

Stagoll, B. (1983). Family therapy in Australia: Taking a squiz. *The American Journal of Family Therapy, 11*, 16–21.

Storer, D. (1981). *Migrant families in Australia*. Melbourne: Institute of Family Studies, Working Paper No. 3.

Teasdale, T. (1986). *Parental socialization practices associated with androgyny in adolescents*. Unpublished Ph.D. thesis, Macquarie University.

Weir, R., Silvestro, R. & Bennington, L. (1983). *A study of access patterns between three groups differing in their post separation conflict*. Paper presented to the Institute of Family Studies National Family Conference, Canberra.

Author Index

Robertson, J., 34, *57*
Robson, K. S., *191, 192*
Rockin, N., 201, *222*
Rodgers, R. R., 207, 208, *222*
Rödholm, M., 127, *138*
Rogers, C., 144, *167*
Rolle, A., 140, 144, *167*
Rondal, J. A., 44, *57*
Ronfani, P., 141, *167*
Rosaldo, M. Z., 295, *329*
Rosefeld, A., 295, *329*
Rosenblatt, D., 43, *57*
Rosenfeld, J. M., 213, *225*
Rosenstein, E., 213, *225*
Rousseau, J., 65, *87*
Rowhani, J., 93, *111*
Rubenstein, G., 201, *222*
Rubin, J. Z., 45, *57*
Rubinstein, J., 178, *192*
Ruppelt, H., 104, *113*
Russell, A., 336, 340, 342, 343, 344, 345, *357, 358*
Russell, C., 216, *224*
Russell, G., 11, 15, 16, 21, *24*, 47, *57, 192*, 212, 215, *225*, 333, 335, 336, 339, 340, 342, 343, 344, 345, 347, 348, 349, 350, 351, 354, 355, *356, 357, 358*
Rutherford, E., 12, *24*
Rutter, M., 7, 15, *25*, 33, 50, *57*, 213, *225*

S

Sagi, A., 13, 16, *24, 25*, 109, *113*, 201, 204, 205, 208, 209, 211, 212, 215, 216, 217, 218, 219, 220, *222, 224, 225, 226*
Saitoh, H., 248, 265, *268*
Saitoh, K., 252, *268*
Sameroff, A. J., 178, *192*
Sandqvist, K., 122, 126, *138*
Santuccio, M., 141, 144, 145, *165*
Saraceno, C., 142, 144, 147, *167*
SAS, *192*
Sasso, S., 139, 148, 151, 153, 156, 159, *165*
Saunders, G. R., 142, 144, *167*
Sawin, D., 178, *191*, 205, *224*

Sayers, P., 174, *192*
Schaffer, R., 54, *57*
Schenk, M., 103, *113*
Scheper-Hughes, N., 175, 176, *192*
Schildkrout, E., 280, *293*
Schmidt-Denter, U., 93, 94, 95, 98, 105, 106, 107, 108, 109, 110, *113*
Schmidt-Kolmer, E., 98, *113*
Schnapper, B., 65, *87*
Schooler, C., 263, *268*
Shenohara, T., 249, 256, *268*
Sherrod, K. B., 296, *328*
Shinsakur, Y., 260, *268*
Schreiber, J. M., 142, *167*
Schrepf, N. A., 12, 14, *23*
Schütze, Y., 99, *112*
Scott-Heyes, G., 37, *57*
Sears, D. O., 199, *222*
Sears, R. R., 12, *25*
Segalen, M., 60, 73, *87*
Sepkoski, C., 179, *192*
Sessler, G., 120, *138*
Settle, S. A., 217, 218, *226*
Sharon, N., 201, 219, *226*
Shepher, J., 203, *226*
Shoham, R., 204, 205, 208, 220, *225, 226*
Shorter, E., 146, *167, 172, 192*
Shorwal, R., 207, 208, *222*
Shwalb, B. J., 258, *267*
Shwalb, D. W., 258, *267*
Siddque, C. M., 198, *226*
Siebert, R., 142, 146, *167*
Sieder, R., 97, *112*
Siegal, M., 346, *358*
Sigman, M., *191, 192*
Silverman, S., 140, *167*
Silvestro, R., 354, *358*
Sims, M., 49, *57*
Senger, P., 78, *87*
Sirey, A. R., 140, 141, 144, *167*
Smith, C., 49, *57*
Smith, K., 263, *268*
Snowden, R., 78, *87*
Sofue, T., 256, *268*
Soliman, P., 216, *226*
Solnit, A., 217, *223*
Solomon, R. H., 233, 235, *245*
Sorifu, 250, 251, 252, 253, 254, 255, 256, 257, 258, 259, 262, *268*

Subject Index

372   SUBJECT INDEX

221, 339–340 (*see also* Division of housework and childcare)
Transfer isolates, 261–262
Transfers, job, 261–262, 264, 267

U

Unemployment, 11, 16, 29, 31–32, 42, 49–50, 54, 149, 352
United States, 3–22, 34, 73, 97, 108–109, 138, 235, 240, 248, 255, 258, 295–297, 316, 320, 322–327
U.S. history, 4–7
Urban, 177, 287, 289
Urban-rural differences (*see* Rural-urban differences)

V

Visitation, 133, 353 (*see also* Child custody; Divorce)

W

Welfare services, 216, 273 (*see also* Child welfare system; Public policy)
West Africa, 273–291
West Germany (*see* Federal Republic of Germany)
Women's rights, 119, 141, 171, 199, 262
Work-orientation, 47, 256–257
Work roles, 41–42, 72, 124, 263
Work schedules, 22, 41, 124, 153, 184, 233

Z

Zaire, 324

DATE DUE

~~NOT DUE~~ JAN 1 3 2004		
~~NOT DUE~~ APR 1 ~~NOT DUE~~ MAR 2 7 2006		